MW01492746

RANDY BACHMAN
TAKIN' CARE OF BUSINESS

RANDY BACHMAN
TAKIN' CARE OF BUSINESS

JOHN
EINARSON
RANDY
BACHMAN

McArthur & Company
Toronto

Published in Canada in 2000 by
McArthur & Company
322 King Street West, Suite 402
Toronto, ONT M5V 1J2

Canadian Cataloguing in Publication Data

Einarson, John, 1952-
    Randy Bachman takin' care of business

ISBN 1-55278-160-7

1. Bachman, Randy, 1943-   . 2. Rock musicians – Canada – Biography.
I. Bachman, Randy, 1943-   . II. Title. III. Title: Takin' care of business.

ML420.B113E35 2000   782.42166'092   C00-931322-2

Design & Composition by *Mad Dog Design Connection Inc.*
Cover Design by *Mad Dog Design Connection Inc.*
Printed in Canada by *Transcontinental Printing Inc.*

The publisher would like to acknowledge the financial support of
the Government of Canada through the Book Publishing Industry
Development Program (BPIDP) for our publishing activities.
The publisher further wishes to acknowledge the financial
support of the Ontario Arts Council for our publishing program.

10 9 8 7 6 5 4 3 2 1

Contents

AUTHOR'S NOTE

How do you pin down someone as busy as Randy Bachman? Simple: join him out on the road. Following his triumphant appearance with the Guess Who at Winnipeg's Pan American Games closing ceremonies in August 1999, Randy resumed his touring commitments and I accompanied him on the leg from Nashville to Seattle, twelve days on a luxury tour bus wending its way across the highways and byways of the US and Canada, punctuated by concert stops hither and yon. Because his schedule involved a lengthy stretch of travel from one coast to the other, it gave Randy and I ample opportunity to pass the days conducting in-depth interviews as the scenery whisked by our window. More to the point, Randy became my captive on the bus with nowhere to hide from my queries. He proved a willing and cooperative interviewee on our trek, and in the process we developed a close friendship and I managed to gather much of the information and anecdotes that appear in this book.

Initially, the members of Randy's band approached my arrival on their bus with trepidation, viewing it as an invasion into their own private world. There were even some rumblings of resentment toward my hogging their boss's time. However, by the second day we were all fast friends and, to my delight, I was soon accepted as an honorary "Road Dawg." The trip became unofficially dubbed the "Zagnut Tour of America" as each and every truck stop brought a frantic search for the hard-to-find yet delicious American confection. I extend my warmest thanks to "the boys in the band and crew" — Colin Arthur, Donnie McDougall, Rogé Belanger, Michael Shellard, and Andy Bowmer — for putting up with me on that outing.

At every concert stop, it was quite inspiring to witness the audience response Randy and his band elicited. From Manchester, Tennessee, to Moses Lake, Washington, Randy never failed to bring the audience to their feet stomping and singing along to his solid gold set of familiar favourites. His music has touched several generations and remains popular and appealing. Following each performance, Randy remained behind until the final autograph was signed or the last personal tribute from fans was received. He always took the time for those who appreciate his music and felt the need to tell him so. The tour was an appropriate setting to begin approaching this book, given Randy's legendary presence in popular music spanning some four decades. Past and present collided in Nashville where Randy not only headlined a classic rock festival but also spent a few days hustling his current crop of songs to several of the top country music artists. In many ways, that typifies Randy's outlook: keeping his legion of fans happy but still looking forward.

In an ironic twist, wherever we seemed to stop on the tour we would find Randy's son Tal's debut album on display or hear his hit single *She's So High* over the radio. It was a tremendous source of pride for Randy to be witnessing the rise of the next Bachman generation as a musical force while his own career continues unabated.

As you read this book, you will note that the voice changes from time to time. Randy's reflections and anecdotes appear extensively throughout and are set apart from the main text. In addition, the insights and observations of some three dozen others — family, friends, band mates, associates, and contemporaries — add more to Randy's story.

I would like to take this opportunity to thank all those who willingly gave of their time to be interviewed. Their names appear throughout the book. In addition, a special thank you is extended to the following: the ubiquitous Marty Kramer, Randy's manager and a long-time friend of mine who acted as facilitator and confidante; my agent David Johnston at Livingston Cooke/ Curtis Brown Canada; Ron Ade (Fillmore Riley and Co.) for expert legal advice above and beyond the call of duty; Susan Kelly at Stohn-Henderson; Nick Jennings for pointing me in the right direction; my Nashville buddy and host Jeff Dunn; Carny Corbett, the man with the record collection; Paul Whitteker for help with photos; Dr. Larry and Mrs. Shelley Lindquist for medical explanations; Mike Boettcher and Jaimie Vernon for the archival articles; and my friend Marty Melhuish for writing his 1976 BTO biography.

Some people declined to be interviewed for this book because of ongoing litigation or for personal reasons. Quotations attributed to Fred Turner are courtesy of an in-depth interview I conducted with him in the latter eighties for a biographical article I wrote for the *Winnipeg Free Press*. Despite repeated entreaties, Lorayne Bachman refused to speak with me.

Thank you to Kim McArthur for her enthusiastic support of this project.

I would like to thank Randy Bachman for his confidence in me to present his story honestly and thoroughly, as well as his support and cooperation throughout the process of putting this book together.

Lastly, thank you to my family—my wife, Harriett, son, Matthew, and daughter, Lynsey—for their constant love, support, and encouragement.

John Einarson
Winnipeg, August 2000

NOTE FROM RANDY

S ince I was very young, I knew that my gift from God and my des-
tiny was music. It was such a natural and joyful path for me to follow. From my first band to the present, my life has been just "a phone
call away." Sooner or later, the telephone would ring and there would
come an offer from someone to write, play, or produce some music
and I've always been happy to do it all. I am amazed and grateful that
decades later, I am still able to be living this teenage dream. There have
been bumps in the road and I am sure there are more ahead, but at the
end of the day it's a road that I believe I was guided to travel. Where it
will lead, I don't know; the next destination is just a phone call away.

I feel like I still have so much music to create and things to do that
this book seems premature. However, I love to read books about people I admire and am interested in and John Einarson had kept me so
entranced with his books on Neil Young and The Guess Who that it was
hard to refuse his invitation to collaborate. So I accepted. John is one
of the lucky ones who was in a band in Winnipeg in the sixties and
lived through the "happening" we all had. It was a magical and marvellous time. John knows almost more about the facts of my life than I do,
and his patience and understanding was appreciated by all who participated in this book. Many things in my life have come full circle in
recent years, so now seemed to be the time to talk about it.

Thanks to my songwriting partners all over the world, the bands
that ask me to play or produce on their records, the people who use

my music in movies, television, and commercials, and the fans for their continued support. It all keeps me going.

To the people who have been a part of the trip, I thank you for the great ride and will remember you always: Burton Cummings, Jim Kale, Garry Peterson, Chad Allan, Bob Ashley, Fred Turner, Tim Bachman, Robin Bachman, Blair Thornton, Bruce Allen, Neil Young, Sammy Hagar, Eddie Van Halen, Chet Atkins, Lenny Breau, Gordie Johnson, DOA, Farmer's Daughter, Prairie Oyster, Lenny Kravitz, Don Burkhimer, Jack Richardson, Phil Ramone, Tony Hiller, Ralph Murphy, Ringo Starr, Marty Kramer, Lorne Saifer, Colin Wiebe, Donnie McDougall, Rogé Belanger, Paul Whitteker, Andy Bowmer, Jonathan Conrad, Susan Abramovitch, Graham Henderson, Carl Wilson, John Austin, Trooper, Lorayne, Gar Gillies, Russell Gillies, Jim (Jumbo) Martin, London Bus Stop, and Sam Feldman.

To my mother and father, Anne and Charles Bachman, and my brothers Gary, Tim, and Rob — thanks for the great fun time growing up in our family.

My deepest thanks and all my love to my wife Denise for everything. A special thanks for the most precious thing I have in life, my children and grandchildren: Tal, Kezia, Lorelei, Bannatyne, Brigham, Emilie, Callianne, Kierra, Tanner, Jeddy, Ashton, Matthias, Enoch, Lael, Lorenzo, Madison, Gabriel, Christianna, and those still to come. The joy they bring me is endless and immeasurable.

Randy Bachman
August 2000

Preface

The sun shone brightly on Sunday morning August 8, 1999, boding well for the much-anticipated gala closing ceremonies of the 13th annual Pan American Games that evening. For two weeks, Winnipeg had been the focus of attention as athletes from the two Americas competed in more than two dozen events. But by show time ominous dark clouds had moved in as light drizzle turned to downpour minutes before Winnipeg's own Guess Who was set to take the stage for a much-touted reunion. As the athletes vacated the south end bleachers to assemble en masse in front of the enormous canopied stage, crewmembers uncovered the equipment and dried off the amplifiers. Some twenty-five thousand fans (with an estimated 200 million more via satellite broadcast) had sat patiently through speeches from the mayor, premier, prime minister and various dignitaries, choral numbers, flag waving, geese flying, and Caribbean dancing, all in anticipation of that one moment when the local-boys-who-made-good would take the stage. There was no doubting why the crowd was there. Despite the inclement weather no one left his or her seat.

Backstage, the four members — guitarist Randy Bachman, singer/pianist Burton Cummings, drummer Garry Peterson, and bass player Jim Kale, now all in their fifties — stood nervously awaiting their introduction by local impresario Sam Katz who, in his haste, flubbed Garry's name, calling him Randy Peterson.

When we were backstage waiting to go on, I was grabbing everyone's shoulders and yelling, "Adrenaline! Adrenaline! It's Shea Stadium and we're the Beatles!" That got Jim up. And when we hit those first notes, man, that was indescribable! It was a hundred and ten percent overdrive with each guy just exploding. It was the most surreal event of my life. I never thought it would happen.

When we started to play, I don't know if anyone could see it on camera, but I could barely hold back the tears. I was literally trying not to cry on camera. To sing those first lines, "No time left for you," and hear Jim kick in with that harmony, it was magic. I can't describe the feeling but if there is a fountain of youth, that was it. I felt like I was twenty-three years old playing Daniel Mac Collegiate or River Heights Community Club and we were young and nothing could stop us. We owned the world for those few minutes and we were kicking it with our music. It was so incredibly powerful. After all the years of bickering, misappropriated recognition, other bands getting all the accolades, this was our moment to finally show everyone how good we were. And we really did. My wife and kids thought we were lip synching to a CD because it was so note-for-note perfect.

With the opening drum beat of *No Time*, the crowd let out a thunderous roar that shook the stadium as the band kicked into high gear nailing the harmonies perfectly, with Randy's lead guitar soaring over the other instruments. On their feet from the moment the group took the stage, the rain-soaked audience sang along with every word. "Here's a song written right here in the North End," announced Burton proudly before playing the familiar chords to *These Eyes*, Jim's strident bass runs propelling the song to its climax. In the VIP seats Premier Gary Filmon, who had been instrumental in coaxing the four members into appearing, stood up and danced. Gesturing toward his former writing partner, Burton acknowledged the next song as one of the finest numbers the group had ever recorded and its composer the man who taught him more about music than anyone else. Randy nodded, Burton picked up his flute, and the guitarist strummed the jazz-flavoured chords of *Undun*. Then came the bluesy intro to *American Woman*, Burton on harmonica motioning the crowd to join in. "I say A, M, E, R, I, C, A, N. American woman gonna mess your mind." Over and over, building momentum, it was like a steam engine picking up speed before those three pounding power chords and mass hysteria. This was the number the young athletes had been waiting for, the one they knew best. Everything old was new again. Randy let loose a barrage of guitar riffs as Burton genuflected before the one true guitar god. And then it was over. The group stood together, waved to the crowd and exited.

Afterwards Randy reflected,

Being together with those three guys was such a magical thing, if I knew how to bottle it I'd make a zillion dollars. It must be that Keith Richards–Mick Jagger thing; no matter how much they fight and disagree or do their own solo things, when they get together with Charlie Watts it's the original recipe, the Rolling Stones. It's the sum total of those individuals.

Despite several glitches involving transportation and security and failing to meet the man responsible for their reunion, Premier Filmon, everything involved with the performance went off perfectly. Still riding an adrenaline rush, the group and their families and friends were hustled back to the downtown Holiday Inn Crowne Plaza Hotel only to be disappointed when no one was there to congratulate them or share in their triumph.

When it was all over, I honestly expected to meet the premier or the mayor of Winnipeg at a reception where you get a triangular sandwich and an olive and someone saying thanks for coming.

That didn't happen. We never saw Filmon or anyone. You would think they could have rented a room in our hotel for us to meet all the dignitaries. It would have been great publicity for the city and a thrill for us. As it was, when we finally got back to the hotel, Prime Minister Chrétien was in the lobby surrounded by all his security. When he saw us come in though, he pushed past them all and came over to meet us. We had our photograph taken with him.

There is no doubting that the Pan Am Games reunion left a lasting impression on the four members of the Guess Who. That they could surmount decades of acrimony and personal problems to stand together was a feat in itself. As the final notes of *American Woman* reverberated through Winnipeg Stadium, offers for a reunion tour doubled, tripled, and quadrupled. At last count, $2 million was on the table. Whether they toured or not was up to them alone. Of far greater significance was the residual affection the four felt toward each other from the experience.

I came away from that reunion feeling like I have three close friends, three old friends. When you start a band, you are literally closer to those other guys than to your own brothers because you are usually the same age within one or two years, whereas with your brothers you might be years apart. You have more in common with these guys. And you are thrust into the same car and van and hotel room with these same guys for endless months and years sharing the same dreams. You have to learn to work things out, learn to fight, break up, and make up. The Guess Who must have broken up a hundred times, but the next day there was no one else we would rather play with in town who had our common musical bonds and musical education. We had the same musical references, which were the records we had from England or from the Deep South. These were our libraries, our reference books. I could say to Garry or Jim or Burton, "Can you play this like Georgie Fame?" and they would instinctively know and play it. If I said that to another musician he wouldn't know what I was talking about. We had this incredible bond between all of us. The true story of what we shared together and the bond we forged is truly unique and incredible.

Early the next morning, Randy was scheduled to fly out of Winnipeg en route to Shreveport, Louisiana, to resume his tour commitments. Accompanied by Marty Kramer, Randy strode purposefully through Winnipeg's airport. As he checked his bags, a familiar-looking middle-aged man approached the burly, bearded guitarist and thrust his hand out toward him.

I recognized him as a guy I knew from one of the hundreds of bands that used to play the community clubs in Winnipeg in the sixties. He congratulated me on our superb performance the night before. I could see he was very emotional, he had tears in his eyes, and I realized something for the first time in my life. For him, the dream was gone; he had never gone any further than the community clubs. But in the four of us he had been able to live out that dream in our success. We were the four horsemen who rode out of Winnipeg to find glory and fame and had come back one more time. We had lived the dream of a thousand other kids growing up in Winnipeg. To them, we are still the heroes.

CHAPTER 1

Prairie Town

Takin' Care of Business. More than mere disposable pop fluff, the song has transcended the pop charts to become not only a classic rock anthem and guaranteed crowd-pleaser, but a surefire jingle pitch for everything from hamburgers to office furniture, movies to music compilations. It has become synonymous with the gentle bear of a man who composed it almost thirty years ago as a paean to the working-class daily grind that he himself managed to escape with his guitar in hand as a teenager. Though Canadian rock music elder statesman Randy Bachman didn't coin the phrase, he nonetheless transformed it into an icon in our popular culture lexicon. One of Randy's earliest mentors, Elvis Presley, the "King" himself, paid Randy the highest form of praise by adopting it as his personal motto, going as far as to have a belt buckle custom made with the letters "TCB" engraved on it and bestowing TCB pins on friends and fans.

For Randy, taking care of business had been a personal credo long before he ever penned lyrics to go along with that phrase. His business is music and as the song says he's been "workin' overtime" for four decades. How many of us can boast of doing nothing else in life than what we truly love? From the moment he picked up a guitar at age thirteen, and even earlier as a preteen violin prodigy, music had been his singular focus and obsession. You can count the other jobs he has had on the fingers of one hand, most barely lasting a day or two. Everything in Randy's life is benchmarked by music — what records he was listening to, what guitar he was playing, the band he was in, the studio he recorded this or that hit, what musical hero he met. Sports teams? Adolescent hijinks? Teenage crushes? Schoolboy pranks? Nope. Ask Randy Bachman to recount his life and you'll receive a concise history of rock 'n' roll itself punctuated with colourful personal asides about the triumphs and tragedies he has experienced. He is a walking encyclopedia of music; don't ever play *Rock 'n' Roll Jeopardy* with this man!

"Everything is about music for my Dad," states eldest son Tal, a recording artist in his own right. "He's not very social, not a real party guy. But if you get him turned on with the right question, on things he is interested in, he'll go on for the rest of the day. He's full of these great stories about his musical experiences."

"I always call Randy the one-trick pony," smiles his second wife, Denise. "All he lives for and all he has ever done in his life is music. But he does that one trick really well. If they could dissect his brain, the part that represents the creative impulse and music would be like a grapefruit and everything else would be the size of a pea. He doesn't have any other interests than music.

"He can get a bit blinkered at times not seeing what is going on around him because he is so focused on what he is doing. For that reason sometimes he doesn't hear things people say to him. One of the complaints in our family is that Randy doesn't listen to us all the time. It's not that he doesn't care, he cares a lot. It's just that he becomes preoccupied and tunes the rest of the world out. I asked him once if he was ignoring me on purpose. I started going through all those doubts like "Oh, he doesn't like me." At that moment he came out of his inner private world and said "Huh? What? Oh no, no. I was just thinking about a song." I realized what he has in his head is music all the time. It would be like having to listen to someone talking to you when you have headphones on playing music. There's music going in his head all the time; it never stops whether he is thinking about a lyric or hearing a song line. There is a radio on in his head constantly. He doesn't hear the normal buzz of side talk or conversation that most people pick up on because he is so focused on music."

"Everybody knows who Randy is," acknowledges Canada's foremost music journalist Larry LeBlanc. "He is instantly recognizable as a Canadian icon. An entire generation of people has grown up with Randy Bachman. Even teenagers today know who he is. But despite the fame, Randy remains a complex person. I have known him more than thirty years but I don't think I know him. He is a very hard person to be a friend with. Who are his friends outside the music business? I don't think he has any. I can't imagine Randy having a social life without music in it. He lives and breathes rock music at all times, from morning until night."

More than just music, Randy is enamored with the music *business*. From his earliest bands he was the one who collected the fees at the end of the night, paid out the expenses, disbursed the salaries and managed the accounts. He learned the hard lessons of that business with the Guess Who, a band that not only provided the all-important blueprint for every successful Canadian artist that followed but who also wrote the book on the pitfalls of the music industry. The Guess Who made every mistake conceivable, and paid dearly for it. The message was not lost on Randy who vowed to avoid retracing those steps when he launched Bachman-Turner Overdrive in the early seventies. If the Guess Who were the poster boys for mismanagement of their own affairs, BTO became the role model for today's bottom line, corporate rock ethic.

"Randy was never into music for the groupies, the hangers-on or the parties," states his brother Gary, one-time manager of Randy's pre-BTO group Brave Belt. "He played because he loved it but he also wanted to make a living from it. The money was always important to him."

That focus on business, however, has brought Randy almost as many detractors as admirers. Respected as a gifted musician, talented writer, and skillful record producer, he has nonetheless earned enmity throughout his career for his tough-minded business acumen. Former band mates, colleagues, associates, even his own brothers have found themselves in dispute with the guitarist over matters related to the business side rather than the creative side of the music industry. For them, *Takin' Care of Business* takes on an entirely different tone. Randy has his own agenda and woe be it to anyone who gets in his way.

"No matter who is managing Randy Bachman, he calls the shots," suggests former Guess Who road manager Jim "Jumbo" Martin, who developed a close relationship with the guitarist during his tenure with that band. "Randy and Burton have guys like Marty Kramer and Lorne Saifer around to deal with the things they don't want to deal with." There are those who maintain that when push comes to shove, Randy brings in the big guns and steps back. "Randy has pulled a lot of moves by having someone else be tough and doing the heavy stuff," adds BTO manager Bruce Allen, now one of the top managers in the music business, "with me being the spokesman or business manager Graeme Waymark, or lawyers. Randy is always nice. He's humble and self-deprecating, soft-spoken. But he has more lawsuits than anyone I know."

Sometimes perceived as standoffish, self-absorbed, and aloof, Randy instead chooses his words carefully as if measuring the value of each syllable and phrase, doling them out sparingly. He does not engage in small talk for its own sake, preferring the silence of his own thoughts. He is diplomatic, sometimes evasive, but rarely badmouths anyone in public. Even at the height of the much-publicized Cummings–Bachman feud, Randy tried to take the high road. "Randy has always been very careful not to say bad things about people in the media," attests Denise Bachman. "When Burton trashes him in the press, Randy has never responded in kind. That's just not him." But he is not above revenge. While BTO enjoyed the rarified air of pop music's upper echelon, he penned *Hey You*, a thinly veiled put down to his former Guess Who partner as if to say "I'm up here and you're not."

Colleagues attest to what are referred to as "Randy's Rules of the Road," a no-nonsense code of conduct that emphasizes a spartan work ethic. "Randy is known as a tough guy to work for," acknowledges Denise on Randy's consummate professionalism, "but he isn't that way as long as you do your job. That's all he expects of anybody. He doesn't even care what people do in their private lives as long as it doesn't interfere with their job. But the problem is it always does get in the way. He's always there, he doesn't let people down, and he expects the same from them. It's not that high a standard. "If it's your job, do your job." That's it. He has always had a very professional attitude. Randy cannot bear to be around when someone doesn't show up for rehearsals or goes onstage drunk and misses the cues. It looks bad not just for him but for everyone involved. It's his name up there and he does not want to be associated with that kind of thing. To him it's a business and you have to have a professional attitude."

"The hardest thing about working with Randy," maintains former partner Fred Turner, the "T" in BTO, "is that he is a steadfast business-man. It's a business. If you aren't a hard worker, you won't get along with Randy and that's all there is to it." For some, living up to Randy's high standards has not always been easy. Even kinship has not always been sufficient if you aren't measuring up. But for those who do, the rewards can be great.

"I think one of the reasons Randy has remained successful," continues Denise, "is that he never bothered with drugs or alcohol. He never wasted his time with any of that. So while others were falling down drunk or stoned partying, he was still plodding ahead which is why he left a lot of them behind. That's all it takes is that dogged determination without being distracted. He didn't blow his money or his career on the excesses of the music business." And who can argue with his track record? Amongst the hundreds of boxes of memorabilia Randy donated to the National Library of Canada a few years back were some one hundred gold, silver, and platinum singles and albums Randy earned his career. Only Bryan

Adams and Celine Dion can rival Randy's gold rush.

Yet to those who know him intimately he can be caring, sensitive, generous to a fault. "Randy is like a big teddy bear," reflects Jim Martin. "He has a real good character and personality to him. I always thought of him as a good friend. He loves to talk if you get him going on something he is interested in. He gets carried away sometimes but that's just his genuine enthusiasm getting the better of him."

"I've never understood how he has been perceived in the media as having a hard edge, difficult to work with and very businesslike," emphasizes Randy's first girlfriend, Claudia Senton Anderson, who remains a close personal friend to this day. "He was always an extremely loving human being. Even when I see him now he'll still give me a big hug. His children must adore him. Yet when I would read all this about him I would think 'What is this all about?' because I don't get the connection between the person I know and what I read in the papers. I don't think people change that much from who they are inside no matter what we have gone through. Anyone who knows Randy well doesn't see anything else in him but the person he really is." She is, however, quick to qualify, "But he certainly isn't naïve. The other stuff is just business."

Randy Bachman remains a fascinating figure on the Canadian music landscape. A true legend who has seen and done it all, he looms large in the development of Canadian popular music and continues to be a force to be reckoned with. As former confidante Bruce Allen characterizes, "Randy is a walking contradiction, partly truth and partly fiction," borrowing from a Kris Kristofferson lyric. Like all legends, myth and reality often become obscured. "Randy is the Great Gildersleeves," laughs Garry Peterson. "He could tell a story and embellish it to the point that even if you knew he was exaggerating, it was still a good story and you believe it. He is a great storyteller and can spin a yarn. But he does it in such a harmless way and he gets so enthusiastic." In Randy's case, however, the truth of his amazing career reads like the stuff of fantasy.

"Randy is an eternal optimist," concludes Denise. "That has not only driven his career but also his personal life. He sincerely believes that there is always going to be something better coming along. And more often than not it's true if you have the stamina to get through the tough times. Randy has always had that stamina."

Randolph Charles Bachmann comes by that dogged determination honestly. Born to first generation Canadians of hardy eastern and central European peasant stock he grew up imbued with the same immigrant work ethic that so many brought with them to Canada in the late nineteenth century.

I'm not afraid of work. I enjoy working. That's an ethic I learned from my Dad and my grandfather, my Mom's father. They both worked hard and never complained. My grandfather was a labourer and did a lot of physical work all his life. He would come home then go outside and work in his garden. My Dad would come home after working all day, have dinner, change his clothes and work all night building our house, adding rooms, building an attic, building a garage. I learned to work at his side. If you wanted to be with him you had to go down to his tool bench in the basement. And when he wasn't working around the house he was working for the community as an alderman for West Kildonan.

The community of West Kildonan traces its origins back to the early nineteenth century and the Scottish settlers who first homesteaded on the land near the confluence of the Red and Assiniboine Rivers (known as the Forks). Concerned for the welfare of his fellow countrymen forced off the Scottish highlands with the advent of sheep enclosures, philanthropist Thomas Douglas, the fifth Earl of Selkirk, acquired a parcel of land in Western Canada. Here he brought the first of the Selkirk Settlers in 1812. As more arrived the settlement spread northward along the Red River and was given the very Scottish name Kildonan. An uneasy mix of Scottish settlers, Metis (half French, half Native) buffalo hunters and the indigenous tribes of the Plains resided in the community that grew around the Forks. A bloody skirmish between Selkirk Settlers and Metis hunters in a field near Seven Oaks in West Kildonan in 1816 revealed the tensions rife within the community. Kildonan was later divided along the Red River into East Kildonan on one side and on the other side the community of West Kildonan.

By the time of its incorporation as the City of Winnipeg in 1872, the demographic nature of its residents was split fairly evenly between Anglophones in the west and south and Francophones across the Red River to the east. Into this mix the Canadian government sought to throw in hardy peasants drawn from the landless rural masses of Eastern Europe. With the completion of the transcontinental Canadian Pacific Railway in 1885 the push was on by the government to fill the new western lands with suitable settlers. Several times a week the CPR train would pull into Winnipeg from the East laden with hundreds of Polish, Russian, Lithuanian, Rumanian, and Ukrainian émigrés. Although most continued on to the free land in Saskatchewan and Alberta, one in ten chose to disembark and seek their fortune in the Gateway City. By the turn of the century, the ethnic character of Winnipeg had altered drastically as the city's North End became the European immigrant enclave, a colourful cosmopolitan community of diverse languages, foods, customs and religions where Protestant mixed with Orthodox Christian, Jew, and Roman Catholic. What these new Canadians had in common however was a determination to make something of themselves and to provide greater opportunities for their children than they had in the old country. And to do so most often meant backbreaking work.

Stephen and Lena Dobrinsky had both come from Eastern Europe as children, Steve from Poland and Lena from the Ukraine, and they met in the community of West Kildonan. Steve, a labourer for the municipal authority, was no stranger to hard work yet always found time for his and Lena's nine children, five girls and four boys, as well as to enjoy the company of neighbours and friends. The Dobrinsky home at 522 Hartford Avenue near McKenzie north of Main Street in West Kildonan was the kind of place you felt comfortable and at home in. There was always plenty of food and hospitality.

My mother was born Anne Dobrinsky in Winnipeg on September 16, 1920. Her parents were from the Ukraine. Her mother, my grandmother Lena, came over to Canada when she was barely an infant and married at fourteen. That's what you did in those days. My grandparents both spoke Ukrainian and Polish around the house and like any little kid they would talk to me in that language and I would understand them. But as we grew older, my parents discouraged them talking to us in Ukrainian. They wanted us to speak good English. I wish I had had more interest in learning the language and had carried it on. Basically the only people who retained the ethnic language and culture back then were my Jewish friends who went to Hebrew school every day from four-thirty to six. But for everyone else, they simply wanted to blend in and become Canadian.

My mother's maiden name was Dobrinsky but I did some genealogy years later and found Dobransky and Dobranskj. I don't know what happened to it but it was Dobrinsky by the time my mother came along. I also found that all her life my mother had been a year and a day off from her actual birth date. In those days my grandfather couldn't read or write English and must have made a mistake.

My mother grew up in that little house my grandparents had on Hartford Avenue. Back then it was pretty much a one-room shack with wilderness on the other side of McGregor. Even when I was going to play at my grandparents' house there was nothing but prairie near it. The sidewalks were wooden with packed mud roads and big ditches surrounding them. Since no one had plumbing everyone dumped their waste in the ditch. When it rained it all washed away to the Red River. But plants would grow out of the ditches because of the natural fertilizer and composting. When they put in sidewalks we took the wooden planks to the ditches and floated on them like Tom Sawyer rafts.

As they had more kids, my grandfather kept adding on rooms. Then came the big event: they got indoor plumbing. I can still recall that. Before then there was no running water in the house and you had to go to the standing pipe, just a pipe sticking out of the ground on a little mound on Hartford and every one had a key, a little octagon key, to turn it on. You'd fill up your pails and carry them home. Everybody did this from blocks around. In winter you had to leave the water running for an hour or so to keep the pipe from freezing so you would get this incredible ice slide. I remember going with my grandfather who would take old newspapers and cardboard boxes, put them around the pipe and light them to melt the pipe for water. Neighbours would see the fire and come out with their pails. Otherwise it would freeze again.

My grandfather was, I think, a garbage man. They never told me because in those days there were no terms like sanitation engineer but he used to come home from work with all these things that people had thrown away. Lamps, mirrors, purses, jewellery, shoes. Later on he dug ditches, fixed potholes, and laid sidewalks, things like that so I guess he worked as a municipal labourer for the city of West Kildonan which was a separate city before the amalgamation of the various communities into Winnipeg. In winter he would go out with teams of workers to shovel snow for the schools and hospitals because there were no snowblowers or ploughs.

From an early age I had a real sense of a close extended family. Because they lived closer than my other grandmother, Grandma Bachman, we would go to my Grandma and Grandpa Dobrinsky's more often. It was about a half-mile from our house at Seven Oaks and Powers but between us there was nothing, just prairie. When I was little and my grandmother wanted me to go home she would hang a red blanket out on the clothesline. There were no phones so she and my Mom used a kind of semaphore. My mother would see this red blanket and know little Randy was on his way home. And I'd walk through the open field alone with the prairie grass almost as tall as me. When I got home my mother would put a white blanket out on the line to let my Grandma know I had arrived safely.

Like everyone growing up then, my grandmother was the greatest cook in the world. She cooked our family's comfort food. No one could make that Ukrainian peasant food as good as she could until she passed away and the torch was passed to my mother. Grandma would cook these enormous meals every weekend. She would literally start cooking Friday night for Sunday dinner. She would make her own sauerkraut and she didn't make a dozen cabbage rolls, it was a giant turkey roaster stuffed full of them, eighty to a hundred holobchi with cabbage and rice. Another roaster would be full of perogies. What didn't get eaten on Sunday they would have for the rest of the week. It was the same food every Sunday and that's why it was comfort food because we ate it every week. It was the family meal. I can still smell it. Their house had that Ukrainian smell to it and it was great going there.

The unofficial boundary line between West Kildonan to the north and the neighbourhood known simply as Winnipeg's North End was Inkster Boulevard named for John Inkster who homesteaded on the land that later bore the street. With its boulevard of trees dividing the lanes of traffic, Inkster had a more stately air to it than its adjacent thruways and residential streets. It was on Inkster Boulevard that the five Bachmann boys resided. Born of German-Austrian immigrants, the boys lived with their widowed mother and maiden aunt. In a time when opportunities for women were limited and pay scales discriminatory, these two managed to raise five strapping young men, one of whom was Charles Bachman.

I never knew my grandfather Emil Wilhelm Bachmann and

neither did my Dad. He died of appendicitis when my Dad was about three or four. So here was this woman, Grandma Louise Bachmann, with five sons and no husband. This was before and during the Great Depression when these boys were growing up so it had to be tough for her. My grandmother had a sister, Mary Kendall, who never married. Instead she dedicated her life to helping her sister raise those five boys. And it couldn't have been easy. There are photos of the Bachmann boys, my Dad and his brothers, at the YMCA, all big muscular guys who ate like horses. These two women raised them to be honest, hardworking men. My grandmother stayed home to raise the children and Mary went out to work and there wasn't a lot of work for a single woman back then.

Somewhere along the way Randy's father dropped the second "n" though Randy's birth certificate lists him as "Bachmann," the traditional German spelling. Years later when he toured Germany as a solo artist, Randy found the promotional posters had restored the double "n." To this day, Randy's surname elicits a variety of pronunciations depending on where he happens to be. Is it "Back" man or "Bach" man? It's all a matter of geography.

It's actually pronounced like "Backman" but in the States it's always "Bachman," like Johann Sebastian Bach. I recall a funny incident. After BTO I went solo and released the *SURVIVOR* album and was invited to go on Dick Clark's *American Bandstand* show. I was doing *Is the Night Too Cold for Dancing* and also, as a tie in, *You Ain't Seen Nothin' Yet*. When you are a guest you get to go sit in the audience with Dick. I'll never forget what happened. He leaned over to me and I'm thinking "He's going to ask me something about the record." Instead he says, "So what is it: Backman or Bachman?" I'm trying not to do a "um ana um ana um ana" like Jackie Gleason's Ralph

Kramden character because it just threw me.

There is a difference in pronunciation between the American and Canadian way of speaking. If my manager Marty Kramer is calling on my behalf to someone in the States and says, "I'm calling for Randy *Back*man" there's nothing, no bells ringing.

I'll say, "Marty, are you calling to the States?"

"Oh yeah, Randy *Bach*man."

The response back is invariably, "Oh, Randy Bachman, Bachman-Turner Overdrive!" There is immediate recognition. Also, in England, Ringo Starr calls me BACKman with an emphasis on the "Back."

There was a time when I wanted to change my name simply to Mann because I thought Bachman sounded too ethnic. I loved the name Shelly Mann, the jazz drummer with the nightclub Shelly's Mann Hole. I wanted to drop the Bach and be Randy Mann. It seemed like a cool stage name but my father told me in no uncertain terms, "This is a proud family name. If you change it, you're out of this house." So I never changed it and I'm glad I didn't.

Anne Dobrinsky met Charles Bachman, three years her senior, in the winter of 1940. Anne recalls their chance encounter. "My brothers used to go to the Red River and slide down the river bank in winter time. As one of my brothers was sliding down, another boy came down and he fractured his leg so they had to bring him home. Charles came with a bunch of other boys to the house and that's how we met." The couple wed the following year. For the first two years, Charles and Anne resided in a tiny apartment on Cathedral Avenue in the North End until the arrival of their first son, Randy, on September 27, 1943, at St. Joseph's Hospital on Salter Avenue near Mountain in the North End. Moving in with the Dobrinskys for the first year, they soon after purchased a house at the corner of Seven Oaks and Powers and set about raising their family. Brother Gary arrived nineteen months after Randy.

Much later in life Randy would learn that he had been a twin.

Following his delivery, Anne complained of severe abdominal pain but was told she would be fine. Two hours later a check by her obstetrician revealed that a second fetus had suffocated in the interim.

My mother's favourite cowboys were Randolph Scott, Gary Cooper, and Tim Holt so it was Randolph, Gary, and Tim. I think Robbie was Robin Hood. She would go to the movies and swoon over these guys. So we were named after the cowboys. And I literally saw every Randolph Scott movie.

"You're named after this guy so we're taking you to see him."

I really loved those cowboy movies because the good guy always won and then he would pull out a guitar and sing. That stuck with me. The romantic guy in a white hat who got the girl and rode off into the sunset. And they played and sang.

In today's vernacular, Charles Bachman would likely be termed a workaholic. Skilled in the precise art of lens crafting, grinding the lenses to fit the frames and making the eyeglasses, he worked long hours at Imperial Optical on South Osborne Street in Fort Rouge, travelling by bus to and fro five days a week. As a dispensing optician, he later founded Benson Law Opticians on Kennedy Street downtown before setting up his own business, Charles Bachman Optical, in the Boyd Building on Edmonton Street. When not at work, Charles kept busy refurbishing and renovating the family home at 356 Seven Oaks adding rooms as more boys were born. The long, wood-framed bungalow at the intersection of Seven Oaks and Powers went through several building phases before the family relocated to 655 Hartford when Randy was in his late teens. Evenings were also spent on civic committees as an alderman for the City of West Kildonan serving in a variety of capacities as deputy mayor, police commissioner, fire commissioner, justice of the peace, and following the incorporation of West Kildonan into Unicity, as chairman of the provincial lotteries board. In nine years of service Charles Bachman demonstrated a strong sense of civic duty and community responsibility. He was ultimately rewarded with a street named in his honour.

The Bachman household was typical of its time. In postwar Canadian society, dad went out to work while mom stayed home, looked after the house, and raised the children. Disciplinary matters were left to dad when he returned home each evening. "You just wait until your father gets home," was enough to strike terror in the heart of any mischievous youngster. By all accounts Charles was a good provider managing to raise four boys on a modest income allowing them all the necessities as well as sports equipment and music lessons. "Money was precious in that family," recalls Claudia Senton Anderson, a school friend of Randy's who spent many hours at the Bachman home. "There wasn't much of it in that house. Anne Bachman was extremely frugal, always trying to make ends meet for everyone. Those four boys ate their mother out of house and home. She used to take the bus somewhere to go to this bakery and buy two- and three-day-old cakes and pastries for her boys. If Randy has a weakness for baked goods, it came from back then with his mother. I used to laugh at how frugal she was, saving everything like plastic containers. But she was a great mom. Anne Bachman was a real traditional Ukrainian mom who cooked all those wonderful ethnic foods like perogies and holobchi."

Despite having three other sons, Anne Bachman remained closest to Randy. He, in turn, describes himself as a Momma's boy as a youngster and according to his brothers was the favoured son. "Randy was a quiet baby," recalls his mother. "He didn't cry a lot. He was a good boy. He never gave me any trouble. He was the only baby around the family at first so he was fussed over. As a young boy he was always polite and soft-spoken."

"They were a close family," continues Claudia, "but I think Randy was his Mom's boy and certainly was his Mom's favourite child. Gary was the one who seemed to spend the most time out of favour and that's probably why he left early. He stuttered profoundly as a child to the point where it was absolutely awful to see the pain he went through. Gary was more bullied and intimidated by his father than the other kids. As a result Gary was more of a loner in the family. I think he felt like he lived in Randy's shadow. His Mom had a closer relationship with Randy than Gary or even the two younger kids. In that family the dynamics happened between Randy and Gary and their parents. The two little ones were just sort of kids. No one paid a lot of attention to them."

Growing up without a father, life had dealt Charles Bachman a cruel hand. He had endured a tough life and set high standards for himself. The same went for his boys, especially the eldest, Randy. Discipline meted out could be harsh and his rules strict, yet the boys never complained. Earning and maintaining the respect and admiration of their father was paramount to them as they grew up. "In spite of what the boys will tell you," confides a family friend, "there were a lot of unresolved issues between the boys and their dad. Their dad could judge harshly and wasn't always supportive or if he was it was in a hard way. When that hand came down that was it. He could be very tough on the boys, Randy and Gary especially. They loved and adored him but the way I saw it, he was very hard on them." It wasn't always easy for Randy living up to his father's expectations. Around the house it was Anne who ruled the roost and the quick flick of a dishtowel was often enough to assert her authority. "Randy's mother was definitely the boss of that family," laughs Guess Who drummer and boyhood friend Garry Peterson. "She was sterner than Charlie. You were scared to go into Randy's house if she was home. Charlie was a good-hearted guy."

A gap of several years between sets of brothers created the sense of two families in one. While Randy and Gary are less than two years apart in age, there is an eight-year distance between Randy and Tim with Robin almost ten years Randy's junior. Despite the demographics, the four generally got along well though the youngsters were more often the brunt of their older brothers' hijinks. Before the arrival of television, computers, and video games, young boys and girls had the whole outdoors as their playground and the only limitation was your imagination. It was still the playground of the mind. Adventures could be created just climbing a tree or running through a field. In late 1940s and early 50s West Kildonan, there was still plenty of both.

"There was a creek that went through Seven Oaks behind our house before they filled it in and built Smithfield and Enniskillen streets," remembers Gary. "We used to go fishing in the creek or catching tadpoles. There were open fields behind us and not all the streets were paved so we could ride our bicycles all over. There were lots of trees to climb. Just typical boys stuff."

"Robbie and I shared a room and Gary and Randy shared a room," remembers Tim Bachman warmly. "Randy played with us quite a bit. Gary wasn't home much between the ages five to about ten so Randy was around to play with us. Being bigger he could do lots of things to us. I'm sure he was having fun but there were times when it wasn't fun for us. We would be afraid when our parents would buy us toys because Robbie and I knew that the bigger guys would use them on us. Each summer we would pile into the family car, a '51 Chevy, and head off to places like Bemidji, Detroit Lakes, Bismarck, Mount Rushmore, all the cowboy places. On one of these trips my Dad bought us these whips like Lash LaRue who was a big cowboy hero then. We felt safe while we were with our parents but dreaded going home because when Dad would be at work and Mom would be busy, Randy and Gary would make us run back and forth and try to whip our feet out from under us."

Growing up, I was a fearless kid, bold and adventurous, full of schemes and plans, not aware of consequences. When I think back on some of the misadventures I got into and I tell my own children and grandchildren, their mouths hang open in disbelief.

They think I'm making this stuff up.

Being the oldest of four boys I was put in charge if my parents ever left the house.

"I'm just going to the store. Randy, watch your brothers."

We'd be at home after school watching *Howdy Doody*, but the minute she closed the door it was wrestling matches, pillow fights, all hell would break loose. I was their fearless leader. They looked up to me and anything they suggested they knew that if I did it, guess who got in trouble? Not them, me. "Randy started the fire! Randy broke the window! Randy threw me through the air!"

One Christmas my brother Robbie got a bow and arrow set with rubber darts and suction cups. We discovered that these arrows would stick on the fridge. That was wonderful. That's how Robin Hood started on television each week, the arrow flying through the air and "thwung," sticking in a tree. I had this notion, "Wouldn't it be cool if the arrow went whizzing by Robbie and Tim as they were running by and stuck on the fridge just like on Robin Hood?" So my little brothers ran back and forth across the kitchen as Gary and I shot arrows at them from the living room.

By the time my parents returned I had shot the arrows so often that the shaft had worked its way through the rubber suction cup. As the back door opened my Mom and Dad heard screaming. An arrow had, by chance, hit Robbie in the temple and he was bleeding a little because it was the stick not the rubber tip that hit him. Knowing my parents were there Robbie was hamming it up holding the arrow in the air and shrieking "Aah, I'm hit, I'm hit." I'll never forget the look on my parents' faces. And there I was standing in the kitchen holding the bow.

In our living room the old couch we had was stuffed with straw; this was before foam rubber padding. When we acquired a new couch, the old one was put in our backyard to be taken away by the garbage men. We asked our parents if we could use it until they took it away. It was out beside the garage next to the garden where corn and potatoes were growing. They agreed. For the next few days that couch became our playground. I was older by then, fourteen or so, and Gary was twelve. Timmy and Robbie were still kids. So when my parents went out it was "Randy, you're babysitting your brothers." In those days there was no danger in the neighbourhood, people didn't lock their doors, everybody knew one another, parents and kids. It was safe. Since we were on the corner of Seven Oaks and Powers we had friends going both ways on all four corners.

"Hey everyone, my parents are gone. Come on over. We've got a chesterfield in our yard!"

All the kids in the vicinity were bouncing off it, doing flips, jumping off the garbage cans onto it, wrestling, pretending we were on a raft and falling into the garden, just having a grand old time. The whole neighbourhood was there.

Somebody had the idea to have a wiener roast. I had been told a million times not to play with matches but, what the heck, my parents weren't home. They weren't gone long, maybe an hour. My friend Shelly brought over these incredible kosher wieners, we lit the fire and there we were sitting on the old straw-stuffed couch roasting wieners and marshmallows. As it turned dark, with my parents due home soon, all the kids left. I told my brothers to get into bed while I went outside and stomped on the fire until I thought it was out. As I was getting into my bed waiting for the sound of my parents coming in the door I saw this flickering from my window off the garage coming from the backyard. I looked out the window and the entire couch was ablaze with flames shooting two feet in the air above it.

"Oh my God! Gary, Timmy, get up! The couch is on fire!"

We rushed outside in our pajamas not knowing what to do. We couldn't call the fire department for fear of our parents finding out. Confusion reigned supreme. We grabbed the garden house and doused the flaming couch but as we were doing so the garden became soaked and we were slipping and covered in mud. Meanwhile the lady in the house behind saw the flames licking toward the wooden garage and called the fire department. Suddenly we heard sirens. At the very moment the fire truck pulled into our driveway, my parents came home with the groceries. Busted. The woman from behind ran over and told my parents how we had been getting into mischief with a fire in the yard. As the firemen blasted the couch with a hose, the fire chief noticed that all the paint was blistering off the adjacent garage. So they blasted the garage too. It was filled with lumber. My Dad was always building things, so it would have gone up like a torch. I received a severe tongue-lashing and was put over my Dad's knee for that one.

Another time I went to the circus and saw an acrobat riding a bicycle on a tightrope. My grandfather had a shed in his backyard known as "the shack." In the summer my grandmother would cook on a wood stove in there and can preservatives in fall. At the other end they had a woodshed where he stored all the junk he would collect from his garbage job. The structure had a flat roof. So I assembled all my friends in my grandparents' backyard and placed a plank on the ground going up to the roof of the shed. As they all cheered me on, I rode back a half a block on my bike and headed full speed toward the plank. "Kaboom." I was on the roof riding around as all the kids cheered. It was a Sunday evening and the whole family was in the house playing cards or just visiting after dinner when they heard the commotion and came outside.

"Get down from there right now! You're going to break your neck."

Well, did I get off my bike and climb down? No, instead in grand circus fashion, I decided to ride off. As I was doing so my bike hit the edge of the plank sticking up above the roof pushing it off and I went careening off the roof headfirst into the woodpile. I split my lip, my nose was bleeding, and my crotch was beyond belief because it hit the crossbar of the bike. As I lay there moaning, all my friends applauded like it was part of the act.

I went on doing things like that not because I was bad, I just had a vivid imagination. My Grandpa took me to a Tarzan movie and when I came home I bugged my mother, "Make me some

Tarzan trunks! Make me some Tarzan trunks!" Over and over. I wanted the leopard skin–style loincloth trunks just like Johnny Weissmuller. She was always sewing but replied, "I don't know where to get that kind of cloth."

"Well, I do."

I ran out to my father's car which had leopard skin seat covers and cut a big swatch about two feet square out of the back seat and took it into my mother. Thinking nothing of it she made me the coolest-looking Tarzan trunks. There I was up in a tree on Seven Oaks and I'm Tarzan. I made a little platform and had taped apples and bananas to the branches so I could simply reach out and grab some fruit just like Tarzan. All the kids on the street were down below pointing at me. "Isn't he cool!" I would ride my bike under the tree and swing up on a branch as the bike carried on.

As my Dad came walking down the street from the bus, he spied this commotion under the tree. Looking up, he smiled, "Wow, you're just like Tarzan up there. Come on down for supper." As I came down from the tree he noticed my loincloth. "Where did you get that?" I hadn't even thought about it.

"The car seat," I told him, frowning. He proceeded into the house and had some heavy words with my mother before another severe over-the-knee whacking for me.

I rarely thought of the consequences before I acted. I would just impulsively do things. Years later I went to the Winnipeg Arena to see Lonnie Mack who played a V-shaped Gibson guitar. I had never seen anything like that before. I went home with the idea that I wanted a Flying V guitar too. My Dad was building our new house; we had moved to Hartford and Airlies over the railroad tracks near my grandparents. The doors had been delivered for the bedrooms and I looked at one and thought "Man, what a great piece of wood." So I took my door downstairs, cut it in half because I only needed three feet, traced a V shape, cut it out, carved out where the pickups and bridge from my Telecaster

should go (I had a Fender Telecaster at home that I wasn't playing), bundled the wires with scotch tape, and stuffed the pickups
in. Amazingly it worked. I thought it was the coolest thing. My Dad
came home from work, and since he was a builder I wanted to
show him what I had created.

"Dad, look what I've made!"

He looked at it and said, "Son, that's incredible. Where did you
get the parts?"

"From my old Telecaster."

"Where did you get the wood for the body?"

And then it hit me. "The wood for the body? Oh, oh."

He walked through the house, and the door was missing from
my room. I really got it for that one.

My Dad belonged to the Legion and he came home one day
and said, "They've got a new flag. Do you want the old one?" And I
said, "Sure." He had no idea what I was planning to do with it. I cut
a hole in it and I wore it as a poncho onstage at the Winnipeg
Arena opening for the Jefferson Airplane. Later it came out in the
local paper: "Alderman's son desecrates union jacket flag." It was
near Remembrance Day and all the veterans were upset. Once
again it was done without thinking.

Randy's Mom was raised in the Orthodox Ukrainian Catholic
Church while Charles Bachman had been brought up Lutheran.
When it came time to choose a religious affiliation, the family opted
for Salem Chapel, a tiny non-denominational affair close to the
Dobrinsky home. Sunday mornings were spent at Salem Chapel fol-
lowed by a traditional Ukrainian family dinner at the grandparents'.
The combination of the two reinforced in Randy a strong sense of
the bond between religion and family.

I came from a background of going to church every Sunday.
We were a fairly religious family. We lived on the outskirts of West

Kildonan at the time and there was a little place on Jefferson
Avenue, Salem Chapel, way out near the tracks that back then was
all prairie. It was this little white building with windows like an
old-fashioned rural schoolhouse. It was a non-denominational mission. They just told stories and we would sing *Yes, Jesus Loves Me*.
There was a lay preacher, Mr. Clayton, who was not a minister in a
clerical collar, and his wife, who played the organ. They both
taught Sunday school. We would sing all these joyous songs and
then split up into little circles by age and study all the Bible stories, like Noah's Ark and Daniel and the Lion's Den. These were
real stories with morals where the good guys win and the bad
guys burn. I never missed a Sunday. It wasn't slanted toward one
particular Christian faith but it gave me a solid foundation and a
warm feeling about religion, a feeling of security and belonging.
So I had this comfortable indoctrination into the values, morals,
and ways of religion.

Afterwards we would walk two blocks to my mother's parents,
my Ukrainian grandparents' house, and have the most incredible
Ukrainian prairie dinner. The whole family, all the aunts and
uncles, would be there. This was my Sunday every single week
growing up and I loved it.

My parents were not fanatical until I turned thirteen or fourteen and by then a Lutheran church had been built in West
Kildonan. The reverend knew my mother and father so he managed to convince them that I should be confirmed in the
Lutheran church. I had to endure all these lessons a couple of
times a week and learn all this weird Martin Luther stuff that I
didn't like. It wasn't fun compared to Salem Chapel. Religion
became strict and formal. As a result, I rebelled and drifted
away in my mid-teens but I never felt a great loss. I knew that
from an early age I had been taught to be a good person and I
lived that in my life and the way I dealt with people. It was a
solid grounding and seemed a natural thing to me.

Randy's introduction to music came at the tender age of three when he appeared on a local radio talent show, *King of the Saddle*. Each week precocious little kids would compete for a five-dollar prize and the honour of being crowned King as determined by audience applause. In the pre-television years, vaudeville entertainment — singers, jugglers, acrobats, comedians, with a live orchestra in the pit — was presented from several theatres in Winnipeg, often between movie features. Randy's Aunt Nerky, Anne's youngest sister who often looked after him as an infant, took the lad down to the Dominion Theatre near the corner of Portage and Main for the live show. It would kindle in him a lifelong ambition.

My big showbiz break came when my mother taught me *You Are My Sunshine*, put a little guitar around my neck, and Aunt Nerky took me down to the Dominion Theatre. It must have been early 1947. There I was singing my little song strumming this guitar tuned to an open chord and it was "Isn't he cute!" The audience applauded me vigorously. I can recall this quite vividly, and I won. The host came out and gave me a brown envelope and when I opened it there was a five-dollar bill. Wow! I had no idea what money was, all I knew was I was King of the Saddle. That little event would serve as a defining moment for me. People were applauding me and I knew it.

But the thrill of victory was short-lived and I was soon to learn the agony of defeat. The next week my mother taught me a new song, *My Best to You May Your Dreams Come True* and dolled me up once again to defend my title. I got up onstage and promptly lost to a little girl who wasn't any better than me, but was cuter with Shirley Temple ringlets. The experience must have imprinted itself on my subconscious because I never wanted to taste that feeling of defeat again. I wanted to bask in the applause.

At age five my parents announced, "We want you and your

brother Gary to play a musical instrument. Randy, what do you pick?"

"Drums!"

"No, too big, too noisy. What's your next pick?"

"Piano!"

"Sorry, can't afford it. What's your next pick?"

"Guitar!"

"No, too noisy. How about a little violin?"

"Well, okay."

So I was given a little half-size violin because I was only five. Gary received an accordion. Actually I had a false start on Hawaiian guitar, playing it flat on my lap like a steel guitar with metal finger picks and a bar but after a couple of lessons that wasn't for me. Instead, I took violin lessons before I had even begun school and the next thing that happened simply astounds me to this day. I couldn't imagine my own kids having to do this at that age. After about a year of lessons, I was required to ride the bus alone — six years old and I couldn't even read the street signs because I was just in grade one. I would look for the soldiers outside Toyland at Eaton's department store, get off the bus with my transfer, and wait there right downtown all alone for a bus that had "Cor" on it. I could read that much. That was the Corydon bus and I would take it all the way to the south of Winnipeg until I saw a big school and playground. I would get off the bus and walk two blocks to Mr. Rutherford's house for a one-hour lesson and retrace my steps, transferring at Eaton's to my bus, which took me near my home. Then I would walk the rest of the way. I did this every Saturday. I didn't even know where I was going but I remember being terrified that if I daydreamed even for an instance I might miss my stop and then what would I do?

Lo and behold, on one occasion I wasn't paying attention and missed getting off at the soldiers. I ran to the driver crying, "Stop! Take me back to the soldiers! I have to get off at the soldiers!"

"I can't, it's a trolley bus. It doesn't back up."

I was inconsolable figuring I was lost forever. So the driver stopped his bus in the middle of the street, let this hysterical little kid with the violin case off, and I walked back to the toy soldiers. As I was doing so, the Corydon bus passed me by. Now I'm panicking thinking that if I miss that bus it was the only Corydon bus ever and I would never get home. I was terrified. I started running and as I did, the driver saw me and stopped to let me on. He was the regular driver and knew me from every Saturday. That moment of sheer terror has never left me.

My first violin teacher, Mr. Rutherford, could be quite cruel. He used to wear a dinner jacket; he was a prim and proper Englishman who wanted me to win the Royal Conservatory and play in competitions, which is the most horrendous thing to put a child through. I had to stand properly but as you tire, your elbow starts to sag. When that would happen, he would hit me with a yardstick. One day I was practising at home and my Dad looked at me and asked, "What are all those marks on your arm?"

"Mr. Rutherford hits me."

"What?! With what?"

"A yardstick, if my arm gets tired and goes down."

"Next Saturday I'm coming with you to your lesson."

So my Dad waited outside while I had my lesson, but he could see us through a window. Sure enough Mr. Rutherford hit me and my Dad caved in the door, grabbed the guy, and shook him.

"Don't you ever do that again." As we were leaving, he informed the other parents about this guy. Next week I had a new teacher.

Randy's first day of school was equally memorable. Built following World War I and named in honour of the valiant efforts of the British Empire, Victory School was a sombre red brick building modelled in the proper British school tradition. Each morning a bell rang at precisely 8:55 a.m. Students would promptly line up, boys on one side, girls on the other, and march left-right-left into the building to the strains of the *Victory March* blaring from an external loudspeaker. Recess time would reprise the formality. The school was located just one block over from the Bachman home, and this allowed young Randy to sleep in longer than other children and then make a mad dash to join the lineup once the bell sounded. Though he did well enough in elementary school, higher education was not his calling. Randy Bachman wanted to be a musician.

My first day of school was traumatic for me because I was without my brother Gary. Up to that point we were inseparable. I couldn't sleep the night before worrying about the first day. I didn't know what to expect. I had heard from older kids in grades two or three about detention and I was petrified. I thought it was like jail.

On the first day, the teacher came down the rows approaching each student asking them their name, what their father did for an occupation, and what they wanted to be when they grew up. What did we know? We were only six. So it was "My name is Iris Freeman and I want to be a nurse. My name is Ronnie Brown and I want to be an accountant like my Dad." Then she stopped in front of me.

"My name is Randy Bachman, my Dad is an optician, and I'm a musician."

Silence. Then "What do you want to be when you grow up?"

I repeated, "I'm a musician."

So she said it again with a little more sternness in her inflection: "Randy, what do you want to be when you grow up?"

"I play violin." I was six and had been playing violin for one year, a fifth of my lifetime.

Slowly and deliberately, as if enunciating the syllables would make a difference to my response, she posed the question once again. I got up crying and ran all the way home. I remember throwing up on the way. As I approached the house my mother was outside hanging up the laundry.

"What are you doing home?!" It was only nine thirty in the morning.

"I don't want to go back to school. I quit."

"You can't quit, you're in grade one."

So she took me back and explained to the teacher how I had won King of the Saddle and had been playing violin for a year. Obviously in my head and heart I was already a musician, whereas the other kids weren't anything yet. They were just kids.

Around age five, Anne and Charles noticed something was wrong with Gary. His walking became increasingly laboured and painful for him. Quite simply, his bones ached when he walked. A trip to the doctor revealed the boy had Perthese Disease or more formally Legg-Perthese Disease, osteochondrosis of the femoral head, a crippling condition that leads to the disintegration of the hip bone and tends to strike predominantly boys between the ages of four and eight. The news certainly altered the close relationship Randy and Gary had enjoyed because over the next five years Gary would spent lengthy stretches at the Shriners' Hospital on exclusive Wellington Crescent in south Winnipeg. When he was home, it was up to big brother Randy to ensure that Gary got to school and back.

I was close to Gary but something happened in his life that brought us even closer together but in a way also separated us at the same time. At the age of five he was diagnosed as having Perthese Disease. If the weight is kept off of the leg for a lengthy period it would grow back to full form with nice rounded edges. But if you put weight on the leg, the hipbone would become flat and you'd have a limp and a funny gait the rest of your life. At the Shriners' Hospital he received crutches and an aluminum brace. He walked with one shoe that had a lift and the other shoe was like a big brace with aluminum piping on it. When he put his

weight down, his left foot was suspended in this aluminum har-
ness. So he walked with a kind of shuffle. But he is one of the few
who recovered from Perthese Disease and to this day all he needs
is about a half-inch lift in the sole of his shoe. Most end up with
one leg four or five inches shorter. That was thanks to my parents
getting him the therapy he needed early on.

As a result of his handicap, I became his mode of transportation. Wherever he went, I pushed or pulled him. We had a little
wooden wagon and he would sit in it and steer and I would push
it. He was five and starting school and I pushed him to school
every day. I was like the workhorse. This went on for four years.
On the back of the wagon was a salmon tin nailed to the frame so
I could put the end of a hockey stick there and push him. In winter I pulled him in a toboggan. Every single day, back home for
lunch, four times a day. I did it and didn't complain but a part of
me wanted to go off and play with the other kids and I must confess that for a time, I was kind of sorry he was my little brother.
I'm embarrassed to say this now because I love him dearly but I
was saddled with this responsibility at the age of seven. I watched
out for anyone making fun of him too. Though I never got into
any fights I would stand up for him and threaten kids and they
would back down. Gary would wave his crutches at guys who
teased him. There are some very sad photos of him with his
crutches at these baseball games wanting to play. He could have
walked on his legs but my parents wouldn't let him because if he
did, the bones would be deformed and he would walk with a limp
the rest of his life. So it was "Do this for four years now and you'll
be okay."

The Shriners were terrific. They covered all the expenses,
provided care for him, and gave us tickets to the Shrine Circus.
I would go and visit him at the Shriners' Hospital. He would go
in for a week or two at a time. But they wouldn't let me in so I
would sit outside his window and he would hang out the window

and I would talk to him. It was really disturbing for me not to be able to go in to see him.

Gary also used to stutter, and as an older brother I used to tease him about it, sad to say. I'm not sure if it was a result of his dealing with Perthese Disease or not.

As Gary recalls, "Life for me at home was different than for Randy. It became his duty as my older brother to look after me when I was home. It was tough on him and I think he might have resented it. I wasn't as footloose as others until I was ten and finally came home for good. During that time, my relationship with the family was different. My brother Tim was born while I was away. I came home from hospital and he was already three months old.

"When my parents bought me an accordion, Randy got a violin and we actually played the last vestiges of vaudeville in Winnipeg performing at the Beacon Theatre at Selkirk and Main. They would show a newsreel and a feature movie and then have a couple of vaudeville acts followed by another movie. Randy's violin teacher was in the pit band and she arranged for Randy and I to play between features.

With Randy on violin and Gary on accordion, the Bachman boys were groomed for the stage. Hardly your typical stage mom, Anne Bachman was nonetheless enamoured with the idea of a performing family. Later, once Tim and Robbie were old enough, they too were parachuted into the act with their big brothers accompanying them.

Every year at the Imperial Optical Christmas party, my brother Gary and I were the entertainment. Instead of being thrilled to go to the party like all the other kids to receive presents from whoever was dressed up as Santa, we would be nervous because we had to get up and perform before everyone. We would play *Oh Holy Night*, me on violin and Gary on accordion. It was terrifying. Looking back though, it was good training for being in front of people and performing, being able to turn it off and on at the same time. Then as we got better we were invited to perform at other events. Our whole Christmas holidays would be spent playing ten or twelve parties.

As I got older and switched to guitar, Gary was still on accordion, Robbie would play Ogilvy Oats tins, those round cardboard containers that I cut down to different sizes to make tom toms using wooden spoons, and Timmy had one of these little guitars with a crank that played *Twinkle Twinkle Little Star*. I was fifteen, Gary was thirteen, Timmy was eight and Robbie was five. We were like the Von Trapp family except now Robbie and Timmy were the cute ones and Gary and I were just the backup musicians. We weren't cute anymore. My mother taught Robbie and Tim to shake like Elvis to *Tutti Frutti* and everyone would guffaw "Aren't they cute!"

But the plus side was that we would be playing all these Christmas concerts at the Polish Legion Hall, the German Club at Mountain and McGregor, the Foresters and so on and when it was all over we would get another present from the Santa. "Play your little numbers and, butta boom, here's a present." An event didn't go by we didn't play at in West Kildonan. There is a little clip of us, the Bachman Brothers, performing in the video for the slower version of *Prairie Town* that my Dad had taken years ago. I'm about fourteen playing my Harmony guitar, Gary's on accordion, and there's Timmy and Robbie with their hair curled like Bugs Bunny in the front and they're doing their little Elvis schtick out front. It's priceless.

While Randy relished the attention, Gary was less than enthused. "My parents always had us as the entertainment at these functions and I hated it. It wasn't that I hated performing, I just wished I played some other instrument than accordion. Back then it was all polkas and Lawrence Welk so it wasn't a cool instrument to be saddled with." The family would travel to Charles's uncle's farm in Woodridge, where the boys would entertain for community functions. As the train pulled in, the whole town would come out to greet them.

Following Randy's abrupt departure from Mr. Rutherford's tutelage, Anne Bachman heard of another violin teacher, Iris Spencer, who played in the pit orchestra at the Beacon Theatre on Main Street. Iris was more to the young lad's liking with a hip approach to the instrument veering him away from the formal classical lessons towards fiddling and popular tunes.

Iris was real show business, not classical. She had me playing King Ganam stuff, the cool fiddle player from *Country Hoedown* on CBC who always dressed in black with a little moustache. Country fiddling reels, Irish and Scottish jigs, this stuff rocked. I would watch *Country Hoedown* to see King Ganam who would do this thing where he would go around in a circle while he played. This was musical liberation for me. Iris made music fun. Mr. Rutherford was like prison camp.

When I was a little older Iris would say to me, "Will your Mom let you come to a show next Friday night?"

"Who's playing?"

"Ray Price."

"Ray Price?!"

Every Ray Price song started the same way with the two-string fiddle intro. My aunt Nerky used to take me to these shows. While everyone was enjoying Ray Price or the other country and western acts I'd be watching the fiddle player. But I soon discovered I was increasingly distracted by the electric guitar players, these guys playing big brightly coloured Gretsch and Gibson hollow body guitars and I started thinking "That's wilder than the violin."

The arrival of Elvis Presley was an epiphany — the liberation of millions of teenagers from the music of their parents and the start of a whole teenage subculture, the culture of rock 'n' roll. Randy took to it like a duck to water. Witnessing Elvis on a neighbour's television altered the course of his young life. Soon he, too, wanted to play guitar.

Television had just arrived in Winnipeg. We didn't have it yet, and I had a friend who had the first set on the block. His dad was an electrician I think. I was invited to this kid's birthday party on a Sunday night and afterwards we watched television. Ed Sullivan was on and Elvis Presley was a guest. When I saw him I thought to myself "Wow, what was that?!" The audience was screaming and they had the screen blocked off from the waist down because he shook his legs and hips.

My Mom was always close to her sister Nerky who was like twenty when I was a kid; blonde peroxide hair cruising around in a big red convertible with her boyfriend playing the radio blasting out Bill Haley, Chuck Berry, all the rock stuff. It was a scene right out of the movie *Grease*. So it was Aunt Nerky who had the hip music. My parents had the typical late forties/early fifties fare: Patti Page, Glenn Miller, Tommy Dorsey. When Elvis came along, my mother didn't mind him. On the other hand, my Dad thought this was terrible when we first saw him on television. I was transfixed. I saved up my money and bought that first Elvis Presley album at Woolworth's next to Eaton's. That was my first record album. On it was *Lawdy Miss Claudy, Tutti Frutti*, all this fabulous rock. There was a wildness to the music — the singing, the rhythm, and playing — that leapt off the grooves. And the guitar playing by Scotty Moore was fantastic.

My brother Gary had some friends who went to the Proteen club, a teen dancehall on Pritchard Avenue off Arlington Street in the North End, a really hip spot for dancers. These guys had dropped out of school and worked so they could afford the coolest clothes. Proteen wasn't blue jeans and t-shirts. Guys dressed up in the hippest white shirts with button-down collars, cool sweaters, pointed shoes that could kick the eye out of a snake polished so you could see your reflection. They went to dance and pick up chicks. These guys were way hipper than I was. Gary brought them over one day and they said to me, "You like Elvis's *Tutti Frutti*?"

"Yeah!"

"Have you heard Little Richard?"

"No. Who's that?"

"He's the guy that wrote *Tutti Frutti*."

So the next weekend they brought over a Little Richard album and, man, if I thought Elvis was wild, this was out of this world. Same songs as Elvis — *Ready Teddy, Rip It Up, Tutti Frutti* — but ten times wilder, screaming and shrieking. I had never heard anything like this, the intensity and ferociousness of that sound. When I played classical violin it was all very structured and formal, playing the notes on the page written hundreds of years before. Now to hear rock 'n' roll and hear the freedom in the notes and playing was liberating to me. Forget the violin, I wanted to play this!

Charles Bachman's relatives, the Dupas family out in the town of La Broquiere near Woodridge southeast of Winnipeg, had two boys a little older than Randy who by 1957 bore the distinction of owning their very own Martin acoustic guitar. Though most often a reluctant visitor to the rural community, once Randy learned of this treasured possession, he couldn't wait to make the trek. And when the Dupas brothers upgraded to a blond, jumbo-sized Gibson hollow body electric guitar, the kind Scotty Moore and Chuck Berry played, Randy was beside himself. By age thirteen the violin was soon supplanted by the guitar.

Their parents were my Dad's cousins but it didn't matter. To me they were as close as my brothers because they had a guitar. Later when they acquired that blond Gibson electric guitar I was overawed by this thing. It was the coolest instrument I had ever seen.

While the grown-ups would be visiting, these guys would let me play their guitar and show me things.

They would teach me Johnny Cash tunes because they were into country music. That fall, being farm boys, they were about to go away hunting for a week so I asked to borrow their guitar while they were away. Before they left I asked them to show me the chords to Johnny Cash's *I Walk the Line*. "Sure." They came back a week later and I could play better than they could. I had taken the chord structure from *I Walk the Line* and turned it into *Be Bop I Love You Baby*, *I'm Sticking with You*, and *Honeycomb*.

I knew that on violin you play positions that become like a capo as you move up the neck. So I applied that same principle to the guitar. "If this is an E chord, if I move it all one fret up and use my other finger like a bar that must be F." All the Dupas brothers knew were open chords and here I was playing up and down the neck. I played the lead line to *Sixteen Tons* for them. They were amazed. They told my Mom, "This kid's a natural."

The advantage I had was my years of violin training. I had the dexterity in my fingers and the all-important brain-to-finger coordination. I was never very good at playing baseball and hockey because my brain-to-legs-and-arms' coordination was clumsy. I was always the worst guy on the team. But my brain-to-finger coordination was incredible. I also knew that the notes moved up the neck like a violin and there was a logic to the chord formations as you moved up. Furthermore, because violin was a lead instrument, you played melodies. Any song I would hear I would listen to the various parts as melodies and apply what I heard to the strings of the guitar.

Soon after that I got my first guitar, a Harmony arch top acoustic which I soon discovered wasn't loud enough for me so I moved up to a black Silvertone guitar from Simpson-Sears, never realizing that an electric guitar also needed an amp. I would press the head against the kitchen cupboard to get the resonance through the cabinet.

Gary's friends would still come over to practise dancing before going to Proteen and bring their records. Although I never stopped loving Elvis, my allegiance was soon divided. I couldn't buy enough records. I didn't have enough money. Whenever I could beg, borrow, or steal records I would absorb the music and learn the guitar parts. School became secondary to me and I began hating to get up every morning.

A firm believer in the value of earning your own rewards, Charles Bachman wasn't about to hand his eldest son an expensive guitar. No, Randy would have to earn it. After many years with Imperial Optical, Charles and Lorne A. Walsh founded Benson-Law Opticians (Benson from the optical company in the States and the Law from Lorne A. Walsh) on Kennedy Street right next to the Salisbury House restaurant around the corner from Portage Avenue. Working downtown was a step up for Charles. On Saturdays Randy would come visit him at the office, have a Mr. Big Nip at the Sals, then stroll down Portage to Winnipeg Piano to ogle the electric guitars hanging on the walls. When it came time for him to earn enough money for his own electric guitar, Charles came through with a lifeline.

My Dad got me a job at Imperial Optical as a messenger boy delivering the finished glasses downtown. Even though he had left, he still had contacts there. With it came a bus pass. Man, that was something. I could go anywhere, anytime with that pass. I would do my deliveries during the day and use the pass in the evenings. I had a briefcase and I would take the bus to their offices on Osborne, pick up the lenses and glasses, hop on the bus to The Bay, get off and all around The Bay and down Portage were the optometrists' offices. I would make my deliveries and pick up the orders, the prescriptions, and frames, from them and take them back to Imperial. I would do five or six trips a day. It wasn't big pay but it was a very responsible job for someone at a young age. On weekends I would babysit and deliver the *Kildonan Post* twice a week, Wednesdays and Saturdays, scrimping and saving up for that guitar.

Tim Bachman recalls something special about his brother's first job. "Just about every payday Randy would buy Robbie and I a little Matchbox toy. That was extremely generous of him because he wasn't making that much. It became a very significant gesture for a teenager to think about his younger brothers and became very special to us."

The remarkable thing about Randy's guitar playing, friends and family earnestly attest, is that he became so good so fast. Part of that had to do with his years of violin training that gave him an ear for melody and a fluid dexterity. Another factor was his commitment to the instrument. Once the guitar came into Randy's life, he literally gave up all else to devote every waking hour to practising and learning songs. "Randy became obsessed with the guitar and music," marvels Gary. "He and I shared a bedroom. As a teenager I would go out in the evenings. As I left, Randy would be sitting on his bed, back against the wall playing his guitar and when I returned several hours later Randy would be in the same position still playing, no matter what time I came home. I got used to falling asleep to his playing so much so that to this day I still love falling asleep to the television or music. One of the reasons he became so proficient was because he learned to play in the dark without looking at his frets. My Dad would holler 'Lights out' and he would keep playing."

In grade seven came the shock of my young life: I had to go to Edmund Partridge School which was probably two and half miles from my house. I took my bike a few times and my spokes got kicked in so I would have to walk there and back four times a day. There was no place to have lunch so we went home, had lunch, listened to CKY, and hoofed it back to school. In grade eight I had

started playing guitar and the next year I met Garry Peterson at
Edmund Partridge. Garry was two years behind me but he played
drums. He was already a boy wonder in the community. Every
time there was a hockey or sports banquet at the end of a season
the entertainment would be a big band record and out would
come this little ten-year-old kid who would do a drum solo like
Gene Krupa in the middle.

Garry was the only kid I knew who played drums. All I'd seen
was Elvis's drummer or Bill Haley's drummer in those rock 'n' roll
movies. I asked Garry if he wanted to drum with me so we could
be like Elvis or the Everly Brothers and he said no. "No?!" So I asked
him why he refused and he said it was because he already played in
a band and made lots of money. I hadn't been thinking about
money, I just wanted to play *Bye Bye Love* and *Don't Be Cruel*.
Garry said "I play weddings and make twenty dollars a night."

"Wow! What do you play?"

"Polkas, schottisches, waltzes, old-time Ukrainian weddings
out in the country with Nick Wally."

Nick, whose name was Wallichinsky or something like that,
played accordion and guitar and knew all the traditional European
wedding songs. Garry said "I'll tell you what, I'll play in your band
for free if you'll come play in mine and you can make some
money." I had my little black Silvertone guitar from Simpson-Sears
but I didn't have an amplifier. Nick Wally had something I could
plug into so I learned *Rebel Rouser*, which basically was a polka
anyway, *Guitar Boogie* and *Under the Double Eagle*, which was a
pedal steel song you could polka to. And I learned *Tennessee
Waltz*, a three-four waltz. I used to back my brother Gary on
accordion so I knew those songs. I played with Garry Peterson in
this polka band on weekends and would come home with thirty
or forty dollars. My Dad at the time was making fifty-five dollars a
week and feeding a family of four. So that was really something. I
was fifteen and Garry was thirteen.

Subconsciously, I must have been influenced by all those
Ukrainian and German polkas with their heavy, stomping, four-on-
the-floor dance beat that drove everyone mad at dances and
socials filling the dance floor. That became BTO's music, that
pounding beat. I'm sure subliminally I was drawing on those early
influences.

I played my first rock 'n' roll dance with Garry Peterson at
Edmund Partridge. It was a Christmas dance and we were called
The Embers — me, Garry and another kid, a schoolmate of mine
named Perry Wauksvik — and we were going to play *Bye Bye
Love* and *Be-Bop A Lula*. I had a guitar cord made with a screw-on
jack that allowed me to plug into the school PA system in the
gym, not realizing that this is the PA for the whole school. I play
a chord and I could hear this echo coming back at me from all
these empty rooms. "Wow! This is like Gene Vincent's *Be-Bop A
Lula!*" The principal introduced us and as we walked out from the
wings, the cord I had hooked into the PA tangled around the
Christmas tree and it started tipping forward as I walked toward
the front of the stage oblivious to the imminent disaster. The kids
were going "Whoa!" watching the tree bend as I strutted forward
thinking "Wow, this is all for me?" I was wearing a little sparkle tie
and cool shirt. "They think I'm Elvis!" The only thing that kept the
tree from toppling over on me was the electrical cord for the
lights plugged into the wall. The tree momentarily suspended on
an angle as I looked back and jumped out of the way just as the
cord gave way and the tree smashed to the floor breaking all the
glass ornaments and bulbs. All my buddies applauded "Yea for
Bachman!" The principal pushed what was left of this decorated
tree out of the way and we play our two songs. What an auspi-
cious debut.

Two years Randy's junior, Garry Peterson was born May 26, 1945,
and lived with his parents and brother Randy on Kilbride Avenue in

West Kildonan. Their friendship predates their early musical endeavours. "I first met Randy playing little league baseball in West Kildonan,"
recalls Garry. "His father was managing the Red Sox and Randy was
playing first base. I was playing for the Tigers. That was preteens. I don't
think Randy really liked sports though. He was a big kid so they always
wanted him to play because he was so imposing, but he was never really into sports, especially after he discovered music. Once he got into
rock 'n' roll that was it for him.

"I started playing professionally in 1949. I was known all over the
city. I played shows at the Playhouse Theatre with the likes of the Ames
Brothers, the Four Lads, the Andrews Sisters, Lionel Hampton. It was
vaudeville with a variety of performers. They had a pit orchestra and I
would come on and do a couple of numbers with them taking drum
solos in the middle. It was all jazz stuff. When I was nine I joined the
Winnipeg Junior Symphony Orchestra made up of all the best high
school musicians who were sixteen and seventeen. When I was eighteen I played with Lenny Breau at the Towers at the Town and Country.
That was amazing."

Never a basher or pounder, Garry's formal training and jazz experience later served him well in the Guess Who as his light touch
became a distinctive feature of the group's sophisticated style. "When
I worked with Nick Wally I had to go sixty to a hundred miles out of
town, play four hours, then get home at three in the morning. That was
tough for a kid of ten or eleven years old. Nick was a good friend of
the family so it was okay with my parents."

I didn't really have a best friend like other guys did. Instead I
had a best friend in school, Dennis Tkach, and a best friend outside of school and that was Garry Peterson. I had two lives, school
and music. I didn't play a lot of sports because I was very awkward. My father wasn't very athletic so we didn't do a lot of that
at home and I didn't learn the rules. I'd play football and the ref
would be blowing the whistle at me and I wouldn't know what I

was doing wrong. "What do you mean there's three downs?" When I sprouted from about five-foot-four to six-foot-two around age thirteen or fourteen, all of a sudden guys wanted me to play football because I was husky. "Nobody'll get by you." But I didn't like it because my fingers would get hurt. I had discovered the guitar and that's all I wanted to do. I told my mother I couldn't wash dishes because it would soften the calluses on my fingers. The next day she threw me a pair of rubber gloves and said, "Your turn for the dishes."

The friendship Randy and Garry have enjoyed since their early teens remains firmly planted. Even today, despite all the water under the bridge, they can still share a laugh together. "I always looked up to Randy. He was two years older but he was also, in my eyes, a cool guy. He was my closest friend growing up. I think we were both shy so we did a lot of things together. We walked to school every day, I lived over on Kilbride and would go down McKenzie to his house. Later we would double date, Randy and Claudia, me and Nadia. Those were magical times, so much innocence. We had nothing to lose and everything to gain. After school we would go over to Randy's house and he would play me all the latest records. But he used to piss me off because he would never play the song all the way through. He would get so excited he'd be moving onto the next song before the first one had ended. I'd say, "Yeah, I love this one but I want to hear the whole song!"

With no formal instruction, Randy would attend all the rock 'n' roll shows that passed through Winnipeg to glean licks from the guitar players. On one occasion he even met one of his earliest heroes and brought him home.

For me growing up, besides Elvis there was Gene Vincent who had *Be-Bop A Lula*. My aunt had the 78 and I would play it all the time and I learned the guitar part. It was a simple riff but very effective. The flip side was *Woman Love*, which was banned

41

because everyone thought it had an obscenity in it. It didn't, it was just the way he sang "Huggin" that people misinterpreted as something else. I would buy Gene Vincent records because they were very similar to Little Richard, very simple chord structures but powerful rock 'n' roll. The guitar playing was terrific and all these guys yelling "Go cat go." It was wild stuff.

I had a friend named Victor Zahn and we both loved Gene Vincent. I would play the guitar parts and he would do the Gene Vincent screaming and dancing. Victor had an old army motorcycle, a brown Harley-Davidson that we used to ride around on.

One day we saw in the newspaper that Gene Vincent was coming to Winnipeg. This was April of 1958. We were beside ourselves with anticipation. He was playing the Dominion Theatre near Portage and Main where years earlier I had been King of the Saddle. It was Good Friday and Victor and I went to the show. There was nobody there. Here he was with three songs in the Top Ten and hardly anyone was there. Maybe thirty people. Back then there was no security so after the show Victor and I went backstage and met Gene and his band the Blue Caps. They gave me a blue cap and signed it. I still have it. I talked to the guitar player about some of the things he had been doing and met Gene Vincent. I noticed he had a brace on his leg.

"How come there aren't any people here?" he asked.

"This isn't a good weekend. It's Passover and Easter."

"Man, we've got three more shows, Saturday afternoon, Saturday night, and Sunday."

They ended up cancelling all but the Saturday night show. Victor and I went again and the band was really rockin'. Again there was hardly anyone there. After the show we went backstage to talk with Gene and the band.

"What are you doing tomorrow?" I asked Gene.

"Nothing. The gig's cancelled."

"Would you like to come over to my house for Easter dinner?"

Being a family with four boys, my Mom was used to us bringing
friends over for dinner.

"Sure. I'd love a home-cooked meal."

"Great."

"But I'll come on one condition: Victor picks me up and drives
me over on his motorcycle." He had spotted Victor's Harley and
was marvelling over it.

"Fine," Victor agreed. Meanwhile, the band was all shouting,
"No, don't let him on this thing! He'll kill himself. He's already got
a brace on his leg."

I went home and told my Mom that we were having one more
for dinner and she was okay with that.

The next day Victor pulls up to our house with Gene Vincent
on his motorcycle and he joins my family for Easter dinner. My
mother had no idea who he was. There we were, four boys in
striped t-shirts and jeans and here's Mr. *Be-Bop A Lula* himself sitting at our table decked out in a puffy black shirt with silver
sparkles like Elvis, his mop of curly hair done up in a cool do, zoot
pants with the long chain hanging down, a leg brace, and big boots.
My parents thought nothing of it. "Just one of Randy's friends." After
dinner Victor picked Gene up and took him back to the hotel.

A further factor in Randy's rapid ascent from novice strummer to
nimble picker in record time came via a rather serendipitous
encounter with someone who would not only become a personal
mentor but go on to be acclaimed as one of the greatest guitar inno-
vators the world has ever seen and may not ever see the likes of again.
Lenny Breau was about to enter the young rock 'n' roller's life.

These days the epithet "genius" is thrown around far too easily. But
when it comes to guitar, Lenny Breau was truly a genius. Born in 1941
of French-Canadian ancestry to show-business parents in Auburn,
Maine, young Lenny became obsessed with the guitar at age three. He
left school at fourteen to join his father and mother, Hal Lone Pine and

Betty Cody, on the road as accompanist in their country and western act under the nickname Lone Pine Junior. The Lone Pine Jamboree travelled the rural country and western circuit throughout the northeastern US and across Canada becoming a popular attraction both live and on radio. Settling in Winnipeg in 1957, the outfit began a lengthy stint as hosts of the CKY Caravan broadcast live from a different location each Saturday morning. Young Lenny idolized the guitar stylings of Chet Atkins and by the time he joined his parents' gypsy-like life on the road he had mastered Atkins' distinctive finger picking perfectly. When Lenny played, it sounded like a whole band. Restless to explore new vistas, Lenny soon moved on from country licks to jazz stylings progressing from the town hall hoedowns to smoky jazz clubs.

Saturday mornings I would listen to the CKY Caravan hosted by Hal Lone Pine. It was pretty hip because he actually had records out on the charts. He would cover maybe Ersel Hickey's *Bluebirds over the Mountain* or a Ray Price song that hadn't crossed the border and he'd get the Canadian hit. He recorded at CKY studios. The Caravan broadcast mostly from car lots throughout the city hustling used cars. You could go down, watch, and have coffee and donuts from the CKY trailer.

Every Saturday I would listen on my radio and after a few numbers Hal Lone Pine would say, "Now we're going to take a break and let Junior play." It wasn't the normal band; they'd all leave the stage area for a cup of coffee. The next thing you would hear was the most marvellous guitar music coming over the airways. It sounded like a whole band, three or four guys playing, so I thought Junior was the name of a band. I was used to playing single notes on guitar like a violin. Each Saturday I tuned in listening for Junior and lo and behold at the end of one show they announced:

"Next week, we'll be at Gelhorn Motors folks. See ya there."

"That's just down the street from me!"

The following Saturday I rode my bike down to Gelhorn

Motors on North Main across from Kildonan Park and waited around watching the group set up. They all wore those typical Nudie-style cowboy shirts with fringes and cactus sequins, but among them was this little guy, really young, about my age, very slight and fragile-looking, sporting dapper clothes and a string bow-tie. His hair was well groomed and he had a pencil-thin moustache. He was playing the most beautiful guitar I had ever seen, an orange Gretsch Chet Atkins model 6120.

The group played its set, which was pretty rockabilly, rockin' country, then, true to form, they announced a break to let Junior play. I waited to see this other band take the stage but instead it was this little guitar player with the moustache and his enormous orange guitar. He started playing and I looked around to see who was playing bass and rhythm guitar but there was no one else there. It was just him. He had an Echoplex amp and he played *Caravan* covering all the parts simultaneously by himself. I'm sure he must have noticed my mouth hanging open and my eyeballs affixed to his fret board. "This sounds marvellous!" He had a Bigsby vibrato arm and every once in a while added soaring vibrato to the notes. He segued into *Liza* starting out slowly with chords and slap-bass rhythm then soloing over it all at the same time.

By now he knew I was watching him. Guitar players always know when another player is watching their fingers. When I would go see Lonnie Mack or the Ventures I would bring binoculars and a note pad. "Twelfth fret, fourteenth fret." I'd take notes, go home, and figure out what they were doing. So there I was gawking at Lenny and when he finished I approached him.

"Can I ask you something?"

"Sure."

"My name is Randy Bachman. I play guitar."

"Mine's Lenny Breau."

"What? I thought you were Junior?"

"Oh, that's just my stage name. This is my Dad and Mom's band."

"What's that called, what you're playing?"

And Lenny replied coolly "It's called Chet Atkins."

I thought it was one big word like flamenco. Chetatkins.

"How do I learn that?" I inquired.

"You have to get it into your head first. You have to get a record."

"Where?" I was ready to do just about anything to learn that style.

"Go to Eaton's record bar and ask for a Chet Atkins record."

The next Friday after school I took the bus down to Eaton's on Portage Avenue and asked the woman at the record bar, "I need a chetatkins record."

"You mean Chet Atkins?"

"No, no, chetatkins. It's a kind of guitar style like flamenco."

So she replied slowly and deliberately but with a grin, "I think you mean Chet Atkins. He's a guitar player."

"No, I talked to this guy and he told me it's chetatkins."

She went behind the counter, pulled out an album and told me, "Listen to this," and put it on.

"Yes! That's it. What's his name?"

"Chet Atkins."

I bought the record, took it home, and learned *The Third Man Theme* by myself, figuring out first the bass line then the melody and putting them together.

Two weeks later, the Caravan played a car lot around Arlington and Mountain Avenue, which is a bit far from where I lived but I made the journey anyway. In the meantime I learned that Lenny had moved across the street from two schoolmates, the Schmollinger twins, Carol and Karen, on Airlies right there in Garden City just north of West Kildonan. After their set, I asked him if I could come over to his house sometime.

"Sure. I don't do anything from Monday to Thursday. I'm practising guitar."

Besides his guitar prowess, I was further enchanted by the fact that this guy, who was not much older than me at the time, was not in school. This was like one of these community service announcements: "You Too Can Quit School." Like Lenny, I wanted to quit school and play guitar all day. What a life!

I went to school the following Monday morning and at lunch I made my way to the Schmollingers' house. Then as they returned to school, unbeknownst to my mother, I went over and knocked on Lenny's door. He was just getting up, it was after one, and was in his bedroom with his guitar and a record player. That first day I showed Lenny what I had worked out, *The Third Man Theme*. He was impressed that I had done it on my own and saw that I had a desire, a determination and aptitude for the guitar. He showed me what I was doing wrong because I didn't know the proper chords so my fingers would be crunched up. "This note here is also over there on that string." From that moment on I was the hunger and Lenny was the nourishment. I visited his house many times over the next couple of years.

Everything I wanted to learn I would struggle at and then have Lenny show me what I couldn't get. He would then show me the slicker way to play it; there is always an easier way to play it on the guitar and I would remember it. I have no cassettes of him, no tapes, no notes, no pictures of him and I together, only my memories of this gentle, soft-spoken young man sitting in his bedroom showing me where to move my fingers. It was probably the greatest couple of years of my life in terms of my learning curve and it gave me the foundation for my playing style today because I started integrating those ideas and styles into my stage playing soon after with the Velvetones, Jurymen, and Allan and the Silvertones. Suddenly I could play more than Duane Eddy or Chuck Berry or Hank Marvin because I had this little edge. I could play this really cool country Chet Atkins style.

I never took any formal guitar lessons so I didn't know the names of a lot of the chords. I would just figure them out using my ear for melody. When I would go hang out with Lenny Breau,

mostly weekdays because he would be out on the road on weekends, he didn't know what some of these chords were called
either. Some young guitar player would say to me after a gig, "Can
you show me that C9?"

And I'd say, "What's that?"

"You played it three times in that last song."

I would be playing these chords without knowing their technical names. Lenny was the same way until he taught himself to
read music. Rock 'n' rollers like me could fake it and Lenny was a
great faker too because he had an incredible ear, he could literally
hear something once and play it, invert it, solo over it, everything.
But in order to make the leap to jazz and classical he needed to
read. I never learned to read. In those days it was just listening to
records, picking up the needle, finding that note by trial and error,
replacing the needle, listening to the next note methodically note
by note over and over. If you had a decent turntable you could
slow an album down to 16 rpm, which left it in the same key but
an octave lower and slower so you could figure out the notes
much easier.

When I would be in Lenny's bedroom watching him, trying to
move my fingers where he did, Lenny spoke very little. Music was
the common language we shared. He had a stutter so it was very
embarrassing for him to talk, but every once in a while he would
simply reach over and move my fingers to the right spots. I didn't
have to move all over the frets, he would show me other notes
closer.

Lenny was extremely disciplined. He would do three hours of
classical practising with Montoya records and then three hours
with Howard Roberts or Tal Farlow doing jazz. He would practise
twelve hours a day. Sometimes I'd have to wait outside because he
was in the middle of one of these disciplined practices and didn't
want to be disturbed. He would even go as far as to put on a cool
coloured shirt and practise jazz, then change to a white flamenco

shirt to practise classical.

One thing Lenny taught me that has remained with me throughout my career is that if you can sing the notes in your head then you can play them. To this day I always sing my solos before I record them. I make up a melody — a melodic line — not just a bunch of scales and licks. He also taught me that the spaces are as important as the notes. Leave some holes and make people anticipate the next note. BB King told me that too years later. What I learned from Lenny was a playing etiquette — not to go berserk with a barrage of notes.

Lenny played some rock, too. He was Scotty Moore to Ray St. Germain's Elvis for a time and recorded *She's a Square* with Ray, but he didn't have the passion to play rock 'n' roll. It was more emotion, more groin than cerebral for him, and he was a thinking player more into esoteric jazz. He could play Chuck Berry but it wasn't him. Lenny was more the ultra-cool beatnik hipster sitting on a stool, cigarette smoke curling around his head, playing Miles Davis or John Coltrane on guitar. He looked so sophisticated, his little Dartagnion moustache, long fingernails, beatnik tam.

As he bridged off into jazz I went off to play in rock 'n' roll bands. By the time I was in the Guess Who in the mid-sixties I would be out on the road a lot. Lenny had left his parents' band, married Val St. Germain, Ray's sister, and was living down around Furby Street. I would call him up and ask if I could come over for a lesson because I would see him playing incredible jazz at the Stage Door. I'd go over to his place for an hour and I'd pay him three bucks.

But by then I had learned pretty much everything I wanted to know about playing Chet Atkins and Merle Travis. I could take a Chet Atkins record, listen to it three times and play the whole thing. I was into rock so I would get him to show me tricks and jazz stuff which I still play to this day, some icings for my cake. But that's life. Friends drift apart and take different paths. But it

has meant so much to me throughout my career to know that I
knew Lenny Breau and learned literally at his feet. He went on to
become a true guitar genius. Players would travel thousands of
miles to see him play and beg for lessons. When I was a kid visiting his house on Airlies he never charged me.

Consumed by his passion for music and cutting classes to hang out
with Lenny Breau, Randy's grades plummeted. School no longer held
any interest to the avid guitarist who nurtured a dream to be a professional musician, a career choice one notch up from pimp or bootleg-
ger in the eyes of his father.

Up until then I had been an A student in school. My parents
told me I had to get A's so I did. But all that stopped in grade eight
and nine when I discovered the guitar. By grade ten I was earning
F's and I failed. After Edmund Partridge I went to West Kildonan
Collegiate until I was asked to leave. I just wasn't applying myself.
I failed grade ten and grade eleven and was well on my way to
flunking grade twelve too. School by then was boring. All I wanted
to do was play in a band.

Any grade is easy when you are repeating it. First time through
I learned about 45 percent and flunked, so the next year my
teacher sat me down and told me, "How stupid can you be to not
learn another 10 or 15 percent? I don't want you flunking again.
Learn another 10 or 15 percent, get fifty-five or sixty and you'll
pass." I just had to take some other things like typing which I'm
forever grateful for. I actually had a very well-rounded liberal
education because when I flunked a grade I would have to take
other courses I hadn't taken the year before. So along the way I
took Shops, Latin, French, Chemistry, Biology, and Physics. I'd flunk
them but I would remember 45 percent of the material.
So I had a smattering of this and that. I could build a hat rack and
conjugate a Latin verb.

In grade eleven I had a revelation. My teacher came to me and said, "You can play anything on guitar. Do you have music in front of you."

"No." I replied quizzically.

"So you play by memory?"

"Yes."

"So you have a great memory. Then why don't you just memorize these four History essays and memorize these twenty theorems in algebra. It's okay when you go into an exam to write down your tables, theorems, and your essay outline. Why don't you memorize them and do that? There are only certain key events they are going to ask you in History so if you memorize four of them you'll be okay."

"Wow, I'll do that."

I realized I had a phonographic rather than photographic memory. If I hear something I can remember it. Just like on guitar, if I can hear it and sing it I can play it. So suddenly on my next Geometry paper I had an A and on History another A.

In grade twelve my friend Dennis Tkach and I would sit at the back of every class and play hangman. We would do this in English class and we had this strict teacher from Britain who believed in caning. He carried a riding crop around under his arm that he would use to wake you up by rapping it across your desk and splitting your paper in half. Dennis and I made the mistake of dating our hangman games each day so in May this teacher strolled down the aisle, opened my notebook and saw that every class since the start of the year we had been playing hangman. He whacked my desk with his riding crop and promptly expelled me, just before the final exams.

So I went home. It was about two in the afternoon and my mother inquired, "What are you doing home?"

"They threw me out of school and told me not to come back."

"What do you mean, it's May. There's only a few weeks left."

"They said I couldn't…"

"Go back, right now!" She had a broom — she'd been sweeping the floors — and she started prodding me with the broom out the door.

West Kildonan Collegiate at that time was all windows and all the kids were watching this scene of me reluctantly running as my mother was banging her broom on the sidewalk behind me chasing me back to school. She went into the principal's office, old O.V. Jewitt, and banged the broom on his desk.

"Take him back, right now! I don't want him at home."

O.V. replied, "I can't take him back. I have to set an example."

So I ended up at St. John's High in the North End where Burton Cummings went and only lasted an afternoon there. My mother then took my case to a new school opening up in Garden City, a newer part of West Kildonan where she knew the principal, Bobby Bend. She had gone to school with him. She went to Bobby and begged, "Please, please, do me a favour and take my son. He's really a good kid. He had all A's until he went crazy over this guitar. Please give him a chance." Bobby looked at me, pointed his finger in my face, and in this James Cagney-like voice threatened, "I don't think you're all that bad. I'm going to give you a chance. But if you blow it…"

"Okay," I nervously replied.

"I don't want to see you skipping classes or getting into any trouble."

And I did quite well. I honestly need to thank him because he saved my high school education. That was at Garden City Collegiate. That's where I met my girlfriend Claudia Senton — my high school sweetheart and my first real love.

By his own admission, there have only been three women in Randy's life. Claudia Senton, now Anderson, was the first. Claudia had moved from River Heights in the south end to Garden City the year she entered grade ten. Her father Glenn worked at Birchwood Motors while her mother worked as a nurse. Claudia and Randy shared a homeroom but because Claudia was in the matriculation stream aiming at university while Randy opted for the general program, the two did not share many classes together. An odd couple — Randy at well over six-foot-two with Claudia barely five-two — the two teens nonetheless found in each other a kindred spirit and soon became inseparable. "In his early years it was his guitar and Claudia," notes Gary Bachman. "She was his first love, his first real girlfriend. She was a bit more forward, outgoing, and friendly than he was. With her I saw a Randy that I didn't know. He was always rather quiet and withdrawn and didn't like company much because he lacked confidence and social graces. She brought him out of his shell. Claudia would arrange double dates and social activities that involved him because he could never do that. He wasn't the instigator."

"Randy and I connected because I think we knew we were different," reminisces Claudia. "We both came from very humble, average backgrounds but we knew in each other that we had gifts. We were very unusual teenagers. We didn't do the usual things other teenagers did at that time. We didn't drink, we didn't have sex, and we lived totally in our own belief systems that we could accomplish something. And we talked about that all the time. How many teenagers in those days would sit in a parked car on a cold winter night out on the Perimeter Highway for hours with the car running so we didn't freeze to death talking about our dreams, hopes, goals, and aspirations? Most kids would have been making out, wrapped up in the lust of it all. Instead, we had this incredibly deep relationship of understanding, like two old souls.

"It was like we were always the king and queen of the May, the golden couple. When we walked down the halls, other students used to tell me the crowds would part and there was an aura about us. We were lucky because we had a great teen life. Not all teens had that. And we were so lucky, as well, to be growing up in Winnipeg in the late fifties which was a very magic time and place.

"Randy had the classic characteristics of an obsessive personality," stresses Claudia. "I don't know what he did before he connected with music because I met him just as that connection was starting but it became an obsession for him. Writing songs and lyrics became his form of self-expression. Until he discovered music and it became the vehicle for his own personal growth and development, Randy struggled with who he was. He considered himself to be not very bright and in today's standards you might consider that he suffered an attention deficit because he would get bored so fast it was unbelievable. He still does. But if it was something he was interested in, he had this incredible capacity to suck up everything about it. His learning and knowledge base were only geared to things that interested him and if it didn't interest him you couldn't get him to learn it if his life depended on it. Consequently he didn't do well in school, didn't like school, and daydreamed a lot.

"As a teenager Randy was shy and lacked confidence unless he had a guitar in his hand. He relied on me to do the social things that most teenagers would do in their lives. He really didn't like crowds so if we went to a dance he did not enjoy himself unless he was playing at it. He liked arriving, playing, and leaving. To get him to come down to the floor and dance with me was like pulling teeth. He was too self-conscious. He really didn't like to be around a lot of people so we didn't have a lot of friends outside of the band. We just hung out with each other.

"Everything was in the context of music to Randy. It's funny because with the degree of recognition he has achieved, people would recognize him and would have all these connections to him based on their lives, but he would have no connection to them other than what was going on with the band, the music he was writing, and where the band was playing at the time. Thank goodness he had the courage to embrace his passion because the world didn't make it easy for him."

With both parents working, Claudia became a fixture in the Bachman household every day after school, with Anne treating her like the daughter she never had. "She was like my other Mom," smiles Claudia. "She was wonderful. She had these four boys who did nothing else but eat. Back then Randy was a big kid, tall but in those years he didn't have a lot of body weight on him. He was lanky and pretty slim. Rather than go home to an empty house, I would go to Randy's house and eat my way through the next two or three hours and often stay for supper. And in-between eating we would do homework together. I always felt very much at home there and I think there was this belief that Randy and I were going to live happily ever after. His mother thought we were going to be together forever."

Claudia tutored me endlessly, hour upon hour every evening, word by word, phrase by phrase, in French vocabulary and Math and instilled in me the importance of caring about school and how it would mean something to my self-worth to complete grade twelve. She drove it into my head to complete high school because before that I didn't care. I just wanted to play music. The big thing then was to finish high school and not be a dropout. Who knew, maybe this music thing might not work out and I might want to go to college.

At the end of the school year, 1963, Claudia was picked the sweetheart queen and I was the sweetheart king. At the prom, my band was playing so in order for me to dance with her as the king and queen, I had to leave the stage and the band carried on without me for one song. After that, I scrambled back onstage to finish the night.

I almost flunked grade twelve but rather than repeat it again instead I went to the dreaded summer school. There were two subjects I didn't pass and luckily one was History which I had aced the year before. In grade twelve I had gambled and learned the wrong essays. So in summer school, the instructor advised me, "If they asked those topics on the June exam, chances are they'll ask the other ones for the August exam so learn those." And so I did and passed.

With school finally behind him, Randy set his sights on a future in music. His parents, however, had different ideas.

CHAPTER 2

Shakin' All Over

For teenagers growing up in Winnipeg during the fifties and sixties, two factors shaped their lives offering escape from the routines of school and family: the radio and the community club. Radio became their window to the world while the neighbourhood community club served as the socializer where boys met girls, listened to records, danced, and shared a first kiss. For some, it was the place to make music as well.

Located on the basin of the Great Plains, Winnipeg crackled on a clear night with AM airwave signals from across the continent. You could lie in your bed, twirl your radio dial, and through the static pick up stations from exotic locales that filled your head with strange new sounds and enticing images — Shreveport, Louisiana; Albuquerque, New Mexico; Chicago; Buffalo; Memphis — places you had never been to nor were likely to visit except via radio wave. You could listen to those sounds and dream of going to Shreveport with visions of bayous and juke joints beckoning. Names like Gatemouth, Stan the Man, Hound Dog, and Wolfman Jack furthered the mystique. It was like belonging to some secret club, a cult, where you were privy to all these incredibly unique sounds that no one else had heard.

I don't think I slept a lot as a teenager. I was always glued to the radio at night. I would be a zombie the next day at school but all the kids were like that.

"Turn that radio off and get to bed!"

I would take my rocket radio under the covers and carry on with my nightly ritual. Just like kids nowadays surfing the Internet, in the fifties teenagers surfed the radio dial.

For as long as I can remember my greatest teacher was the radio. When I sang in *Prairie Town* "We didn't have much but a radio" literally that's all I had, a little white radio my Aunt Nerky gave me that wouldn't work unless I put my hand on it. It was a tube radio and somehow I grounded it with my hand. If I took my hand away I would hear all this static. To this day I can put this right hand in an oven and not feel anything because it became so used to all that heat from the tubes.

Radio in Winnipeg in the late fifties and early sixties was incredibly exciting. At night I could pick up signals like WLS from Chicago, or KLOS in Los Angeles, WNOE in New Orleans, or Wichita, Kansas. I would run to school the next day and tell my friends "I got Wichita, Kansas, on the radio last night and they played *Rock Around the Clock*!" I would stay up until three in the morning listening. I ordered records from Stan the Record Man in Shreveport, old 45s of rhythm and blues guys. There were no rhythm and blues records in Winnipeg. Those records gave me my initiation into blues guitar. So the radio became my educator and it still is.

My mother always had the radio on around the house. We would come home at lunch and tune into CKY or CKRC for a whole hour listening to rock 'n' roll. CKY was a big 50,000-watt station and they received all the new records. They were still country music but played rock 'n' roll at certain times of the day. I would return to school with my head pounding with these wonderful rock 'n' roll songs. One lunch hour I heard Chuck Berry's

School Days for the first time and was completely blown away. I had never heard guitar like that.

I used to go to all the country and western package shows at the Winnipeg Auditorium and on one occasion they introduced this fellow with neat blond hair who sat down at the piano and played *You Win Again* and a Johnny Cash song. Then he jumped up, kicked the piano stool aside, and started pounding *Whole Lotta Shakin' Goin' On* with his hair falling over his face. It was Jerry Lee Lewis. I'd never seen anything like him. It was a country show where people sat there and politely applauded Kitty Wells or Patsy Cline. The next day on the radio Doug Burrows at CKRC played *Whole Lotta Shakin' Goin' On*. Rock 'n' roll was just catching fire in Winnipeg and the phones lit up. So he played it again back to back. I was mesmerized. I would sit by the radio with my Silvertone guitar and try to play these incredible songs.

I didn't hang out with other teens at the usual spots. Instead I hung out with guys who had records. Music was the attraction for me. I didn't like to go to the YMCA because it was too far downtown but a lot of my friends were Jewish — Richard Sheps, Carol Sprintz, Henda Plosker — so they would invite me to the YMHA. Didn't matter to me. Great pool, nice restaurant, and dances every Saturday night with great-looking Jewish girls, dark and gorgeous. Whoa! At fourteen these girls were like women already. To see them in bathing suits and then at the dance later that evening was something else. I met a lot of people at the Y who thought I was Jewish. With a name like Bachman, I could be. We would ride our bikes down Salter to the Jewish Y or take the bus and accompany the girls home afterwards on the McGregor bus. For us, bus transport was everything back then.

I used to play some of the dances — Garry Peterson and I. I would get on the bus with my guitar and amp and two stops later Garry would get on with his drum set. We would ride the bus down to the Y and play a gig. Maybe his Dad would pick us up because as a musician himself, Ferdie Peterson was always out playing gigs. Or my Dad might drive us home. Otherwise at midnight we rode the last bus home with a whole gang of kids and our equipment. It was just so simple and innocent then.

Like most metropolitan centres, Winnipeg is a collection of diverse communities and neighbourhoods united as a result of urban sprawl under a common banner. Though now incorporated into Winnipeg proper, West Kildonan was a separate community when Randy was growing up, along with East Kildonan, Fort Garry, St. James, and St. Vital, to name a few. These communities retained a strong sense of individuality and local identity back then. Indeed, Winnipeggers thought of themselves first and foremost as hailing from their own community. Furthering that sense of distinctiveness was the community club located in each neighbourhood. With a baseball diamond, soccer pitch, outdoor hockey rinks, canteen, and social hall hosting everything from cub scouts to bingo to wedding socials, the "club" was the hub of the community where both parents and kids congregated. Loyalties and neighbourhood club rivalries could be quite fiercely defended. When North End hockey teams played teams from the South End like River Heights or Crescentwood, pitched battles could erupt in the stands. Bands would emerge from these neighbourhoods to become popular on their home turf and just like hockey or baseball teams, rivalries carried over. Battle of the band competitions could sometimes be just what the name implied; rarely did an interloper from outside the neighbourhood upset the local favourites. If they did they might have a tough time getting out of the building in one piece.

When you take stock of the impact Winnipeg, alone on the prairie boondocks, has had on the international music scene in the sixties to mid-seventies, the tally is staggering. Together the Guess Who, Bachman-Turner Overdrive, Neil Young, Randy Bachman, and Burton Cummings account for in excess of sixty million records sold.

I am often asked the question, "Why Winnipeg?" There are a couple of reasons. One is the city's remoteness. It's pretty much dead centre in the continent, and the nearest city, Minneapolis, is still quite distant. In winter Winnipeg is even more isolated. Therefore Winnipeggers have often had to go it alone rather than following national trends. Another factor, I think, is the multicultural nature of the population, the diverse ethnic mix, a smorgasbord, and to this day each retains a distinct identity within the city. There are Polish clubs, Ukrainian clubs, Italian clubs, Belgian clubs where they hold weddings and socials. Hand in hand with these cultural identities, each neighbourhood had its own focal point, the community club. So when teenagers got together at their local high school or on their block to form bands in their basement (it was too cold to practise out in the garage) they had all these venues available right in their community. On any given weekend there were literally hundreds of dances organized throughout Winnipeg at community clubs, ethnic halls, church basements, and schools. It was a great city for breaking bands, especially in the community clubs.

I couldn't dance fast, most boys couldn't, but I could handle a slow dance. Just grab a girl in a bear hug around the waist, hold on as tight as she would allow, and shuffle around the dance floor to *In the Still of the Night*. That was my favourite song because it was long and slow and great for clutching. Generally, it's an older sister who teaches you how to dance but I was the oldest and had all brothers so I never really learned. I loved the music and wanted to dance but I was too self-conscious of making an idiot of myself in front of the girls. Usually the last dance was a slow waltz so you would wait all evening making eye contact with the girl you fancied and when they played that final song you would pluck up the courage to ask her onto the floor and slowly sway around the room.

What began simply as neighbourhood kids spinning their

favourite 45s soon evolved into live bands playing the popular
music of the day. As an alderman, my Dad often ran the dances at
the West Kildonan community centre on Friday nights, so I asked
him if I could be the deejay sometimes. They had a little PA and a
mike so I would introduce the songs then put the mike in front of
the record player to blast the music out. That's how I started out
and I began thinking maybe I could play here with a band. Back in
1961 Neil Young was the deejay at Earl Grey Community Club, his
neighbourhood club, and when he formed his first band they
played at Earl Grey. That's how everyone got his or her start.

If there was one thing that set the Winnipeg music scene apart
from every other major centre it was the community clubs. With more
than fifty community clubs scattered throughout the city, they offered
music at a grassroots level for aspiring young musicians. "The community club scene was really unique back then," remarks Neil Young,
recalling his glory days on the local club circuit. "There was nothing
like it anywhere else. Kids would dance or just watch the band playing." BTO's Fred Turner adds, "If anyone ever asked me when the best
times were in music for me, it was back in those early days in the community clubs. The first real gig I ever played was at Orioles Community
Club for a soft drink and a chocolate bar. With everyone plugged into
one or two amps there would be so much racket on stage you had to
kick guys in the ankles to get them to change chords."

It was a natural progression for me to move from playing the
records to actually performing at my community club, first with
Garry Peterson and then the two of us with Mickey Brown.
Eventually we learned enough songs to play an entire evening,
three or four one-hour sets with a ten-minute break in-between,
and we were off and running. Nothing could stop us.

The community club was an incredible beehive of excitement
and a nurturing ground for musicians. Initially you would play

dances at your own neighbourhood community club then get invited to community clubs outside your neighbourhood like River Heights in the south end. And River Heights bands like The Squires with Neil Young would be invited to play in your area and it grew from there. What we went through in Winnipeg in the sixties would make such an extraordinarily glorious, joyous movie people wouldn't believe it. It would be better than the Tom Hanks movie *That Thing You Do*. It was so wonderful the sense of family, community, and music all together.

I heard about this guy, Mickey Brown, who played at Eaton's fashion shows and wore sweaters, white bucks, and a Frankie Avalon hairdo. Somehow he heard of Garry and me and came to see us. "I want you guys to be in my band." It was ridiculous. I played guitar and didn't even have an amp. Garry played drums. We had a piano player; Mickey sang and played rhythm guitar. That was the band. Nobody cared that we didn't have a bass player, nobody knew about bass players in Winnipeg then anyway. Mickey knew how to get his hands on a Silvertone amp with two channels so I could plug my guitar into one channel, it had reverb and tremelo, and Mickey ran a microphone through the other channel. We also put the piano through the amp with a contact pickup so the band had a bottom with the bass keys. With that we went out and played the community clubs on the west side of the Red River regularly. In those days we could get the whole band into a station wagon — the drums, amps, and all of us. This was essentially my first formal band that had a stable lineup.

At age sixteen, Randy, along with his faithful sidekick Garry Peterson, joined singer Mickey Brown and piano player Ron Edgar to become the Velvetones, one of the most popular groups on the burgeoning community club circuit in 1960. "That was Randy's first real serious band," recalls brother Gary. "I saw them for the first time at the Playhouse Theatre for one of those multiband events like a battle of the bands with Roy Miki and the Downbeats featuring Fred Turner, The Jury, and all the bands at that time. But when Mickey Brown came out there was screaming from the girls as if Frankie Avalon had just come onstage. That band was hot." The Velvetones also backed a singer named Gary Cooper, a shoe salesman from Portage La Prairie, on a 45 record. *Heartaches and Disappointments* backed with *Come On Pretty Baby* marked Randy Bachman's vinyl debut.

One of the Velvetones' most requested numbers was a little something called *Randy's Rock*, an original instrumental Randy concocted.

Randy's Rock was the intro to *Johnny B. Goode* and *Oh Carol*, just Chuck Berry licks strung together. Rather than call it *Johnny B. Goode*, Doc Steen at CKRC said, "Why don't you call it *Randy's Rock*?" I played it for Jim Pirie who was the hot guitarist around town working with the CBC before Lenny Breau and he wrote out the transcription for it.

"Why is it called *Randy's Rock*?" Pirie asked me.

"Because I wrote it."

"No you didn't. It's all Chuck Berry stuff."

That shattered me. Someone had found me out.

Mickey Brown was a teen heartthrob and girls actually screamed at him. We were playing Jerry Lee Lewis, Elvis, Gene Vincent, Fabian kind of stuff. Eventually I threw Mickey out of the Velvetones because he was more interested in girls than the music. We would be onstage playing and he would disappear into the audience lining up dates with likely young ladies. Garry and I just wanted to play; we were totally committed to playing, one hundred percent. Mickey was in it for the chicks, we weren't.

"We don't need a singer. We'll do instrumentals."

So we dumped him, picked up a tenor sax player, Joel Shapiro, and changed the name of the band to the Jurymen.

Instrumentals were the big thing then: the Ventures, Johnny and the Hurricanes, the Champs, Duane Eddy. I had acquired an amp and a big orange Gretsch guitar like Lenny Breau's so I turned my old Silvertone guitar into a bass by putting bass strings on it so my brother Gary could join us on bass. We didn't need a PA system; we could just walk out onstage and play instrumentals. I would do *Walk, Don't Run* and I took *Chapel in the Moonlight* and gave it a Ventures' arrangement. We also did *Sleepwalk*. We were smokin'. We'd do three fast songs and a slow song, that order all night. It was great because it got us into a whole other kind of music.

Drafting siblings into his band would become a pattern for Randy later on in his career. "Gary didn't have much interest in it," suggests Claudia Senton Anderson, "but Randy would spend hours and hours with him teaching him to play so he could be in the band. It was always intriguing to me how Randy made such a conscious effort to bring his brothers into the business." For Gary, though, playing onstage did not hold the same allure. "Playing with Randy and Garry Peterson, I had no idea of how good these two were. They were amazing players at an early age. It was a pretty hot band. The biggest gig we ever did was backing up Canadian teen star Bobby Curtola at the Transcona Arena before about three thousand people. It was at that point that I realized I would rather be in the crowd watching than up onstage playing. I just didn't have the same drive as Randy. I had a girlfriend who I thought I was in love with and didn't want someone else dancing with her or something like that. That was the last time I played."

More independent, with an eye to striking out on his own, Gary had taken a job at the Canadian Wheat Board downtown where he chanced to meet two young employees as keen on music as his big brother. "I was working with a guy named Jim Kale from St. Vital who had a Fender bass and a Fender amplifier, one of the only guys in town with this kind of professional equipment. His band was playing all the time but when he wasn't working and the Jurymen were, I would borrow his bass and amp. Jim Kale was a great guy, very generous and kind, always willing to loan out his equipment to other players. As a matter of fact Neil Young once remarked to Randy that if it hadn't been for Jim Kale's generosity and equipment he wouldn't have played nearly as often as he did in those early days. Bob Ashley, who played piano, also worked at the Wheat Board. He and Kale lived near one another in St. Vital and had joined Allan Kowbel from East Kildonan as Allan's Silvertones, named for the Sears guitar. At some point they needed another guitar player and Jim mentioned this to me one day at the Wheat Board. So I told Randy about it."

The Silvertones were from the other side of the Red River and were a popular East Kildonan group whose reputation was already beginning to spread around the city. I had heard of them. Allan Kowbel, who later became Chad Allan, was the leader and was playing lead guitar at the time so I was asked to audition for rhythm guitar. The group's repertoire consisted largely of material from Cliff Richard and the Shadows from Britain whose guitar player was Hank Marvin. I had never heard the Shadows until I met Allan. They gave me a couple of Shadows EPs to learn from which, I think, had *Kon Tiki, Man of Mystery, FBI*, and songs like that. I learned the chords no problem, I had a few days to figure them out. But the melodies were a piece of cake for me so I learned them too just for fun. With my background in melody from years of violin and my time with Lenny Breau, moving on to the Shadows seemed natural for me.

At their next rehearsal, Allan was playing lead and singing, with me playing rhythm. We rehearsed in a cubbyhole by the stairs at Bob Ashley's house and in the middle of a song Allan broke a string. Instinctively switching from rhythm to lead, I finished the song. When it was done I sheepishly looked at Allan figuring that was it, I had stepped on his toes. They were all looking at me when he said, "It's so hard to play lead and sing at the same time. I'll just play rhythm. Randy, you're now the lead guitar player." Boom. I was in.

Bob Ashley had an old German Kortung tape recorder and he mentioned that if you turn the heads out, one is record and the other play, you could get an echo. "Really?!" I lit up. Hank Marvin used echo in the Shadows. We didn't know what an echoplex was and even if we did you couldn't buy one in Winnipeg. I begged and pleaded with Ashley and finally he parted with it and I had special patch cords made and plugged my Gretsch guitar into this tape recorder and from that into Jim Kale's Fender Concert amp. I got the most incredible echo sound from that little homemade system. Even Neil Young commented on my cool echo sound I used to get. That became my sound.

After I played one or two gigs with Allan and the Silvertones, I went to Allan, Jim, and Bob and informed them, "I can't play with your drummer anymore." Brian "Ducky" Donald had no backbeat. All he did was military-style drum rolls. Every song sounded like *Wipe Out*.

"I've got this friend, Garry Peterson, who's a boy wonder. He can play anything and he can read music."

This was a Tuesday and we had a big dance booked for the coming Saturday at Daniel MacIntyre Collegiate.

"Yeah, Ducky isn't that good but how are we going to fit in another drummer before Saturday? We can't do it."

So I jumped in with, "How about right now?"

It was about eleven thirty in the evening when I phoned Garry's house. His dad, Ferdie, gruffly answered.

"Yeah, who is this?"

"Mr. Peterson? It's Randy Bachman."

"What do you want?!"

"I'm at a rehearsal with my new band and the drummer isn't very good. I would really like Garry to be in the band."

"Yeah? So what's the problem?"

"They need to hear him now. Tonight. The gig is Saturday and we only have one day to rehearse, Friday after school."

Pause. "Okay, come on down." Being a musician himself, bless him, Ferdie Peterson knew this was an opportunity for his talented son.

We were out in St. Vital on the southeast side of the city. Kale phoned a friend who had a car and by the time we arrived at Peterson's with our guitars and Kale's amp it was almost two in the morning on a school night. I knew I was going to catch it from my parents when I finally got home but this was the moment and we couldn't let it pass. We went down to the basement where Garry's drums were set up. Ferdie put on a tape of Louis Belson or Buddy Rich, big band music. Garry took his seat at the drums and as the music swelled toward the drum break, Ferdie stopped the tape and Garry who was all of fifteen but looked eleven launched into the most incredible drum solo. Bob, Jim, and Allan dropped their jaws. We did a number together, Floyd Cramer's *On the Rebound*, a recent radio hit. For the first time these guys felt a solid backbeat behind them. As the song ended everyone looked at each other and said, "You're in."

It was three in the morning as I snuck into the house. My Dad confronted me with, "What are you doing coming in so late on a school night?!"

"I wasn't doing anything wrong," I replied confidently. "It was the chance of a lifetime. We were getting my friend Garry into the band. You can phone Mr. Peterson and check it out." He did and everything was fine.

At school the next day I gave Garry the records I had with the songs the band did and showed him the ones I didn't have records for. By the end of Friday's rehearsal he knew the thirty songs we had for our set and at the Saturday gig we were incredible. And that solidified the lineup: Chad Allan, Randy Bachman, Jim Kale, Bob Ashley, and Garry Peterson. Soon after we changed the name to Chad Allan and the Reflections. Playing mostly British material set us apart from the other bands around town.

Taking the name Reflections from the Shadows, the group was the toast of the town in short order. As Jim Kale once remarked they were the best jukebox band in the city. "We always went to see them play," says Burton Cummings on the stir the Reflections caused at the community clubs. Cummings was fronting his own North End band, The Deverons, but was in awe of Randy's group. "I must have seen them eight or ten times before I even talked to them. This guy Bachman on guitar, well you just had to see him. We'd stand back about a hundred feet because we were so intimidated. They were so great." Drawing on a hitherto untapped source of material, the Reflections had the novelty of uniqueness coupled with raw talent.

"Randy was definitely the biggest influence on me in the city," acknowledges Neil Young, one of many neophyte guitar players smitten with the melodic Shadows sound after witnessing a Reflections performance. Young quickly became a Bachman disciple, following his mentor from dance to dance to watch his fretwork. "He was the best. I'm like an axe compared to him. Back in those days he was light years ahead of anybody else. He had a homemade echoplex from a tape loop on an old tape recorder and he did that Shadows style better than anybody. He was playing a big orange Gretsch guitar and I got one like his. I bought it from Johnny Glowa who was the guitar player in the Silvertones before Randy." Neil's Squires were soon introducing Shadows material into their repertoire.

I know of a lot of players in this city who took up their instruments or were motivated to form a band because they saw the Reflections play somewhere. They were thirteen or fourteen. We weren't much older but had a head start. That lineup was so talented, head and shoulders above the local rabble, because we could really play. No one could do Floyd Cramer piano licks like Bob Ashley or play Duane Eddy, Shadows, or Ventures guitar like Chad and I. Other drummers couldn't play a drum solo like Garry. He'd been doing that since he was four. We had training in harmo-

ny, arrangement, structure, tempo, and playing in time so that
when we listened to a record we could copy it perfectly, not just
the notes but the phrasing, tonality, and delivery, and sound identical to the record. And it was all done by ear. We could literally play
a song after one or two listenings.

I remember playing a dance, probably at River Heights or somewhere in the south end, where I was introduced to Neil Young. He
was a skinny, dark-haired kid who had come to the dance with
Lorne Saifer who was managing him at the time and he stood to
the right of the stage, my side, and watched me. I had heard of
him because in Winnipeg you tended to know of other guitar
players who were good. I ran into him a few times at the
Paddlewheel Restaurant at The Bay where all the musicians hung
out or at Winnipeg Piano checking out the guitars. Even from
early on, I noticed in him a determination and a sense of direction
that set him apart from most of the players on the local scene. He
later told me he saw the same in me. Neil wanted to be better
than Chad and me. He had something in his eyes that told me he
knew what he wanted to do. From that early age it was obvious
he had a dream and nothing was going to stop him from fulfilling
it. My only regret is that he and I never played together back then.
If we had teamed up on double lead guitar it might have been
incredible but I guess it was never meant to be.

Once we started going further afield, Neil wanted to know
what that was like. He would ask us questions about our experiences. "Neil, there's life outside of Winnipeg. Rock 'n' roll does
exist out there," Jim Kale and I told him. When he left Winnipeg
most people laughed at him. "We'll never hear from him again."
But he certainly proved everyone wrong. I thought he would
make it somehow. He had such drive.

Besides talent, the Reflections boasted versatility. Garry Peterson
had learned to play a decent alto saxophone and would come out front

to wail on *Wild Weekend* while Chad or Randy manned the drums. Chad could play lead and also handled keyboards with Jim often singing a few numbers. "I was always impressed with the fact that they were able to switch instruments," marvels Burton Cummings. "They were the only guys who could do that." The group was frequently augmented by female singers Carol Barnes or later Carol West to give their repertoire further depth. In the nucleus of the Reflections were the finest young musicians Winnipeg had to offer.

Garry Peterson was like a brother to me. We had known each other since we were kids and had grown up in the same neighbourhood. On the road we shared a room, sometimes even having to share a bed when times were lean. We had a lot in common coming from strong family backgrounds. I had a younger brother named Gary; he had a younger brother named Randy.
We were used to hearing those names.

Jim Kale was more distant because he came from another part of the city, St. Vital, but I had an affection for Jim because he was a generous individual and a really good guy. Everybody borrowed Jim Kale's amp; he had the only Fender Concert in town, and when he wasn't playing guys would be calling him to borrow it. Some bands literally couldn't play if Jim had a gig that night. He also loaned out his Fender Precision bass that, for a time, was the only one in town.

Chad was very introverted and quiet. Being an only child he never learned how to act around other guys — kibitzing, pranks, practical jokes, or helping each other out. He couldn't relate to those situations and seemed removed from that, aloof and in his own world separate from the rest of us. Bob Ashley was even more removed from us, introverted to the extreme and painfully uncomfortable around people.

The Reflections brought a whole new repertoire to other musicians and bands. As a result, Winnipeg had this little enclave of

Hank Marvin fanatics playing *Kon Tiki* and *Wonderful Land* when
no one else on the continent was doing it. No one had heard the
Shadows instrumentals, Mike Berry and the Outlaws, Shane Fenton
and the Fentones in Winnipeg until we played them. We recorded
that stuff too, like *Tribute to Buddy Holly*, a Mike Berry and the
Outlaws song, or *It's Just a Matter of Time*. Even some of our early
original songs were derivative of those obscure British artists. *Shy
Guy* was basically Shane Fentone's *I'm a Moody Guy*.

Spurred on by the Shadows sound and Hank Marvin's melodic guitar
style, Randy composed his own Shadows tribute, *Made in England*, a
catchy instrumental that mimicked all the trademark nuances and hooks
of the British group. Randy's nimble fretwork so impressed Neil Young that
he penned his own Shadows style instrumental, *Mustang*, acknowledging,
"*Made in England* was the kind of sound we were trying to imitate."

Brazenly, I sent a copy of *Made in England* to my heroes the
Shadows in England. I figured they might want to record it. I
received a rejection letter on the group's own letterhead, which
featured the four guys in silhouette. It read: "We received your
record but unfortunately we do not feel it is appropriate to record
at this time." That was the thrill of my life at that point. Me, a kid
from Winnipeg, sending the Shadows my own composition and
receiving a reply. Didn't matter whether they recorded it or not.

With an eye to the business end of operating a band and armed
with his parents' sense of frugality, Randy managed the group's finances,
collecting the fees at the end of the night, paying the expenses, and
watching the bottom line. In that capacity he became the group's de
facto leader, and over the years the group's various managers learned
that decisions had to be vetted through Randy first. The other band
members acknowledged his role and deferred to his authority.

"Randy was the dad of the band," observes Claudia Senton

Anderson on the dynamics of the relationships within the group, "the guy who worried about everything: getting the equipment to the gig, getting it back to his house to be stored. He was fastidious about everything. He had to pack the same way and unpack exactly the same. It used to drive the other guys nuts, especially Jim Kale. They couldn't understand that about him.

"It was always amazing to me that Jim stayed in the band with Randy because he was always threatening to walk out, always going to quit. Randy would get so pissed off. I remember driving home from gigs with Randy and he would be just beside himself about Kale, complaining that Jim wouldn't want to try something or change something. Jim was extremely stubborn and that drove Randy up the wall.

"Garry Peterson and Randy were the closest. Garry was always upbeat and enthusiastic, keen to learn and grow and saw in music a wonderful opportunity for a career. Randy would spin the dreams and Garry would get on board. Garry was dependable and always willing to do whatever it took whether carrying the equipment or loading, all the dirty work that wasn't fun whereas with Jim you never knew what he was going to do from one day to the next. Garry contributed a hundred percent and in those early years he was a good partner for Randy."

"Chad Allan was an interesting guy," continues Claudia, "reclusive, introspective, almost a geeky kind of kid. Randy liked him because he was bright and could write and contribute on a creative level. When they would be putting stuff together Chad was always interested in how to make it different and better. That became a connection between him and Randy. The two worked well together in the first few years but Allan couldn't stay committed. I remember the others would be on the phone trying to find him just before a show.

"It was pretty much Randy that was driving that band. But he used to get frustrated and fed up with them because he had a vision and they didn't always share the same vision. They had pieces of it but at that time it really wasn't possible for kids from Winnipeg to make it. The odds were so against it. It seemed almost impossible, except in Randy's eyes."

In December 1962, the Reflections became one of the first local groups to record, journeying the 800 km in the dead of winter to Kay Bank Studios in Minneapolis to cut several sides for the Canadian-American label. By February, *Tribute to Buddy Holly* backed by the group's original piano instrumental *Back and Forth* was #7 on the local CKY charts.

This was the big time for us. We had bought the Trashmen's record *Surfin' Bird* and on the label it said "Recorded at Kay Bank Studios, Minneapolis." Winnipeg lacked a decent studio. CKY and CKRC had recording studios but the best you could get was mono or two-track recording. We phoned down to Kay Bank and inquired about the facility. To our amazement it offered three-track recording. "Wow, one more track!" So we asked what the hourly rate was, pooled our resources, and booked a couple of dates over a weekend in late 1962. Claudia Senton's Dad, Glenn, worked at Birchwood Motors and he loaned us a Buick to use and I borrowed my Uncle Jack's little box trailer, which didn't have a cover to put over the equipment. My Dad had a canvas tent because we used to go on tenting trips so we set up the tent in the trailer, put the equipment inside it and collapsed the tent over it all with a couple of bricks on top to keep it from blowing away. And off we went to Minneapolis.

"I couldn't believe that these guys from Winnipeg were cutting records and writing their own songs," remembers an enthusiastic Burton Cummings. "I still remember how lucky and jazzed I felt the first time I got to talk to them. Talking to guys who lived in Winnipeg and cut records! Yes, the dream was there. It could be done."

"When we had a chance to record, we recorded," notes Garry Peterson. "We had to hawk an amplifier once to pay for a recording session but we did it. We always invested in the band, money and time. That was probably one of the contributing factors to our making it,

73

that and our willingness to look beyond Winnipeg."

We started going out on the road by 1963 because of the airplay we were getting from our records. We'd tour western Canada — Brandon, Regina, Saskatoon — we were pretty adventurous. My Dad lent us his station wagon but we ripped the ceiling liner by pushing the drums into the back. We didn't have drum cases so the legs and lug nuts would poke into the ceiling material. We would literally leave school after four on Friday, drive to Rainy River, Ontario to play a high school prom, play all evening, pack up, and drive right back getting home the next morning, all for $150. We thought nothing of piling into a car and driving literally for several days straight. We were young, what did we know? It was just part of being a musician, what you had to do, and we loved it.

With the release of further singles cut in the early British rock mold, the group's reputation spread and Chad Allan and the Reflections began venturing farther afield, travelling as far west as Alberta and east to Thunder Bay. In those days travel for the band was a fairly simple affair, but the group soon found the need for an extra hand so Jim Kale's buddy Russell Gillies signed on as the group's first road manager. Glenn Senton arranged for the group to lease the vehicles they required. "The guys came back from Birchwood Motors with two brand new Buick station wagons," recalls Gary Bachman, "and my father exclaimed 'What are you going to do with these things?' The guys replied, 'This is how we get around as a band.' My Dad just scoffed, 'How are you going to pay for them? You aren't making enough money. You're going to get stuck with these and you're going to be coming to me for money.' He just didn't understand that a musician or a band could make a living at what they did."

It was difficult for Charles Bachman to accept his eldest son's dream of being a professional musician. The prevailing sentiment among postwar, fifties-era parents who themselves had lived through the Great Depression was, "It's a nice hobby, a sideline, but you'll never make a living out of it. Have something to fall back on." That something for Charles meant a vocation. "My parents encouraged Randy's music, and in fact encouraged all of us in music," maintains Gary, "but up to the point where Randy wanted to do it for a living. In their eyes you had to go to school and then get a real job. Being a musician wasn't considered a real job in those days because it offered no security or financial stability. They made Randy sell shoes or suits and would only let him play at night because even selling shoes was an honest man's job. That was their attitude. To them, a musician was like an artist, a painter, and they never made anything of themselves living hand to mouth. 'Not having a profession, what was Randy going to amount to? He would be playing beer parlors all his life' Nobody knew the scope or the magnitude that a band could rise to at that time."

I was already playing in the band but I needed money to buy a new amplifier so a friend of mine from West Kildonan named Marvin Hoffer, whose uncle owned the North Main Car Wash at Inkster and Main, got me a job there. He said, "Be there at 5:30 in the morning and you'll get $10 an hour." So I arrived at the crack of dawn and worked like a wet dog soaping down cars and chamoising them until eight at night. When I was done the boss handed me $15. I never went back.

My Dad then got me a job at Bata Shoes, a retail outlet around the corner from his office. There's nothing worse than your Dad getting you a job because you feel obligated. When you are the new guy the routine was you got the worst customers or the toughest tasks. It was a trial by fire to see if you could handle the job. So when some farm Baba with gigantic feet like Goofy's comes in, her nylons rolled down to her calf and she hasn't washed her feet in a month, I was the one who got to fit her for shoes while the other guys watched. Swallowing my pride, I managed to sell her the shoes she wanted so I was in. The next day this drop-dead gorgeous, ten-out-of-ten chick came in, short skirt, long legs and I served her. While I was kneeling at her feet looking up at her I got an erection and couldn't get up to fetch another pair of shoes. I tried holding a shoebox in front of me as I manoeuvered across the floor. Meanwhile, the other salesmen were killing themselves laughing at this scene. It was an evening shift starting at 5:30. I took my break at 7:00 and never went back. I got on a bus to East Kildonan where we were playing a dance that night and made $35.

The next morning my Dad woke me up at nine.

"Why are you still in bed? You have to get to work."

"I'm not going," and rolled over.

"What do you mean you're not going?"

"It was terrible. I made $35 in the band last night. What would I have made at Bata? Maybe $6 or $7."

He went in on Monday to pick up my cheque and it was for $7. You have to remember that in those days most parents were earning maybe $50 to $70 a week. I could make $50 playing two nights. But my Dad's generation believed you had to work a legitimate job. Being a musician wasn't a real job to him. Only jazz musicians did that and as far as he was concerned they were all on drugs.

I briefly worked at Simpson-Sears in the men's wear department where the philosophy was if someone came in looking for a shoelace you tried to sell them a suit. If they wanted a tie you tried to get them into a matching jacket. I couldn't hustle people to buy things they didn't want. I lasted two days standing on my feet all day trying to squeeze Bigfoot into a new suit. It made no sense doing this for maybe $20 for a weekend and still playing dances in the evening. I was further ahead just staying home, practicing all day and playing evenings.

I had no interest whatsoever in working for a living, so what do you do to placate your parents and avoid work? You stay in school. I told my Dad I wanted to continue on with my education and he told me about this new place opening up called the Manitoba Institute of Technology where I could take business administration. Being in a band, I thought it a good idea to learn how to handle the finances. I didn't want to go to university and I wasn't interested in learning how to do anything with a wrench so my Dad took me there to check out the courses. "Yeah, I'd like to take business law, banking, insurance, accounting, and economics." It seemed pretty easy and practical enough — everyday kind of topics that I had an interest in. But it was the same story: "With your abilities, you're not applying yourself." I was playing in a band, that was all I wanted to do.

"Neither of Randy's parents wanted him to be a musician full-time or make it his career," confirms Claudia. "In fact, there was quite a bit of pressure put to bear on him not to pursue it and they even involved me in some of those conversations. So the year I went to university, Randy went to the Manitoba Institute of Technology, or Red River Community College as it's known today, to study business administration. That was totally driven by his Mom and Dad giving him a rough time because I was going to university and he wasn't. It was sort of 'What's wrong with him? He can't possibly make a living out of music so why would he even try?' Randy went to college to please his Dad. He always wanted to please his Dad. But he was very unhappy at college and didn't do very well. It was hard on him and he never finished. He was very dispirited and we would have long conversations about why everyone was pushing him to do this when he didn't want to. I used to tell him that he needed a business background to manage his music business. He was pretty good at Math, that was his strong suit and in the long run I think that served him well."

Garry Peterson faced a similar speech at home. "My father didn't want me to be a musician either. He wanted me to be a dentist. We had many fights over that. All parents who lived through the Depression said, 'My children are never going to have to suffer like this. I'm going to give them every opportunity to get an education.' For my father's generation, being a doctor, lawyer, or dentist were the careers to strive for because they were the most secure and didn't have to worry about money. So it was only natural that they wanted us to go further in school. As it turned out, what Randy studied proved to be far more valuable than what I took, which was matriculation with Latin and Physics and into pre-dentistry at University. Randy went to MIT and took business and typing, which was far more valuable in life than what the hell I learned. What can I do today with organic chemistry?"

Irv Applebaum shared classes with Randy and the two rode to school every day for the two years Randy attended MIT. "We were both from the North End; he was from West Kildonan and I grew up on Mountain Avenue," states Irv. "Randy was generally a very well-liked guy not because he played in a band but because he was genuinely a nice person that people liked being around. No ego, just fun to be with."

Irv recalls Randy's strong sense of priorities. "He had two obsessions that I recall back then: music and money. Randy was quite focused on his musical career and where he wanted to be financially. I always thought business administration was an interesting avenue for someone who wanted to follow a musical path. Randy was like the consummate businessperson back then, always wearing a sports jacket, a green one with leather patches on the elbows. He looked like a banker and the son of an alderman not a rock musician. He seemed to be immersed in his courses, more so than I was at the time. I never had the assignments done; Randy always had them done and still had time for his music. He didn't have great marks but he did okay; he worked very hard at it. He spent a lot of time with the instructors and seemed to have a rapport with them. That was different than the rest of us. Randy was personable enough and focused enough to approach them for help.

"Randy always had his head together. He would have made an incredibly successful businessman if he had pursued that direction. Most of us were somewhat foolish and free-spirited like most nineteen year olds, but Randy had his head set in the right direction. He didn't seem like a guy who was in a popular band, he was a very normal guy. In spite of everything that was happening with him in the band, he was anything but aloof or arrogant. He was extremely down to earth. His communication with us at MIT had nothing to do with the band. If he ever talked about what was happening with the group it was more from a sense of awe on his part, like he couldn't believe it. There was nothing totally radical about him whatsoever. What was radical was in his head and that was always music."

Irv was a well-known North End pool shark who could pull in more money than Randy just from a few games. But that environment never suited the quiet guitarist. "Randy never hung out at the pool hall. We all hung out at Sportsman's Billiards on Main Street where I hustled pool. Burton Cummings was just a kid playing pinball all the time and he used to drive me crazy with all the noise from the pinball machine when I was trying to play. I would holler at him to stop it. I tried once to teach Randy to play pool but he couldn't do it. He was useless at it."

With a pipeline to the British pop charts, it was no surprise when the Reflections began introducing a new sound to Winnipeg audiences. A year before the Beatles took North America by storm, the local quintet were already performing *Please Please Me, I Saw Her Standing There*, and other numbers from the Fab Four's debut album. Marvels college friend Irv Applebaum, "Randy had a picture of the Beatles in his locker long before they hit here in North America and anybody knew who they were. He loved the Beatles. He was in touch with everything that was happening musically in England before anyone. He once told me the Beatles were going to be a major group. I just thought 'Who are these guys?'"

Once again the Reflections were at the forefront of musical trends leading the way for others to follow. "Randy used to haul out all his records and play them for me after school," laughs Claudia, "and I remember the first time he played the Beatles and asked me what I thought of them. I don't even know how he got that album because it wasn't out in Canada yet but I remember him playing it over and over ad nauseum trying to learn the guitar parts."

The transformation to Beatlemania was rather sudden for us. At a dance we played before the British Invasion hit North America, we combed our hair over our foreheads. The kids were laughing at us. We did a complete set of Beatles songs and it was quite a change for the crowds. Overnight it was like we were a different band. They came to hear our usual repertoire which in itself was unusual because we still did a lot of obscure British music but when we did the Beatles stuff they weren't prepared for it. We did almost the entire first Beatles' album song by song. We had been so in love with England we just latched onto the Beatles as another cool English group. "Wow, a whole new British music to capitalize on!" That was a year before they debuted on Ed Sullivan. Winnipeggers heard those songs first from us. Neil Young's introduction to Beatles songs came from us. Months later when Beatles records began being played on local radio, some kids actually thought it was us.

Chad and I promptly went out and bought Rickenbacker guitars like John Lennon and George Harrison. And when you change guitars, you change the sound of the band. I wrote *Stop Teasing Me* emulating the Beatles' sound on *Do You Want to Know a Secret*.

One of the things the Beatles did that affected the Reflections was that now all of us could sing. In the Beatles, George did a tune like *Do You Want to Know a Secret* or *Roll Over Beethoven* and Ringo sang *Boys* and *I Wanna Be Your Man*. So I could now sing a lead or Garry could, plus the harmonies were much more diverse than before. The Beatles had this incredible vocal blend of three voices that were all different in timbre yet fit so well together. Overnight, we sounded like the Beatles or the Hollies or the Fortunes. I handled the high harmonies while Jim and Garry took the middle.

Once the Beatles hit North America, we would be playing our shows then when we were about to launch into a Beatles number, Dino Corrie from CKY would come onstage with a gigantic comb and comb our hair forward Beatle-style. The kids would go wild.

When *A Hard Day's Night* opened in Winnipeg at the Garrick Theatre in the spring of 1964, I was right there on opening day. I went with a few friends for the first afternoon matinee and in those days you didn't have to leave the theatre between shows. My friends went home but I stayed, mesmerized, memorizing everything. I completely lost track of time. It was like a how-to video for me: how to be a rock star. How to run from crowds of screaming girls, how to write songs in a boxcar, how to be cheeky to a reporter. Sitting in that darkened theatre, I decided that this was what I wanted to do for the rest of my life. I must have seen the movie five or six times when I felt a tap on my shoulder. It was Phil Brown, the chief of police in West Kildonan, and my Dad. They had been out looking for me after the other boys had returned home and I hadn't. My Dad had phoned the hospitals and police looking for me. They decided to go check the theatre and there I was.

With the arrival of the British Invasion, the Winnipeg music scene literally exploded as hundreds of bands emerged from basements sporting Beatle haircuts, suede Beatle boots, and velvet-collared waist-coats playing decidedly British-influenced repertoires. It was a mini Liverpool. Burton Cummings remembers at the time trying to list all the bands he knew of who were actively working the local scene before stopping at 250. "The British Invasion gave all the bands more options," he suggests. Everyone wanted to tap the youth market — stores, theatres, restaurants. As kingpins of the local scene, Chad Allan and the Reflections kept busy playing movie theatres, wrestling match-es, fashion shows, Blue Bombers football team rallies, track meets, on the roof of a KFC in East Kildonan, on flatbed trucks in car lots, everywhere teenagers could be expected to congregate. "The band scene was the central core of Winnipeg's teenagers at that time," postulates Cummings, "and represented a wonderful social interaction between kids from all the areas of town in all the areas of town."

In the fall of 1964 the group changed their name once again. This time it was to Chad Allan and the Expressions after a Chicago group named The Reflections had scored a hit single with *Just Like Romeo and Juliet*. Signed to Toronto-based Quality Records, it was time for the band to cut another single. With little money to spare and reluctant to trek to Minneapolis again in December, manager Bob Burns, a local impresario and television celebrity as host of *Teen Dance Party*, arranged for the group to cut their next single at CJAY TV's recording facility. It was early morning on a cold December Sunday when the five weary musicians straggled into the television studio. They would emerge several hours later with a piece of music history.

Allan Kowbel's friend Wayne Russell had an amazing record collection from overseas as well as reel to reel tapes of the British hit parade. As a Christmas present, his cousin in England would tape her favourite 45s and send them to him. For rock 'n' roll-crazed kids like us it was like discovering buried treasure, songs you never ever heard in Winnipeg, A and B sides. We used to learn the songs right off the tapes, sometimes without knowing the title of the song. That's how we learned *Till We Kissed* and found out much later that the title was actually *Where Have You Been All My Life*. That's how we first heard the Beatles in early 1963, a full year before their records hit in North America. And among Wayne's collection we found *Shakin' All Over*, a hit in Britain for Johnny Kidd and the Pirates in 1960 that never crossed the Atlantic.

It was wintertime, Chad had a sore throat, and we had played a dance earlier where he had sung for three hours so his voice was totally gone. He was taking antihistamines and was so dizzy that he sang laying down flat on his back on the floor. We had to lean the mike over him. You can actually hear his raspy voice on the final recording. There was just one microphone in the middle of the room and the entire band plugged into Jim Kale's Concert amp — all the instruments, two guitars, bass, and piano. That was our mixing board — if we wanted to change the balance we'd turn the channel volumes up or down. When we heard the first playback, the drums were too loud so we left the mike where it was and moved the whole drum kit further back.

It was against the station's regulations to use the facility for private recording sessions, but Bob Burns went ahead and paid an engineer, a moonlighting CJAY employee, to come in. We set up in the *Teen Dance Party* set, a big concrete room with a large black curtain used for background that helped deaden the cavernous concrete sound. It wasn't set up as a normal studio because there weren't any playback monitors so we would have to record a take, put down our instruments, run into the little control room, and hear the playback on the tape-recorder speakers. The engineer had to unpatch two plugs from the mike in the room and patch them into the speakers so we could hear a playback. He kept doing this back and forth and by this time it was two-thirty in the morning and we were all very tired. One of these times he forgot to pull out the patch cords and when we went in to hear the playback it was feeding back into itself and had this slapback echo on it, the instruments, drums, voice, everything. We heard it and yelled, "That's like Elvis!" It was like *That's All Right Mama* or Cliff Richard's *Move It*. We told him, "Leave it, that's the take!" It was all totally by accident but that was the sound on *Shakin' All Over*.

With its trebly guitar riff, clinkity-clink piano, manic drum fills, and solid rhythm, *Shakin' All Over* was a natural for a single. Nevertheless, when the band submitted the tapes to George Struth at Quality

Records in Toronto the following week, *Till We Kissed* — an Arthur Alexander number recently given the British Invasion treatment by Wayne Fontana and the Mindbenders — was the quintet's choice as the A side, with *Shakin' All Over* relegated to the flip side. Struth knew a hit when he heard it and reversed the group's decision pressing up copies with Shakin' as the A side. In a further move to enhance the single's chances, he left the group's name off the label instead printing "Guess Who" under the song title. It was a deception bent on avoiding the trap that Canadian records continually fell into when submitted to Canadian radio. With British and American records dominating the charts, few Canadian acts ever received airplay. Struth's reasoning was simple: the record sounds British; if radio thinks it is a mystery British group they'll give it a spin and once they hear it they'll be hooked. It was a bold bit of subterfuge but Struth's gambit succeeded. Released in January of 1965, by March 22, *Shakin' All Over* had displaced the Beatles' *Eight Days a Week* to become #1 across Canada.

George loved our recording of *Shakin' All Over* instantly because it had an exciting, raw British Invasion sound. But he figured, and rightly so, that putting our usual name on it and stating it was from this Winnipeg group would be the kiss of death so he decided to simply put "Guess Who" on the label and let everyone try to figure out who the artist was. Create a little mystique surrounding the record so people will think it really is a British group. And it worked. When people across Canada heard the record they thought it was a hybrid of one Beatle, one Rolling Stone, one Shadow, this kind of thing. Listeners actually phoned their stations claiming "I know it's one of the Rolling Stones." The record had a mystery surrounding it that piqued the curiosity of radio programmers. Before we knew it, *Shakin' All Over* was #1 in Toronto, then Vancouver, and in every region across the country and people still didn't know the identity of the group.

We received a phone call from George in early 1965 and he said to us "We've got your new name. It's Guess Who!" And we said, "We hate it!" But when we tried to revert back to Chad Allan and the Expressions nobody was interested. We started using "Guess Who? Chad Allan and the Expression" for our next recordings but no one cared. We had become the Guess Who. It was tough on Chad to lose his marquee identity in the new group name.

Shakin' All Over gave us a big, big step to get beyond Winnipeg. We went down and played the grandstand show at the CNE in Toronto in the summer of 1965. Toronto was a big deal. For us kids from Winnipeg, it was like going to New York. Nobody knew we were from Winnipeg. People thought we were a British band.

Canadian music was so regionalized back then. It was that old East-West, Grey Cup football rivalry thing where western Canadian records couldn't get played in the east and vice versa. I would get *RPM* magazine and many of the songs on the charts by groups like Jack London and the Sparrows, the Esquires, or the Big Town Boys I never heard in Winnipeg. We were one of the first western bands to get accepted and gain airplay in Toronto and headline a show at Empire Stadium.

But we had no idea how to capitalize on a hit record. None. We were still playing community clubs. No one was experienced enough to give us any direction.

It was a lesson both the group, and Randy in particular, would not forget.

With *Shakin' All Over*, the Guess Who became the first Canadian group to break out of a regional scene to national prominence by scoring a #1 record right across the country. It was a monumental feat given radio's predilection for avoiding homegrown talent in favour of the imported variety, as well as Toronto's dominance of the music industry. The Guess Who became a Canadian phenomenon.

In the 1960s, the Canadian music industry was a fledgling effort living under the looming shadow of its southern neighbour. There were no national booking agencies, promotional representatives, or marketing managers. The limitations of geography had rendered the Canadian music scene a fragmented affair with scattered regional scenes and no national star system. *Shakin' All Over* managed to catapult a little-known Winnipeg group to the national stage. "All the other bands across the country were regional," stresses journalist Larry LeBlanc. "The Collectors, for example, were huge out on the West Coast but meant nothing in the rest of the country. Bands like the Mongrels and Eternals from Winnipeg did nothing in Toronto. JB and the Playboys were huge in Montreal but nowhere else. The Guess Who, on the other hand, was big nationally."

Seeking to translate the Canadian success of *Shakin' All Over* to the American charts, George Struth licensed the single to New York–based Scepter Records in the spring of 1965. Owned by Florence Greenberg, Scepter's breadwinners had previously been the Shirelles and Chuck Jackson with Dionne Warwick their current hitmaker. Released Stateside in late spring, *Shakin' All Over* was slow to catch on, breaking regionally in several areas, most notably the northeastern seaboard after WBZ radio in Boston added it to their play list. By June, the single had peaked at #22 on the *Billboard* charts after an eleven-week run, an unprecedented achievement for a Canadian-based rock group. Prior to that only the Beaumarks from Montreal had managed to dent the US Top Fifty from a Canadian base with *Clap Your Hands*. Paul Anka, The Diamonds, the Four Lads had all abandoned Canada for the US. The Guess Who soon found themselves fielding requests for American appearances.

Randy now faced a dilemma. Playing in a local band and attending classes at college had been tough enough to manage, but now the outside world was beckoning. As Irv Applebaum recalls, "When it came time for Randy to make a decision whether to carry on with his studies or follow music, he discussed it with our Economics instructor. Randy told me the instructor had advised him, 'You only have one opportunity in your life. Go for it.' So Randy quit."

I remember going down to Kresge's next to Eaton's every Thursday morning and the woman there had *Billboard* magazine. I couldn't afford to buy it so I'd ask her where *Shakin' All Over* was on the charts this week and she'd say it was like #32 with a bullet. And I'd still be going off to school every day while our record was climbing the US charts.

Three weeks before final exams were to be written in my last year in business administration, the band got a call to travel to New York. An agent in New York had told us he was going to get us on the *Ed Sullivan Show*. All we had to do was get to New York. *Shakin' All Over* had become a hit in the US and the big time awaited me. So there I was clearing out my locker three weeks before final exams and the head of the faculty came up to me and asked, "What are you doing?"

"I'm quitting."

"Quitting?"

"I'm going to be on the *Ed Sullivan Show*."

"You'll be back," was what he told me as he walked away shaking his head.

Paul Cantor managed Dionne Warwick and in June he called us from New York to come down. He told us we would be on *Ed Sullivan*. But he left out the word "maybe." I literally cleared out my locker at MIT on Friday afternoon and we left that day for New York driving straight through. I remember the five of us arriving in New York on a Sunday evening and somehow finding the Ed Sullivan Theater near Broadway, which was where the show was broadcast from. It was all lit up and Kale and I went to the back door and knocked. Someone opened the door and looked at us.

"What do you want?"

"We're here to do the show. We've driven all the way from Canada."

"Who are you?"

"The Guess Who from Winnipeg."

He looked at his clipboard. "Nope."

"What about next week?"

"Sorry." And he closed the door.

We went to see Paul Cantor the next day. "What's this about the *Ed Sullivan Show*?"

"Well boys, if your record gets in the Top Ten I think I can get you on *Ed Sullivan*."

We were scared to death because all we knew of New York back in Winnipeg was *The Naked City* television show where somebody got murdered every week. We were frightened to go out because we didn't want to be that week's murder. Initially we would go from our hotel to Scepter studios and back. That was it. Pretty soon we realized we weren't going to be murdered so we started venturing out further to see Carnegie Hall, the Empire State Building, and Greenwich Village, which was very cool at the time with the folk thing happening.

We thought Scepter Records was Spector Records so we were going out of our minds thinking we were going to meet producer extraordinaire Phil Spector. We thought he had changed two letters in his name for the label name. That's how naïve we were.

When we arrived at Scepter Records to get our royalty cheque for *Shakin' All Over*, it was $400 for the entire band. We had sold a quarter of a million copies of *Shakin' All Over* in the States. We were ripped off but that's the way it was for everyone back then. We were prairie dogs and just being in New York was a big deal.

We recorded at Scepter Studios for a week then we went out on tour with the Kingsmen. It was just a blur. We worked up and down the East Coast, Jones Beach, Orchard Beach, what you would see in those beach movies, teenagers dancing in these big roller-skating pavilions. We were certainly wide-eyed, innocent kids. That was the biggest thing we had ever done. The package

tour included us, Dion and the Belmonts, and the Turtles. Sam the
Sham and the Pharaohs did some dates with us as did Eddie
Hodge who had *I'm Gonna Knock on Your Door*. Barbara Mason
did some gigs with us too but she was so young her mother had
to accompany her. Dion and the Belmonts would sing do wop
songs all the time on the bus, snapping their fingers and singing
Why Must I Be a Teenager in Love. I hung around Dion all the
time and watched him. He had such a smooth voice. It was fabulous. For us, it was living one of those rock 'n' roll movies. I still
have the program from that tour signed by all the performers.

Scepter was primarily a black label and put a black couple
dancing on our US album cover and didn't include our picture on
it. One of our first gigs in the States was in Washington, DC. We
drove down from New York, went up to a high school, and it was
a black high school. We got to the gate and everyone was staring
at us. We were booked to play a sock hop after school. The principal came up and asked us what we were doing there. "We're the
Guess Who." And he replied, "No you're not." So we had to show
him the Canadian cover and he eventually let us in but it was a
very weird experience.

We worked the eastern seaboard from New York down to
Florida. We would do a fifteen-minute set, *Shakin' All Over*, and a
couple of other songs that nobody knew. They only recognized
Shakin' so sometimes we would open and close with it. The
Kingsmen would do *Louie Louie, Jolly Green Giant, Money, Little
Latin Lupe Lu*. Dion would do all hits. When we got back to New
York, Paul Cantor asked us if we would like to back the Shirelles
and the Crystals. We were good at copying records so we said
sure and we did that for a few months. We had no idea we were
walking into the 1965 race riots. We played places where there
was blood on the floor. It was unbelievable for us, white kids from
Canada. We drove through Georgia and saw the ghettoes, and that
was quite an eye-opener. We would go to gas stations with every-

one in the same vehicle and guys would greet us with shotguns. "You can't come in here with those niggers," and calling us "Nigger lovers." It was scary.

We would do our set, take a break, then come out and back the Shirelles with *Soldier Boy* and all their hits — five white kids backing a trio of black girls. We didn't know any better. We played around New York and it was great. Then we went to Chicago and there was a riot going on right in front of us on the floor, black and white kids fighting. We played in Minneapolis and my parents drove down to see their son and there was a battle going on, black against white on the floor with knives. It was unbelievable. We didn't have these kinds of problems in Canada.

We were away from home a long time, the entire summer into the fall, living out of suitcases in and out of New York. We never knew when it would end and we didn't want it to end. We were able to ride that song for the better part of that year because it continued to break out in different regions of the US and kept getting airplay. The money was terrible but that wasn't the motivation for us. We were actually losing money on those tours and I don't know how we managed to survive. At every stop we would get a room with two double beds and a cot and share.

The touring pace became gruelling as the band crisscrossed the continent burning up the miles. A morning fashion show in Boston, an afternoon sock hop in New York, then on to Washington, DC, or further. They once drove nonstop from Winnipeg to Texas, played a show, and drove straight home. "There was never much time in any town," remembers road manager Russell Gillies. "We would pull in, find the gig, I would phone the radio station to do interviews, play the gig, pack up, and leave right after. We played dates within a five-hundred-mile radius. We would play Chicago then head off five hundred miles to the next gig." Russell recalls the band trekking clear across the continent from New York to Vancouver with a quick stop in Winnipeg to pick up clean clothes. On a Florida turnpike, their vehicle was pulled over for speeding. Holding a suitcase stuffed full of American dollar bills from the previous night's engagement, but fearing it might be confiscated, Russell told the officer he only had Canadian money. The police then took Garry Peterson into custody and held him for ransom until the band came up with the correct currency.

Following a performance in upstate New York, the promoter refused to pay up. As Russell approached the man, he leaned back in his chair allowing his coat to falling open to reveal a pistol in a shoulder holster. "I ain't gonna pay you." Undaunted, the burly Russell informed the promoter that he had better have the cash by the time he finished tearing down the equipment or there would be trouble. Sure enough, on returning to his office Russell was paid in full.

Back in Canada, Quality Records released *Tossin' and Turnin'* as the follow-up to *Shakin' All Over* and despite its rather limp rendition, the single climbed to #3 largely on the momentum *Shakin'* had created. Scepter, on the other hand, rejected the song, instead bringing the group into its studio to lay down tracks for a suitable single and album. After screening the band's batch of original songs, staff writers were dispatched to provide stronger material. "I could see that this wasn't one of the top studios in the world," notes Garry Peterson on their arrival at Scepter. "But it was a larger level than we had experienced from where we came from, a step up. It was primarily a black label and not the right place for us. Scepter weren't going to put any money into the band, they were just trying to capitalize on *Shakin' All Over*, throwing shit against the wall and hoping something would stick."

Not having written *Shakin'*, we didn't know how to write a follow-up. Instead we cut an old Bobby Lewis number, *Tossin' and Turnin'*, which paled in comparison to *Shakin' All Over*. It went down well at our dances but lacked that raw spark. We were still very timid about releasing our own original material as A sides. We had a proven track record for taking someone else's song, like

Shakin' All Over, and redoing it. There was a kind of safety in covering something that had already been a hit by another artist.

Florence Greenberg who ran Scepter Records was quite a songwriter herself. She had written *Soldier Boy* for the Shirelles. She summoned music publishers who came with songs for us to record. Amid the songs pitched to us were Mitch Murray's *I'll Keep Coming Back*. Murray had written hits for Gerry and the Pacemakers like *How Do You Do It*. We were offered Artie Wayne's *Use Your Imagination* and two songwriters named Geld and Udell came to the studio and played us *Hurting Each Other*, which we cut. It later became a huge hit for the Carpenters. When we covered Bruce Johnston's *Don't Be Scared*, the harmony was so bad. We couldn't hit those notes and didn't know enough of the studio tricks like slowing down tape or doing it in a different key. Bruce, of course, later joined the Beach Boys.

Going up in the elevator to the studio, I encountered two men in leather coats and jeans. Turns out they were Burt Bacharach and Hal David who were there to present their latest batch of songs to Dionne Warwick. So I was thrilled Scepter was going to offer us their writers.

Instead, out of the blue, Florence brought in these three black kids playing hookey from high school named Nick Ashford, Valerie Simpson, and Josie Armstead who sat at the piano and sang their songs to us. I think Florence was trying to turn us into an R 'n' B soul group. But we really liked their material and picked *Hey Ho (What You Do to Me)* to record. We couldn't sing the high parts, so the three of them sang on the track and also did the backing chorus on *Hurting Each Other*. Ashford and Simpson later wrote *Ain't No Mountain High Enough*.

Stanley Greenberg, Florence's son, was the studio engineer and he was blind, which really blew us away. He knew the board by feel so we didn't realize he was blind because he knew what he was doing. The studio was four track so we were moving up track by track from mono in Winnipeg to three tracks in Minneapolis and now to four. We thought this was wonderful. We ended up recording quite a few tracks in New York that summer.

Despite a rave-up recording akin to *Shakin' All Over*, *Hey Ho (What You Do to Me)* failed to crack *Billboard*'s Hot 100 and Scepter promptly lost interest in the Guess Who. Though the group continued to make forays into the US for live shows and continued to release records Stateside on tiny independent labels, for all intents and purposes the Guess Who had been relegated to one-hit-wonder status. Canadian acclaim continued, as *Hey Ho* and *Hurting Each Other* posted healthy chart positions. It was still big news for a Canadian act to be touring the States, so the Guess Who had credibility. However, the writing was on the wall. The group was floundering.

Back home in Winnipeg, the Guess Who remained hometown heroes. "People thought we were millionaires," remarks Jim Kale, "but it was the community club and church basement dances that were keeping us alive." For Randy, the notoriety was a double-edged sword. Twenty-two years old and still living with his parents, he was in no hurry to move out. The band's busy schedule gave him independence without losing the security of home. When he would be off the road, home became his sanctuary and he relished the familiarity and routine. His lengthy absences, however, made him almost a guest in his own house. Gary had left home already, had married, and was expecting his first child and the family had taken in a school chum of Tim's, Glenn Horoshuk who was fleeing a bad situation at his home. Glenn would live with the Bachmans for several years becoming almost a surrogate fifth son as each of the boys gradually struck out on their own.

Here he was the same quiet, shy, young man he had always been yet when Randy ventured out in public he quickly became the centre of attention. "We were all extremely happy for Randy when he became successful," recalls Tim Bachman. "He was happiest being up onstage and he had worked very hard for the success he achieved. I never saw him ever turn anyone away. He's never one to say, "I won't sign that" or "I don't want to talk to you." He always had time for people. He knows that every person who comes up to you is your employer in the sense that you owe your success to them. They buy your records and come to your concerts. But I don't think he changed. People around him changed their perceptions of him but to us he was the same. At the house he was still just our big brother. He would bring us gifts from the road like an Indian pouch from Texas. I thought at the time it was cool that he could be out there somewhere in the US playing for how many thousands of people but still remember his little brothers. It was exciting for him to come home and play his latest record for us on the family console. He would often play new songs for us and ask, "What do you think of this?" He always involved us. He and Robbie wrote a song together that was on one of their early albums called *Goodnight Goodnight*.

The constant touring brought matters to a head between Randy and Claudia. Now enrolled in university, she saw her future in a professional capacity. On the other hand, Randy expected a traditional stay-at-home girl, someone like his Mom, to be there when he came home from the road. Stresses Claudia, "Although Randy's family still believe my parents broke us up because my Dad didn't see a future for me with Randy, which wasn't true because he was very supportive of him, the fact of the matter is I broke it off.

"I honestly believe that what happened between Randy and I was that I became scared of how his life was going to be; what kind of a life he was defining for himself in music and what that would mean for me. What really scared me was that I looked at this person who I dearly loved and saw him becoming something I wasn't sure I could live with. Not so much him but the environment he was creating. He was away a lot and when things started happening for the band it was so exciting they just had to run with it and he became engrossed in it. So what it started to mean for me was the person who for the last three years had been everything for me — my mainstay, my best friend, soul mate, companion, brother to me — all of a sudden was gone. I would see him when he would come back home and talk to him but he would be so wrapped up in what he was doing that I didn't see a place for me to fit in other than sitting at the back of the stage waiting for him. And that just isn't who I am.

"I saw myself staying home raising our kids and waiting for Randy to come home. He was very clear about that even back then. When the band started to happen and I was in university he would say to me 'What do you need university for?' I needed it because I loved to learn and I wanted a career for myself. Randy didn't get it. His response was, 'That's okay. You can still do that sometime, but what I really need is for you to stay in one place to maintain the home fires until I come home.' I just couldn't see that role for myself. I had such a thirst for learning and he had the same thirst but for music. He couldn't make the connection.

"It has always fascinated me that he wanted to have a large family yet be away from them so much. He used to say to me, 'We're going to have lots of kids,' and I would be thinking 'Oh no. How's two? I've got other things I want to do. To want all those children must be something in him that he needs to help him stay connected back to reality. It was important to him even when he was nineteen or twenty. I remember distinctly the conversations we had when we broke up centring on things maybe looking different in a few years once I had my degree and worked a little. Then we could figure it all out. But within six months of us splitting up, he had met his first wife and she was more than willing to play the game the way he wanted it. And to her own detriment to some extent in the end, because she ended up staying home and looking after six kids while he was away most of the time. That's what would have happened to me and I knew it because he was very clear about what he wanted. I couldn't have lasted as long as his first wife did."

CHAPTER 3

No Sugar Tonight

Following a whirlwind six months, the newly christened Guess Who found their fortunes ebbing by the fall of 1965. Failure to follow up the success of *Shakin' All Over* left the quintet dispirited, riding an endless treadmill of nondescript gigs. Celebrities on their home turf, they were just another band out on the road living off the dying embers of a former hit record. Plagued by a lack of direction, the group watched helplessly as the momentum of the previous year faded. "I can't blame management," surmises Garry Peterson. "They did the best they could. But what I can say is that we outgrew these people and really should have gone on to the next level. As a result, the band was never marketed properly." Randy knew the group desperately needed a shot in the arm.

The Reflections/Guess Who had managed to ride the British Invasion tidal wave of infectious pop Merseybeat sounds. But by the end of 1965 that tide had been stemmed by a harder-edged, rhythm and blues–influenced style as evinced by groups like the Rolling Stones, Animals, Kinks, Who, Yardbirds, and Paul Revere and the Raiders. Rock 'n' roll was transforming and Randy wanted to follow it. Acutely attuned to AM radio, he heard the winds of change but could he steer the band in that direction?

Keyboard player Bob Ashley had not been happy over the previous months. Classically trained, with an artistic temperament and delicate psyche, the road was not for him. As far back as 1963 when he failed to join the others on a western tour, Randy had questioned Bob's commitment to the group. Irv Applebaum recalls witnessing another side to Randy's character, the dispassionate band leader, while the two were still attending college. "I remember Randy saying in the car one day on the way to school that he felt the group had to get rid of Bob Ashley. That was a different side to Randy that I hadn't seen before, a more calculating businessman even at nineteen or twenty years of age. That was probably the only hard side I ever saw to him and the only person I ever heard him speak negatively about."

While Randy, Jim, and Garry embraced the rock 'n' roll lifestyle with gusto, Bob found the long grind in the back of a station wagon, the loud volume, and screaming teenyboppers at odds with his more refined musical sensibilities. "Everything that was happening with the Guess Who was just going in a completely different direction than Bob ever considered," comments manager Bob Burns. "I think he was content for it to be a local group." By November, Bob had left the Guess Who.

Bob Ashley was quite shy and introverted. He felt uneasy onstage and once said to me before a gig where we had six hundred people waiting for us to go on, "There are twelve hundred eyes watching me." It was a strange statement but revealed what was going on in his head. Bob had perfect pitch so whenever I would bend a note on the guitar he would wince almost in pain. He once asked me not to bend any notes. He couldn't stand my solo in *Tuff E Nuff* because of all the bending. It drove him crazy. Bob missed a few nights because he didn't want to be on the road so I sensed he wasn't destined to be with us much longer. He just didn't have what it took to be in a band and wasn't interested. The success we were enjoying only deepened his discomfort on- and offstage. One night the Crystals dragged him out front in the middle of *He's a Rebel* and that mortified him. They thought he was cute and were tickling him under the chin. For Bob, it was humiliating and shortly after that he left.

Chad played keyboards for a while but we knew the band needed a permanent replacement. We were missing something. At the same time Chad, too, was also beginning to show reluctance at going out on the road. He was in college and had a girlfriend who wanted him home. The rest of us were married to the band. We had girlfriends but the band always came first.

On a swing through Wisconsin in mid-December, Chad Allan did the unthinkable: he abandoned the group leaving the other three high and dry to complete a two-night engagement. The contract stipulated a quintet so with Ashley gone, road manager Russell Gillies took the stage armed with a tambourine for the first night. "The next day, Chad got on a bus and went home," recalls Russell still steamed at the singer's unprofessional attitude. "Didn't say nothing; he was just gone. I knocked on the hotel room door and discovered he had left. I not only had trouble with the promoter but also with the other three guys who didn't want to play. I managed to convince the promoter that Chad was ill and the band would play instrumentals. Then I had to tell the other three that they were playing. I remember pinning one of them over a pool table and insisting 'You're playing tonight!' It was a weekend at a monstrous college bar in Madison full of kids who wanted to party. They didn't care if anyone was singing as long as it was loud and they could dance to it. The band actually went down well. They got the kids singing along and we ended up getting most of our pay." On the return trip home, the three vowed never to be stuck in that kind of predicament again. If Chad's commitment was waning they needed another member, someone who could play keyboards but more importantly someone able to take the pressure off Chad and cover the vocals if he ever ducked out again. Back in Winnipeg, Randy, Garry, and Jim met at Bob Burns's office and put in a call to Randy's one and only candidate for the job, Burton Cummings.

In looking to replace Bob Ashley, I felt we had an opportunity to be less adult, less grown up. Bob was like an adult; he was this prim and proper stiff British young adult. He never really let down his guard and had fun. Chad Allan was similar, kind of old before his time. Peterson, Kale, and I liked a lot of fun. We were the rebel rousers in the group. And the music was changing too. The British Invasion had initially been polite young men in suits like the Beatles playing pop songs. By 1965–66, the rougher R 'n' B groups were now leading the charge and they were far less stuffy. They were scruffier-looking and raucous-sounding. I thought we needed to get back to that. We were too grown up
in our approach and we needed an infusion of youth.

Having heard Burton's reputation as a rebel rouser and read the write-up he received in the local newspaper after scuffing up a grand piano with his Beatles boots at the Winnipeg Arena opening for Gerry and the Pacemakers, I thought he was the guy for us. He was young, hungry, aggressive, making headlines for his brazen attitude, and didn't give a damn about anything but the music. Burton wasn't afraid to be a little cheeky and shake things up. He was exciting. All that appealed to me. He had a voice and could definitely play keyboards. He wrote songs, he looked good, and had cool hair. Added to that, he was a couple of years younger.

We checked Burton out with CKY's Dino Corrie who worked frequently with the Deverons, and Dino vouched that Burton was reliable and dedicated. Furthermore, Burton was a North Ender; he was one of us like Garry and me. We knew what we wanted so we scouted him out only once, I think it was at a Bay fashion show, and that's all we needed. There was no doubting Burton Cummings had the goods.

Born on New Year's Eve, 1947, Burton Lorne Cummings grew up

an only child on Bannerman Avenue in Winnipeg's tough North End. Abandoned by his father before he was barely a year old, Burton had been raised by his mother, Rhoda, and her parents, the Kirkpatricks. Rhoda Cummings worked at Eaton's downtown department store in the finance department and although her single income was meagre, she managed to provide her son with everything he needed for a proper upbringing, except a father. "You can't miss what you've never had," related Burton in a 1981 interview. "So I didn't miss having a father, except on Father's Day when all the kids in class were making cards for their dads and I'd get bummed out because I didn't have a dad to make one for. Or the first day of school when you had to stand up and say what your dad did for a living. That was a nightmare for me. I didn't have the guts to say I didn't have a father so I'd make something up." Nonetheless, Burton grew up amid the comfort of a close-knit extended family that enjoyed get-togethers where music played an integral part. "I started piano at age four. I loved rock 'n' roll but I didn't much care for classical piano. I hadn't put the two together yet. But the minute I found out I could play *Diana* by Paul Anka, that was it. Next thing I knew, my mother couldn't tear me away from the piano."

Burton starred in several productions of Gilbert and Sullivan operettas at St. John's High School and sang in the church choir. His interest in popular music was piqued at a tender age, fostering both an obsession and a dream. "I started buying records very young, about seven or eight years of age. My mother gave me *Hound Dog* and *Don't Be Cruel* for Christmas one year, so I must have been seven or eight. Once I started buying records I went nuts. I would cut lawns and deliver newspapers to save money to buy more records. I started thinking, 'What a great way to make a living, making records.'"

It was Burton's alto saxophone, however, not the piano, that brought him his first taste of acclaim in a rock 'n' roll group. That group was the Deverons formed at St. John's High around 1962 by Burton's classmates. "Ed Smith and I were really good buddies from school," recalls Burton. "Then suddenly he started going to these band practices and I was really jealous. I thought, 'I'd like to be in a band too.' But, no matter how much I hinted, I wasn't invited." Undaunted, Burton began hanging around the novice group's practices, gradually insinuating himself into their ranks, first on saxophone then a bit of piano and finally as lead vocalist and front man. "From that moment on, the band became mine," he acknowledges.

By 1964, with their youthful vitality, talent, and good looks, the Deverons were a popular attraction throughout the city and heirs to the throne behind Chad Allan and the Reflections. "Probably we were next in line in terms of ranking below them in the city," boasts Burton. "We were never a threat, they were always number one, but we were right up there." Burton had found his salvation. "Music was the only thing in my life once I was in the band. I just ticked off the minutes in school from Monday to Friday. I couldn't care less about anything until four p.m. on a Friday, then it was, 'We're on tonight!'"

A featured moment in the Deverons' energetic set was when Burton would stand on the community club's rickety old piano in his Beatle boots and belt out a rocker. "All the community clubs hated me because I scratched up their pianos." By mid-1965, the Deverons were being managed by another North Ender, Marty Kramer, and signed to the Reo label, a subsidiary of Quality Records, which released the group's debut single, *Blue Is the Night*, a cover of an obscure British ballad. The flip side offered Burton's own original composition, the harder-edged *She's Your Lover*. The single raised the group's profile considerably and the Deverons were invited to open the show for Gerry and the Pacemakers at the Winnipeg Arena. The Reflections were also on the bill. Cummings's antics that night on top of a grand piano brought him considerable attention.

Then came the phone call in December 1965 that would forever alter the course of Burton's life. "I had just come back from Minneapolis. The Deverons had gone there for a recording session. Something had gone wrong with the train car that we were returning on and we were five frozen little kids. It took something like seventeen hours to get home. I just wanted to go to bed. I did manage to get to bed for about an hour and a half when the phone rang. It was Bob Burns, the Guess Who's manager, and he said, 'We have an important meeting and I'd like you to come down to my office immediately.' My initial reaction was, 'Good God, can't this wait a day? I'm exhausted and cold, I've got no voice.' But he insisted it was very important. On the way down in the taxi I figured that maybe the Guess Who were going to use some of their power and experience to help The Deverons, sort of help from the big guys. As I got to the office, I walked in and Bob Burns was there with Jim, Randy, and Garry. And they just came right out and said, 'How'd you like to join our band?' I think I said, 'Gee fellows, I'd love to but The Beatles just asked me to join last week' and I walked out the door. I reacted like a smart-ass. I obviously thought it was a cruel joke to play on a young lad. I then came back in and realized they weren't kidding and I said 'Yes' right on the spot. I really didn't think twice about it. They were the biggest band in the country." By the start of the new year and his eighteenth birthday, Burton Cummings was a member of the Guess Who.

Conspicuous by his absence at the meeting was Chad Allan who wanted no part in the decision to recruit Burton. "Burton was brought in to augment the band and maybe Chad would be happier and stay," maintains Garry Peterson. "But it never worked that way. Chad was threatened by Burton. It had been Allan and the Silvertones and Chad Allan and the Reflections so I guess in his mind he felt he was being pushed aside. Here was a younger, wilder guy. It's too bad we didn't keep it together because it was a stronger band. Any chance you have to get a better person in your band why wouldn't you take it? It's going to make the band a better band. But lead singers always worry about the other guy taking the spotlight away from them and not being the big guy anymore. I think Burton intimidated Chad."

Burton wanted Chad's throne. Definitely. If Chad had made the decision, Cummings would not have been in the band. We still needed Chad to fulfill gigs, but the writing was on the wall. How could a talent like Burton Cummings have remained second fiddle for long? No way. The three of us — Garry, Jim, and I — wanted to play the harder rock songs and Cummings could do them. The music was changing and Chad couldn't roll with it. He had gone to a doctor and knew he had nodules on his throat and was looking ahead to having his throat scraped. He just couldn't do four fifty-minute sets a night. We were asking Chad to scream and he wasn't a screamer. Burton had a much stronger voice and a serious commitment as well as the attitude we needed. The three of us welcomed the change.

For those five months when we had Burton and Chad together in one group, we were convinced we had the best band in the world. We could do anything. We had five voices so we could do all the Hollies' and Beach Boys' material. Chad could do the softer numbers; Burton could scream the Eric Burdon and Paul Revere songs. We could cover everything from Cliff Richard and the Beach Boys to the Kinks to Georgie Fame's pop jazz. The dances we played at that time were incredible. Our repertoire tripled with Burton because he could do the harmony numbers and all the rougher, harder rock that I now wanted to play.

Suitably re-energized, the new lineup proved short-lived. Following the recording of a third album, *IT'S TIME* (the first two being *SHAKIN' ALL OVER* and *HEY HO*) in Minneapolis, Chad Allan bowed out for good. Despite the hasty recruiting of fellow Deveron Bruce Decker on rhythm guitar, by September 1966 the Guess Who was down to the familiar quartet of Bachman, Cummings, Kale, and Peterson.

Much of the *IT'S TIME* album is just us trying to be everybody else, all the groups we liked. We were still imitating the styles we liked in our own songwriting. I was simply taking my influences and putting my own stamp to it. I copied the Raiders, Kinks, and

the Animals. That's how everybody starts off. But the individual
writing styles were starting to emerge. We weren't collaborating
yet. At that point I had made up my mind that I really wanted to
be a good songwriter. I figured there were younger guys who
were better guitar players than I was so I decided to focus on my
songwriting. I felt more confident as a writer. I was now using a
Fender Telecaster that had this incredible grungy sound through
this tiny Fender amp and as a result much of the material on *IT'S
TIME* had a biting guitar. I didn't have the clean Rickenbacker
sound like on our previous albums. Usually you tend to write for
your singer and suddenly I could write for another singer's style,
not just Chad Allan's. Now we had an Eric Burdon in the band. *So
Believe Me* was the Kinks and Raiders and *Clock on the Wall* was
House of the Rising Sun done slower. That was Burton's first
vocal with us. Neil Young once told me it was one of his favourite
songs from that period. He even wanted to record it at one time.

The relationship that developed between the older, more experienced Randy and the teenage neophyte Burton is complex, rooted in
deep-seated subconscious needs, and more than thirty years on still
remains a source of controversy. From that alliance would emerge
some of the greatest songs of the latter sixties as the two would forge
a unique creative bond to become Canada's best-known composing
team. On the other hand, in spite of the creatively charged partnership
the two enjoyed, their divergent personalities and experiences would,
like some centrifugal force, repel one from the other the closer they
became. It is a scene that has played itself out time and again in the
intervening years since the two first came together. They are drawn
toward one another for creative reasons, recognizing the unique chemistry the Bachman–Cummings combination possesses, only to disinte-
grate in acrimony soon after their personalities come into play. Theirs
is a multifaceted bond, a love-hate relationship: Randy, the father figure
to the fatherless Burton; Burton, the rebellious son or younger brother

to the patriarchal Randy. "It's a child and his father, that's Burton and Randy," asserts Garry Peterson. "Randy and Burton remain the longest-running soap opera in Canadian history," suggests journalist Larry LeBlanc, who has known the two musicians for some thirty-five years. As mentor to the younger Burton, it would be Randy who would teach him to play guitar, encourage him to pick up the flute and add it to the band's arsenal, and initiate the songwriting partnership by planting Lennon–McCartney dreams in the young lad's head.

Already the undisputed leader with regard to the group's business affairs, with Chad Allan gone Randy now assumed the role of musical director. Jim and Garry were quite comfortable deferring to Randy's authority; Burton idolized Randy and looked to him for guidance and wisdom. "Everybody in that band considered Randy to be the leader," Garry emphasizes. While Burton assumed the role of front man singing all the songs, Randy quietly called the shots from behind.

The group had taken on a new road manager by this time, Jim "Jumbo" Martin, a notorious North End tough guy whose ample muscles could easily hoist several heavy amplifiers at once as well as intimidate the most insufferable of rowdies. "It wasn't like I went out looking for fights, they came to me," smiles Jim. "People used to come to the North End Salisbury House and guys would walk in and say 'Which one's Jim Martin? I'm here to beat him up.' I wouldn't dare walk away from it. Next thing I knew I had a reputation as this tough guy."

Jim Martin confirms Randy's role in the group. "He was the leader. He was the guy that went out and found Burton. He was the guy I dealt with when it came to money if I needed expenses or road advances. Even back then he was a capable businessman. If I had been given $500 for gas expenses for a tour and afterwards gave Randy receipts for $499.99 he would say 'Jim, where's the penny?' I would look at him funny but that's the way he had to do it. At first, I think Cummings looked up to Randy. We all did. He was our leader. If I had a problem I went to him. Somehow he was always able to solve everyone's problems." Over the next few years Jim Martin and Randy would develop a close professional and personal bond.

To say that Burton was in awe of Randy in the early months would be understating his admiration and respect for the guitarist. "One night just after I joined the Guess Who, Randy came over to pick me up and as usual I wasn't ready yet," relates Cummings. "I was still living with my mother and grandmother, and the whole family, my aunts and uncles, were over. Randy went out to the car and brought out an old nylon string classical guitar and proceeded to mesmerize my family for an hour playing Broadway show tunes. He was brilliant and everyone was spellbound." Despite all the turbulence over the years, Burton is always quick to acknowledge that no one taught him more about music and songwriting than Randy.

After Burton agreed to join the Guess Who, unbeknownst to him, his mother, Rhoda Cummings, contacted me through my Dad. She knew our family because my Dad was an alderman and was well respected in the community and she called him to ask what I was like. She wanted me to be a big brother to Burton, to promise to look out for him, to bring him home after gigs and to make sure he stayed out of trouble. She said to me, "I will let Burton join your band if you will be his big brother. He has never had a father and I want you to look after him because I respect you." I couldn't tell him this but she made a pact with my Dad and I to look after him. I had to promise his mother I would look after her son. I think she was a bit naïve about Burton but worried that he might go astray. He was younger than all of us. He was still under age and couldn't even sign anything without his mother's permission. So after we finished a gig, I would bring him home. Having grown up as the big brother to three younger siblings I treated Burton like a younger brother. She didn't want him hanging out with certain guys of dubious reputation from his neighbourhood.

This circumstance allowed Burton and I to develop a close bond. In the first few months we spent a lot of time together —

rehearsals, at Bob Burns's office for our weekly meetings, gigs, afterwards out to the Sal's or Marigold for a bite to eat. I had a car and so I picked him up and dropped him off every night.

After a while though, I think Burton sensed that I was more of a presence in his life than he wanted at the time and gradually began to rebel. He didn't have a father or older brother to break away from so I took on that role. Initially, he couldn't get enough from me in terms of musical knowledge and experience. But at some point he started avoiding me. Once he got his own car, he would drop me off and I discovered he wasn't going home. His mother would get on my case the next day because he wouldn't come home until the next morning. He would head off to Ari Perlmutter's or meet up with a bunch of guys at the Sal's.

I don't know if Burton ever knew that agreement between his mother and me because she told me never to tell him. But like my own kids, sooner or later they have to leave the nest. I was Burton's authority figure, I was his nest, and he had to assert himself to me. "Screw you and your rules, I've got to live my own life." It gets to a point where a guy's got to break away from his father or tell his big brother he's an ass and make his own life. Burton figured he had learned all he needed from me and we started growing apart.

Initially, the two enjoyed a close companionship, with the more adventurous Burton bringing out a wilder side in Randy. Though Jim Kale was already a seasoned imbiber, Randy's experience with alcohol was limited. With Burton, Randy's obsessive nature got the best of him, but only for a short time.

Burton wasn't smoking at home in front of his mother and if he was drinking it wasn't out in the open. Rather than me being a drinker or smoker or influencing him the wrong way, my father assured his mother that I was a decent boy who didn't smoke or drink. Burton and I did drink together early on but that was over by the time we began writing together.

During our drinking spell though, Burton and I used to drink until we fell down. I remember once a friend, fellow Winnipegger Jack Skelly who came along with us once in a while as our bouncer, picked me up in a hotel hallway and carried me back to my hotel room. I had drunk so much I passed out in the hall. We used to have competitions to see who could stand up the longest. He usually beat me. We really used to get into it.

A couple of weeks later we had a party at someone's house for Chad Allan who was leaving the band. I really got drunk that night, so drunk in fact that I actually drove over my own foot with a car. Try to figure that one out. I don't recall whose car I was moving so someone else could get their car out of the driveway but it was one of those old two-door cars where the doors are really long. I kind of sat myself half in the car and half out with my rear end partly on the seat and one foot on the ground. And it was slippery. So I had this big door ajar and it blew all the way open in the wind. There I am hanging out of the car as I put it in reverse. As I did so, the wind pulled me further out of the car, my foot slipped and as the vehicle rolled backwards, my left foot went under the front wheel. I immediately put on the brake and yelled for help. Who should come out of the house but my father. He reached in and put the car into forward; it lurched ahead, and then he put it in park. As I got out he looked at me and said, "I'm ashamed to call you my son."

I was the oldest son and you always want your father to be proud of you and say "Good job, you've done your best." When my Dad said that to me, I was devastated. That was the last night I ever drank.

My smoking experience was even shorter-lived. When I went to MIT, in my mind I thought "Here I am a cool college guy" so

I assumed I should smoke a pipe. Garry Peterson smoked a pipe and showed me what to do so I bought one, a little pouch, and some tobacco. I remember going home and sitting in my Dad's living-room chair, the proverbial Archie Bunker chair that when he entered the room you didn't say anything, you just quietly vacated immediately. It was his territory and when he was home that chair was off limits. There I was sitting in his chair feeling very sophisticated and mature as I filled my pipe with apricot-cherry–flavoured tobacco and lit up.

A few minutes went by as I puffed away confidently when my mother yelled from the kitchen, "Something's on fire! Something's on fire!" My mother and father didn't smoke.

"It's okay, I'm smoking a pipe now."

"Not in this house you're not!"

Just then the phone rang; she picked it up and called out, "It's for you." I got up from the chair and as I turned toward the kitchen I fell down on my face dizzy-headed and having trouble breathing.

"I'm never going to do this again," I moaned and I never did smoke. That was my lone smoking experience.

The other guys in the band all smoked and I found I wanted to be around it less and less. One of the hazards of playing in a rock group was that we would play smoky clubs and I hated it. We would get on airplanes, and back then people would smoke on them and I would be trapped. It didn't matter where I sat, the smoke would be all over me and I couldn't stand it.

During the summer of 1966, the Guess Who undertook a gruelling six-week tour of one-night stands in rural Saskatchewan. Using Regina's Westward Inn as a base, the group would venture out every afternoon to destinations like Weyburn, Estevan, Yorkton, Melford, Moosomin, even as far as into Alberta returning to Regina in the wee hours. A Kentucky Fried Chicken outlet adjacent to the hotel provided the group's main source of sustenance. "We had four of us in one room and three in another and we would share beds," remembers Jim Martin. "There was nothing funny going on, that's just the way we had to go because we couldn't afford anything else. We used to get $6 per diem and had to get through the day's meals on that. It was ridiculous all the driving we did. The vehicles were always breaking down and using up all the money. Our Buick sedan broke down one night in the middle of the prairies and we ended up towing it behind the GMC truck. Cummings and Bachman stayed in the Buick and we hooked it up with a chain. There we were driving down the Trans-Canada Highway pulling this Buick. I got into the rhythm of the night driving and when I eventually looked back in the mirror there was no Buick. They were gone. I said to Kale 'Where'd the car go? It's not behind us anymore.' So we turned around and drove literally ten miles before we found the car off on the side of the road. Cummings and Bachman had pushed it onto the shoulder and there they were sitting there. We hadn't even realized they were gone. 'What happened?' 'The chain broke.' 'Where is it?' 'I don't know. Somewhere back there on the road.'

"So we had to drive the truck slowly with me lying on the hood looking for this chain on the road. I found a dead skunk before we eventually found the chain and hooked the car up once again."

Burton vividly recalls the rigours of that summer odyssey. "We played twenty-eight nights in a row in twenty-eight different Saskatchewan towns, four one-hour sets a night with a ten-minute break in-between each set, for $400 per night and had to cover all our own expenses from that. It was physically exhausting and I don't know how my throat put up with it but when you're young and ignorant, you can endure unbelievable physical demands. With all that adrenaline and youth I was ready and willing to do anything." Adds Jim Kale, "We were supposed to be making $400 a night, six nights a week. But after reading the contract a second time, we discovered that we received the first four hundred in paid admissions. If that didn't come, we got what was there. Sometimes it wasn't very much."

That tour underscored the rut the group found itself in due, in part, to manager Bob Burns's limitations. "We travelled all day and night to get to Peace River, driving and driving," recounts Jim Martin. "It was the town's fair so we figured it was a big gig. We got to the hotel and a parade was going down the main drag, five kids on bicycles with streamers. They had a dunk tank set up in the middle of the street and they had Cummings sitting there and people were throwing balls trying to dunk him. Then Randy got up there. Here was the whole town trying to dunk the Guess Who. These were the kind of bookings Bob Burns took. The act who was always either following us into town or had just been in the town we were in was Reveen the hypnotist. It was almost like we were following each other."

On a night off in Regina, while the others partied back at the hotel, Randy and Jim Martin chanced to drop into a local coffeehouse, the Fourth Dimension. Here Randy encountered the second love of his life. Jim Martin remembers that evening well. "The 4D was downstairs in what used to be a bowling alley. Randy and I were sitting at a table when he spied these two girls at another table. Randy immediately started in on me.

'Man, look at that girl. She's beautiful. I gotta meet her.'

'Well, go and do it. Go over there.'

"Then he got on my case because he was very shy with girls. 'No, you do it. Come on Jumbo, you've got a way of talking to girls.'

"He kept at me all evening bugging me to go over and talk to this girl for him. As the evening wore on it became obvious somebody had to make a move because he was desperate to meet her. He kept claiming it was love at first sight. Finally I relented and told him I'd go over. I walked to their table, introduced myself, and asked if I could sit down with them. Meanwhile Randy's eyes were glued to their table watching me intently. They invite me to join them and introduced themselves. They were sisters, Lauralee and Lorayne Stevenson. Lorayne was a strikingly beautiful girl. I chatted with them for a while and as I looked back, I swear Randy had broken out into a sweat. He was giving me gestures like 'Get me over there!' So I finally said, 'There's someone who would like to meet you.' Lorayne could see Randy over at our table so I gave him the wave to come on over. I've never seen anyone move that quickly. 'Vroom.' He was at their table in a split second. I did the introductions and Randy just melted right there in front of her. He was in love."

A striking, dark-haired beauty, Lorayne Stevenson was an American from Salt Lake City, Utah, up in Regina that summer to visit her parents who had moved there earlier. While in town she had modelled for various ad agencies and was a runnerup for Miss Saskatchewan Rough Rider. Lorayne neither smoked nor drank, a further factor that appealed to Randy. What he was yet to discover, though, was that Lorayne Stevenson was a member of the Church of Latter-day Saints, a devout Mormon.

As I was sitting there at the 4D, in walked two girls looking very non-Regina, very classy. One was blonde, blue-eyed like Suzanne Somers, the other was dark like Raquel Welch. Jumbo and I looked at each other and I said, "These two aren't Regina stock." I told him, "I want the dark one; you take the blonde." It turned out the blonde, Lauralee, was already engaged to another guy so Jumbo lucked out but I got to see Lorayne the next day. She was slated to go back to Salt Lake City after a week but she phoned and extended her vacation while we were in town. A friend of the band's, Terry David Mulligan, an ex-Mountie now a deejay at CKCK in Regina and host of several of our dances, had dated Lorayne before I did.

When the Saskatchewan tour came to an end, I went back to Winnipeg but felt this longing for Lorayne. I wanted to be with her. She, in turn, had decided to stay on with her parents in Regina. Garry Peterson was getting married and I was in the wedding party so I invited Lorayne to be my date. I asked my parents if she could stay over in my room and I would sleep in the basement. They hadn't met her but agreed. Lorayne came for the wedding and stayed a few days while I showed her off around town to all my friends. She was like a 10, drop-dead gorgeous, so I wowed all my buddies with this beautiful American chick. Shortly after her return to Regina she called me.

"My Dad's got a job in Florida. We're all moving to Florida."

"I don't want you to go."

"What does that mean?"

And I found myself saying, "Let's get married."

It was a whirlwind romance. We were pretty intense while I was in Regina but after that it was a long-distance relationship. We had only known each other a couple of months at best when I asked her to marry me. I didn't really know her that well but I was certain I didn't want to let her go.

Suitably smitten, Randy began to investigate the Mormon faith. "I don't know when Randy found out Lorayne was a Mormon but while we were in Saskatchewan he started getting into it," recalls Jim Martin. "He was saying 'I gotta be a Mormon.' Obviously, he loved the girl and was ready to do whatever to be with her. When the tour ended, Randy left Lorayne in Regina but planned on going back to see her soon. I remember we were driving back to Winnipeg and while we were sitting in the car on the highway, Randy pulled out the Book of Mormon and handed it to Burton. 'Man, you have to read this.' He was trying to convert us. We all thought he was getting a bit carried away with this stuff. Burton looked at the book but didn't want any part of it. He brought it home and put it in his freezer. And I swear, when Burton and I moved from Winnipeg to LA ten years later, that book was still there in his fridge."

Founded in the early nineteenth century by Joseph Smith of Palmyra, New York, the Church of Jesus Christ of Latter-day Saints, better known as the Mormon Church, is a Christian religion based on the Book of Mormon translated by Smith and first printed in 1830. The tenets of the Mormon church are found in the Thirteen Articles of Faith drawn from this book. Smith maintained God, through the angel

Moroni, had directed him to uncover the book in the hills of upstate New York. Mormons believe in the pre-existence of one's spirit and salvation through leading a good life but it was their practice of polygamy that drew the ire of others. Persecuted, the Mormons moved westward where, under the leadership of Brigham Young, they established a Mormon community in Salt Lake City, Utah. More than merely a doctrine of spiritual beliefs, the Mormon Church demands strict adherence to a particular lifestyle with a focus on the family and missionary work.

Several coincidences happened in my life before I met Lorayne that summer. I had met a real cool-looking blonde named Marge in Winnipeg. I took her home and met her family and I noticed something about them and their home. I asked if she wanted to go out and she said, "Sure. Do you want to go to church on Sunday?" I thought, "That's a weird thing to suggest." I ended up being busy and never went, but the next time I saw her she asked me again to go to church with her. "Well, what church do you go to?" And she said "the Mormon Church." A couple of months later I met another girl named Myrna. Her parents seemed pretty secure about her and interested in whom she went out with. She asked if I wanted to come to a dance at the Mormon Church. And now the third girl was Lorayne in Regina. It was like a series of meeting girls I was attracted to who belonged to the Mormon Church.

After I met Lorayne in Regina, I came back home and looked up the Mormon Church in the Winnipeg phone book. It was on Academy Road so I went there alone. When I walked in the door it felt like I was home. They had missionaries who welcomed me with open arms.

"Welcome, I'm Brother Tom. Who are you?"

"I'm Randy Bachman."

They seemed like average people. I asked someone, "Where's the minister?"

"We don't have a paid minister."

"What do you mean, every church has a paid minister?" I replied.

And they responded, "This person is a businessman. He does this because he really believes."

That seemed really cool, someone who was not paid to tell me what to believe and ordinary people up there relating stories about how to be good Christians. It reminded me of Salem Chapel.

As I was leaving the meeting, the two guys at the door who were about my age asked, "Would you like to learn more about the Mormon faith?"

"Yeah."

"We're missionaries, we'll come to your house."

So I went home and told my Mom, "Some gentlemen are coming to our house tomorrow, they're missionaries."

She went, "Oh okay," not realizing they were from the Mormon Church.

The next day at eleven as they came walking up to the door, my Mom shouted, "Oh no, Mormons" like they were Jehovah's Witnesses or something. In those days people feared Mormons because they didn't know about them.

"Yeah, they're coming to see me."

"What?!" she exclaimed in shocked disbelief.

Two young men came in and gave me the first lesson, which is fairly general and gets more specific as you go through the teachings. They used a felt board to illustrate the hierarchy. My mother suddenly decided to vacuum in the middle of this so I moved them into the bedroom.

At the end of the meeting they said to me, "We usually close with a word of prayer. Would you give us a closing prayer?"

I didn't know what to say. In the Catholic and Lutheran churches that I had grown up in, everything was scripted. I was at a loss for words.

"We'll get on our knees and wait until you feel like saying something."

As these two guys got down on their knees in my bedroom I started to cry.

"What do I say?"

"Talk to God. Talk to Jesus. Are you thankful for anything? Do you need anything?"

This was an amazing thing for me. Nothing like it had ever happened to me before. When I was a kid and you said a prayer it was "Now I lay me down to sleep..." — the Lord's prayer, all scripted. But this was me talking to something I had believed in and respected as a little kid and learned the commandments and laws and suddenly it was like meeting a great uncle or grandfather you never met who sent you gifts and suddenly you can talk to him. It was an incredible sensation.

"I have never felt like this before in my life," I told them when I was done. "I'm in. What do I have to do?"

"You have to know what you are getting into, you have to go through a series of discussions, and you will have to be baptized."

I had been baptized as an infant but this was different. It was baptism by immersion, washing clean all that you had done before and starting fresh. To account for your wrongs you actually had to call people and tell them what you had done to achieve the burden of relief. They had to tell you they understood and forgive you. I spoke to some people and even went to the record store on Selkirk Avenue where I had stolen a few records as a teenager and left a hundred dollars on the counter.

"I owe this to you" and left.

The fellow at the counter said, "Thank you" as if he knew.

That burden being lifted was incredible. I called Lorayne and told her my experiences and that I felt wonderful.

"I've found myself," I announced. "I don't want you to go away. Let's get married."

There was a need in my life — something was missing. But you never really know it until you are confronted with it. You don't know a lot of things exist in the world until you are exposed to them. We all live isolated lives, so to speak. I lived a sheltered life in West Kildonan with my parents. I already knew there were things I didn't want to try like drugs. I had tried smoking and drinking and knew I didn't want to do them anymore.

My parents barely knew Lorayne and didn't like the fact that I was considering a change of religion and lifestyle. But I really wasn't my Mom's Catholic or my Dad's Lutheran. They tried to talk me out of it, laying out the potential problems; however, you can't talk someone out of something if they believe they are in love. You just have to accept it.

In the Mormon religion, Randy discovered a faith and a set of principles compatible with his own lifestyle choices. Garry Peterson had mixed feelings about his best friend's sudden conversion. "Randy and I were very similar. We were never really wild guys. I remember Randy telling me he had gone out with a Mormon girl in Winnipeg and when he met Lorayne she was a Mormon too so he figured 'If I can't beat 'em, I gotta join 'em.' It was almost like an omen to him that this was the direction he should go. In my opinion, I think Randy found a haven for his shyness, a place where you didn't have to smoke or drink. He found a place where he could fit in."

"Even before he met Lorayne, Randy was already becoming a quiet, reclusive person," offers Gary Bachman. "He was never an open, gregarious guy who mixed well with others. He didn't have a fondness for smoking or drinking but when he did drink it made him withdraw even more. I think the times he drank were to avoid talking to people. Randy was very impressed with the sense of close family that the Mormon Church offered so I don't think it was that hard a switch for him when he met Lorayne and converted to being a Mormon. Love will do amazing things to any guy and Lorayne was a wonderful girl, so my parents had no problems with her or the relationship."

As with all things in Randy's life, his wedding to Lorayne had to be scheduled around band commitments.

The nearest opening between tour dates was in early December so we set the date for December 5. Lorayne came to Winnipeg earlier with some of her belongings, furniture, and clothes, and I think Nadia Peterson hosted a shower for her. The wedding was in Regina and we all pulled up in the Guess Who bus we had recently purchased secondhand — my parents, family, and friends, with Jumbo driving. Burton wore his sparkly burgundy Gerry-and-the-Pacemakers–style suit from the Stag Shop and sang *Ave Maria* at the ceremony. But we had an unwedding-like reception as far as my parents and the guys in the band were concerned. We were from a European family and Ukrainians were great party people at weddings, singing, dancing and eating for days on end. The weddings I had attended as a kid were like Genghis Khan and the Barbarian hordes, guys leaping in the air dancing, partying straight through until no one could move from all the food and booze. Ours, on the other hand, was subdued to say the least: no drinking, no smoking, a barbershop quartet moving from table to table serenading. Afterwards we drove home to Winnipeg in the freezing cold in her little Studebaker Lark with a coat hanger holding the trunk closed. The band and my family followed in the bus.

Like all recent converts embarking on a life-affirming transformation coupled with his own compulsive nature, Randy embraced the tenets of the Mormon faith with fervent missionary zeal. Tim Bachman, who accepted the Mormon faith into his own life a decade later, understands his big brother's ardour. "Lorayne had grown up with it so she was more used to it by then but this was all new for Randy. When you have a spiritual experience like that, when you come to believe something is the truth, you have this desire that the people you love feel the same thing you do. I remember when I became a Mormon, in those first early moments I wanted everyone I knew to have those feelings, to feel what I had too. You forget that not everyone has had the same experiences you have and that they have to do it for themselves. You can't do it for them. I think Randy felt that this was such a wonderful thing for him at that moment in his life that everyone else close to him should have the same experience. Randy goes at everything full bore. He would never go at anything partway."

Younger brothers Tim and Robbie were not invited to the wedding but came to know Lorayne soon after. "Immediately after they were married," states Tim, "Lorayne came to live with us for a while because Randy went out on the road right away. I was at school and one day someone came up to me and sneered derisively, 'Your brother Randy's a Mormon.' I had no idea what that meant. I had never heard the word before, didn't have a clue, but the way he said it to me made it sound bad. I just figured it couldn't be good so I replied, 'No he's not.' And we got into a fight until the teacher broke us up. I went home that night and said to my mother at the kitchen sink, 'Can I ask you a question?'

'Sure.'

'What's a Mormon?'

"She whipped around and whacked me in the chops with the dishrag.

'You've been talking to your sister-in-law haven't you?!'

"I was completely puzzled. 'What are you talking about?'

'You've been talking to Lorayne.'

'No. What's she got to do with this?'

'Where did you hear that word?'

"I told her so and so at school had called Randy a Mormon. 'It sounded bad because of the way he said it.'

'Well what did you say?'

'No he isn't.' I wasn't about to look stupid and ask this kid what a Mormon was.

'Wait until your father gets home.'

"I thought 'Holy cow, this must be a bad word if I have to have my father deal with me.'

"My father came home later that day, we had dinner, and afterwards he summoned Robbie and me to the living room. I had told Robbie what had happened at school and he was just as in the dark as I was. My Dad then called Lorayne to the living room and said, 'Okay, explain it to them.' She spent almost two hours detailing her faith to us. We both sat quietly listening, waiting for the other shoe to drop, the bomb to hit. Finally she finished and we were just as confused. We understood the religion but couldn't figure what was so wrong that someone would taunt me at school.

'Is that it? Where's the bad part?'

"My parents just looked at one another and shrugged their shoulders. And that was that. It was out in the open now but it was no big deal to me."

Gary Bachman recalls Randy's sole attempt to indoctrinate father Charles Bachman. "My parents were supportive of our decisions as long as we were happy and it wasn't breaking the law or wasn't a cult. Mormons believed in God, as my parents did. It wasn't Hare Krishna or anything strange so that was okay with them. As long as Randy was happy. Not long after Randy and Lorayne moved into their first house they invited my girlfriend and me and my parents for dinner. After dinner there was a knock at the door, Randy got up and in came two Mormon missionaries. They set up their little easel and proceeded to give us all a Bible lesson right there in the living room moving these felt pieces around the board. My Dad immediately got up and called us aside.

'Randy. Gary. I want to talk to you in the kitchen.'

"He looked directly at Randy and said, 'I don't know what the heck you're trying to do here. You wanted to become a Mormon and I thought that was fine. I'm a Lutheran, you were a Lutheran before. You want to switch, I'm not going to tell you why you should or shouldn't or what's wrong with it. But I don't expect you to try to convert me. So one of two things has to happen right now. Either you have to go in there and, politely as you can, ask those two gentlemen to fold up the easel and sit and visit with us, or we're out of here never to return.' The two men folded their easel and we had a pleasant evening with them. And that was the end of it."

Lorayne and I found a little house at 160 Luxton in the North End. Being a musician and not having any credit, no one wanted to rent me an apartment or house. They assumed it would be party central. My mother knew a Rumanian fellow, a butcher, who played accordion and used to perform at all the Ukrainian weddings. He had a house on Luxton. His sons were musicians too so my Mom figured he would rent us the house because he knew who I was and knew my family. Lorayne and I went to look at the house, a tiny green two-bedroom affair, full basement, porch, on a lovely tree-lined street, much like my grandmother's house and Burton's mother's house. We met the owner, he liked us, and he agreed to rent us the house for $75 a month. It was a great house.

Lorayne had previously lived in Salt Lake City where she had an apartment so her things were brought up. Initially that's all the furniture we had. We bought a television and a stove. Because her parents were moving to Florida they gave us the contents of their pantry, their food storage, which kept us going for months: dozens of canned hams, boxes of Kraft Dinner, sacks of wheat, rice, and sugar. One of the policies of the Mormon Church is that all members must have a supply of foodstuffs and medical supplies in case you lose your job or suffer some crisis. We inherited the Stevenson's storage contents.

In September, the Guess Who recorded their next single, the first as a quartet. Composed by Toronto songwriter Johnny Cowell, *His Girl* was cut as a favour to Bob Burns. None of the band members thought much of the soft ballad. While the single brought the group back to the Canadian charts, it also brought them some unexpected attention overseas. Quality Records licensed the recording to the independent King Records label in Britain and after overdubbing a lush string score, acoustic guitar, and additional drums, *His Girl* cracked the coveted British Top Fifty by early February 1967, peaking at #45. Elated at their newfound acclaim, Bob Burns post haste set about arranging a trip for the group to the UK to capitalize on the record's chart showing. No one bothered to notice that the single promptly disappeared from the charts after a mere two-week run. Instead it was "We're off to London!"

Suddenly we came face to face with our dream when *His Girl* charted in England and we had the opportunity to go there to tour. We got a hold of the British pop charts and there we were. It was stunned disbelief on all our parts. "We've got a hit in England!" Then we started receiving phone calls from England. Whoa! We had been dying to go there. Naïvely we thought we would actually see Cliff Richard on a street corner or The Shadows playing at the London Palladium. This was our Mecca. We couldn't wait to go over.

Ray Levin had been a schoolmate of mine from Garden City Collegiate. He had emigrated from England so naturally I struck up a friendship with him. He and his father Cec, who was in the furniture business, along with Bob Burns, formed Transcontinental Productions to arrange our excursion to London.

We borrowed enough money for airfare, fancy new stage clothes from the Stag Shop, new equipment from Garnet, all totally financed. It cost a fortune to ship the gear over but we figured we were about to hit the big time. The streets of London were paved with gold. We thought we were going to be the next Beatles.

Our send-off at Winnipeg airport on February 20, 1967, was a major media event covered by television and newspapers. Everyone was out to see us off: wives, girlfriends, mothers, fans, all in tears. It was like we were going off to war. Many of our contemporaries on the local music scene showed up to bid us good luck because we were living their dreams. Accompanying the four of us were Bob Burns, Russell Gillies, Terry David Mulligan (who

came along for the fun), and a photographer from CJAY named
Bob Hickey.

After a day of oohing and aahing at Piccadilly Circus and
Buckingham Palace, we made our way to the offices of King
Records run by Phillip Solomon who was also involved in one of
the pirate radio stations operating just outside British waters.
Waiting in the outer room were other wannabes like us. When we
met Solomon he laid out his plan which was no different than
what most young, upstart, hungry bands were offered in those
days. The difference was we had already been through the mill
with Scepter Records so we were wary. The proposal was for us
to sign with his booking agency and we would record additional
singles on the King label. It was the typical English club circuit
with jaunts to Germany to play the dives in Hamburg like the
Beatles had done. Our question was simple.

"What will we be getting out of this?"

"You'll get your weekly salary," came the response.

"What if we sell a million records?"

"You'll get your weekly salary."

"What about touring profits?"

"We already told you. You'll get your weekly salary."

Over and over he kept repeating this mantra to each of our
questions. Finally it was presented as "Take it or leave it." I looked
at Jim who was doing a slow burn. We all knew without even dis-
cussing it what our response was.

"We'll leave it."

We got up and walked out. They thought they had us by dan-
gling a British tour before our eyes. When we hit the street we
stopped, looked at each other, and realized "What have we just
done? We have no tour, no label, no money. Zip." We were furious
with Bob Burns because he had failed to secure any contracts
before we left. Neither us nor our management team had gotten
anything signed before we flew off to England. If we had seen the

one-sided agreement submitted to us we would not have gambled our future on an ill-fated trip. Our only saving grace was that we had return-trip tickets.

Despondent but determined to make the most of our predicament we said, "How long can we stay? Twelve days? Okay, we're here, let's get into England." We pooled our money, checked out of our rooms at the Regent Palace into one room with two single beds, pushed them together and slept width-wise across them. We each had different lifestyles so while the rest of us would be getting up each morning, Burton and Jim would just be coming in after a night of carousing. Burton had hooked up with a girl he knew from Regina who was living in London. I checked out some of the clubs but would head back each evening to write to Lorayne because it was the first time we had been that far apart.

It was the custom in English hotels to serve a full breakfast — bacon, sausages, eggs, kippers, toast, cereal, muffins — so we befriended the Spanish maids who pushed these breakfast trolleys from room to room. When serving was over they would bring the leftovers to us. We literally lived on cold bacon and toast — bacon sandwiches — for the two weeks we stayed there. The routine was get up, have a bacon sandwich; come home, have a bacon sandwich. Once in a while we treated ourselves to a Wimpy's hamburger that was about the size of a quarter.

I had a subway map and each day I would venture out around London walking, riding the tube, and observing London life: Carnaby Street, Soho, record shops. I figured "Who knows if I'll ever be in London again." I soaked in all the sights, sounds, and smells of the city and would arrive back at the hotel each night exhausted and have a bacon sandwich.

We weren't able to get around to see a lot of bands because we didn't have the money but we did manage to meet The Who at the Marquee Club in Soho one afternoon. They were recording a live set for one of the British pop television shows. We were strolling by, heard the noise, and just walked in and sat at a table to watch.

"Who are you? What are you doing here?" asked one of their crew.

"We're the Guess Who from Canada."

"Oh."

"We need to talk to you."

"Well, just sit there."

The Marquee is like someone's basement, it's so small. The Who had stacks of Marshall amplifiers and were playing so loud our ears were ringing like someone had fired a gun beside our heads. We didn't want to look rude or uncool by plugging our ears but it was painful. They were smashing their gear and smoke bombs were going off. The director kept stopping them.

"Turn it down!"

"Okay."

Then they would just crank it up again blasting away. John Entwistle was playing his bass guitar with a metal pick cut from the aluminum trim around an Arborite countertop or table, whacking the strings like a hammer.

Finally they finished, the director had enough footage, and they laid down their instruments and came over to talk with us.

"We need to straighten out the name. We're the Guess Who and we're getting confused with you guys."

John Entwistle looked us up and down and simply mumbled, "Oh bugger off. There's the Byrds and Yardbirds so there can be a Who and Guess Who, so bugger off."

That became a running prank with Entwistle and I. Years later we were staying at the same hotel as the Who and Kale and I went up to Entwistle's room and knocked on his door. He was just getting up.

"Who is it?" he sheepishly shouted from behind the closed door.

"It's the Guess Who. Bugger off!" And we ran off laughing. We'd phone his room and do it again.

Years later when John and I met for the Ringo Starr tour, I went up to greet him with, "I'm Randy Bachman from the Guess Who.

Bugger off." He roared with laughter. We then went off to play *Shakin' All Over* together at the Hard Rock Café in Vancouver.

Once, in 1969, we were checking into the Continental Hyatt Hotel in Los Angeles and as we were signing the register, the manager asked us the name of our band. We told him "The Guess Who." Moments later two security guards confronted us.

"Unless you pay this outstanding bill for damages, you are not allowed into this hotel and we will prosecute you. Which one of you is Keith Moon?"

"No, wrong band. We're the Guess Who from Canada."

"Oh, you sure you're not The Who? You're not Mr. Moon?"

"No."

"If you are then we'll require you to post a $10,000 bond." "Moon the Loon" was notorious for hotel room demolition and banned from most American hotels.

"It's not us. We're Canadians." We showed them our passports. So they let us stay.

Settling into my room, I proceeded to make a few phone calls. As I sat in this lovely antique wooden chair, it immediately fell apart on me. So, after declaring that we were not notorious roomwreckers, there I was in the lobby, red-faced, with a broken chair in my hand. Turned out the chair was faulty but it didn't erase my embarrassment.

In the midst of our London dilemma, Bob Burns suggested we contact Mills Music who had published *Shakin' All Over*. He reasoned that since they had made a considerable sum off us maybe they could throw us a bone. Tony Hiller, who worked for Mills Music, came to our hotel and we laid out our situation to him. Tony had heard *His Girl*, liked it, and offered us an opportunity to cut some demos for him.

At Mills Music I met Ralph Murphy, a Canadian songwriter originally from Ottawa, and he and I wrote a song together. Because of contractual obligations I adopted the pseudonym Spencer Charles

— Spencer for my favourite band, the Spencer Davis Group, and Charles for my middle name. Our song, *A Little Bit of Rain*, was later recorded by a guy named James Ray. That was such a thrill for me at the time. "I wrote a song in England!" The chords in the middle eight later showed up unconsciously in the middle of *Takin' Care of Business*.

Tony Hiller took us into Regent Sound Studios in Soho as a demo band to cut two Mills Music songs written by their staff writers Jimmy Stewart and Jerome Langley. These two writers had presented us with *Miss Felicity Grey* and *This Time Long Ago*, which we thought were decent songs. Tony also allowed us to cut two tracks of our own so we recorded Neil Young's *Flying on the Ground Is Wrong* from the first Buffalo Springfield album and right there in the studio I composed a Walker Brothers'-style number on piano called *There's No Getting Away From You*. It had a Phil Spectorish-echoed piano flourish to it. Burton sang it in an Anthony Newley/Gene Pitney vocal style at first before modifying it to his own voice. It's a great song that Burton even considered re-recording years later on one of his solo albums.

As we were recording at Regent Sound, I happened to look up at the acoustic tiles on the walls and spotted a little pattern where the dots had been punched out creating a funny little caricature of a person. I followed the dots and at the bottom was a signature: J. Lennon.

"Were the Beatles ever here?"

The engineer told me they were once there doing some demos. I asked if I could have the tiles but because they were tongue and groove I'd have had to take the whole wall. Nonetheless, I was elated at knowing the Beatles had been where I was now.

We recorded over two days in early March just before we had to go home cutting the tracks on the first day and overdubbing the next. Being in a London studio was intimidating; however, as soon as the engineer counted down the track, we rose to the occasion and played professionally. Tony Hiller thought we were great. We were already better than the average British band because of our years of experience. The arranger, Cy Payne, wrote a score for fluegelhorn and Tony added glockenspiel and a few other things to sweeten the tracks, another layer of icing to make our four-piece rock sound more radio-friendly. Despite our initial dislike of the fluegelhorn, it added a contemporary pop sound like that of the Fortunes or even the Beatles who were using orchestration by then. Tony Hiller took the tapes to Fontana who worked out a licensing deal with Quality back in Canada to release them in the UK. The singles did nothing there but *This Time Long Ago* and *Flying on the Ground Is Wrong* later became hits for us in Canada.

The four recordings from the London sessions revealed that in the hands of a skilled producer and arranger, the Guess Who could present an accomplished, professional, and original pop sound as opposed to merely emulating their mentors. These tracks were light years ahead of *IT'S TIME* and served as an important step for the band.

The group returned to Winnipeg in early March demoralized, tails between their legs, with a crippling $25,000 debt from their impetuous London adventure. A meeting was convened at Ray Levin's house where, with Randy speaking for the four, Burns and Levin were tersely dismissed. A lawsuit was considered before the band realized they had no money to mount such an undertaking.

We snuck into town avoiding the media who had been led to believe, by Burns and by us before we left, that we were going to be on a major tour over there. There was no press about us arriving home. Instead we hid in our homes for several days. We then called a meeting at Kale's house and agreed that was it. We decided to break up. The humiliation seemed just too much to bear.

The problem was we still owed some $25,000. Divided four ways we each would be responsible for $6,250. That was a lot of dough in 1967.

"I'm not going back to Bata Shoes or Sears men's wear to pay off my share of our debt. I can make more money playing in a band so I'm going to start a band. Do you want to be in my band?"

Jim said, "I'm in."

"I'm in, too," came Garry's response.

"Me, too," chimed in Burton.

"Great, we're a band again. We're going to pay this off and get back on our feet."

We couldn't afford to keep a manager on so I took over our affairs and contacted the booking agents.

Faced with financial ruin, I couldn't ask my parents for help. I had to work it out myself. This was my life, my decision. I was twenty-three years old and on my own. Before we went away I had a few guitar students that I met on weekday evenings, some guys from other bands around town. I decided now I would charge them $15 for an hour's lesson; four students took lessons, one per night. That brought in $60 a week that really helped us get by. Lorayne and I survived for weeks on our pantry supply from her parents. We devised a variety of ways to liven up Kraft Dinner. I was very grateful to have that supply. Lorayne had modelled in Regina and now did the same in Winnipeg for Sears and The Bay. But when she received an offer to model at a local car show in a bathing suit and two days later I overheard some guys talking about her, I told her, "No more modelling." I did not want anyone gawking at my wife.

With few options available, the Guess Who set about doing what they knew best, working. "We looked good and sounded good," offers Burton, "but we were broke and terribly in debt. It was so far down the line for us that there was only one way out and that was to make it.

That's what kept us going." The band soon found a whole new audience with their sound. Once again, Randy and the group were at the forefront of English music introducing the sound of 1967 England to eager Winnipeg fans.

We still had to stickhandle around London trip questions. When asked about our adventure, we would put out a smokescreen: "We recorded in London!" Every band wanted to do that and we had. So we were able to save some face, at least among our peers on the local scene.

Besides that, we brought back the latest records from the UK by groups like the Cream and Jimi Hendrix. I took the first Hendrix record up to Doc Steen at CKRC and told him this was what was happening. He listened and concluded, "I can't play this on radio." We brought England to Winnipeg. We started playing this stuff around town and smashing our equipment like The Who. People thought we had lost our minds. Initially, audiences didn't like this music, but within two weeks they were coming back to hear it again. We had smoke bombs going off and I would ram my guitar through a fake Garnet speaker cabinet that Russell Gillies would re-cover the next day. The kids never knew because it all looked brand new when we started the night. Gar Gillies, Russell's dad who owned Garnet amplifiers in Winnipeg, built me a special pre-amp unit so I could get all the distorted Hendrix and Clapton sounds. I named it the Herzog and I would put it on full blast and it would be making howling noises like a wild bull's testicles being crushed with pliers. Gar also made me a custom whammy bar that was longer, like a propeller, that allowed me to do the Hendrix "Wild Thing" sounds.

Before we knew it, the deejays were all on the air hyping us. "They're back from England! Come hear their new English sound." Our fans became legion. We went from a few hundred a night to thousands trying to get into the tiny little halls to see our incredible show. We were hip again because, like years before in the Silvertones and Reflections, we were ahead of the pack having access to English music before it hit these shores. Burton back-combed his hair like Hendrix, I had my whammy bar on my guitar sustaining and bending feedback notes, and all of a sudden we were heavy. Winnipeg had yet to witness any psychedelic music. Once again we were trendsetters. Out of the ashes of an unmitigated disaster we managed to find some saving grace.

Another lifeline came via the local CBC television affiliate CBWT. *Music Hop* was a popular Canadian television pop music showcase weekdays at 5:30 from a different city each day. Although the very nature of the series underscored the fragmented regional state of Canadian music, it ultimately helped break down those barriers by creating national audiences for artists from all parts of Canada. The Thursday Winnipeg edition had previously featured former rockabilly-turned-nightclub singer Ray St. Germain backed by a chorus and the Lenny Breau Trio. By 1967, producer Larry Brown was on the lookout for something much more hip to go with the name change to *Let's Go*. He had already tapped former Guess Who front man Chad Allan to serve as host, but the show needed a backing band. Who better than Canada's greatest hit makers, the Guess Who?

Larry Brown asked if we could read charts, sheet music, which were to be written each week by the show's musical director Bob McMullin. I said, "Yes, of course!" It was a desperate bluff. Garry and Burton could read but Jim and I couldn't. We learned everything by ear from records. In a subtle move a few days before the scheduled audition, I called Bob and asked about his progress in writing the charts. He was nice enough to tell me both the titles he had finished and not yet finished. I promptly went out and bought the records, called a band rehearsal and we learned all the songs to a "T." Two days later at the CBC audition, the charts were put in front of us, we smiled at each other, and not only did we play the songs perfectly, we sounded exactly like the records. Larry Brown came up to us and said, "You got the gig." Our ruse worked. The show paid us $1,100 a week, which we put directly toward our debts. The gig lasted through two years and some seventy-eight national weekly TV shows and by the end we were out of debt.

Some of the stuff we did on that CBC show was quite incredible. We would go from Blue Cheer's *Summertime Blues*, heavy metal screaming guitars, right into a pop number with the Winnipeg Symphony and from that into *Friends of Mine* with a Gerry Mulligan avant-garde sax solo. We even did the Sgt. Pepper album with the orchestra. Because of the weekly national exposure we were voted the top band in *RPM* magazine several years running.

At the start of the second season, Larry Brown came to Burton and me with a proposition.

"You guys are established national television stars now. Here's a perfect opportunity for you to perform original material. Why don't you and Randy write and if I like it, I'll let you do it on the show."

It would be impossible to place a monetary value on the benefits accrued to the four members of the Guess Who from that weekly CBC television show. It allowed the band to regain a solid financial footing, provided national exposure and name recognition along with a forum to promote their latest singles, took them giant steps toward forging their own sound, gave them studio experience with producers and arrangers, and became the catalyst for the Bachman–Cummings songwriting partnership. "Randy and I owe Larry Brown a real vote of thanks," acknowledges Burton. With Larry's encouragement, the seeds of the Bachman–Cummings collaboration were planted.

Jim Martin feels the *Let's Go* show saved the group from falling apart. "The band became part of the CBC family. Everyone became very close, from the producer right down to the makeup girl, Anne. Larry

Brown really loved the band and became such an important input to the guys and encouraged them to do their own thing. In two years, the group was back on its feet. If that show hadn't been there I don't think the group could have stayed together."

The Guess Who became the darlings of the local CBC affiliate, resulting in further work in radio that included a memorable northern tour of airforce bases sponsored by the Department of National Defence that was broadcast live to remote communities above the 60th parallel. It was a bitterly cold December morning when the group arrived at CBC headquarters on Portage Avenue for their northern journey.

We thought that would be a cool experience and the money was good so we agreed to go along. In those days we would play just about anywhere. We were booked alongside Ted Komar and his orchestra. Ted played accordion, and the other players were well-established jazz players from around town like Reg Keln and Ronnie Halldorson who had both backed up Lenny Breau. Headlining the mini-tour was "Our pet, Juliette," star of her own long-running CBC television series and a former Winnipegger. A magician and a comedian rounded out the troupe. We were the token pop act.

Prior to departing, we were urged to wear our warmest clothes. It was the middle of winter, forty below in Winnipeg, and we were heading north towards the Arctic Circle. I had this cool sheepskin coat that was quite bulky but warm. We all wore scarves, toques, mitts, and boots. When we showed up wrapped up in our winter wear these airforce guys proceeded to give us more clothes to wear over our own parkas and coats telling us, "Where you're going you'll need these extra clothes." As big as my feet are, size thirteen with big bulky winter boots on, they then put them into another pair of sheepskin-lined boots with galvanized rubber on the outside. I could barely walk with six pounds on each foot. They then gave us parkas to be worn on top of our parkas. As he was handing me mine, the officer told me, "By the way, the buttons are made of compressed, dehydrated soup and inside the hood is an aluminum lining. If you take it out, put some snow in it and place it in the sun you can heat up the buttons and eat the soup. In your pocket is some sterno and matches to start a fire." This coat was a walking survival kit. I thought to myself, "Where are we going?!"

After fitting us with our additional outer garments, we were loaded onto a bus and driven to the airport to board an airforce cargo plane called an Atlas, the kind where the entire front end lifts open and jeeps drive right on in. In the middle of the fuselage they had a couple of rows of theatre seats bolted to the floor. We took our seats and off we went. We were flying pretty low, you could see the ground, but it was freezing onboard so we were glad to have the extra warmth of the survival coats.

Our first stop was Churchill on Hudson Bay. As we were about to taxi into the airport, the pilot informed us that there had been a terrible accident nearby just prior to our arrival. A polar bear had killed a schoolkid in the playground. Apparently the school had been built in the traditional path of the polar bears. We played our show in Churchill then headed off to places like Inuvik beyond the Arctic Circle.

Most of the guys in Ted Komar's band were there for the party. They were being paid well and the music charts were a breeze to play so they were drinking pretty good. In the vernacular of the day, they were pretty sauced most of the time. It soon turned into high school hijinks all over again. For the crowds, seeing Juliette live, watching a magician make rabbits disappear, and seeing a real live rock band that appeared on television was a real treat. The whole community would come out to the shows, old, young, Moms and Dads, Native and non-Native.

One night at another of these remote outposts somewhere, Juliette was onstage singing backed up by the Komar band who were half in the bag. Burton decided to have some fun. He proceeded to make this huge cardboard sign three feet wide. On one side he printed "Applause" and on the other he put "F*#k You." In the midst of one of Juliette's numbers he strolled right across the stage between her and the musicians. The crowd saw "Applause" and erupted; Juliette figured it was for her and became really jazzed by the audience response. She couldn't see Burton. Meanwhile the band cracked up and fell over in hysterics because they saw the other side of the sign. The music momentarily fell apart as these guys cut up. Juliette turned around to see what was happening to her accompaniment but by this time Burton was already offstage. The players managed to pull themselves together just in time for Burton to stroll out again and crack them up. There were a lot of pranks like this on that trip.

At another gig, we were guests at a massive banquet where we feasted on all the local delicacies like moose and otter. Following the meal, the booze began to flow and being a nondrinker, I asked to be taken to a barracks to sleep. The guys in the band would just pass out where they sat. As they were escorting me to the barracks I couldn't see a thing. There was no building, just a bump in the ground with a stovepipe sticking out. The structure was half underground with the other half covered in packed snow. The entrance went down into the ground to a bunkhouse with about forty bunks on either side and at the end a pot-bellied stove with a stack of wood and a bucket of coal beside it. The room was white and I realized the windows had thick frost all over them, from the inside. The guy stoked the fire for me, got it warmer in the room, and I removed my bulky outer parka, my sheepskin coat, my scarf and mitts. He then turned to me and with a cautionary wag of his finger warned, "Whatever you do, don't let this fire go out." Normally they had someone each evening maintaining the fire every hour or two throughout the night but because of the special occasion, everyone was at the party. He bid me goodnight and left. I threw another log on the fire and promptly fell asleep.

When I woke up I was so cold I could barely move. The fire had died out, there was no one around, and I couldn't see a thing out the windows covered with frost a half-inch thick. I couldn't leave so I put on all my winter clothes and piled up the mattresses from the bunks into an igloo to keep my body temperature inside. There I huddled underneath my mattress fortress praying to stay alive. The top caved in on me but I figured I was okay and fell back to sleep again.

The next thing I knew I was awakened by someone touching my neck to see whether I was still breathing. It was morning and I was close to being frostbitten but luckily the mattresses had kept the heat in. So I managed to survive my Arctic experience. The other guys were oblivious to what had happened.

At the end of the tour, the Canadian Armed Forces presented each of us with plaques showing a map of the north and little flags where we had stopped.

At Larry Brown's urging, and with the prospect of national exposure, Burton and Randy began composing songs in earnest. To this point they had both written alone but soon found they needed each other, and a unique partnership was formed.

We found we were running out of whole songs alone and started to share our fragments. I needed a voice for my songs because I couldn't sing them. When we tried it and it worked we immediately knew the sum was greater than the individual parts; one and one made three. We felt that there was something special there.

Burton and I developed a weekly ritual. We would do a gig on a Friday evening, go out to the Sal's, then I would drive him home. "See ya tomorrow." I would come over to Burton's at eleven the next morning carrying my little Hilroy notebook filled with song ideas jotted down throughout the week. We would work at the piano in Burton's front room putting our ideas together crafting songs. At two in the afternoon, Granny Kirkpatrick would bring us cookies and 7-Up and we would be done by four, go outside and enjoy the sun, play our latest efforts on guitar, bid farewell to each other, and I would go home. A few hours later I would swing by and pick him up for the gig that night.

We had this regimented routine every Saturday. We would show each other the ideas we had come up with or borrowed from other songs. We didn't live in a vacuum and weren't working in isolation; we were subject to the influences of the latest radio hits or records we purchased. We wouldn't copy directly but the feel or some chords might be drawn from another song. By the time Jim and Garry added their parts it was far removed from the initial influence though that first inspiration remained the spark.

The thing about Burton and me was that we had similar musical experiences and tastes. If I said to him, "I want an Eddie Cochran bridge here" he instinctively knew what I was talking about. Or he would say, "Remember that song from the Hollies' album, *Fifi the Flea*? I like that hook." And I would say, "Oh yeah. Then let's go from that into a Georgie Fame thing." We had this inner connection, a private vocabulary drawn from the music we loved, the shared musical library in our heads that allowed us to take a lot of shortcuts and save a lot of time explaining things to each other.

There was a certain magnetic attraction to each other at first because I wanted to be songwriter and needed an alter ego, a balance, a collaborator, and he also wanted to be a songwriter and needed the same thing. I became McCartney to his Lennon, the missing piece to his puzzle and he to mine. I would bring a nearly completed song to him and he would love it up to a point or not like it to a certain point then love the remainder. He would then play me one of his songs until the point where it fell apart for me. We would then take the strengths of each song and piece together a completed song.

Those Saturday sessions together were something we looked forward to, getting together with scraps of songs. It was the excitement of creating our own music that spurred us on. We wanted to be like Bacharach and David or Lennon and McCartney, those really great songwriting teams. Even with the differences in our personalities we still clicked. We really can't explain it even today. There was just a chemistry that happened and the result was some great music.

"Randy would write half-finished songs and I would write half-finished songs," acknowledges Burton, "and nine times out of ten we'd put them together and they would work. We had an invisible language that we could talk to each other with that was an intuitive, expedient means of communication. It was like a pipeline to each other's brain." Notes Garry Peterson, "The trust Randy and Burton had together and the relationship they enjoyed was closer than with the rest of us because they wrote together. Burton learned to write songs with Randy. They had so many experiences together and were closer."

With his creative juices flowing, Randy began looking further afield than the Guess Who to market his songs. Not everything he composed would earn Burton's nod of approval so with a growing surplus of completed songs, fragments, riffs, and lyric ideas, he set about establishing himself on the thriving Winnipeg music scene as a writer/producer for hire. With his reputation as one of the elite of the Winnipeg crew, his name had cachet with aspiring rockers looking for a little of that Guess Who magic. Randy knew well that the real money in the music business came not from performing or touring, not even from recording sessions. It was in songwriting and publishing. He who wrote the songs and published them made the money. Lennon and McCartney earned vastly more than the other two Beatles; Jagger and Richards' income far outstripped the other Rolling Stones. Mills Music had made far more money than the Guess Who from *Shakin' All Over*.

At twenty-four with a pregnant wife at home, Randy was already looking toward a more stable career in the music business and less road work.

Randy's status was further elevated when, on the back liner notes to the Buffalo Springfield's second album, *BUFFALO SPRINGFIELD AGAIN*, released in the fall of 1967, Randy's name appeared as an "influence and inspiration" to the seminal California group, the darlings of the folk-rock crowd. Formed by ex-Winnipegger Neil Young along with Stephen Stills and Richie Furay, the Springfield had not only scored a hit record but an anthem for a generation with *For What It's Worth (Stop, Hey What's That Sound)*. Earlier in the year Young had tried in vain to entice Jim Kale to join the Springfield in Los Angeles. Randy was in illustrious company on the album sleeve. Among the other names acknowledged as mentors to the group were the likes of the Beatles, Rolling Stones, Jimi Hendrix, the Byrds, Chet Atkins, Hank Williams, Ricky Nelson, and Neil and Randy's early hero Hank Marvin.

Burton and I loved the Buffalo Springfield. Neil came back to Winnipeg at Christmas 1966 to visit his mother and we received a call: "Come down to CKRC, I'm playing an acetate of my album for Harry Taylor and Doc Steen." So Burton and I went down; Kale was there, and Neil said, "You won't believe this. It's recorded in eight track. You can record guitar after guitar." We were in awe. As we were listening and really digging the album, we got to a track in particular.

"Who is that singing?" I winced.

"It's me."

"What?"

"It's like Bob Dylan," replied Neil. "If you've got a really weird voice, somebody out there will like it. As long as you deliver it with honesty and go for the notes, people really don't care what it sounds like."

I never forgot that. Neil took a lot of ribbing for his voice yet he stuck to his guns and has one of the most distinctive and recognizable voices in rock music. All you need to hear are two bars and you know it's Neil Young. Later on in BTO when I was pressed into singing lead like on *Takin' Care of Business*, I tried to put a character into my singing rather than worry about tonal quality because I think my voice's tonal quality is terrible, as is Neil's. But despite not being great opera-trained voices, we both have individuality.

When the Springfield's first album came out in Canada, we learned that album inside out. We played

What It's Worth in our shows as well as what we thought was kind of a hidden gem, *Flying on the Ground Is Wrong*, which we later recorded. The Springfield were the most ultra hip, cool band, so when their second album was released and there was my name on the back listed as an influence I went "Wow!" It was an unbelievable thrill. Even though it was spelled wrong, Backman, everyone knew who it was.

Lorne Saifer had managed several south Winnipeg bands including Neil Young's Squires before Neil flew the coop for Toronto and ultimately Los Angeles. By the latter sixties he was attempting to groom the Mongrels to become the next Guess Who. The only problem was that none of the five Mongrels was much of a songwriter. Lorne turned to Randy Bachman for suitable material to launch the group's recording career. Lorne was also connected with Winnipeg booking agent Frank Weiner who had his own house label, Franklin Records. It was a perfect match: Weiner and Saifer had the artists all hungry for original material. Weiner had the record label; and Randy had the songs and studio experience that could be parlayed into a role as writer/producer. Together Randy and Lorne formed Sabalora, a production and publishing company to market their services to Winnipeg artists. One song, *Funny Day*, recorded by the Mongrels, was co-written by Randy and his London acquaintance Ralph Murphy. "We called them Randy's Rejects," smiles Mongrels' guitarist Duncan Wilson, describing the source of material Randy offered Sabalora artists, "the songs the Guess Who had rejected." Besides the Mongrels, Sabalora was responsible for songwriting, publishing, or production for the Sugar And Spice, Love Cyrcle, and Mind Explosion among others. None of the records or artists came to anything but the experience served Randy well for future endeavours and revealed his desire to branch out into other facets of the music business. It would also become a bone of contention within the Guess Who.

I was looking for an outlet for my songs. I ran into Lorne Saifer one day and indicated that I'd like to work with his band as producer or writer. He liked the idea but wanted a piece of the action. I figured I could use Lorne to pitch my songs to other acts so we formed a publishing company. Sabalora was SAifer, BAchman, LOrne, RAndy. One of my songs the Mongrels recorded was *Good Good Man*, which was originally titled *The Ballad of Willy Loman* based on *Death of a Salesman*. I received a letter from Arthur Miller's attorney insisting I desist from using Willy Loman's name. But I had to keep my writing with Burton for the Guess Who separate from my Sabalora work. It brought in a few bucks now and then. As a matter of fact, when Tally was born, I was in Toronto and Lorne was there at the hospital with Lorayne. He still needles me about the fact that he held Tally before I did.

CHAPTER 4

Wheatfield Soul

With the group's profile raised considerably as a result of their weekly exposure on *Let's Go*, Coca-Cola approached the Guess Who to record a radio commercial. Coke's jingles coordinator was Toronto-based Jack Richardson, a veteran bass player and producer. Jack contacted the band with the offer and took an instant liking to the quartet. The positive experience cutting the commercial encouraged Jack to recommend the Guess Who for a more elaborate project.

"I was with McCann-Erickson, the advertising agency for Coca-Cola," Jack recounts on his initial contact with the Winnipeg group, "and we developed this youth radio campaign whereby we decided to use younger spokespeople for our product. You couldn't reach a fifteen or twenty year old with the same message as a sixty year old. Bobby Curtola was our first exercise in this campaign and that proved to be very successful so we expanded on that. We next did a series of radio commercials using Canadian acts like JB and the Playboys, David Clayton Thomas, and Robbie Lane and the Disciples. The jingles were based on the songs these artists were relatively well known for. The Guess Who was one of the acts we approached. The outcome of that was that the agency recommended we put together a compilation album from the catalogues of these artists. I suggested it would be better to go with something original. The first one we did was with Bobby Curtola and it was so successful they decided to do it again." That second effort became *A WILD PAIR* with the Guess Who on one side of the album and the Staccatos from Ottawa on the other. Released in the spring of 1968 as a promotional item, the album was ordered from Coke with ten bottle caps and one dollar.

"That *WILD PAIR* album proved to be extremely successful," continues Jack, "selling over 85,000 copies, which was quite a feat for the Canadian market." Jack, together with his business partners, arranger Ben McPeek, accountant Allan MacMillan, and lawyer Peter Clayton formed Nimbus 9 Productions Ltd. and Nimbus Records to market the album.

Despite the presence of a new manager, Don Hunter, Jack found himself dealing with Randy as the group's spokesman. "My feeling at the time was that Randy was definitely the force behind the group," acknowledges Jack. "When I got involved with them Burton was still a teenager and Randy was older and more experienced and as such was making most of the decisions as far as the group was concerned."

What attracted Jack Richardson to champion the Guess Who's cause was the songwriting of Randy and Burton. With the *WILD PAIR* album, the two songwriters entered a prolific writing period that would yield not only the five tracks for that album but also at least two dozen more, Many, such as *I Found Her in a Star* and *Six AM or Nearer*, were destined for subsequent Guess Who albums once the group found success. In total, the Bachman–Cummings songwriting team, either individually or collectively, submitted more than thirty demos to Jack for consideration on *A WILD PAIR*.

"The *WILD PAIR* album gave Randy and Burton something to write towards, a project where they had to provide sufficient original material for as opposed to just writing for the sake of writing," recalls Jack. "They had good songs, they were good players, and I felt that Burton had a charismatic quality to him that seemed ready to explode. There were few bands at that point in time who had any profile nationally across Canada. The Guess Who had that with the CBC television show and their previous records. *Shakin' All Over* had been a hit. The problem was that either from lack of support from their label — who weren't prepared to provide any additional financial backing — or because the group hadn't come up with a follow-up, they had failed to capitalize on that initial momentum. Bob Burns really didn't have as much production experience or musical background as the band now needed. I had been in the music business since 1947 and probably had more experience than most producers in the country at that time. Our coming together was a very compatible situation for both of us. We both had something to offer each other."

Recording *A WILD PAIR* in early 1968, we travelled to Toronto and got to work with the Toronto "A team," the top players on the scene, mostly from the jazz world, like Guido Basso, Ed Bickert, Don Thompson, and Moe Kaufman. Some of these players looked down their noses at us because we couldn't read music but were pulling down more money than they were. One guy who was decent to us was Hagood Hardy. When it came time to write another song for the sessions, Burton and I each wrote a song around his unusual name. Burton's was better so we cut it for the album. I did some incredible Hendrix-style guitar with my Herzog and wah wah pedal but it was mixed out. I was disappointed they only left a little bit in the fade out. *I Need Your Company* was my attempt at being Jimmy Webb using major seventh chords. Burton's vocal on that was absolutely perfect and the orchestration was understated enough to complement the song. The middle eight was me copying *You've Lost That Lovin' Feeling*. *Heygoode Hardy* was over the top in terms of arrangement with wild trumpets everywhere. *Somewhere Up High* was my own *Walk Away Renee* with cellos.

Jack brought in a new young guy to mix the album and we

said, "What"s a mixer?" He balances the sounds, we were informed. That guy turned out to be Phil Ramone whom we met for the first time. Phil, of course, went on to great success with artists like Billy Joel. That's why *A WILD PAIR* sounds so darn good. The sound is incredible, largely because of Phil Ramone.

A WILD PAIR would have been the first Canadian gold album but because it wasn't sold through retail outlets for $3.98 we didn't qualify. Still, it was one of the biggest-selling albums in Canada up to that point. Its significance to our evolution was immeasurable. The album was a further progression in terms of our level of sophistication. Everything was incremental from *His Girl*, to the London sessions with Tony Hiller, to *A WILD PAIR*. Working with producers who knew what they were doing was a major step for us. And receiving critical praise and positive consensus from fans boosted our confidence and gave our egos a real shot of bravado.

"I recall the first session we did at Hallmark Studios in Toronto," offers Jack. "I brought back the tapes to my partners and we listened. I told them I thought it just wasn't good enough and that we should scrap it and go back to the drawing board and start over. I was met with incredulous looks because we were still an embryonic company and had spent considerable money already on this project. I called the group together and said "Look guys, we're scrapping that other material," and I remember Randy brightening up and saying that was what they had come in to talk to me about. So we went back to square one and redid the session. I think that was one of the things that cemented the relationship between us, that we were as interested in their well-being and satisfaction as we were in getting product into the marketplace. I don't think they had ever encountered that before."

Suitably impressed, Jack and his partners at Nimbus determined to stake their future on the Guess Who. A pitch to the group was made, they agreed to sign with Nimbus Productions, and the band's existing contract was bought from Quality Records for a paltry $1,000. "I felt there was a tremendous amount of latent talent in the group but in those days there really wasn't a Canadian music industry like there is today. A Canadian group would beg, borrow, or steal enough money to go into a studio to cut a record then give it to a Canadian label and, more often than not, it ended up in the wastebasket. I just felt there was more to it than that. We approached both the Staccatos and the Guess Who. The Guess Who agreed. The Staccatos chose to stay with Capitol Records so it was one of those 'win one, lose one' situations but I think we won the best one."

The first order of business was a single to capitalize on *A WILD PAIR*'s success. The group assembled at Hallmark Studios in Toronto to cut several tracks including the Bachman–Cummings compositions *Of a Dropping Pin* and *When Friends Fall Out*. Both failed to make much headway on the Canadian charts. Nevertheless, Jack believed the band needed an album to showcase their diverse sounds. Financing the project, to be recorded in New York at Phil Ramone's new studio, required a leap of faith on Jack's part. "I took out a second mortgage on my house," states Jack. "It was $5,000 which in those days was a serious amount of money. That paid for some of the *WHEATFIELD SOUL* sessions, not all of them. The total cost was about $9,800. When you are young and fearless and you believe in what you are doing, you take that chance. I would be very, very hesitant about doing the same thing today. But the marketplace is very different today. Back then it was really the birth of an industry in Canada." The gamble paid off in spades.

Jack Richardson instructed Burton and I to write more songs for a whole album. To us, that was validation that we were indeed songwriters. And we, in turn, had confidence in Jack. He saw something in us that no one else did, or would admit to, and was willing to put his money where his mouth was.

When Jack felt we had enough material he arranged for sessions in New York. Before we entered the studio though, Jack informed us that because he was mortgaging his house to finance the album and launch the new label, he needed to own our song publishing. We told him no. Burton and I had Friends of Mine Music to publish our tunes. We shared everything equally if it was a collaboration or a hundred percent if alone, but it was ours. Jack persisted, stating that if we had a turntable hit, meaning a lot of radio play but not selling many records, he needed to recoup his investment. It was a deal-breaker and presented as "Accept it or no recording." Reluctantly, Burton and I acquiesced and gave him a full percentage with the stipulation that this arrangement remained only until he earned some money, then a lesser percentage until his investment was paid back. We would then get our publishing back. The plan was not in perpetuity but merely to help pay Jack back his investment. We knew we needed this break.

So Jack took 100 percent of our publishing (which is 50 percent of what a song earns) and Burton and I got nothing besides our writers royalties. Friends of Mine Music was given credit as a token but not paid any money. In terms of songwriting royalties, Nimbus earned 50 percent and Burton and I split the remaining 50 percent. When we started having hit singles we would see Nimbus earning big money, more than Burton and I individually. Nimbus 9 also took half the record royalties as a production company.

After a time, I saw what was being earned by Nimbus and it was a pretty hefty sum. I suggested to Jack that they must have earned their stake back by then. I received a letter back giving us 40 percent of their 50 percent but only on the BMI performances; that meant on radio, not the mechanicals which is on the sale of each record, at the time, 2 cents. It was better than nothing. I wanted it to increase more a year later but that never happened.

"I make no apologies for the fact that we controlled the publishing of their songs," counters Jack. "We were gambling our money on the band." The publishing issue would become the focus of a bitter feud between the two songwriters decades later.

Meanwhile, the group and Jack, along with arranger Ben McPeek, journeyed to A&R Studios in New York in mid-September 1968 to record *WHEATFIELD SOUL*, the name derived from the band's defence of their humble prairie roots. "We used to go to Toronto and get looked at as prairie hicks, farmers, and country bumpkins," laments Burton. "We were really white bread compared to all the Toronto boogaloo bands. So I just said, 'Hey, you can call us down all you like but we've got wheatfield soul.' It was our way of fighting back."

As the sessions progressed, *WHEATFIELD SOUL* emerged as a diverse collection of styles rather than a cohesive sound, from lush ballads and jazz-tinged numbers to heavy rock and psychedelic trips.

The *WHEATFIELD SOUL* album was a pastiche because that's what we thought you had to do. We thought it should be a well-rounded album that represented a potpourri of styles showcasing our various influences and current genres. But what we ended up with instead was no clearly defined Guess Who sound. *WHEATFIELD SOUL* was a bunch of vignettes, a sampling of sounds allowing the public to choose which direction for us.

We were simply building on the experience and knowledge we had accrued. There were no books to tell you what to do. Nowadays you can get a book on anything: how to record, how to write a song, how to go on tour, how to make a video. We were just blundering around. And all of these little things we did that were false starts or errors or mistakes were all very important learning tools.

Sessions completed, Jack approached RCA in New York. "Nimbus had a distribution deal with RCA in Canada," relates Jack, "and *Of a Dropping Pin* was the first single. Although it wasn't a huge success, Andy Nagy at RCA in Montreal felt there was something there and called his head office in New York. I flew to New York to meet with Don Burkhimer at RCA based on the single *Of a Dropping Pin*. There was no mention of an album in the pipeline, we had just completed it. Don wasn't aware of the album. He was an A and R man and a great guy. I brought along an acetate of *WHEATFIELD SOUL* and after our conversation, I asked him if he would mind listening to it and giving me his opinion. Don sat and listened to the entire record which was very unusual for an A and R man, let me tell you, and when it was done he looked at me and said 'Jack, *These Eyes* is a smash hit.' I came back to Canada and told the boys that we were going with *These Eyes* as the single, that RCA felt the same way, and that we had a potential deal with them on that basis. That's where it all started."

As head of Artists and Repertoire for RCA in New York, Don Burkhimer was always on the lookout for new talent. The label had been slow off the mark in terms of signing the current rock scene but Don heard something in the Guess Who. "Not too many record executives paid much attention to Canadian talent at that point," recalls Don, "but RCA was already a presence in Canada with offices in Toronto and Montreal. I saw Canada as an untapped source. What I saw with the Guess Who were two very strong personalities in Randy and Burton, both of them creative, who complemented each other well. There was a chemistry between them. Neither one seemed to take on a leadership function in the studio. It was actually very democratic. Burton's voice and musicianship coupled with Randy's guitar figures were very instrumental in making hit records. The Guess Who were good for the label in more ways than one. They were a rock band, and RCA at that time — other than Elvis and Jefferson Airplane — needed more exposure in the rock field. The Guess Who gave us a presence that encouraged other artists to consider the label."

RCA in the United States offered Nimbus a contract for the group. "The Guess Who signed a record deal with Nimbus and then we went and negotiated the deal with RCA with the group's full approval," qualifies Jack Richardson, which meant that Nimbus retained control over the group. "Nimbus never acted as middle men between RCA and the group in terms of getting paid though. There was a total point situation and the band portion of that overall pool went directly to them and the production portion went directly to our company. The only time that varied was in Canada where we made the distribution on any Canadian royalties that came in. The split between the band and the production company, Nimbus, was a 3/8-5/8 split, with the 3/8 going to Nimbus and the larger portion going to the band. It definitely wasn't a 50-50 thing. We originally controlled the publishing until the first period of the contract when we got them together and, in essence, gave the publishing or ownership back to their company, Expressions Music, and we administered it."

I think we got a dime or twelve cents on every album sold — that was the old royalty. In those days it was very low. Our contract was with Nimbus 9, a production deal with them, so they took a big chunk of the money. They financed the album and took half the money as well as getting the publishing. We split up what was left. Nimbus 9 —Richardson, McPeek, MacMillan, and Clayton — became wealthy on the Guess Who's success. They built a recording studio in Toronto with Guess Who money. I talk to Jack Richardson's kids once in a while and they thank me for putting them through college.

A battle soon ensued over the choice of debut single. With its lush orchestration and smooth vocal delivery, *These Eyes* was a natural for the pop charts. The band wanted a rocker. "I had a very strong conviction that *These Eyes* was a smash hit and so did RCA," recalls Jack. "The band, on the other hand, did not want to release *These Eyes* as the first single. We had some pretty hot and heavy words over that one."

I wrote the piano part for *These Eyes* in Regina one night waiting to take Lorayne on a date. That was back in the summer of 1966 and we hadn't known each other long. She wasn't ready so as I waited and noodled around on her parents' piano in the living room I came up with the chords. The words I had were actually "these arms" with the line "These arms long to hold you." I later showed Burton my new song called *These Arms*. I also had the descending progression down to the A minor chord. He wanted "these arms" to be the second line and he had a song that started with the rhythm pattern da da da dut dut da, da da da dut dut da. It was almost like the chords in Archie Bell and the Drell's *Tighten Up*. We put the parts together and added "These eyes are crying" and made the title make sense telling the story. *These Eyes* was just a song written by a guy who could only play piano in the key of C and that's why the beginning is so simple. That's all I could play on the piano.

We saw ourselves as a rock 'n' roll band and fought against *These Eyes* being the first single. We wanted a rocker like *When You Touch Me*; Nimbus and RCA wanted *These Eyes* and they won. Over our vehement protests, Jack sat us down and bluntly pronounced, "This is the best song on the album. You have no other chance. I've mortgaged my house for this and we are standing at the edge of a precipice. We either take the leap or you go back where it is safe and never get any further." He was right. RCA paid less than ten grand for the *WHEATFIELD SOUL* album. Don Burkhimer told me years later they would have paid ten times that after *These Eyes* hit.

Up until the last two decades, the Canadian music industry has suffered from an extreme case of inferiority complex, almost a penis-envy, directed at our powerful neighbour to the south, the United States. "They're bigger, they must be better." Canadian talent rarely got a break up here until they had somehow proven their worth to American audiences. With that stamp of approval or validation, Canadian radio then embraced its own with vigour. In the sixties we lost so many talented Canadians simply because they couldn't find support at home. Paul Anka, Neil Young, Joni Mitchell, David Clayton Thomas, Zal Yanovsky,

Denny Doherty, The Band, the list goes on and on. Once these talented Canucks found favour with American audiences, however, the rush to welcome them back home became a stampede.

In a sense, the Guess Who defied that familiar routine with *Shakin' All Over*'s massive Canadian success coming well before its entry on the US charts. The group managed to ride that tide through to the end of 1965; however, after the initial momentum of that hit died down, the Guess Who found themselves having to fight tooth and nail for airplay and recognition despite national prominence on television each week. Recalls Canadian music journalist Larry LeBlanc: "The Guess Who had been off the radio for two or three years by the time *WHEATFIELD SOUL* and *These Eyes* came out. Nobody had been playing the Guess Who. The *WILD PAIR* album didn't get any airplay. They were so cold to Canadian radio. I saw them playing at Maple Leaf Gardens during that period at one of the worst shows I have ever seen. They were on a bill with groups like The Happenings on a show called Summer Cool Out and only a hundred people turned up. There were more police-men than people in the audience." Radio is not very forgiving and the Guess Who were perceived as has-beens.

When *These Eyes* first came out in Canada, it didn't do well. CHUM radio in Toronto and some of the other so-called Canadian supporters wouldn't play it. However, as was the custom in those days, Rosalie Trombley at CKLW in Windsor/Detroit, who is responsible for breaking a lot of Canadian product over the years, including BTO later, started playing the song into the Detroit vicinity. The station had a huge market area all the way to Toledo, Ohio. Soon after, we received word from them that there was a groundswell of interest and maybe we should promote it more. So we hired our own independent promotion men in the US at our own expense — us and Nimbus 9 with a little support from RCA — to push the record. We spent $1,000 a week on our own inde-pendent promo men.

Although we had balked at releasing *These Eyes* as the first single off *WHEATFIELD SOUL*, once Jack and RCA made that decision, we knew it was a good song and believed in it. There is a magical quality to that song still today when you hear it on the radio. It's timeless. So we were willing to spend our own money to give the single a chance.

These Eyes managed to gain a toehold in the northeastern US through Detroit, Toledo, Buffalo, and into New York. Regional programmers picked it up and the ripple effect started as it gradually rolled across the US. Other programmers would read *Billboard* and see *These Eyes* listed as a regional breakout hit in the northeast and a week later in the south. It wasn't an instant hit. *These Eyes* took three months to climb locally, regionally, and finally on the national charts. By the time it hit LA the record was everywhere. We took the risk and it worked. But CHUM and other influential Canadian markets didn't pick up on the record until the momentum had already gathered steam in the US. Then they jumped on the bandwagon. That lack of initial support frustrated us.

As we watched *These Eyes* climbing the *Billboard* charts we were hit with three distinct feelings. First was disbelief. Then déjà vu because we had seen this happen before with *Shakin' All Over*. And finally a determined resolve to not let it slip away like we had done with *Shakin'*. We were wracked with a mix of fear and trepidation. "What do we do next? How do we build on the success of *These Eyes*?" We did not want to be a one-hit wonder again like what had happened with *Shakin'*. Here we were with a song that we hadn't wanted to become the hit, but now it was so how do we capitalize on that? "I remember to this day where we were when *These Eyes* first broke," smiles road manager Jim Martin, "the first time it charted. We were sitting on our bus waiting for the ferry in Vancouver to go to Nanaimo, British Columbia. Randy said, 'I'm going to call the office and see what's going on.' Our manager, Don Hunter, was back in Winnipeg so Randy got off the bus and went into the terminal to find a payphone. I kept looking in my rearview mirror just checking the cars behind us when all of a sudden I saw Randy running toward the bus like he was in a hundred-yard dash. I was thinking to myself, 'No one's getting on the ferry yet. What's his problem?' As he ran up to the bus I opened the door and he leapt up the steps like a kid who just found buried treasure. He shouted to everyone, 'I don't believe it! Detroit/Windsor just broke *These Eyes*!' Despite everything the band achieved afterwards, that has to rank as one of the greatest moments of my life. Randy was three feet off the ground. It was such a thrill for them."

Jim Martin also recalls first hearing *These Eyes* on an American station. "I was driving through the States coming through Chicago. We used to drive from Winnipeg to Toronto and back through the States because the roads were easier. It was about two o'clock in the morning when I heard it on WLS, a big Midwest station. I had to pull the vehicle over to the side of the road and wipe away the tears."

Released in January 1969, by April, *These Eyes* had peaked at #6 on the *Billboard* charts earning the group its first gold record (*WHEATFIELD SOUL* made #45 on the album charts). Recalls Garry Peterson, "The odds of making it from Winnipeg, let alone Canada, were incredible. Who could ever have thought that would happen? Especially still living there. Neil Young had to leave. We made it purely on our music, writing, and performance. We never had any money behind us, no hype. It was all about the music." Jim Kale recounts ruefully, "We took ten years to become an overnight sensation. How many bands release eighteen records before making it?"

Suddenly the old Greyhound bus was insufficient for the tour demands placed on the group. The Guess Who hit the ground running, playing everywhere across the US throughout 1969. No longer enduring long, cold highway odysseys, instead the group was flying first class, meeting the equipment at the gig. "Everything changed," notes

Jim Martin. "I remember not long after that coming into a hotel in Detroit and the RCA promotion man coming up to us and saying, 'Hey, what do you want? Cigarettes, booze, girls? Just tell me.' Everything was being handed to us on a platter. At first we all were excited about it; Randy, too. There weren't any problems right away. Sure, Randy was a Mormon and the other guys were living it up. The edginess was there but it wasn't a major obstacle yet. Here they were, a bunch of ordinary guys from Winnipeg, and they were making it, so the attitude was 'Let's enjoy it.' Randy was still 'Johnny Businessman' and maybe there was stuff going down that intimidated some people, but initially they didn't want to lose the fact that they had a hit record. Everybody wanted to enjoy it. But as they had more hits then things got crazy."

Garry had a problem flying whenever his ears were plugged from a cold. If you've ever flown with your ears not clear, the air pressure is like a knife going through the side of your head. We would be flying first class, businessmen around us reading newspapers, and suddenly here's Garry writhing in pain, screaming, clutching his head and holding his ears as if someone had stuck him with pins like a voodoo doll. Stewardesses would bring him hot tea bags in cups to put over his ears, scalding him. There were times when Garry couldn't fly, so while we flew to the next gig, he drove, sometimes a thousand miles and he would arrive just minutes before the gig. Burton had to play drums on one occasion because Garry just couldn't fly. We played as a three-piece. Burton sang and played the drums, came out front to the piano for *These Eyes*, and then went back to the drums. Garry had such a head cold the pressure would have been too much to bear.

After that incident, Garry came to us and said he wanted a helmet made and he wanted the band to pay for it. The thing cost several grand. It was a space helmet that looked like a fish bowl over his head that allowed him to adjust the pressure as we ascended and descended. We thought he was nuts. There was no way we were going to get on a plane first class with *My Favourite Martian* wearing a bowl on his head. So he ended up driving whenever he couldn't fly. The poor guy did a lot of driving, leaving immediately after one show, driving all night to arrive just in time for the next gig exhausted. On a couple of occasions, his brother Randy Peterson actually filled in for him.

No longer playing community clubs and rural dances, the Guess Who catapulted to theatres, concert halls, and arenas. The group signed with the prestigious Willard Alexander Agency in New York (a move that later proved a mistake that the group was forced to buy their way out of). On July 25 the Guess Who appeared at the Seattle Pop Festival before 150,000 people alongside the elite of the pop world. "The Seattle Pop Festival was a better festival than Woodstock," maintains Burton, "but the problem was that no one filmed it. I was pretty nervous because anybody that was anybody in pop music was there. With Jimmy Page and Robert Plant backstage, Jim Morrison wandering around, and Gary Brooker from Procol Harum standing at the side of the stage watching me, I was quite nervous. It was the first time that I could look out and not see the end of the audience. There were so many people there. It was just a sea of heads."

We were one of the only acts booked for all three days at the Seattle Pop Festival so we were at the site each day wandering around backstage and catching all the acts. I saw the Byrds with Clarence White playing his string bender, the Flying Burrito Brothers with Gram Parsons. They were both doing glorious country rock and later on I jammed with them in a backstage tent. The Doors were there, Ten Years After, Led Zeppelin, It's a Beautiful Day, Chicago, Alice Cooper, Procol Harum, Ike and Tina Turner, a very eclectic bill with a real mix of artists. We were doing our psychedelic thing with *Friends of Mine*.

I remember another time we travelled to Cleveland to appear

on the *Upbeat* show, a local rock showcase where acts mimed to their latest hits. Van Morrison was appearing on the same show. *Brown Eyed Girl* had been a huge hit and here was "Van the Man" joining us on this fairly lame show. Cummings and I were over the moon because we loved Van Morrison from the days of Them and *Baby Please Don't Go, Gloria* and *Here Comes the Night.* We had done all those songs in our sets. We approached his dressing room with star-struck anticipation only to find him almost in tears. En route to Cleveland, his guitar and luggage had been lost. Because of our featured slot on *Let's Go*, we had an endorsement deal with Yamaha in Winnipeg to use their gear — guitars, bass, drums, and organ. So I offered Van one of my Yamaha guitars, this weird-shaped solid body. He was thrilled. He used it for the taping then promptly brought it back to me. "No, you can keep it." He was visibly touched by my generosity. He'd probably never heard of us before but was impressed by the kindness of this Canadian band.

On May 24, the Guess Who made their debut on Dick Clark's *American Bandstand*, the icon of pop music television shows they had each grown up watching every Saturday morning. Returning on August 16, the four were presented with their first gold record by Dick Clark for a million sales of *These Eyes*. Later that same year, popular soul act Junior Walker and the All Stars covered *These Eyes* and took their saxophone-dominated version up the R 'n' B charts. Selling over half a million copies, it earned its writers a tidy sum.

I loved Junior Walker's version of *These Eyes*. It actually saved our lives, Burton and I, in Chicago once. After a gig I went to collect the money and as usual I had a bagful of small bills, three or four thousand dollars in ones, fives, and tens. I always figured it was safer carrying it in a grocery bag because it was less conspicuous than an attaché case that was like carrying a neon sign saying "Money." At about three in the morning I received a phone call in my hotel room that Burton needed to be picked up. I can't recall what he had done but he had been detained at a police station. I picked him up in the station wagon we used. The bag of money had been stuffed under the seat until I could get to a bank the next morning.

I soon realized I was lost. It was a hot summer night and people were out in the streets drinking and partying, doors open, music blaring out into the streets. I drove around for a while and realized we were the only white people in the area. Being innocent Canadians, Burton and I entered a juke joint to ask directions back to the hotel. There was a party in progress as we entered and we sought out the bartender. Before we could locate him, several large black gentlemen accosted us.

"What are you doing here, Whitey?"

Sensing trouble we tried to pull back but were immediately encircled. Suddenly Junior Walker's version of *These Eyes* came on the jukebox.

"What are you guys doing in here?!"

"We're lost," I managed to stammer. "We're the Guess Who. We wrote that song."

"No you didn't. Man, that's a black group."

"No, really, we wrote it."

One guy went over to the jukebox and looked at the record label.

"What's your name?"

"Randy Bachman."

"What's your name?"

"Burton Cummings."

He looked at the label again.

"You wrote that song for a black group?"

"Yes."

"Okay, well you go out here, turn right, go down Cicero and that'll get you back downtown."

Armed with our directions, and our hides, we left.

With *These Eyes* beginning to fall off the charts, RCA clamoured for a swift follow-up. Knowing full well that momentum can be lost all too easily, the group obliged. Rejecting other tracks off *WHEATFIELD SOUL*, including Randy's *A Wednesday in Your Garden* tipped in many circles as a logical successor to *These Eyes*, Don Burkhimer instead pressured the band for a new single, another soft pop song. "He took us out to a New York deli and begged us to give him one more and we'd never have to work again," recalls Burton. "We were sitting on our bus waiting for the ferry to Vancouver Island in early 1969. Randy started playing the opening chord and *Laughing* was finished in about fifteen minutes."

Much to our chagrin, RCA had asked us for another one like *These Eyes* as a follow-up after it went gold. We wanted to rock. We wanted an *American Woman* when they were pressuring us for another *These Eyes*. But we were stumped to come up with a follow-up in a similar soft rock vein. I was enthralled with the opening strumming minor chord on the Bee Gees' *New York Mining Disaster* so I took that triad, turned it into a major chord triad, and placed that before a Dave Clark Five chord pattern from *Because*, which was a well-worn pattern in dozens of songs dating back to Irving Berlin. We then took the background vocals from the Platters' *Twilight Time*, the ascending "ah's," and put them in behind the lyrics. We did all this on the spot. That was enough to get us started; the rest was original, the idea of laughing at someone who broke your heart.

Laughing illustrated Randy's "erector-set" approach to songwriting, drawing from his own influences and current pop trends by taking the best nuances and constructing something that is at once both familiar and original, a formula he would put to good use throughout his career: "What makes that song a hit? Figure it out and adapt it."

Always attuned to AM radio, Randy could analyze every song he heard for the key factor that made it a success. His skill at arranging allowed him to deconstruct a song and rebuild it the way he wanted it.

The flip side of *Laughing* would become Randy's crowning song-writing achievement and go a long way toward the integration of jazz and rock.

Despite the fact that *Laughing* was calculated to be in a similar mold to *These Eyes* in terms of style, the flip side was totally alter-native. There was nothing like *Undun* on Top 40 radio. It was so left field as a single. It had no chorus to sing to or guitar riff to stick in your head. It just was so different from anything else at that time. Certainly, songs like it existed on albums but not on AM radio so when radio did embrace *Undun* it was quite a feat.

Undun was based around chords I had learned from the Mickey Baker Guitar Chord Book that Lenny Breau had urged me to pick up years earlier. He had learned chording from it. It was like the first tablature book that showed you pictures of where to put your fingers to form all these incredible jazz chords. The book illustrated the standard jazz voicings, the chords to put in the mid-dle of a jazz song, the turnarounds they called them or the stan-dard endings with ten different chord patterns. It was the primer for every jazz guitar player. I took some of these turnarounds as the basis for *Undun*. I played the chords to Burton who thought it was a great progression but he couldn't come up with a melody or words because the chords changed so fast that trying to place a melody over them was difficult.

On one of our trips to Vancouver in 1969, I woke up one morn-ing in our downtown hotel on English Bay. Everyone else had gone out. I stayed back to write letters home and I turned on FM radio. I heard a Bob Dylan song, *Ballad in Plain D*, and one line, "She came undone." That was the spark I needed to write the lyrics as if I was telling a story of a young girl losing control of herself. Previous to this, we had met a girl in Vancouver who, after a particularly bad acid trip at a party, fell into a coma and didn't come out. We had all been at that party and knew her — her name was Marcy. Her tragic situation became my inspiration and the Dylan line provided the catalyst. It was a true story that also held a lot of meaning for the time. I reached over, turned the radio off, and started to write the words out. They didn't even rhyme. I played it for Burton later and he responded, "That's incredible. I can't add anything to it. You've written a gem of a song all by yourself."

Once *Laughing* stopped selling at 750,000 copies we thought we were finished. We were destined to become one-hit wonders all over again until a deejay flipped *Laughing* over and before we knew it *Undun* was a hit pushing the record over the million mark.

Because we had been around almost ten years by the time *These Eyes* and *WHEATFIELD SOUL* became hits, we were much better prepared for a follow-up album. If you look at *CANNED WHEAT*, some of those songs had already been in our sets dating back to the *Let's Go* show. We had a reserve to draw on and even re-recorded *Of a Dropping Pin* and later *When Friends Fall Out* because we believed they were good songs that hadn't been heard by more than a handful of people outside Canada.

Laughing and *Undun* had emerged from sessions for the group's sophomore RCA album, *CANNED WHEAT*. Recorded in May 1969, the album was plagued by recording problems and technical disputes. "Oh god, were there sound problems," sighs Jack. "I actually broke down and cried over that one. When we made the deal with RCA, one of the things we had to live with, and believe me it was very difficult, was the fact that any artist signed to the label had to use their recording facilities and their staff. So when it came time to record *CANNED WHEAT* we did it in their studio on 24th Street in New York, which was a real archeological discovery. Beforehand, I sat in on a session with the engineer who had been assigned to us and asked a few questions about the design of the control room and overall feel of the place. I then went before RCA's entire technical division and told them what I felt was wrong with their studio. Now I don't claim to be a technical wizard, but my opening line to them was 'Okay guys, what was the last hit you had come out of this studio?' I was met with dead silence.

"We ended up doing the session dates there and I had serious problems with the way the tracks were recorded. The sound was horrible. We finished recording and went to mix it and the damn thing wouldn't come together at all. I tried to mix it twice and it was dreadful. I did not want the band to go down the tubes with this. RCA brought someone else in, he worked on it and pronounced, 'I think we've got it. There's a little bit of distortion on it.' I said 'A little bit? Holy shit.' So I flew down from Toronto that night, listened to what they had and it was just garbage. It was Memorial weekend in the States and the band was playing the Felt Forum in New York. I happened to be walking down the street and ran into Jumbo Martin. I said to him 'Jumbo, get the band together and have them over at A&R studios tonight at midnight. We're going to re-record *Laughing* and *Undun*.' I went up in the morning to the office of the head of RCA. I hadn't shaved or changed my clothes since flying down from Toronto, and I told him, 'The facilities are terrible, the engineer is terrible, I've got a session booked at A&R tonight and we're going to re-record those two songs.'

'You can't do that.'

'Just try and stop me.'"

The sound of much of the *CANNED WHEAT* album was terrible and we felt we could do a much better job re-recording it. The sound on *WHEATFIELD SOUL* was wonderful because we cut it at A&R Studios with some of the guys who are the top engineers in the business now but back then were just getting started: Phil Ramone, Elliot Scheiner, David Greene, Shelly Yakus. But that album was recorded independently with Jack Richardson's money.

When we signed with RCA we had to use their recording facilities in New York that had these giant rooms with high ceilings for orchestras. But for rock drums the sound was dead. Garry would hit his drum and you'd hear a tiny click rather than a solid thump. No matter how much we tried we couldn't get a sound we liked. We had ten days to do the album and spent the first two frustratingly trying to find a comfortable sound. We were used to working in the CBC studio or at Kay Bank and being able to do an entire album in two days. Here we were two days later gnashing our teeth with nothing to show for the time spent. We wanted to go back to A&R Studios with Phil Ramone to do the album. We wanted the sound we achieved on *These Eyes*.

At our behest, Jack approached RCA with a request that we be allowed to record the album at A&R rather than their own facilities. But the contract stipulated that when you signed with a label back then you had to use their studios. In response to our demand, the RCA engineers walked out. NABET, the association of broadcast engineers, pulled their RCA members in what was known around the label as "the Guess Who strike." The work stoppage lasted a couple of days until we acquiesced and agreed to use their facilities. We returned to RCA studios, set up, puttered around for hours, yawned, then at midnight after the sessions had ended, we packed up all our equipment and surreptitiously headed out to A&R studios and recorded a couple of tracks all night. The next day we returned in the afternoon to RCA and carried on the façade of cutting the album there. We did this again the next night where we did overdubs and completed the tracks for *Undun* and *Laughing* at A&R. We paid for this ourselves, Nimbus and the band. Just listen to CANNED WHEAT and you can hear the difference in sound between those two cuts and the remainder of the album. The other tracks have a dry sound to them because we cut them at RCA. No matter what we did, we couldn't get any life out of them.

When RCA learned of our clandestine recording and heard the obvious difference in the two tracks, there was nothing they could do about it because it was too late; the album was completed. Jack had to remix all the tracks to its maximum and actually remix *Laughing* and *Undun* just to bring them down a bit so that there wasn't that tremendous difference between them and the other tracks. But you can still hear it. That's why those two songs are so good.

On the home front, Randy and Lorayne's life had undergone considerable changes in the intervening year. They were still renting their tiny bungalow on Luxton when Talmage Charles Robert Bachman was born on August 13, 1968. By mid-1969, with a toddler on the loose, Lorayne expecting another child, and Randy's income increasing tenfold, the couple felt it was time to purchase a house more in tune with his profile as a pop star writing million-selling records. Randy also wanted Lorayne to feel comfortable and secure during his increasing absences out on the road or recording.

In West Kildonan the street that denoted well-heeled status was Scotia Street bordering the Red River as it winds its way northward to Lake Winnipeg. Scotia ran from the North End up to expansive Kildonan Park, a circuitous, tree-lined route of spacious, elegant old homes. Randy and Lorayne purchased a two-storey, wood-sided, three-bedroom Cape Cod–style house at 199 Scotia at Matheson, with evergreen trees in front and a detached garage in back. The house was located at a bend in the street that jutted out to accommodate the meandering river. The finished basement was turned into Randy's own demo studio. Though hardly ostentatious, the modest house was nonetheless visible evidence to everyone in West Kildonan that Randy Bachman was now successful.

Seldom off the road for lengthy spells, Randy sought solace in the precious days at home with his family — Lorayne and baby Tally, as well as his parents and relatives. Away from the rigours of band life, the four band members rarely socialized together. Each had his own circle of acquaintances. For Burton it meant hanging out with high school and neighbourhood friends or the company of other musicians like Kurt Winter and his group Brother, Greg Leskiw and Gord Osland's band Wild Rice, or singer Diane Hetherington. Randy sometimes socialized with Garry and Nadia or Jim Martin and his wife Lorraine. "My wife and Lorayne became close," states Jim, "almost inseparable. She was closer to Lorayne than any of the other wives and they spent a lot of time together. She didn't try to change our religion or anything. Randy pushed it more than she did. I don't ever recall her trying to convert us. Randy, on the other hand, became more Mormon than she was." Never one to remain far from music, free time for Randy meant writing, demoing new song ideas in his basement, or production chores for Sabalora.

But a finely appointed house and growing family could not obscure the fact that Randy was spending less and less time at home. It would be a familiar refrain played out throughout his career. It wasn't easy for Lorayne but when they married she knew full well the lifestyle of a musician.

We had always lived the dream, now we were living the rewards: the money, gold records, adulation, and acclaim. But when you are in the middle of it all, getting up each day in a different city and travelling all the time, you don't see the bigger picture. You don't realize the success. Back home all your friends are aware
of your success because they are hearing about it on the radio or reading about it in the newspapers and pop magazines. They're seeing you do it, while you're so busy doing it you don't even realize you are doing it. At least until you come home for a few days then you discover everyone is treating you differently, yet you aren't any different as a person or friend. That was strange.

Suddenly we had more money in our bank account, which

allowed us to do some of the things we couldn't before when the band was making $400 a night. For Lorayne and I it meant we stopped looking at price tags. We could just walk into a store, see something we wanted and put it on the counter without bothering to check the price. Or we could buy three of something, each in a different colour. After years of scrimping and saving, living a fairly meagre existence, we became a bit more self-indulgent. It was like putting in ten years at a job and finally, in the last two years, earning your ten years of pay.

Our big indulgence was the purchase of the house on Scotia Street. Being a kid from Seven Oaks and Powers, Scotia was our Wellington Crescent, the toney end of West Kildonan. The houses were spacious and elegant, running like a ribbon along the Red River. Not concerned that the river overflowed every spring and dumped sewage in the backyard, we felt it was prestigious to be along the river. My parents were just down Hartford; my grandparents still lived in the vicinity; my Grandma Bachman lived a few houses away on Inkster; I was near the North End Sal's and all my friends. I hadn't strayed far from my roots. Burton was living nearby. We were so close we could have shot an arrow between houses.

Our house on Scotia developed quite a history. When I moved out in 1972, I sold it to Jumbo Martin. When he left Winnipeg in 1976, he sold it to his brother-in-law so we kept it within our circle of friends.

Up to that point I had been driving an old '56 Pontiac I had purchased from Jumbo. We called it the Bee because it was yellow and black. It had a transmission that kept slipping. You would get it going doing twelve miles an hour and there would be nothing happening, then you would hear this noise and feel the thrust as the car suddenly slipped into another gear. You would find yourself instantly doing thirty or forty miles an hour. It was like in *Star Trek* when they suddenly go into warp drive. The Bee also had a faulty alternator that caused it to stall frequently. In winter I could never get it started. The best investment I ever made was joining the Manitoba Motor League because I wore out my membership getting the Bee jump-started every winter.

The house on Scotia had watermarks four or five feet up the walls from the notorious 1950 Winnipeg flood that submerged much of West Kildonan. As a result, the detached garage was all rotted wood from being so waterlogged. But I still kept my old Pontiac in it. Typically, one winter morning it wouldn't start so I called the Motor League to come out and jump it. Anyone who has ever lived in Winnipeg knows the ritual. But I had to get the car out of the garage first so I put it in neutral and lay across the hood using my legs to push on the walls of the garage to move the vehicle out. As I began pushing, the wall collapsed into the snow with just the 2x4 studs left standing. Lorayne came out and said, "You can't go on with this car." So I called BMI and got an advance on my publishing income to purchase a 1968 Buick Elektra. I didn't go nuts buying all sorts of frivolous things. My indulgences were rather more practical.

One of the most memorable moments during that period, when things were really starting to happen for the band, was coming home in the summer of 1969 and playing Rainbow Stage, the outdoor theatre in Kildonan Park just down the street from my house. We knew at that point that we stood poised to scale a measure of success that no one in Winnipeg or possibly even in Canada had ever achieved. We were now being accepted on the level of an American band like The Doors everywhere we went whether in the US or Canada. So to come home and play in the park where I had run around as a kid and where my son now played — before the hometown crowd, all the people who had grown with us and supported us, our families, friends, and contemporaries — was a very unforgettable moment for the four of us. It was a gorgeous night under the stars and we played an inspired set.

Money and adulation can do peculiar things to people, especially those who are young, impressionable, and searching for some meaning to their lives. Suddenly everything you dreamt of is now before you. Cautious with his money, his material needs modest, Burton and several acquaintances from the local music scene — singer Gary Maclean, Gord Osland and CFRW deejay Jim Millican, who later became the Guess Who's publicist — lived together. Burton purchased an old prewar wood house at 97 Lansdowne Avenue in his beloved North End just south of Main Street, a block over from Inkster and a stone's throw from Burton's favourite hangout, Sportsman's Billiards. With Burton away so often, the others house-sat and looked after his possessions, not the least of which was his enormous record collection and portrait of his idol, The Doors' Jim Morrison. Burton nurtured a fixation on Morrison for several years and prior to moving out on his own had turned his bedroom at his mother's house into a virtual shrine to the Lizard King.

Although Burton remained thrifty with his material accoutrements, it was still the sixties and drugs were de rigeur in the rock music world. There was an inherent assumption among the rock cognoscenti at the time that drugs enhanced one's creativity and expanded one's horizons.

Winnipeg wasn't much of a drug city then but we would go to Vancouver or San Francisco on tours and you would shake someone's hand and when you took your hand back there would be a joint in your palm or some purple capsules or a chunk of hash. "What's this? This guy put a piece of rabbit droppings in my hand."

There was the prevailing belief at that time that you had to take drugs to be creative. That was the sentiment put forth by the subculture of the San Francisco bands like the Grateful Dead and Jefferson Airplane, and the British bands picked up on that. It was nothing new, jazz musicians had that same notion in the forties and fifties, only in the sixties it was LSD.

It became frustrating dealing with Burton and Jim on the road partying all night. When it was time to leave a city after a gig, Garry and I would always be ready to go. Garry was the most prompt, but Kale and Cummings were usually late. We would hang around for a while then phone their rooms again only to discover we had woken them up again. They had fallen asleep between the two wake-up calls. So we would have to wait for them to shower and pack up. It was terribly frustrating and inconsiderate because they often kept Garry and me waiting.

I no longer partied all night, and I went to church on Sundays. I know the guys in the band found this distancing us. They weren't gung ho about it because by the time I left they were glad to see me go. What I kept saying to them was, "What I have chosen to do, the lifestyle I have chosen to live, is not harmful to you as a person or to the group. It can only be good. I don't cheat, I don't lie, I don't smoke, I don't drink, I don't drink coffee or tea, I don't do drugs. I write songs and play guitar and will always do that to my fullest capacity, one hundred percent heart and soul." What else can you ask of a musician? But in choosing that lifestyle, I wasn't their party companion anymore. After the gig it was no longer "Let's split a case of beer." Instead it was "You guys go ahead, I'll have a 7-Up."

With my obsessive nature, if I had done drugs I would have probably become an addict or if I had continued drinking I would have been an alcoholic. I don't smoke, I stopped drinking, and have never done any drugs. You don't need it to be creative and those like Jim Morrison or Janis Joplin who thought they did might have been more creative without it, or might still be alive today.

"All of a sudden," recalls Jim Martin, "there was no more drinking or smoking around Randy. He became so adamant about it that it did cause problems. He never bothered me with it. I still really liked Randy, so our relationship didn't change. But I felt the relationships within the

band changing. Randy increasingly became more on the outside looking in rather than a part of the four. It was just because he wasn't
appreciated. It became 'Ha, ha, we can do this.' At first the guys would
have a drink or have a toke of grass but they would go off and hide to
do it. But later on they stopped hiding it. They didn't care about what
he thought."

In an interview in *Hit Parader* magazine conducted in mid-1969,
Burton downplayed the growing rift within the group. "The members
of the Guess Who never have been and never will be in love with one
another. We get along alright, though. We do things together on the
road but we have our own personal lives. Everyone digs different
things. The point is that even if you hate each other's guts, you have to
forget it, keep the thing going. It's like a business, the relationship
between employer and employee. We all respect Randy's outlook. He
married a Mormon girl and he's very much into religion and that
whole trip."

Despite the polarization developing within the group, Randy
retained his role as undisputed leader. "These guys should remember,"
emphasizes Jim Martin, "that when things changed, when Bob Burns
was fired and Don Hunter came in as manager, Randy was still there
running things, controlling the band. Randy kept everything together.
He made it all click. With Randy, the band dug its way out of the hole
they were in after the England trip. When it came to business, if Randy
said it was red it was red. Don Hunter wouldn't argue because he was
scared of Randy. Randy knew what was going on and knew the books
too well. Hunter approved things through Randy."

After three soft rock hits in a row, the Guess Who were eager to
break free of that tag and show the world they were no bubblegum
band. Sessions in November of 1969 for their third RCA album were
conducted in that frame of mind. Adding to that heavier sound was
Randy's instrument of choice for the sessions, a vintage 1959 Gibson
Les Paul Standard guitar with a denser sound that became known as
the Guess Who sound.

We had played a lot around Vancouver and the West Coast in the late sixties and that's where I acquired my Gibson Les Paul. I had broken my Rickenbacker and was using a blue sparkle Mosrite, which was a funny-shaped guitar that the Ventures used. It looked cool but the neck was like a bow and arrow. I had it along when we played a church basement gig in Nanaimo. We were onstage playing our set when from the back of the hall came a young man with a little brown case. I knew what was in that case, every guitar player back then knew what a Les Paul case looked like. The Les Paul guitar was the sound of Eric Clapton on *BLUESBREAKERS* and Cream, Jimmy Page in Led Zeppelin, the heavy blues-rock sound. I was playing the Mosrite at the time and the kid opened the case and I could see it was an original '59 Les Paul with a factory-installed Bigsby tailpiece. He gestured at the Mosrite and back to the Les Paul. I knew what he wanted. In mid-song I took off the Mosrite, he handed me the Les Paul, I tuned it up and played it the rest of the night. It had incredible sound. It was heavy to hold but it rocked. After the show, I handed it back to him saying thanks for letting me play his guitar.

"You mean you don't want to trade with me?"

"What?! You want to trade me your Les Paul for my Mosrite?"

"Yes. My uncle gave me this guitar but I saw you on TV playing that Mosrite and I wanted a guitar like yours. It's so cool with the blue sparkles."

"Just a minute. This isn't a fair trade. I've got $75 in my pocket. I'll trade you the Mosrite and $75, but I want someone to witness the deal and to sign a paper attesting that we both agreed to the trade."

"Okay."

The minister signed the paper, the kid went home happy and I got the guitar that would become the sound of *No Time* and *American Woman*. That guitar became associated with my sound, the sound of the Guess Who.

Many years later while I was playing in BTO, out of the blue I received a letter from a lawyer seeking redress claiming I had taken advantage of the kid who was now his client. I sent him a copy of the letter signed by the minister and never heard back from him.

RCA's Mid America Recording Center on Wacker Drive in Chicago had been built more recently than the label's New York facilities and could accommodate the Guess Who's requirements. In fact, Jack Richardson had done the final mixing for *CANNED WHEAT* at Mid America with engineer Brian Christian who became the Guess Who's exclusive engineer. To satisfy the needs of the group and Jack, RCA fitted the studio with the latest technology. The studio had much to do with the sense of renewal the group felt going into sessions that fall and the consistent sound they ultimately achieved. Not satisfied with the version recorded for *CANNED WHEAT*, the first track the Guess Who tackled at Mid America in November was a reworking of *No Time*. Released in December prior to the album, the Guess Who finally got their rocker when *No Time* peaked at #5 in January, 1970, earning the group another gold record. "*No Time* is probably my favourite Guess Who song," acknowledges Burton, "because it proved that we could rock 'n' roll and it gained us a whole new respect and credibility."

It was unheard of at the time to record a song twice but we believed *No Time* was a great song and deserved another shot. It was our Buffalo Springfield song. The riff was pinched from *Hung Upside Down*. It originally had a country rock style to it, especially in the bridge. It was very radio-friendly at the time.

We saw the pop singles scene coming to an end and people digging FM radio and longer tracks with wild jams and psychedelia. We had toured with the Jefferson Airplane and saw this coming in and we wanted more of this in our music. Each of us was a capable enough musician that we could get into some really good jams, some really intricate things. *WHEATFIELD SOUL* had been just a bunch of singles, a collection of weird different songs, as had *CANNED WHEAT*. But with the *AMERICAN WOMAN* album we wanted more of a theme, a sameness, a whole album. We finally achieved a cohesive sound with that album. There is a unity of sound and songwriting that gives that album a cohesiveness. It truly represents the Guess Who at their peak.

With the transition from *These Eyes* to *Laughing* to *Undun* we were gradually getting tougher. We had come from Hendrix, Cream, and the Who. We didn't want to be Gary Puckett and the Union Gap, we wanted to rock. That progression set it up for *No Time* and *No Time* set it up for *American Woman*. We couldn't wait to unleash those songs to prove that, despite our pop singles success, we were a rock band.

Prior to arriving in the studio, the group had just completed an exhausting round of US gigs before returning to Canada for selected dates. One was in Kitchener, Ontario, in August 1969.

We had been touring the States, in the Midwest around Chicago, on some multiband dates doing five or six songs a night with groups like the Buckinghams. We then had a gig in Kitchener, Ontario, at the Bingeman Park Roller Rink, the local arena. When we got there, we found it was a dance like in the old days where we'd play three sets of dance music. We were thrilled because we could play our Beatles, Doors, and Animal songs, the old jukebox sets.

We had been onstage for a while, I can't remember how long, when I broke a guitar string on my Les Paul. In those days I didn't have a spare guitar or a guitar tech to change it for me so I said, "We have to take a break," to allow me to change the string myself. The way we would sometimes signal each other that the break was over was one of us would go up onstage and begin playing the first song of the next set. We'd all recognize the number and end our various conversations and join the others onstage. I started to play this chord pattern "dum dum dadada dada dada dada dum dum dadada dada da dum" and Garry and Jim joined right in behind me on this riff. They were pretty tired of playing the same six or seven songs a night over and over again and wanted to stretch out more like the Airplane, Quicksilver, and Grateful Dead and jam a bit. I soloed over their rhythm and got back to the riff to keep it in my head and we just kept going, really digging it.

Meanwhile, Burton was outside the arena having a cigarette or talking to some guys when someone walked by and said, "Why aren't you in playing with the band?" He looked up and didn't recognize the song. So he ran up onstage and yelled to me, "What are we doing?!" I replied, "We're jamming in E. Play something". He grabbed his harmonica and played a solo then moved to flute and piano. I took another guitar solo. He came toward me onstage and I yelled, "Sing something!" and as he stepped toward the microphone, the first words he uttered were "American Woman, stay away from me." Right off the top of his head. He sang it maybe four times, I soloed again, he sang it again, and we ended the song. The place went crazy, everybody felt the chemistry of a song being created out of thin air from a jam. We didn't really know what it was yet; it wasn't a song that Burton and I had sat down and written with a form and structure. It was just a riff. We played it again at other gigs and it began to take some kind of shape. The song got better and better and took on its form as we played it.

Later, when we went into the studio, Burton strung together lines like "war machines and ghetto scenes," just rhyming words. I had part of the lead guitar line but didn't have the end. Burton had the final four-note riff for *New Mother Nature*, "da do do da" so I just used that. It wasn't a natural line that you would do on guitar because it wasn't to the next string but a drop down and over. When I tried that, everybody just perked up. But we couldn't get the song right in the studio because it had been just a jam and didn't have its own tempo yet. *Laughing*, for example, had started with a tempo. *These Eyes* had a tempo. This thing was all over the place, speeding up, slowing down, stopping and starting. I remember we had a whole frustrating day of working at it in the studio and it just wasn't happening.

Garry and I went in the next day and I just plugged my Stratocaster into a Fender amp with tremolo and a much cleaner sound. That seemed to get the groove going. Then Jim came on and Garry added some tabla and that became the basic band track. I overdubbed another guitar doing the lead using my Les Paul and Herzog, and Burton put the words on. So *American Woman* was born onstage but ultimately finished in the studio.

People say it's a real heavy song, a heavy metal guitar riff, but it's really not that heavy. Guitar players think I'm using a 200 watt Marshall stack and grinding out these heavy power chords but it's not so. It's a fairly light rhythm track. But there's a thickness to the lead guitar lick that gives it the heavy sound and Burton's vocals are like he's yelling in defiance as if he really means it. "American Woman, stay away from me." He really meant it.

Several months earlier, we had problems where US authorities tried to draft us. We had green cards by then and we were crossing the border at Pembina on the Manitoba–North Dakota border. On this one occasion, I remember the American customs official telling us to pull in half a mile beyond the border under the sign saying Selective Service. Before that was a gas station and US gas prices were lower than Canadian so we always filled up in the States. We drove in to fill up and started talking to the attendant. I said to him, "How far is the Selective Service station?"

He looked at me puzzled and replied, "Why do you want to go there?"

I told him we had been directed by the customs authorities to check in there.

He looked me in the eye and stated in no uncertain terms, "You don't want to go there. They took my son three weeks ago and I'll probably never see him again. I suggest you turn around and head east to Duluth and get back up to Canada. They've probably got your licence number and will be looking for you."

So we did that and didn't dare try to cross the same way again. Part of that might have been the sentiment for that song. *American Woman* wasn't the woman on the street, it was more the symbolism of the Statue of Liberty. It was easier to say than "Uncle Sam, stay away from me." But it wasn't planned; Burton just sang that line onstage. RCA used that imagery, though, in their promotion of the record, the Statue of Liberty with the face of an old woman superimposed over a New York alleyway with trash everywhere.

The timing was perfect — Vietnam War, student protests, anti-American sentiments — but we had nothing to do with that. It was just one of those things, fate or whatever. Somebody at RCA had the idea to put it out after *No Time*. It was a powerful song leaping off the album, so they put it out. There was no grand scheme behind it, no vision.

Unlike many of their contemporaries who would often take many months to complete an album, the Guess Who were an efficient recording unit. Years of studio experience and careful rehearsal helped to minimize the down time and cost. The *AMERICAN WOMAN* album cost less than $20,000 to make and sold over two million copies. Artists do not see any financial rewards until the label recoups its costs. With the Guess Who, the returns were almost immediate. Also, Randy and Burton generally came to the studio with songs clearly mapped out rendering the producer's job much easier.

"When we went into a studio they were not long-drawn-out dates," confirms Jack Richardson. "We were usually in and out in two weeks or not much more. Because we did a lot of pre-production, working

Grandma
Louise
Bachman

...arles and Anne Bachman - wedding, 1941

Randy with his Grandparents Dobrinsky -
Lena and Steve

...ndy at 6 months

One Wheel Drive - Randy at age 3
with a toy made by his father
and grandfather

Gary and Randy Bachman -
age 2 and 4

Randy and Gary
on Seven Oaks Avenue, 1948

Mischievous Randy with an unhappy Timmy

Left to right: Anne, Robbie, Timmy, Gary,
Randy on a family camping trip

Victory School, grade 4 – Randy second
row from top, first left

Gary in Shriners' Hospital with Randy outside
(he wasn't allowed in, so they conversed
through the window)

High School 1960

doing his
homework, 1959

Clockwise from left: Charles Bachman, Gary,
Randy, Timmy, Anne Bachman, Robbie, 1959

Randy and Claudia Stenton,
1965

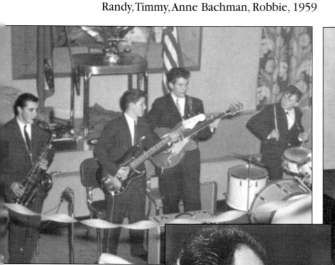

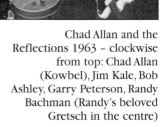

he Jurymen 1962 – left to
right: Joel Shapiro, Gary
Bachman, Randy, Don
Maloney (filling in for Garry
Peterson), playing a North
End legion teen dance. Gary
is playing Jim Kale's Fender
Bass with Kale's Fender
Concert amp that Neil Young
used to borrow

Chad Allan and the
Reflections 1963 – clockwise
from top: Chad Allan
(Kowbel), Jim Kale, Bob
Ashley, Garry Peterson, Randy
Bachman (Randy's beloved
Gretsch in the centre)

Lenny Breau –
Randy's early mentor

Recording artists - Chad Allan and the Expressions/Guess Who Clockwise from top left: Randy, Bob, Jim, Chad, Garry - trading his Gretsch for a Rickenbacker

Packing their station wagon for another road trip, 1964

Randy and Chad on tour in the US - fall 1965

The Guess Who on tour in the US, fall 1965 - left to right: Ashley, Bachman, Allan, Kale, Peterson

SHAKIN' ALL OVER

GUESS WHO?

The deejay single

Silver discs in Canada for Shakin' All Over with manager Bob Burns and CKRC deejay Doc Steen

17-year-old Burton Cummings joins the Guess Who, December, 1965

The Guess Who, fall 1966 - clockwise from left: Burton Cummings, Randy Bachman, Garry Peterson, Jim Kale

parting Winnipeg for London, England, Feb.
, 1967. Left to right: Garry, Randy, Jim, Burton

C's *Let's Go* – The Guess Who and
st Chad Allan – September, 1967

e Guess Who taping the
's Go show – fall 1967

ndy recording music
cks for *Let's Go* –
rly 1968

At Piccadilly Circus, London – Feb. 21, 1967 –
before the ill-fated meeting with King Records

Early winter 1969 following the release
of *Wheatfield Soul* and *These Eyes*

Randy draped in British flag,
Winnipeg arena, November, 1967

Randy in his fringed "Buffalo Springfield" look, 1969

Gold record for *These Eyes*, America[n] Bandstand - August 16, 196[9]

Performing *No Time* on the Wayn[e] & Schuster show, early 197[0]

Cover of *Cash Box* the week *American Woman* topped the charts, May 1970

Photo session for Randy's *AXE* album, spring 1970

Randy performing at the Fillmore East on his last night with the Guess Who - May 16, 1970

Randy holding
Talmage Bachman,
August 1968

The house at 199 Scotia

Randy and Tal,
winter 1970-71

oking glum at the after concert/after
ng Randy party at Sardi's, May 16, 1970
vith producer Jack Richardson and
A's Don Burkhimer

Between bands –
Randy and Tal in
his basement
tudio, 199 Scotia,
fall 1970

Randy and Tal
at the Mongrels
recording session,
Chicago, August,
1970

Randy with Tal, Lorayne with Kezia – fall 1970

Randy in the studio with the Mongrels, August, 1970

The first incarnation of Brave Belt, January 19'
- Randy, Chad Allan, Robbie Bachman

Brave Belt with Fred Turner
(next to Randy) - 1971

Randy with Brave Belt playing
The Garage, Vancouver - fall
1972 after relocating to
Vancouver

Bachman-Turner Overdrive, 1973 - Robbie,
Randy, Timmy Bachman, Fred Turner

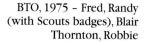

BTO, 1975 - Fred, Randy
(with Scouts badges), Blair
Thornton, Robbie

through the songs, the sessions were pretty smooth. The *American Woman* song was one of the exceptions where we built that in the studio. They came into the studio with the cassette of the live *American Woman* jam that some kid in the audience had taped which consisted of Randy walking up onstage and playing some guitar, everybody else wandering up and joining in, and Burton adding some scat. It was about ten-and-a-half minutes long. We started on it but I told them it needed some structure. They thought they could just go with it because the crowd loved it. But that was in front of ten thousand people, half of whom were stoned and the other half wanting to get there. So we had to pull it together into some form. I flew in some tablas, the Ravi Shankar thing was happening, and those are the thumps in the stops between chords near the end. We did some lyric changes and constructed the song in the studio. It was an example of one of those rare occasions when something comes together in the studio from merely an idea or concept."

There was no denying that *American Woman*, co-credited to all four members — Bachman, Cummings, Kale, and Peterson — was destined to be a hit. "I remember hearing *American Woman* in the studio in Chicago," recalls Don Burkhimer, "and I picked up the phone and called my boss in New York and told him we had a #1 record. That's how sure I was about that song. I knew it was a hit and RCA put a lot behind it." With considerable FM airplay already, RCA released the song as the follow up to *No Time* but not before the group pulled a ruse on Burkhimer. "We cut an out and out country thing called *Close Up the Honky Tonks* for laughs with Jimmy Kale singing," laughs Jack. "We had just finished the *AMERICAN WOMAN* album in Chicago and we phoned Don Burkhimer to come out and hear it. He flew in, walked into the studio, and we said, 'We've got a great single here for you, Don!' We played him this country number and when he heard it, Don's face began to fall. By the time it was over his face was down to about his knees. He looked at us bewildered and said 'Is that all you've got?' Then we played him *American Woman* and had a good laugh."

Perhaps no song on the *AMERICAN WOMAN* album illustrated the
unique qualities of Randy and Burton's songwriting partnership than *No
Sugar Tonight/New Mother Nature* presenting Randy's pop sensibilities
and ear for a catchy hook juxtaposed with Burton's increasingly oblique,
drug-referenced lyricism and bluesy chords. Together they are a remarkable feat of songwriting. Unfortunately, a unilateral decision by RCA
turned *No Sugar Tonight* into another bone of contention with Burton.

Although the Bachman–Cummings songwriting team was a collaboration, we also wrote on our own. If we couldn't add anything
to a song idea we would tell each other and leave it alone. That
happened with *Undun*, for example.

I had finished *No Sugar Tonight* and Burton had *New Mother
Nature*. Then we had the idea to put these two completed songs
together because when he sang "Lonely feeling" there was an
empty space there that suited "Jocko says yes and I believe him."

I remember when the idea to combine the two songs came to
us one afternoon at Burton's house. "Let's do my song then your
song and when we get to the end, let's do the two together." It
was the Beatles' *A Day in the Life*, like a suite or a collage of
ideas. We both flipped when we first did that.

Unfortunately, when *American Woman* was chosen as a single,
the label went looking for a B side. *No Sugar Tonight/New
Mother Nature* was too long so they edited it down to just *No
Sugar Tonight*. Suddenly I had the B side which was flipped over
and got a lot of airplay like a double A side.

Confirms Jack Richardson, "To be quite honest I thought *No Sugar
Tonight* was a better song. The progression is the same as *New Mother
Nature* but overall it is a better song. Lyrically it has a much clearer picture of what is going on in the song and it was more radio-friendly. The
record company has the final say. There was no question that of the
two songs, *No Sugar Tonight* was the one creating any kind of excite-

ment. It was never Randy's decision." After Randy's departure from the Guess Who, Burton would excise *No Sugar Tonight* from the group's set, performing New Mother Nature on its own.

Released in March 1970, *American Woman* tore up the charts everywhere including Europe and Asia and by the second week of May was firmly lodged at #1 on the *Billboard* charts where it remained for three weeks, ultimately selling over two million copies. The *AMERICAN WOMAN* album also went platinum. In the span of just over a year the Guess Who had notched up five Top Twenty singles, scored a coveted #1, sold close to eight million records, singles, and albums, and become the vanguard of what the media had dubbed "The Canadian Invasion" of the American pop charts.

Every Tuesday I would phone the record label to find out what position we would be on Thursday's *Billboard* charts. It all came by teletype to the labels late Tuesday. We were fighting the Beatles' *Let It Be* and songs like that on the charts. I spoke to Don Burkhimer in early May and he said to me, "Congratulations, you've just hit number one." I summoned the guys together and told them, "We've got a serious meeting." So we went back to a hotel room and I told them we had hit #1. We held hands like girls at a pajama party screaming and jumping up and down on a bed until it caved in then we went to the other bed and jumped on it until it caved in too. That was the sum total of our room wrecking in the Guess Who. Then we went out and played a gig.

"When *American Woman* reached #1 in *Billboard*, the stigma of Canada being inferior died forever," maintains Burton. "Someone had to do it and I'm proud it was us in the Guess Who." In his controversial 1971 book *Axes, Chops and Hot Licks*, a state-of-the-union address on the fledgling Canadian music industry, journalist Ritchie Yorke pointed out that "more Canadian records made the world charts in 1970 than in the previous ten-year period. A total of sixteen Canadian singles and six albums reached the *Billboard* US sales charts during 1970. In 1968, Canada didn't even rank among the first forty international record producers. In 1970, we were third!" The Guess Who as a group, and Bachman–Cummings in particular as songwriters, accounted for a whopping three-quarters of those Canadian records. In *Billboard*'s annual year-end survey of the one hundred most successful records of 1970, *American Woman* stood at #3, with *No Time* pulling in at #70. And all this without benefit of the CRTC's benevolent dictating of 30 percent Canadian content on Canadian airwaves. The Guess Who's hits succeeded solely on their own merits — quality music that could stand up to anything produced by the international recording industry.

"There really wasn't another group on a national level in Canada like the Guess Who," maintains music journalist Larry LeBlanc. "They were Canada's national band. If *American Woman* isn't the Canadian rock anthem then *Takin' Care of Business* or *You Ain't Seen Nothin' Yet* is. That's one of the reasons the *OH WHAT A FEELING* box set celebrating Canadian rock music, released in 1996, starts off with *American Woman* because that's where modern-day Canadian rock begins. It started with *American Woman*. Yes there was rock before that but the importance of the Guess Who was that they did it from Canada and their recordings still stand up today. Any Canadian rock recordings before then simply don't stand up today. I used to call them 'tiny perfect singles' and they were."

What Randy and Burton had succeeded in doing was to take an American music form, filter it through their own Canadian experience and keen understanding of the genre and all its antecedents, and play it back to Americans in such a way that it sounded American. Who knows Americans and Americana better than Canadians? "Living in Canada you are exposed to the whole of US communications, therefore you do, as a matter of course, write US-oriented songs," posits Burton. "It's a subconscious thing. You get to understand the US mentality and you program your stuff to it." As America's premier rock critic Lester Bangs noted, the Guess Who represented "a graph of the Canadian fascination with America" and in so doing manage to "catch the essence of American rock 'n' roll."

The Guess Who *was* the Canadian music industry in the sixties. We sold more records ourselves than the entire Canadian music business put together to that point. But we didn't really know or understand at the time what we were achieving. We just had a dream to make records, get them played on the radio, and sell them and be "famous. But what is that? We were famous in Winnipeg. Then we were famous in Canada. Then the world. There are different levels of fame and we didn't really see it much further than each level. It's the same music. You just take your dreams to different cities and different people join in the dream with you.

We were kind of fearless, naïvely, stupidly fearless. Whenever someone said it couldn't be done we said, "No, it can be done" and we would just go ahead and do it. No matter what it took, how long, or what we had to go through, we would just do it. We wouldn't take no for an answer.

I always had it in my mind that if a young truck driver from Memphis could do it, or four working-class guys from Liverpool could do it, so could four prairie dogs do it too. Then once we made it, other Canadians said, "If these guys from Winnipeg can make it, so can we." We became an inspiration to others just as I recall thinking that if a kid from the Lakehead named Bobby Curtola could get his records played on the radio, then why not me? Or if the Diamonds or Paul Anka can be successful, we can too. They were our inspirations before us. I'm grateful for everyone who took that chance and didn't take no for an answer because just as Curtola, the Diamonds, and Anka served as our role models, we opened the doors for Canadians like Bryan Adams and Rush.

Back in the sixties there was no road out of Canada unless you left for good. But with our own bare hands we knocked down the trees to make that road, the road everyone has travelled on ever since. Since the Guess Who, there has been a barrage of Canadians enjoying international success and it's not stopping. And the great thing about Canadian music is that it's all different. It's not a cloning thing like in Seattle a few years ago with grunge rock or Merseybeat in the sixties. Canadian music reflects the diversity of Canadians.

CHAPTER 5

Undun

A t the moment of the Guess Who's greatest triumph in early 1970, the group was wracked by internal dissension. Over the past two years, Randy had steered the band on a path toward success only to watch it spin out of control, due in part to differences in lifestyles and his increasing inability to contain the excesses of the other members. The choice of lifestyles had altered the dynamics between the four, creating an ever-widening rift. Acclaim, adulation, and wealth had opened a Pandora's box and the growing gulf between Randy on one side and Burton and Jim on the other (with Garry remaining neutral) threatened the uneasy détente that had held the group together over the past year. With the world at their feet, Burton and Jim saw less of a need to hide their indulgences and began flaunting their abuses in the open as if to say to their father/big brother-figure, "We don't care what you think." Frustrated, Randy found going out on the road with his two band mates increasingly uncomfortable and dreaded having to leave home. Driven by his own obsessions, he found comfort in the creative process — writing and recording. He began to envision a future for himself away from the grind of the road and the compromises it required of him, dealing with two other individuals who did not always want to see things his way. Those pressures would manifest themselves in serious health problems that would ultimately pull Randy off the road. As well, his desire to expand his business interests beyond the confines of the group itself would force a nasty confrontation.

When you go from being poor prairie kids to making millions of dollars and everybody everywhere is treating you like Elvis or Paul McCartney, weird things happen to you. Your values get distorted; you lose track of who you are. There were a lot of pressures on us from every angle of the business and they became astronomical.

From the middle of 1969 onwards was very stressful for me. The band was getting more and more into partying. We really didn't have any management or direction.

I used to go to parties after pop festivals or gigs to meet people who were making the music like Robert Plant, Sly Stone, Alvin Lee, or who were part of the business. It was a gathering of musicians. But when the drugs came out, I felt a darkness descend over the room and I would say "No thanks guys. I'm leaving," and go to my room. All these parties with Led Zeppelin and other people I admired and respected were going on and I would have to leave. It wasn't easy but it seemed to me to be the right thing to do. And it wasn't just the musicians bringing the drugs. Often it was the music industry people, the record reps, and the accountants who wanted to appear hip and ended up acting like idiots falling over their superstar clients. It was all over the industry.

"Randy tried to impose his mores on the rest of the band," confirms record producer Jack Richardson, "and with rock 'n' rollers that's the wrong approach to take. They were stars by then and enjoying everything that came with that. Randy was a much more reserved person, and the others certainly were not."

As younger brother Tim Bachman recalls, "By 1969–70, the contact we had with Randy was less because he had his own family and lived over on Scotia. He had his own life but I knew from conversations I had with him and other family members that he was unhappy. There was a level of dissatisfaction he felt in the group. But it was difficult to walk away from something he had worked so hard for. He had dedicated his life to the Guess Who and I'm sure in the back of his mind he was thinking 'This is a once in a lifetime opportunity. How can I walk away from it?' On the other hand, I also knew the other guys in the group well. But the change for Randy had been drastic. His life had changed 180 degrees. When I converted, I recall friends telling me, 'Yeah, sure. We'll give you six months.' I was way worse than Randy in terms of my bad habits. So I can imagine people thinking the same thing about Randy and banging on his hotel room door in the middle of the night saying, 'Come on Randy, we've got a couple of chicks and a bottle. We're on the road now, no one will know.' It gets very tiring putting up with that kind of thing and he got to the point where he just said to himself, 'I can't take this anymore. I don't need this.' At the same time, the other guys weren't happy with Randy and the choices he made either."

Even the indomitable Bachman–Cummings writing team, the most successful collaboration in Canadian music history, was showing signs of fatigue. Differences in personality had always served as fuel for the creative tension that sparked their partnership: Burton's yin to Randy's yang. That was now threatened by Burton's resentment toward Randy's patronizing role in the group and Burton's belief that he alone possessed the single most distinctive feature of the band. Burton Cummings was the voice of the Guess Who. With the burgeoning counterculture and album-oriented rock finding a forum on FM radio, Burton sought to appeal to that constituency rather than the pop charts. Pop singles weren't hip. Recording sessions that spring revealed little of the creative strength or cohesive sound that marked the AMERICAN WOMAN album. Unhappy on the road and unfulfilled in the studio, Randy began looking for an outlet. Whereas Burton needed a writing partner (and would rely on several collaborators after Randy's departure), Randy didn't. Two of the band's recent hits, *Undun* and *No Sugar Tonight*, were Randy's alone and his backlog of songs for Sabalora artists was overflowing.

"Even before Randy left the band he wanted to be involved in other aspects of the business," stresses Tim. "He wanted to write for others and produce records. He had evolved from playing barn dances to the community clubs and ultimately to becoming one-half of the Lennon and McCartney of Canada, which is how he and Burton were thought of. They created some of the classic songs of rock music. Having done that, he was looking to evolve to the next step which was as a producer. The road can get pretty tedious. I'm sure that if all he had to do was show up in a studio with Kale, Cummings, and Peterson twice a year and produce two albums he might still be in it. But when you are on the road it's like being married to three or four other guys and their lifestyles."

With the band having hit its stride on the *AMERICAN WOMAN* album, Randy seized the opportunity to step aside from the group for his own pet project, one he could control from start to finish. Given his eclectic tastes in guitar stylings and his wide range of influences from Chet Atkins, Lenny Breau, and the Shadows to his uncanny ability to mimic the current heavy blues-rock Clapton-Page guitar sound, a guitar instrumental album seemed a natural project. Certainly his name-recognition as one of the composers in the top group in North America would only serve to further the marketability of such a product. The timing seemed right. He had no intentions of striking out on his own separate from the group. This would simply be a side project just as Jorma Kaukonen and Jack Cassidy had done with Hot Tuna, their offshoot band from the Jefferson Airplane. What emerged was *AXE*, Randy's opportunity to showcase his versatility and virtuosity. But like so many other issues, *AXE* became another lightning rod for the animosity simmering within the group.

Don Burkhimer came to me with a suggestion. "Since you like Chet Atkins and Lenny Breau, would you do a guitar album?"

I jumped at the opportunity. Then, to compete with the James Taylor singer/songwriter thing that was becoming popular, he asked Burton and me if we would like to do an album of our songs performed acoustically: "Cummings and Bachman do Bachman and Cummings with guitar and piano just like you wrote them in Burton's house." And we agreed to do it.

As it happened, I had a weekend between gigs, Lorayne and the kids were visiting her parents, and never one to let an opportunity to make music pass by, I booked studio time to record my guitar album. That was March 16 to 18, 1970. Garry Peterson and I went to Mid America Studios in Chicago where we had recorded *American Woman*. I also called Domenic Troiano on short notice and he flew in from Los Angeles. We went in on Friday evening, set up, I wrote down a rough song list and arrangements on a sheet of paper, and Garry and I recorded the bed tracks alone. It was the first time I was producing myself, telling the engineer what to do, and working on the arrangements. It was marvellous. We did the basic songs and the next day I added bass and some of the guitar parts. On Sunday, Troiano and Wes Dakus arrived and overdubbed guitar and pedal steel. Troiano and I did some guitar interplay together. That night I mixed it and it was done, quick and easy.

All it was intended to be was a sideline from the Guess Who. I hadn't left the band. When I submitted the tapes to Don Burkhimer, he said to call him when Burton and I were ready to go in and record our acoustic duo album. But that never happened. In the interim, events transpired to torpedo that project.

AXE was never intended as a solo album. There's no singing on it, no rock or pop songs, just dumb little guitar things I used to fool around with in a dressing room or on a bus. I wasn't out to be Jeff Beck or Jimmy Page. There was no master plan, just a lot of fun especially being in charge in the studio applying all the skills

I had picked up watching Jack Richardson. It was a really big step for me. Unfortunately, when I left the Guess Who, RCA released *AXE* as my big solo debut which it wasn't, to say the least. There was the Guess Who with *Hand Me Down World* and the *SHARE THE LAND* album and me, the guy who left, with my quirky little instrumentals. The impression in the media was that I had left the band to go solo and here was my debut solo album. And it wasn't that way at all.

The album didn't sell but has become something of a cult album that a few people dug. Over the years I've had people come up to me in the strangest of places and tell me how much they liked *AXE*. Roy Buchanan, a guitar legend, once told me *AXE* was one of his favourite albums because it's not fifty thousand notes a minute. It's laid back and relaxed. Steve Vai told me he liked it, too.

There are some personal indulgences on that album, like naming a song for Tally. *Zarahemla* was a name from the Book of Mormon; *Not to Return* had been written for the Sugar And Spice back in Winnipeg. Not long ago Tally came to me — he had been listening to the album again — and asked me to play *Suite Theam*. So I did and he asked, "Can I write lyrics to that?" He wanted to use the music in a light jazz Harry Connick/Lambert, Hendricks, and Ross-style with lyrics. I was knocked out.

Already somewhat of a guitar legend in Canada for his work in Toronto's "white soul" group The Mandala, guitarist Domenic Troiano was living in Los Angeles when Randy solicited his playing to grace the *AXE* sessions. "Randy and I had met a few times," recalls Domenic, "and when the Guess Who were out in LA one time, we were putting Bush together at that point, late 1969 I believe, we had rented a house out in Thousand Oaks, and Garry and Randy had come over to see us there. But when he called me to play on his album it was quite out of the blue so I was a little surprised.

"I felt very honoured that he called me because I thought Randy was a really good guitar player. I remember it being a lot of fun, pretty loose, and no big deal. It was Garry, Randy, and I when I was there. I remember we did some playing live together in the studio. The way he had the credits on the album cover reads Randy on the left side speaker and me on the right, which I thought was pretty unique at the time. I'd never seen that done. Randy grew up listening to a lot of different kinds of music, like I did. Growing up back then you didn't think in terms of genres. If you were a guitar player in the sixties you listened to everything. Chet Atkins? Great. Chuck Berry? Wonderful. Get turned on to B.B. King? Terrific. There was much more diversity in the sixties than later when things got pigeonholed. Guitar players learned a lot simply by listening. 'Wow, what's that? I want to play that.' You didn't think 'I can't touch that because I'm a rock player.'"

Domenic saw nothing wrong with Randy indulging his penchant for guitar instrumentals outside the Guess Who. "The impression I got was that he wanted an outlet for other facets of what he wanted to do. There are always tensions in every band, it's like a family, and at that point the Guess Who was going through their tensions and Randy was looking for an outlet. I didn't get any sense that he was looking beyond the band though. He still loved being in the Guess Who."

"Let's face it," responds Jack Richardson, "whether Burton liked it or not, Randy had more contact with the brass at RCA as leader of the group. He was perceived as the prominent figure in the Guess Who. He was more business-oriented than the others and that became an issue as to how he handled that. So it only seemed natural for him to be able to negotiate a contract to do his own album, a natural evolution. There was nothing subversive about it. As far as Burton recording his own album, I'm glad he didn't at that point, though it might have been different if I had been involved."

Adds Jim Martin, "That was the businessman in Randy who knew what he wanted and how to go after it."

Following another spell out on the road, the Guess Who returned to Mid America studios to lay down tracks for their fourth album.

AMERICAN WOMAN had become a phenomenon and a tough act to follow. In sharp contrast to those sessions, a lack of commitment pervaded attempts at laying down what in fact was not the best batch of Bachman-Cummings compositions. "The tensions hadn't reached the point of becoming explosive confrontations," acknowledges Jack. "But you could pick it up from conversations. 'You're doing this just because it fits into your schedule,' that kind of thing. There was a groundswell of dissent. I kind of felt it was brewing but hadn't reached the conclusion where I thought anyone was about to leave. There was an undercurrent of unrest that showed up in the sessions. We had done the bed tracks, some overdubs and vocals, and were in the process of polishing everything up when we left." The group intended on returning in mid-May to complete the tracks but in the interim circumstances intervened to scuttle the sessions. The seven tracks would ultimately surface in 1976 as *THE WAY THEY WERE*, an afterthought once the Guess Who had officially folded.

The issue tainting the album sessions was the allegation that Randy was somehow manipulating the band's schedule to accommodate his own interests, whether family or personal business. As well, further accusations were levelled regarding Randy's business interests with Sabalora. "Some of the areas that Randy undertook to take upon himself," suggests Jack, "probably wouldn't have been nearly as disruptive an element when they first started out but as the success arrived it became a sore point. The others became more knowledgeable about what the potential was than before. I think it was a cumulative thing. As they became more experienced and more exposed to the machinations of the industry, they started to realize that maybe what Randy was doing was not necessarily in the best interests of all. They felt Randy was booking dates based more on his own schedule than he did on the group's search for success. As leader of the band, he was able to speak to the agents. I wasn't a party to this but I heard it from the other guys. It caused some irritation for them. As the fame and notoriety became significantly greater, the rest of the guys in the group took umbrage toward some of the decisions he was making. I'm not putting Randy down; under the circumstances I might have done the same thing myself. With a family, I know what it's like to be away so much. But it was just a question of them being young and inexperienced, and as that experience became greater they started to see some of the loopholes in what was going on. There were some concerns about publishing deals as well."

Jim Martin vehemently denies the assertion that Randy manipulated the group. As road manager he knew in advance the group's scheduling. "No one was telling the agents where we should and shouldn't work. The dates came and we went and did them. We worked our asses off during that period." But there is no denying that Randy did have his own agenda though whether that jeopardized the group is speculative. Nevertheless, the claim by several band members that Randy was somehow secretly negotiating a publishing deal for himself with noted Stax-Volt writer/producer and member of Booker T and the MG's Steve Cropper comes as a surprise to Randy all these years later.

This is news to me. Our album had been out, *These Eyes* was a hit, and Junior Walker's version was out and we were booked to play in Memphis. The other guys were seriously getting into partying but I would get up in the mornings and do things. We had passed the Stax-Volt studios on the way to the hotel, which looked very unstudio-like, more like a restaurant or grocery store than a recording studio. So I asked the guys if they wanted to go with me the following day to visit the studio. I was keen to visit it but the others weren't interested. The next morning I got up early, took care of the money, the deposit, and decided to try visiting Stax-Volt studios. I attempted to wake the other guys to no avail. We were scheduled to check out by one. It was ten by then so I phoned the studio, told them who I was and mentioned some of our hits, and received an invitation to come on down. I got there and was escorted through the studio.

While I was there Steve Cropper arrived and introduced himself. He knew of our records and asked me about some of the chords in *These Eyes*. He wasn't familiar with some of the major seventh chords we had used. Before I left I gave him a copy of *WHEATFIELD SOUL*. He expressed interest in recording *A Wednesday in Your Garden* for the Staple Singers. I was thrilled with that. I left and didn't see him again until a few years ago in Nashville.

The idea that I was somehow cooking up my own publishing deals with Steve Cropper is incredible. Maybe that was motivated by the fact that he recorded *A Wednesday in Your Garden*, which was my song. Anything else is preposterous. I was always willing to help other bands or artists and still retained my sense of excitement at meeting musicians I admired, so it wasn't out of the ordinary for me to meet Steve Cropper. What else did I have to do on the road when the other guys were out partying or sleeping? Besides, if I had been setting up a publishing deal with Cropper, how come I never pursued it after I left the band?

Regardless, battle lines were drawn and sides taken. With Burton and Jim on one side and Randy on the other, Garry had refused to take sides. Meanwhile, out on the road, the pressure was beginning to take its toll on Randy's health. On several occasions he suffered such pain that Jim Martin rushed him to the hospital.

The touring was becoming a blur for me. If you ask me specific dates and locations from that period, I can't remember most of them. I was feeling a loss of control over the band's direction and a separation between us. Our differences affected everything we did. I found myself wanting out of the situation because it had become extremely uncomfortable and unpleasant for me. Despite the success, I was unhappy and, I just wanted out. I tried telling them to ease up a bit but it came across as preaching and guys like Cummings and Kale don't like to be lectured to or told not to do something. "You do your thing, I'll do mine." I wanted a way out without having a major, knockdown, drag 'em out screaming fight. But what happened instead to widen the gulf between us and hasten my departure was gallbladder attacks.

During the last tour I did, three weeks of dates, every single night at about three in the morning I would wake up sweating with chills and what felt like a knife in my stomach as if someone was turning it slowly and knotting my back. I would vomit blood and have diarrhea. I used to turn a chair over and lean the weight of my chest on the leg to relieve the pressure. I didn't know what was causing it or what was wrong with me. Jumbo would take me covered in sweat and shaking to a hospital in a different city each night and be told, "He's on a bad trip. Just take him home and stay with him."

"No, you don't understand," Jumbo would tell them. "This guy is straight. He doesn't do drugs!"

I couldn't get proper medical attention because of our touring schedule. We would have to leave for another city the next morning. This kept on night after night.

"Jumbo, I think I'm dying. I don't know what's wrong with me."

No one would tell me what was wrong. The pain was excruciating. I didn't know it was from the pressure and from eating improperly, which had caused gallstones. Anyone who has suffered gallbladder attacks can attest to the degree of pain involved. My daughters have had babies and gallbladder attacks, and claim that having the baby was a walk in the park compared to the attacks. It's an indescribable searing white vision of pain running through your brain and your body. I would literally get high from the pain, my adrenaline peaking into a numbness of shock. Jumbo would come into the room and find me on the toilet and at the same time vomiting blood into the tub.

I would phone home and my wife would be crying. I just wanted to go home. The other members were unaware of my nightly ritual of intense pain and hospital visits because they would be partying all night. They had no idea this was going on. They would be totally gonzoed while Jumbo was taking me to emergency rooms. Finally, I went to them and told them I had to go home.

"Randy was definitely having gallbladder problems and his back was in bad shape in the last year he was in the band," confirms Jim Martin. "But where are you going to go? We would get in the car and go to emergency at hospitals and see different doctors here and there. It was frequently occurring and started getting pretty bad. He was going through a bit of hell and it was hard on him. The other guys were enjoying themselves after the gig, but Randy would go right back to his room. I don't think they really gave a damn."

Following a concert in Westchester, New York, Randy once again suffered an attack and determined that he had to return immediately to Winnipeg to his own family doctor for the proper medical attention he required. That same night, the band chanced to meet a young guitar player hanging around after the gig. Bob Sabellico had a band that boasted they could play every Guess Who song. Sabellico was in the right place at the right time and two days later found himself onstage subbing for his hero Randy Bachman in the Guess Who.

Just who secured Sabellico's services remains contentious. Randy claims he did, while Garry Peterson maintains it was him. Both say they went to jam with Sabellico's band that night after the gig. Regardless, Burton and Jim were informed the following morning that Randy was going home and Sabellico was put forward as a temporary replacement to fulfill the remaining tour dates. Burton, Jim, and Garry then went to hear Bobby play that afternoon and cut a deal with him for $1,000 a week and an MG sports car following successful completion of the remaining two weeks of the tour. A quick rehearsal was convened and the Guess Who minus Randy Bachman carried on for the remaining leg of the tour while their leader flew home for much-needed medical attention. There really was no other choice. With *American*

Woman firmly at #1 cancelling would have cost the group dearly.

I called a band meeting and laid out my health situation and my solution.

"I've got to go home and get proper medical care from the one doctor who has known me since birth, Dr. Lerner. I'm not in one place long enough to get tests done on the road."

Jumbo backed me up telling them that while they had been out partying he'd been driving me to hospitals nightly. I don't recall Don Hunter being there.

"So what does that mean? Are we going to cancel gigs?"

"No. I've made a deal with Bob Sabellico."

"Who?"

"The guy we met last night from the band that plays all the Guess Who songs."

It was a fait accompli. There wasn't anything anybody could say. I had no alternative at that point and the band couldn't cancel on such short notice without risking lawsuits and damaging its reputation. *American Woman* was #1, single and album, and the band's fortunes were peaking. There were only a few dates left on the tour and the band was finally commanding $10,000 a night. The last gig was the Fillmore East in New York. I figured I would be back by then.

"Bye guys. I'm going home. See you in a few days."

Back in Winnipeg, I met with Dr. Lerner who administered various tests and concluded that besides suffering several large gallstones, I had a diseased gallbladder. He booked me for elective surgery in September and gave me a list of foods I could and couldn't eat.

"Stay away from sugar and fats, drink skim milk."

Pressure, too, had a lot to do with it, the pressure of the band's success and our differing lifestyles. A second opinion merely confirmed Dr. Lerner's original diagnosis as I prepared to be cut open

from my crotch to my chest. The combination of the diet and
being off the road for a few days offered immediate relief but the
Fillmore East gig was looming. The band stayed on the road and
did the gigs with Sabellico. I called the guys to inform them that I
would be rejoining them for the Fillmore.

In my absence it was party central for the band. The narc was
gone. No more pounding on the door telling them to shut it
down; no more lectures.

Being home, away from all the stress gave me time to reflect on
my situation and my relationship with the band. I had a son that I
had not seen being born, a daughter about to be born, and my wife
needed me home with her. I thought I had enough money coming
in from my songs that I could exist for a period of time. I wasn't
quite sure about leaving the band but I told my wife that I really
didn't like being on the road with these guys any more. I had been
with Garry for ten years. I didn't like the thought of leaving but I
didn't see any choice: they were not the same guys they used to be
and I wasn't the same guy I used to be. The success and choice of
personal lifestyles had divided us. It was tearing me apart. It
reached a point where, with that issue and my gallbladder problem
that required me to take two or three months off for medical reasons, I decided to tell the band I had to leave.

What transpired next remains a point of deep division between
the four members of the group still today. The other three, along with
Jim Martin, are adamant that while Randy was away ostensibly for
health reasons they discovered, much to their consternation, that he
had flown to New York to negotiate personal music business on behalf
of Sabalora, namely, a recording contract for Lorne Saifer's Winnipeg
group the Mongrels. Randy maintains he was in New York to settle
business matters for the imminent release of his *AXE* album. Needless
to say, the shit hit the fan. In the confusion that followed, Randy's last
ally and oldest friend in the group, Garry Peterson, threw in his lot

with Burton and Jim to oust Randy from the Guess Who.

"I believe Randy made a lot of mistakes," opines Garry, thoughtfully. "The truth of why he left the band has truly never been told, the honest truth. It was his own fault. Maybe one day I would like to hear him say, and I don't say this with any malice because he is still my childhood friend, 'I'm sorry, what I did was wrong.' Because it was wrong. He was a businessman and he wanted to produce records but he started to do it at the expense of the band, his friends, and business partners who had all invested in the band together. All the guys in the band were thinking 'I can't believe he's doing this.'

"This is the true story. He didn't leave the band, he was fired. I didn't really have anything to do with it, I was asleep. Cummings and Kale got all wound up one night when we were out with Sabellico and called Randy's house. They thought Randy was manipulative, wanting to be home with his family, and trying to create his own publishing empire in Winnipeg by signing up bands and writers with Lorne Saifer of Sabalora. Lorayne answered.

'Where's that asshole, Randy?'

"Now she, for whatever reason, did not lie or anything.

'He's in New York making a record deal for the Mongrels.'

"Oh god, that was it. I got blasted out of bed, I think we were in Springfield, Massachusetts, within driving distance of New York. They got me up and they knew exactly where he was staying in New York at the City Squire Inn so I assume Lorayne gave them all the information. We drove there, arrived around nine in the morning, and went straight to the hotel. He had already gone to the meeting so we sat there in the lobby waiting for him to come back.

"He walked in, we went upstairs, and Burton said, 'Randy, we don't want you in the band anymore.' And he said 'That's okay, I was thinking of leaving.' He was fired before he could say he was quitting. He had no idea we were coming there. That is the honest story whether Randy will admit to that or not."

The decision was taken with a heavy heart by Garry. "I believe Randy violated a trust to everybody in the band. And not only business-wise. I hope Randy understands this one day. He was our leader and all of us looked up to him. So we felt personally betrayed. Here we were on tour struggling with this young kid and Randy, who was supposed to be sick and having a gallbladder operation, is in New York making a record deal. So you can understand the feelings we felt. It was very tough on me because we were the closest, Randy and I. But he never came to me and confided in me. I was very hurt but I had to stick with the entity that got us where we were. I didn't get nasty with him, though, because I didn't feel that way. If Randy would have said, 'I'm sorry. I made a mistake. What I did was wrong' I think Burton and Jim would have accepted that and we could have carried on."

I came to a decision to quit the Guess Who and they came to a decision to boot me out. It happened at the same instant. They said they had enough of my religion and all this stuff and were throwing me out. I said, "That's fine, I quit." By the time your boss fires you, you're ready to look him in the eyes and say, "I quit." The departure came by mutual consent. They went their way, I went mine.

Don Burkhimer had called to ask me to meet him in New York to sort out the loose ends for the imminent release of my *AXE* album, things like song publishing and credits. So I flew in to New York a day early to rest before the Fillmore gig and take care of this business. While I was in town the band rolled in. They assumed I was in town early doing something behind their backs. So the situation was tense.

My diversion from touring and writing with the Guess Who was music, my own music. So I would help other local bands that came to me looking for songs or production or just advice. Because I write songs all the time, I had songs to offer. That was my little indulgence, recording the Sugar And Spice, helping the

Gettysbyrg Address, or writing songs for the Mongrels. I had more experience than anyone else in the city. I didn't see it as jeopardizing my position in the Guess Who. When I had my own time that's what I did. I worked with other bands.

But the guys in the Guess Who, for their own reasons, started to perceive this as contrary to the good of the band. That's why they viewed my going to meet Steve Cropper as a direct threat. They saw it as "Randy cutting his own deal." But I wasn't. When I got back to the hotel and told the other guys, once they finally got up, they took on a rather sullen air. I was elated to meet one of my heroes and they were suspicious of my motives. I never saw Steve again until the late nineties and he barely remembered me.

Don Hunter knew I was going to New York a day ahead. Lorne Saifer knew this too and asked me, since I was going to meet with Don Burkhimer could I speak to him about the Mongrels. I said sure. I wasn't negotiating a publishing deal for myself. But it was perceived later by the other guys as me signing some multimillion-dollar publishing deal. Hardly.

When the band came to the hotel, they had fire in their eyes and a nasty confrontation ensued. Immediately beforehand, Lorayne had called my room to warn me that Jim Kale had called the night before looking for me and they were angry. They had all these things conjured up about deals with Steve Cropper, publishing with RCA's Dunbar Music, or negotiating for the Mongrels. They lit into me with daggers drawn. "You so and so. You've been doing all this stuff behind our backs! We've been out on the road and having a great time without you. You're fired." They fired me first. In defence, I immediately replied, "I quit."

Jim Martin confirms Garry's version of events but supports Randy's assertion that he had already made up his mind to leave. "Randy knew it wasn't right for him any longer. In reality, he had set in his own mind that this wasn't where he wanted to be anymore. He was having health problems and maybe that was an excuse for what else he was doing but he wanted out at the same time that they wanted him out. That's how it went down. I've read where Cummings and Kale say they fired him, but Randy was ready to quit by then. It just happened at the same time. It makes me sick when I see them claiming they kicked Randy out of the band. It's bullshit. Maybe it's because it came from them before it came out of Randy's mouth. They got to tell him they didn't want him in the band before he could say he didn't want to be in the band."

The highly charged atmosphere in that hotel room might have been diffused by a cooler head, perhaps manager Don Hunter or RCA's Don Burkhimer acting as mediator, but in the absence of any rational response, emotion ruled the confrontation. Burton and Jim lashed out in anger feeling a sense of betrayal and seeing no other recourse but to fire their leader. It was a rash decision, an overreaction on their part without considering the whole picture. To them, there was no grey area, it was all black and white: Randy transgressed, he's out. Done deal. Confronted, Randy turned defensive and, despite having made a decision that for personal reasons relating to lifestyle and health his days with the group were numbered, he determined that that was the very moment to quit. Possibly the group's story could have turned out differently had someone intervened and mollified both sides. In any event, that did not happen and the meeting turned explosive.

Recently, when I read their perspective of those events for the first time in this manuscript, I cried. I was totally stunned at the perception that Burton and Jim had at the time. I had blocked out all that for decades because of the pain of it all. I was up for three nights troubled by reading this. "They thought this of me? I betrayed them. I was their leader, Jim Kale's brother figure, Burton's father figure, Garry's best friend and in their eyes I stabbed them in the back." For the longest time I couldn't figure out why Garry Peterson kept saying that he thought I needed to make a statement or apologize. Now I understand their anger. All I knew for three decades was my side of the story. So I recently wrote each of them a letter and laid out my side of the story and apologized for hurting them, which I never intended, and for all the misunderstanding. And I admitted, "Yes, you fired me." Afterwards I felt a great weight lifted off me. We had all been carrying this burden for three decades.

I can't change the past, what's done is done, but I think we've cleared the air. It's taken a long time but I hope it's laid to rest.

In hindsight, I think my split from the Guess Who was inevitable. If it hadn't happened that spring it was only a matter of time. The differences between us were too great and I didn't want to be out on the road that much. I didn't like the lifestyle of the other guys and couldn't see it changing any time soon. With the success of *American Woman* it would only increase. I was aching to be home with my family. After missing Tal's birth, I vowed I would be home for my next child's birth. And that was in July, which would have been at the height of the *American Woman* ride.

"Nobody knew what had gone down that afternoon between the guys," recounts Jim Martin on the events of May 16. "RCA didn't know, nobody in the concert hall knew. It all came down before the sound check, the band went and did the sound check, the opening acts went on — Buddy Miles and Bloodrock — and then the Guess Who took the stage. I was there in the wings at the side of the stage and that was the best I have ever seen Randy play. He was a great guitar player and always played unreal. He totally did something to me inside when he played. As I listened, my mind was flooded with all those memories of our time together, the nights alone on the bus when he would sit up with me to keep me awake, just the two of us, him playing his guitar, playing new songs, or getting me to sing *Bird Dog*."

I was feeling under the weather but sufficiently pumped to

play, and our first set was incredible. Between sets I suffered an attack that doubled me over in the filthy Fillmore washroom, down on my hands and knees, before we took the stage again but we played another inspired performance. I played my ass off that night. I had been so hungry on the plane because I was afraid to eat. Every time I ate, the attacks would hit me. When you have that much pain, your body kicks out so much adrenaline to mask it. I came out of the bathroom high on my body's adrenaline and I went and prayed to God to help me get through this because I knew it was my last night with the band and to help me play like I had never played before.

Onstage, I took a solo and when my solo was supposed to end I didn't. Burton looked at me as I went into another solo doing sixty-bar guitar breaks in songs. I looked over and Garry was digging it, pushing me, and driving me along. The audience went crazy as the adrenaline pushed me further. We played until the wee hours of the morning and they were still screaming for more.

The crowd called us back for several encores and began chanting "These Eyes" over and over. This was the Fillmore East, the epitome of hip cool rock so we didn't want to play it. We wanted to be Led Zeppelin or Traffic, not this pop hits band so we were doing *Talisman, Species Hawk*, Burton reciting poetry, our solos doubling and tripling in length. Finally we relented and the audience erupted. This was their hippie love song. We left the stage in triumph.

"As I watched him playing his heart out that night," continues Jim Martin, "I had tears in my eyes. He was playing incredibly. Unbelievable. I can still picture Burton in my mind standing up at the mike doing his Jim Morrison thing and turning to look over at Randy and you could read it in his face: 'Holy shit! This guy is playing his face off.' I started wondering whether the group had made the right decision. I kept looking at Kale and Cummings and they were looking at Randy all night. The crowd was into it, the band was incredible; everything was just magical. It all gelled that night. The group was always great but this was exceptional. There was something different that night. Maybe it was Randy thinking 'This is my last gig guys but here, this is what I am.' Or maybe it was the feeling of relief for him that his freedom was now there, the bridge was open now for him to cross.

"They came offstage and went upstairs to the dressing room. I wiped away the tears from my eyes and came in and went up to Jimmy and Burton. I looked at them and just thought that if these two guys felt the way I felt during that set, the emotion in them onstage the way they were looking at Randy, something had to be going through them. They must be feeling it was all wrong. I went up to the two of them and the first thing that came out of my mouth was, 'Are you sure you're doing the right thing here?' Cummings gave me an icy stare; Jimmy turned around and said to me, 'Are you out of your f*#king mind? Of course we know what we're doing!' I just turned away, looked over at Randy in the other corner of the room and went over and hugged him. Then I had to get out. At that moment I knew it was wrong. That's my own opinion and obviously the other guys didn't think so. But I let it be known and heard by everyone. I know Garry heard me and I think Randy did too.

"I think things could have carried on after the Fillmore," surmises Jim Martin. "They could have worked out their differences. To me at that time it was very important that the band stay together. If there was a way that I could have saved it I would have, but they didn't want to listen. We all can work out our problems. If Randy needed some time off then they should have given it to him. But they disagreed with everything Randy did."

Following the gig, we convened at Sardi's restaurant for a party hosted by RCA. The guys had already formulated their plans to bring in Kurt Winter and Greg Leskiw from Winnipeg in my place but RCA didn't know what had gone down. That's when it turned ugly.

"You gotta go? Great. Screw off. Get outta here. We've got somebody else."

There's a photo Jim Kale recently gave me of the four of us at Sardi's that night and we are glaring stone-faced and expressionless directly at the camera because we knew the band as we had known it for four years was over right then and there. We were arguing, angry, pissed off and at that moment someone stuck a camera in our faces.

Garry and I had the longest history together but he knew where his bread was buttered. He couldn't go off with me and leave the biggest band in North America. Friendship, I don't think, entered into it. It was a band decision: "Bachman's out." I have wondered sometimes why he didn't intercede on my behalf but that was his choice. Perhaps he knew that he, too, was replaceable and didn't want to rock the boat.

At the gala party celebrating the band's Fillmore triumph and #1 record, Don Burkhimer and the other RCA executives were informed of Randy's departure. "I was aware there was a dichotomy of lifestyles within the group," states Don Burkhimer, "Randy being a Mormon and the others not adhering to the same scruples. But I didn't think it would affect the continuation of the band as it was because they were having so much success. Then I found out Randy was leaving the band and I couldn't believe it. It came as quite a shock to me. I had a great deal of concern for the future of the Guess Who at that moment because I knew how important Randy was to the group with his great musical sense. His guitar playing and writing gave the band an identity. With him gone I knew it was very questionable about the group's continued success. I talked to Randy that night trying to convince him to stay but it was a done deal. I was destroyed. I just wanted to get drunk.

"In my opinion Randy was an integral part of the group's sound. And I was proven correct. The Guess Who never scored the same success afterwards that they had with Randy in the band. It was never the same. When Randy left, the magic was gone. He was an enormous talent. The band lost and I knew it was gone when Randy left. After that the personnel in the band kept changing and I don't think the capability to write hits was there."

Jack Richardson viewed Randy's departure more pragmatically. "The band called me, I was down for the gig, and I went over to their hotel. There was a lot of bad blood at that point between Randy and them. They informed me that Randy had left the band; it wasn't presented as them kicking him out. I called my partners about the situation and told them that as long as Burton was there we still had a Guess Who, which is what I told RCA as well. Burton's voice was the distinctive feature in that band. There was no doubting that. The three of them talked it out with me and I said 'Okay guys, let's see what we can do beyond this point in time.' RCA had just appointed a new president of the company, Rocco Lagenestra, who came over to me at the party and introduced himself. He talked about the Guess Who's achievements and I said to him, 'Oh, by the way, Randy's left the band.' This was the new president and an act that represented a significant portion of RCA's success in those days with the #1 record that week. He was speechless. So I said to him, 'Look, let me just clarify something. As long as we have Burton, we have the Guess Who.' Losing Randy did not mean the end of the group."

The next day, Randy met with Don Burkhimer to ensure that his royalties would still be paid dutifully despite his departure then headed to the airport for a flight home. Jack Richardson and manager Don Hunter knew Burton and Jim were flying home as well and rearranged departure times so that all three were not on the same flight. "If they had been on the same plane I'm sure they would have all been thrown off somewhere over Wisconsin," offers Jack. The problem was that the flight to Winnipeg connects in Minneapolis. As Randy took his seat on the connecting flight, Jim and Burton came on board and once the flight levelled off proceeded to subject their former guitarist to a litany of profanity and threats that brought the plane to an emergency landing to discharge the two drunk and distraught passengers.

The next day the headlines in the Winnipeg newspaper read "Bachman Quits Guess Who." Kids were crying on my lawn, others carrying signs. "How could you do this to Winnipeg?" Guys were driving up in cars yelling and threatening me, people phoning up at all hours to berate me for leaving the group, newspaper and magazine stories condemning me. Even journalists I knew for years turned on me. It was like I had broken up the Beatles. The reaction was incredible. It was a very weird time in Winnipeg for me and it was the first time I ever felt unwelcome. I had to get away until the commotion died down. Lorayne's parents were now living in Saskatoon so we decided to pack up and visit them until things simmered down. I gave Jumbo the keys to our house and asked him to look after it in my absence as we went running off to Saskatoon.

"In all fairness, even if they had been drinking, I can't understand why they couldn't have gone up to Randy on that plane, shook his hand, and said to him, 'It's been a great ten years,'" opines Jim Martin. "If they were any kind of decent human beings, that's the way it should have gone down with Randy. To this day I don't think any of them have sat down and thought of it that way. And I have to add Garry to that. If they had any decency or respect they would realize that Randy was half the reason that Garry and Jimmy made it and are where they are. He was the guy that made it happen for them, why they had lots of money and a house on Park Boulevard. Randy was the businessman that kept it together. He and Burton wrote the songs that made the group what it was. Instead it's all bullshit what has gone down over the past thirty years, all the bitterness."

The fact is Burton was uneasy about going it alone without Randy. The sense of unease increased several notches when Randy confounded the odds three years later and returned to the charts with Bachman-

Turner Overdrive. "It's hard for Burton to admit but he did miss Randy," asserts Jim Martin who remained in the group's employ after Randy's departure. "The best writing was when Randy and Burton were working together. The power in the writing was with Bachman and Cummings. The group never had the same success after Randy. Cummings did need him — history has proven that. Look at the group's career after Randy."

They trashed me and I honestly don't know why. It's not like I did anything to sabotage them or screw them up. They went on and had hits with *Hand Me Down World* and *Share the Land*. How do you think my parents felt reading all that stuff? It's not like I took some monumental amount of money. To this day, I still don't know why they felt they had to do that. It hurt. You want to ignore it, you try to, and then you want to show them. They told me I'd never make it in this business straight. I wasn't hip. They said in the press I was thrown out because I wasn't hip, I was straight. So I was determined to show them that hip was a state of mind and using your creativity and talent. That kind of talk was all jive.

"Randy wasn't the kind of person to go out and start defending himself," maintains Jim Martin. "He kept to himself, to his family. Those other two guys were too busy yapping to everybody that Randy was all wrong. You never heard Randy talking to radio about *them*. He didn't have to."

Writing in *Creem* magazine the following month, Canadian music journalist Ritchie Yorke summed up the stunned reaction in the music world to Randy's abrupt exit.

You could compare it to John Lennon having left the Beatles two weeks before Rubber Soul *was released. In terms of musical potential and financial prospects, Bachman's action was one of sheer madness. Nobody but a fool would change teams halfway through a football game when the team he was then on was 30 points ahead. Yet Bachman did it, and full points to him for guts if nothing else. One day we will find out why Randy Bachman left the group, thus committing what one can only describe as the major folly of rock music in 1970. Why?*

Few at the time knew the true story behind the headlines.

Despite the public outcry, the reality is that pop bands have a very limited lifespan. That this lineup of the Guess Who had managed to last four years was, in itself, quite a feat. The nucleus — Randy, Jim, and Garry — had been together since 1961, nine years of slogging it out on the road together. That's comparable to the Beatles entire tenure together. With few exceptions, most bands that manage to achieve a level of success don't stay together more than a few years. Personnel come and go; riffs lead to dismissals or departures. Taken in a wider context, Randy's exodus was not out of step with the norm; that he chose to exit at the peak of the group's acclaim, however, was.

That same year, the Beatles split up amid considerable private acrimony. The public barely knew of all the wrangling between the four. John Lennon ultimately made the decision to abandon the group before flying off to Toronto to debut his hastily convened Plastic One Band at a rock festival. It was left to Paul McCartney to bear the news to the public that the Fab Four were no more. In doing so, McCartney bore the brunt of the millions of fans and media who blamed him for the demise of the Beatles, a specter that has hung over him ever since. Though the decision was Lennon's, McCartney became the fall guy. In the Guess Who scenario, Randy was the fall guy who has been blamed ever since.

While the Guess Who soldiered on with a revolving door of personnel over the next five years (including Domenic Troiano), the group never again attained the level of sustained success it had enjoyed with Randy in the lineup. The chemistry between Randy and Burton and the songs they created together remain the high point in the story of the Guess Who.

"Randy was always dependable, together, and very smart," surmises Don Burkhimer. "He was a very decent person who seemed kind of out of place in the rock 'n' roll business but was talented as hell and had the scruples and wherewithal to go forward. And he did."

With the March session tracks still waiting to be completed, the group instead brought in two of Burton and Jim's friends, Winnipeg guitarists Kurt Winter and Greg Leskiw, and set about recording a brand new album. "We had planned on going back into the studio after the Fillmore gig, but when Randy left, the others made the decision not to have anything to do with that stuff," states Jack Richardson. "At that point, anything Randy had something to do with was on the black list."

In the wake of Randy's departure, the Guess Who seemed to lose direction. The minute Randy left the band a lot of things went down that shouldn't have because we weren't taking care of business. If Randy had stayed, maybe he would have made us all millionaires."

Adds Jim Martin, "When Randy left, that's when everything started going all over the place and falling apart in the band. Don Hunter could do what he wanted because he didn't have Randy looking over his shoulder. There was a lack of leadership after Randy left because of the way the guys looked after themselves and didn't look after the business. Randy kept everything above water. He was the businessman. I don't think the other guys appreciated that."

The Guess Who made Don Hunter, he didn't make us. He came aboard a train that was going full speed ahead and put on a hat that said "Conductor." I don't think he did a whole lot. I don't think any of our success was due to him. He certainly wasn't a Svengali like a Colonel Tom Parker to Elvis or a Brian Epstein to the Beatles. He wasn't an accountant or a big negotiator; he didn't know anyone in the business at the time. He had no legal training. He handled the money after I got too busy to do that and took the phone calls. But we got along with him; he was a good guy. We poked a lot of fun at him and he took it well. Hunter slowly integrated himself into running the band because it was very hard work for me doing all the business. It was getting to be too much as we became more successful. When I left, Hunter had learned to handle the financial end and the booking, which I don't think the other guys were very aware of.

When someone leaves a band there is always some fear involved like "How are we gonna make it without him?" There was a vying for power as well. "Who's going to take control?" I had pretty much made the decisions for the band. I would call the agent every day to find out where we were going. I collected the money at night and since I was the only guy who got up in the morning, I would go put the money in the bank and send it home to our accountant. I did that every day and I wasn't paid any extra. I did it to look after me and in looking after myself, I looked after them.

As a member of a corporate entity contributing revenue to that corporation which was in turn invested in shopping malls and fast food restaurants, Randy should have been bought out of the Guess Who. In 1970, the Guess Who's gross revenues were anticipated to exceed $2 million, rising to $5 million the following year, a major portion of which was contributed by Randy. Indeed, the Guess Who would sell more single records than any other group in the world including the Beatles, Rolling Stones, and Creedence Clearwater Revival in 1970. Nevertheless, when he exited the band there was no settlement or buy out. When David Crosby quit The Byrds in 1967 he was given a $50,000 settlement; Brian Jones was bought out of the Rolling Stones the year before Randy left the Guess Who. All Randy would be entitled to were his royalties, nothing for the goodwill his efforts had earned the group over the last few years. "I wasn't aware of any buy out," claims Jack Richardson who represented Nimbus Productions. "Randy still received his royalties from RCA. I know that the group set up a new company when the new guys came in but as far as I know he received all the royalties due to him."

There is a lag time between a hit record and the pay out from six months to two years. I quit the group when *American Woman* was #1 but I had some nice money in the pipeline that would be due me down the road. The group went on to enjoy success with SHARE THE LAND and THE BEST OF THE GUESS WHO, albums which were big sellers, but it was tapering down by the time I was putting my money into Brave Belt and BTO. It was starting to get a little desperate by then.

I don't remember any talk of a settlement. I had to go myself the day after my last Fillmore gig and meet with my lawyer to put together a document identifying the songs I played on that I should be paid for. I believe after I left the group and they brought in two new guitar players they renegotiated their contract with RCA and possibly grandfathered it, but I didn't benefit from that. If so they would enjoy a bigger royalty on that early stuff than me. What it boils down to is I get a cent a record.

But a settlement was not the biggest thing on my mind at the time. It's easier to think of later, "Gee, why didn't I get a lot of money for all my sweat equity working to achieve that success?" I retained my songwriting royalties, that was it.

With plenty of time on his hands and a pregnant wife, Randy enjoyed the down time at home away from all the pressures of the last year. He puttered around the house with Tally or took him up the street to Kildonan Park to climb the many trees there.

I wanted to go home to Winnipeg, kind of like the wounded dog that struggles home to be among familiar surroundings. I needed that comfort zone, that healing place, and that was back in the comfort of West Kildonan in Winnipeg. I had missed the local restaurants, movies, ball games, family, friends, parks, everything I needed to rejuvenate me. I missed that for so many years as a travelling musician. People envy the lifestyle but don't realize how great it is to be in a house and eat leftover food because all you eat every day is restaurant food. Or crave your mother's cooking or her cookies when you're in Savannah, Georgia. I needed to relive some lost years, go home, and get the vibes back that made me want to play in a band in the first place.

As far as the music scene was concerned, Randy laid low, riding out the storm that continued to rage around his sudden departure from the top group in North America. With his income secure for the time being from his royalties, Randy felt no urgency to jump back into the rock band fray, instead considering various production projects thrown his way.

I wonder what would have happened if I had accepted an offer to join Emerson, Lake, and Palmer. It was the day after the Fillmore gig and I had stayed to meet with Don Burkhimer to ensure that I got what I was due in the Guess Who. Don introduced me to this orchestrator from Britain who was in the RCA building. He had orchestrated an album for a group called the Nice with British keyboard whiz Keith Emerson. He had heard my *AXE* album. It hadn't been released yet but he heard the variety of guitar styles. He didn't hear a Hendrix or superstar guitar sounds, instead it was a classical song, a country song, light jazz, a jamming-riffy song. He didn't know my *No Time* stuff and all that because that wasn't known in England. He liked the album and told me Keith Emerson had a new band but the guitar player never showed up. He thought my playing would be perfect and offered to take the album back to London to play for Keith and suggest I join the new group. But I didn't want to join another band.

Randy did manage to pick up his guitar on July 1, Canada Day, to make a surprise appearance, albeit briefly and unheralded, at Festival Express. The original "Rolling Thunder Revue," Festival Express consisted of a private trainload of musicians partying their way across Canada with stops for performances in various cities. Boasting such rock luminaries as Janis Joplin, The Band, the Grateful Dead, Mountain, Delaney and Bonnie, and bluesman Buddy Guy, the specially equipped train pulled into Winnipeg for a day-long performance at the Winnipeg Stadium. When Randy heard that there might be a jam he headed on down to sit in.

I came out onstage between acts while they were setting up equipment and did an acoustic interlude. No one really announced me, I just strolled out assuming people in Winnipeg would know who I was. I don't think they did for the first few minutes then someone shouted, "Hey, it's Randy Bachman." I was so nervous and scared that I ended up spelling American Woman wrong. I was doing the "I say A, M, E…" and I missed a letter. I was going to do a whole mini set but I got so flustered I walked off halfway through. People thought "Oh, Bachman's stoned" but I was just out of my element. I didn't have my band and I wasn't a solo acoustic performer. It was embarrassing. But I'm not sure anyone really knew who I was so when I left no one cared. I came out later and joined Delaney and Bonnie onstage along with Leslie West for their big jam at the end of their set.

Afterwards, I jammed on the train in this elegant parlor car. I was sitting there with Jerry Garcia and other members of the Grateful Dead, Janis Joplin, Delaney and Bonnie and their band, guys from The Band, Leslie West from Mountain. Players would wander in and out of this designated jam room, pull up a chair, plug into one of the little amps they had, or sit at the drum kit in the corner and just pick up on the flow of the ongoing jams. I sat there and played all this rambling blues rock music. I was beside a window that I'd opened because the smoke was thick. As the joints appeared and were passed around someone would nudge me and offer one. "No thanks" and it would get passed along to the next player. As the drugs and booze circulated round the room the playing got slower, more lethargic, and sloppy. Meanwhile, I was so charged to be playing with these people whose music I respected and enjoyed that my adrenaline was pumping. I had left the Guess Who and just wanted to play with anybody. Someone commented, "Who's the guy by the window with all the energy?" I was pumped while they were stoned.

On July 24, Lorayne gave birth to a baby girl, Kezia Isanne Bachman, the apple of her Dad's eye. Soon after, the family returned to Saskatoon to be with Lorayne's parents.

August in Saskatoon, harvest time just beginning, another prairie town and it was marvellous. For the first time in months, I felt a sense of peace away from the storm. Lorayne's brother, Bob Stevenson, was about to leave on his Mormon mission to France so along with her younger brother Mark, the four of us went to a drive-in movie on a warm summer night. I hadn't had a gallbladder attack since the Fillmore so without thinking I had an orange soda pop. That was a dumb thing to do. In the midst of the feature I could feel the churning inside my gut beginning.

"Mark, you've gotta take me home."

"Why? I want to see the rest of the movie."

"If you don't take me home right now you won't believe what's going to happen to the front seat of your car."

Back at Lorayne's parents' house, they called their family doctor, Dr. Brandt, who pulled up a half-hour later in a Rolls-Royce. As he administered a shot of Demerol for the pain, I began to fade out but managed to utter one sentence through the haze: "I want to buy your car." I really wanted to own a Rolls. I had also never taken anything like that before and I guess it loosened my tongue a bit.

The next morning I was scheduled to go into the hospital with

Dr. Brandt. The night before, my father-in-law and brother-in-law
Bob Stevenson put their hands on my head, anointed me with oil
and administered a blessing. At the hospital, Dr. Brandt informed
me that he needed to run some tests of his own before proceed-
ing. He had my X-rays sent up from Winnipeg but nonetheless he
went ahead and administered barium to me for his own tests. I
had been through all this in Winnipeg back in May. Later in the
afternoon he came into my room shaking his head.

"I want to take another X-ray tomorrow."

"Why? Just do it, cut me open with a dull antler and get it
over with."

"No, I need another round of tests."

The next morning I took the barium again, more X-rays and I
waited to hear from him. Dr. Brandt came to my room after lunch
with two sets of X-rays.

"At first I thought yesterday's X-ray wasn't yours, that it had
been mixed up with another X-ray. But your neck chain is there in
both as well as on the Winnipeg X-rays."

"So what does that mean?"

"Your Winnipeg X-rays show several gallstones present. But
your recent X-rays show no sign of stones or an unhealthy gallbladder. I don't know what happened. Was it a gallbladder attack
last night?"

"I think so."

"This doesn't happen. Those gallstones must be somewhere
else. I need to run more tests."

I stayed in the hospital for the better part of a week and in the
end Dr. Brandt released me. My gallbladder problems had disappeared. He couldn't explain it. I can't explain it in any medical
terms. After all the testing in the hospital, the doctors were bewildered. They showed me the X-ray from Dr. Lerner back in May
with my withered gallbladder looking like a deflated football with
all these spots that he said were stones blocking my ability to

digest food. Then they held up the recent X-ray of my healthy gallbladder. It was a miracle.

That event really solidified my faith. In the Mormon Church we have the laying on of hands for the comfort and healing of the afflicted. I have witnessed dozens of these and participated as an administrator. It's a very spiritual experience that is difficult to explain to those who have never seen it.

Here I was out of the Guess Who, my contracts had been settled guaranteeing me my share of the royalties, I had been off the road for two months away from the stress and pressure, and I was healthy.

As he discharged me, Dr. Brandt turned and said, "By the way, were you serious about buying my Rolls-Royce? I brought it from Ireland and it's no good here in Saskatoon."

"Yeah. Definitely."

So I bought his Rolls-Royce.

Randy cut quite a dashing figure wending his way through Winnipeg streets in his 1954 Rolls-Royce Silver Dawn. Winnipeg rock royalty, indeed.

Healthy once again, Randy set his sights on being a producer. Having spent considerable time observing at the feet of one of Canada's finest, Jack Richardson, Randy had learned his lessons well. He would often remain behind in the studio after the rest of the band headed back to their hotel to ask questions of Jack and engineer Brian Christian. He experimented with sounds and studio techniques all the while internalizing the craft of a producer. He approached songwriting in by, carefully analyzing what made a record a hit and noting the techniques of good songwriting from the masters. Randy tackled record production in that same analytical manner. Once he knew his way around a recording console, Randy let his muse and his keen ear take over. In the end it is the producer who calls the shots in a recording studio and who takes responsibility for the final recorded product.

Randy wanted that role. He had spent enough time in studios to know what he wanted. As he told writer Martin Melhuish,

> I started to study well-produced records. People like the Beatles, James Taylor, and Led Zeppelin had very well-produced records. Creedence Clearwater Revival were another influence. I would listen to the sounds they got and figure out how they did it, so when I wanted to reproduce it later in the studio, I was able to. I used to translate the best techniques from other people's records into what I was writing and make it come out as a finished product.

In late August, Randy returned to Mid America Recording Center in Chicago to produce an album for Lorne Saifer's protegés the Mongrels. Due to contractual complications between RCA and Capitol Records, the album never saw the light of day. Over the next few months, Randy would also handle production chores for Edmonton rock veteran Barry Allen as well as a trio named Noah who had been slated to work with Jack Richardson but turned to Randy after Jack's busy schedule left them waiting. Randy produced their album *PEACEMAN'S FARM* for ABC/Dunhill and contributed one song. He later produced a second album for the group, financing it himself.

That fall, while sitting in with the house band for a weekly local CBC television country music variety show called *My Kind of Country*, backing the likes of country stars Tom T. Hall and Dave "*Six Days On The Road*" Dudley, Randy chanced to bump into an old friend in the corridors of the CBC building. Since last working with Randy on the *Let's Go* show, Chad Allan had completed his master's degree in psychology and was working as a school psychologist. He also kept his hand in music through songwriting and playing lounges with the Sticks and Strings.

> Chad said to me, "I'm doing some recording at Century 21 Studios. Do you want to try and write some songs with me?"

"Yeah."

Here was a singer who would actually sing with me when a lot of others wouldn't. After I left the Guess Who, nobody would play with me. Chad Allan was the only singer in town who would have anything to do with me. I was the guy who had quit the golden boys of Canadian rock. There was a furor still surrounding me.

Chad and I went over to each other's houses and began sharing song ideas. It was a pretty secure feeling because we had a long relationship so it felt good. Initially, I became involved as a producer. Chad was doing his own stuff. But when I started playing on the tracks it began to take on a different feel, more of a band sound. So what started out as a Chad Allan solo album produced by Randy Bachman gradually took shape as a band album.

I had spent a decade being onstage every night and now I wasn't onstage for the longest period in my life. Every night around ten o'clock my body would go through this adrenaline rush where I could have scaled a telephone pole or run around the block. It's like a football player or any athlete who retires from playing; there is a certain rhythm to your body that you get used to. I remember Lorayne saying to me, "I wake up in the middle of the night and you're not there. I look all around the house and can't find you." I would be in the basement with my guitar and headphones on playing to anything, Crosby, Stills, and Nash, Beatles, anything. She finally said to me, "Whatever you have to do, whatever you feel you need to do, go do it. If it means starting another band, do it."

That's all I needed to hear.

"Wow, I can start another band? Great!"

CHAPTER 6

Welcome Home

How do you form a band when no one will play with you? That was the dilemma Randy Bachman faced in the fall of 1970. Feeling blackballed by the mighty Guess Who machine in his own backyard, Randy ultimately turned to his family for players. In retrospect it wasn't that other musicians shunned him. Quite the contrary, there were likely plenty of players keen to hitch their wagon to Randy's star. After all, he was responsible for the biggest hits of the year and was a musician and songwriter of great stature and international prominence. The problem for Randy wasn't availability but suitability. How do you find players who won't smoke, drink, or do drugs, will take direction without question, and toe the line? After the experience of the last few years in the Guess Who, Randy knew that if he ever formed another band it would have to be on his own terms. That meant selecting players who were compatible not only on a musical level sharing his musical vision, but more importantly on a social level.

Although Chad Allan had no intentions of recording a country rock-flavoured album when he first entered the studio in November of 1970, Randy soon steered the project in that direction. Looking to his former acolyte Neil Young for inspiration, Randy sought to fashion a sound along the lines of the Buffalo Springfield and its offshoot bands Poco and the highly successful conglomerate of Crosby, Stills, Nash, and Young. The Springfield had been one of the seminal groups to integrate country music textures into their folk rock as far back as 1966. They were also one of the first rock groups to utilize that bastion of the hard-core country music sound, pedal steel guitar. More than that, the Springfield had a western image — buckskin fringe jackets, cowboy hats, beaded moccasins. They were the epitome of cool and Randy was enamoured with the group. It was an odd reversal of roles: the mentor now taking his lead from the pupil.

Randy's dream of forming a country rock ensemble was a bold gamble and an about-face from his solid pop/rock credentials. Country rock was still in its infancy by 1970. Groups like Poco and the Flying Burrito Brothers were at the forefront of a fringe movement taking a step backward to a more honest and authentic American roots music in the wake of all the psychedelic acid rock excesses of the latter sixties. Country rock would later become a musical force to be reckoned with. By 1973 the Eagles dominated the pop charts with an appealing easy-listening country-flavoured style that became characterized as the southern California sound. Hand in hand with the rise of country rock in 1970 came the era of the solo singer/songwriter, the James Taylor image alone on a stage hunched over an acoustic guitar writing and performing introspective songs. Besides his work in rock bands, Neil Young had managed to carve out a parallel career for himself as an acclaimed solo singer/songwriter.

Country music was always a big influence for me from the time I was a kid and I always admired Neil Young and Buffalo Springfield because they were rockin' but they kept those country influences, whereas the Guess Who was a real pop band. I envied Neil Young having that outlet. He could rock with CSNY and Crazy Horse or be a country-flavoured solo singer/songwriter.
Here I was, 1970, trying to make a fresh start with a new band.

I knew that if I did a pop band again it could never be as good as the Guess Who. I could never match the incredible voice of Burton Cummings. I could never find another singer anywhere that had all that magic or find all the special ingredients that we had that took us where we had gotten to. I wanted to do something different, not just another Guess Who. I could have written those same Guess Who songs but I didn't want to be a second rate Guess Who.

Instead, I went totally anti-pop. What else could I do? I enlisted Ron Halldorson to play pedal steel, Wally Diduk on fiddle, and Chad Allan on the accordion he had grown up playing. I played acoustic guitar and we did kind of a country rock album. I even sang the odd tune. I also produced the album. After being produced and engineered by the best guys in the business now I was on my own.

Nobody seemed to want to work with me. I had left the top band in the world and as a result was branded a lunatic and a loser. Nobody would join my band. So I looked to my family who had always been there. Robbie was playing drums already and later Tim came in on guitar. My brother Gary even managed the band. I had to get my own brothers. The first one I asked was my youngest brother Robbie who was in grade eleven at the time.

Claims Gary Bachman, "I told Randy, 'You want a band made up of guys who don't smoke or drink. You just came from that and you can't live with it. You can't simply find guys that do and tell them they can't. You need to find guys who don't and tell them not to start.' So I suggested he check out Robbie." Although local sticksman Billy McDougall sat in for one or two sessions, Randy sought a permanent drummer for his new band. "Robbie wasn't bad," Gary continues, "though he had a problem keeping a steady beat not speeding up or slowing down. But I figured they could get a metronome and work with him. Randy wasn't sure about Robbie because of his age and lack of experience."

221

Robbie had started out playing a set of porridge boxes cut down to different sizes. You remember those round things with "Ogilvy Oats" on them? We cut them to different sizes with a knife and put the lid back on and these were his drums. By the time I approached him he had an old set of Garry Peterson's drums.

I had wanted Garry Peterson to play on the Chad Allan sessions but it would have been too difficult for him because it would have been perceived as changing sides. We hadn't stayed in touch after the split. He was in and out of town with the Guess Who and I knew if I talked to him they would probably think he was fraternizing with the enemy. I don't think he really wanted to talk to me even though he certainly could have. He didn't want to rock that boat. So I went in with Robbie and recorded some tracks. He was scared to death. At our first recording session I said to him, "Play like Ringo Starr!" That's all I told him. After the first session he came to me in tears exclaiming, "I can't play."

"Well, you play around the house. And I can't find another drummer." He came back and did it and he liked it.

With the album sessions completed by December, Randy, Chad, and Robbie now required a name, an identity, a manager, and a fourth member to complete the lineup.

I was looking for a name that was sort of like Buffalo Springfield: buckskin fringes, Cowboys and Indians, Gretsch guitars, country rock thing, the look the Springfield had. Neil was known as the Hollywood Indian. People thought he was aboriginal. I wanted a name that would convey that imagery and western motif. I almost called the band Peguis after Chief Peguis who was West Kildonan's hero, our very own Sitting Bull or Geronimo. As a kid I would always go to Kildonan Park and look at the statue of Chief Peguis. I tried the name on some people and they responded "Pegasus?" "No, Peguis" They didn't know what it meant. I was there in the park looking at the Peguis statue one day trying to find inspiration when a friend came through the park and saw me by the statue.

"What are you doing?" he asked.

"I was thinking of calling a band Peguis but no one knows what it means, he's not as historically well-known as Geronimo or Crazy Horse."

And this person said, "You know, you've been really hard done by. You've been scalped. When an Indian becomes a brave he carries a brave belt to carry his scalps on to show that he is a brave."

And I thought to myself, "Brave Belt. There it is, that's the name."

I mentioned the name Brave Belt to Neil Young and he said, "Cool." I played him the acetate of the album when he was back in Winnipeg in January 1971 for a concert and he liked it. Next thing I knew I was on a plane heading to LA to meet with Mo Ostin at Warner Brothers and had a contract for Brave Belt on Reprise Records, Neil's label. I just thought "Reprise Records, yeah, Neil Young, *EVERYBODY KNOWS THIS IS NOWHERE.*" I had told Neil I would love to be on Reprise Records. "Call Mo Ostin," was his reply. So I did and I received a call back from Mo while I was in LA. I played him the acetate and he responded with, "You have a deal." I think they called Neil to verify who I was and if I was legitimate. That night I went down to the Dorothy Chandler Pavilion to see Neil in concert and it was a fabulous show.

I have always believed that somehow on the periphery of my life, Neil has been there. My deal with Reprise had something to do with him. I have never asked him about it because I wouldn't want to embarrass him. He did it anonymously, just like years later when he played on my songs, he didn't want any money or anything special. He simply enjoyed the spirit of the moment.

Brave Belt started out as a Chad Allan solo project that evolved into a band. We wanted to do a Chad album then a Brave Belt album kind of like a Neil Young and a Crosby, Stills, Nash, and

Young situation, a solo thing as well as a group. But it was no longer just Chad's project. Although he went along with it, I could feel him starting to withdraw a bit because he was still suffering personal problems in his relationship with his wife coupled with his reluctance to really commit himself to being a touring musician again. These were the same issues that forced him to abandon the Guess Who and they were already surfacing once again.

When the time came to launch the new group, Randy turned to his brother Gary to manage him. With no experience in that field, Gary was reluctant to undertake the role until big brother prevailed. Having gone through an unsuccessful early marriage at nineteen, Gary had followed a succession of jobs to finally land on his feet in the record business. "When Randy quit the Guess Who, I was working for Warner Brothers Records in Winnipeg," recalls Gary. "I was the king of Portage Avenue because Warners was the hottest label with the biggest selling acts and all the record stores were located on Portage. I had a car allowance, a beautiful convertible, and I would escort all the travelling acts around town to their concerts. Life was mine and it was terrific. Then Randy called me up and told me he was getting a group together with Chad Allan.

'I want you to quit your job and be our manager.'

'Randy, I know nothing about being a manager. I've got the greatest job in the world. I've only been doing it ten months and it's fabulous.'

'I need you. There is no one else I can trust, no one else I can turn to. And you're the best salesman I know.'

'I'll let you know.'

"I called him back that same afternoon. 'Okay I've quit my job. What do you want me to do? You have to tell me what to do and how to do it.' He was my brother and he needed me.

"Here I was, a young guy in my twenties flying off to New York and Los Angeles by myself to meet with all these heavy duty record company executives that Randy gave me a list of. I had only been as far as the Black Hills of South Dakota! What did I know? I took a salary because they weren't working yet. Randy was financing the whole band paying everyone a salary of $175 a week and covering all the expenses."

Selling Brave Belt would be no cakewalk for the novice manager. Randy's name recognition helped open doors, but once promoters heard the album those doors were more often closed quickly. Gigs were few and far between. "With Brave Belt, Randy wanted to be a James Taylor, soft country rock kind of artist," adds Gary. "It wasn't easy then because radio didn't play a lot of that stuff. If that was his objective then he had to leave town, move to LA, hang out at the Troubadour, and play to that crowd which was into that stuff. Otherwise up here in Canada, forget it."

When I was in LA the label executives told me I had to have four members in the band. I couldn't tour as a trio. What could I do? I immediately thought of Fred Turner as the fourth guy. I knew Fred was into music as a career with both feet, living the musicians life and still pursuing the dream out on the road with the D-Drifters. As well, we were roughly the same age — he was the same vintage as Neil Young and me. Even though we never played in the same bands together we shared the same local circuit, the same aspirations and experiences. It's like when Neil introduced me to his kids by saying, "This is my friend Randy Bachman. We played together in different bands and went to different high schools together in Winnipeg," what he means is that we experienced the same things, the community clubs and teen scene/high school years in sixties Winnipeg. Fred and I shared that common bond too. Fred seemed like a natural fit to me. The problem was Fred didn't know it yet.

I wanted a guy who could play both guitar and bass and who had a strong, distinctive voice, a guy who could really belt it out. I needed a John Fogerty voice and Fred Turner had it.

Fred was playing with the D-Drifters, which was a country, rock, and polka band, not country rock but country music and rock music. They had a fiddle player and an accordion. I had called my brother Gary to track Fred down and he called back to say, "Fred is out of town in Regina at the Golden Sunset Motel. Here's the phone number." I called him up completely out of the blue and said, "Fred, this is Randy Bachman." We hadn't talked in four or five years, not since the Guess Who took off.

"I'm in LA. I've cut an album with Chad Allan and my brother. I need a fourth player to complete the band. If you want to join our band, I'll give you a fourth of the record contract. On the next album you can contribute some songs. I'll help you write the songs, we'll go through all your songs and everything."

Fred replied, "I need to think this over. This is a shock. I'm in Regina." He hung up.

A short time later he called me back. "I'm in!" He had called his wife in Winnipeg to check it out with her. So I put Fred's name on the contract. We put his picture on the back of the album even though he didn't play on it just to show we were a band. I was literally flying by the seat of my pants.

It was Gary once again who had put the bug in his brother's ear regarding Fred Turner. "Randy knew of Fred from the Pink Plumm and other bands years earlier," he states. "I knew Fred in the D-Drifters because I went to the pubs and saw the bands. I took Randy to hear Fred once at the Marion Hotel and I asked Fred to sing *House of the Rising Sun*. Randy stood by the door, I opened it, and Fred sang that song. Fred had such power in that voice of his. To the guys in the D-Drifters though, Randy appeared standoffish because he wouldn't come into the bar and have a beer with them."

Fred Turner is one of those larger than life characters. Tall, burly, a wild mane of flaming red hair, he can appear at first glance quite intimidating, like some demon Viking biker. Yet Fred, or C.F. Turner as he was better known to fans in BTO, is in reality one of the most affable, unas-suming, self-effacing, and gentlest rock 'n' rollers you could ever hope to meet. He is the antithesis of the rock star persona.

Born in 1943 and raised in Winnipeg's West End, Fred's initiation into music came in the mid-fifties. "I had eight months of accordion but I couldn't stand it," he recalls. "Accordion just wasn't my instrument. I used to play around with Gary Shaw and his brothers' guitars so I decided I wanted to play guitar too. I took the accordion, it was actu-ally my sister's, down to Winnipeg Piano and traded it in for a Gibson guitar and amplifier. I didn't get anything near an even trade and had to carry some pretty heavy payments each month.

"Here I was, a fifteen-year-old kid, no job, and I took the guitar and amplifier home and my Dad just flipped out. As far as my father was con-cerned if I wouldn't play accordion why would I play guitar? To him it was all the same. So he wouldn't co-sign the loan. I had to cart it all back, tail between my legs. The storeowner asked me what was wrong.

'My father won't co-sign for it.'

'You know, I've got a feeling you'll pay for this,' he told me. 'When you get some money, you stop by each week and pay me. A dollar, two dollars, whatever you've got.'

"I couldn't believe it. My father went through the roof and phoned the guy up but he told my Dad he really believed I wanted to play. I would never have played if he hadn't done that. I bought lots of instru-ments from Winnipeg Piano in the years after that.

"My parents really believed it was the wrong thing to get into music. They pushed for me to finish up school and to work. Their gen-eration believed you had to have a job to look after yourself. The D-Drifters was really the first band I played in where I wasn't working on the side. That was in 1970. Before that I used to work five days a week, play six nights a week, and rehearse on Sundays. I had about nineteen jobs over the years. I laid carpet, fixed typewriters, fixed cars, drove trucks, wrote maintenance and parts manuals for Greyhound, washed cars, cleaned out bakery ovens. I couldn't stick with any of them because of band commitments but I couldn't make enough money to live just from the band. You couldn't survive without a day job."

As a journeyman guitarist and bass player, Fred served his apprenticeship in a succession of local bands, including Roy Miki and the Downbeats in the early sixties and the Pink Plumm. The latter recorded for the Transcontinental Productions' TCP label in 1967 with Fred belting out a cover version of the Righteous Brothers' *You've Lost That Lovin' Feeling*. Fred played everything from Ventures instrumentals through British Invasion pop to heavy Cream/Hendrix rock with a group called Purple Haze. For a brief spell he played alongside Garry Peterson's brother Randy in The Unnamed. At the height of the folk boom, Fred even did a stint with a hootenanny trio.

"With all those bands you always try to get ahead but you never do," muses Fred philosophically. "We were all serious but I was five or six years older than the other guys so I think I might have been a little more serious about it than they were. Winnipeg per capita has more talented people than any other city in the world. I played with a lot of talented players but you had to leave to achieve success and that is still the same. The guys who got out of Winnipeg did far better much quicker than anyone who stayed here. The thing about Winnipeg bands back in those days, too, was that we didn't realize we should have been sitting down and writing our own material. We all played jukebox stuff. Even when we recorded we were covering other songs. The only band around at that time not doing that was Chad Allan and the Reflections, the Guess Who."

By the time Randy called, Fred was beginning to write his own songs after more than a decade in cover bands. The problem he faced was finding an outlet for his original material. "One of the reasons I went with Randy was because I was writing songs and no one in the band was interested. I couldn't get any of them to play any of my songs, not that they were any good, mind you, but it was a beginning point for me. When Randy contacted me and asked if I was writing any songs I thought, 'Hey, somebody's interested in my songs!' When the chance came with Randy to give it a try with original material, I just figured I had never really done that before and maybe it was time I took a chance and took a run at it. This was my last shot."

In accepting Randy's offer, Fred was also knowingly buying into Randy's band ethos. It was hardly a problem for the more mature, focused Fred, now married with his wild days behind him. "Randy was never opposed to my having a beer once in a while," points out Fred. "He knew I wasn't much of a drinker to begin with and he knew that I didn't drink when I played and I wasn't into drugs. I've never really done that. I think Randy chose me by my character more than anything else knowing the kind of person I was. The fact that I could sing the way I did was secondary to him. If I had been a great guitar player or a great singer but crazy, I would never have had the opportunity. Compatibility was important to him."

In May of 1971, Brave Belt's debut album was released to generally lacklustre response from the music industry and ambivalence from the music-buying public. The mellow, country-tinged sound of the band was a risky venture for a respected rock 'n' roller reinventing himself in a new genre. Nothing in his previous recording career was even remotely similar to the music of Brave Belt. Those fans expecting the power chording of *American Woman* or the breezy pop jazz of *Undun* were in for quite a shock. For a man who had scaled the dizzying heights of the rock pantheon and ruled the pop charts for the last two years, the reaction was humbling.

I wanted to read in the media "Randy Bachman rises out of the ashes of the Fillmore to form the new Poco" or "Out of the prairies comes the new Buffalo Springfield." I was looking for the new phoenix rising but it didn't happen. The phoenix didn't rise, it tripped and fell.

Maybe I might have had a chance to do some of these things in the Guess Who. Burton and I had a pretty wide palate to draw on. We liked a lot of styles. We did our Buffalo Springfield song, which was *No Time*, and a Doors song, which was *Friends of Mine*. We even recorded a Gram Parsons'–style country number. *WHEATFIELD SOUL* had a diversity of styles representing our wide tastes but by the time of *AMERICAN WOMAN* we had a more consistent sound with less diversity. The next one would have likely been even more so. In creating your own sound, you lose a lot of the freedom to play any style you want. Brave Belt allowed me to indulge in all my musical fantasies, like having a fiddle player on a track and using pedal steel guitar. In my own mind it was neat, cool, I was the prairie cowboy with the LA deal. But it wasn't working.

Sure it was humbling. I had come from the biggest band in the country and now it was "'Show us what you can do." And hearing back "You aren't that good." But I didn't leave the Guess Who because I had a trunkload of fabulous hit songs and a guy sitting waiting for me to start a new band — leaving one thing to take a giant step in my career. It wasn't like that at all. I was down to nothing, ground zero. Here I was spiritually ready to go after it again feeling strong but I was starting out not at rung one on the ladder but below it. Getting up that ladder was going to be difficult. Everything was on my shoulders.

In retrospect, *BRAVE BELT* was a decent effort marred in part by a flat sound. There were glimpses of the Springfield and Poco alongside Beatles-style guitar. Randy made his vocal debut on the countrified *Waiting There for Me* and *It's Over*, delivered in a high pitch reminiscent of Neil Young's distinctive warble. Taken overall, however, *BRAVE BELT* was an inconsistent effort that failed to find a comfortable niche in the pop market. Country rock was still very much a marginal movement, especially so in Canada, and wouldn't find mainstream acceptance for two more years. Suitably chastened by the experience and always one to learn from his mistakes, Randy approached the group's sophomore album less idealistically.

In the wider scheme of things it was all really important. If the band had been really big right out of the chute, I don't know what might have happened on the next album. It was a building process and a discarding of some self-indulgences and musical whims. Being a survivor for all those years in the Guess Who, I knew that no matter how much you like something, if it isn't working you have to change it.

Despite Reprise's best efforts to promote the new group, hosting media events and a showcase in Toronto as well as releasing a single, Chad Allan's rather limp *Rock and Roll Band*, the album was a commercial stiff. Few record buyers were aware that this was ex–Guess Who member Randy Bachman's latest effort — he was obscured by the group identity — thus crossover sales were slim.

In the midst of recording the band's follow-up album, Chad Allan in a familiar refrain bowed out of the group, leaving them a trio once again. "We were in Toronto when Chad checked out on us and went home just before the band went on," recalls Gary Bachman incredulously. "He was homesick. He didn't tell anyone, he simply packed his bags and left. I couldn't believe it when Randy told me he had done this before in the Guess Who." Unhappy over the dismal response to the first album and uncomfortable with the recruiting of Fred Turner to the group, Chad found himself at odds with Randy's push to focus more on Fred's gruff voice over Chad's softer edges in a more guitar-heavy sound. The weaknesses of the debut album had not been lost on Randy. "Chad didn't like the influence I had brought to the band," cites Fred. One cannot help but see the parallel between this situation and Burton Cummings' arrival in the Guess Who camp five years earlier. For Chad, it was a bad case of déjà vu.

The week Chad Allan quit we had a booking in Thunder Bay at Lakehead University's student union cafeteria. The dance was hosted by Mike Tilka, a student at the time, who later went on to play bass in Max Webster. We were being paid $1,200 for the weekend. Out of that we covered our gas, one hotel room, and food which consisted of a bucket of chicken that lasted the two days. We arrived for the Friday night gig as a three-piece band and proceeded to do our usual Brave Belt material, the country rock stuff Chad used to sing. Fred and I switched back and forth on bass and took turns singing. Meanwhile, everyone in the place was yawning and walking out demanding their $2 back. By ten-thirty, the place was empty, so Mike came to us and announced, "You can stop playing now. No one's coming in. I'll have to let you guys go and bring in another band from Toronto. We need a rocking band." Disheartened, we packed up and headed back to our hotel for a few hours rest before the eight-hour drive home. The band had hit rock bottom by that point with the future look-ing pretty bleak.

The next morning as we were getting ready to check out, Mike pulled up to our hotel and asked, "I need a favour. Will you play tonight?"

"What? You fired us."

"That's not the favour. The favour is, will you play dance music tonight? I can't get another band out in time. I need a band that can play dance music."

"Sure, we'll do it." We had nothing to lose.

"Here are the keys to the student union building. Go work up a set."

So we took our gear over, set it up again, and I said, "Fred, what can you sing?"

"Proud Mary, Brown Sugar, The Kids Are Alright, All Right Now."

It didn't matter how good we sang them, what mattered was the beat and that kids were dancing. Robbie and I sang Santana's *Oya Coma Va* without knowing the words. We just made up phrases that sounded Spanish. Who cared in Thunder Bay? Everybody sang along. We could have been singing in Polish but they all knew that line *Oya Coma Va.* We stretched out songs with extended solos; I played David Crosby's *Long Time Gone* with umpteen guitar solos. When we ran out of songs we repeated them. "We've had a request for this song." They didn't care. They were dancing. Mike Tilka was overjoyed.

We instantly saw the difference between playing sit-down music in coffeehouses people could talk over and playing music they would jump out of their seats and dance to. Every song had that primal drum rhythm with the tom toms pounding out that four-on-the-floor Indian beat and a guitar hook that was memorable in the first four bars that gets them up on the dance floor. That became the formula to BTO. It's in every BTO song.

That weekend Brave Belt became Bachman-Turner Overdrive even though we didn't yet have the name.

Their Thunder Bay epiphany notwithstanding, Brave Belt was still a long shot for success. In April 1972, the group's second album was released with a thud. Produced once again by Randy but recorded this time in Toronto with engineer Mark Smith (who would go on to engineer every BTO album), *BRAVE BELT II* boasted an all-round harder rock sound based on guitar riffs rather than keyboards, steel guitars, and fiddles, and it featured several Fred Turner compositions sung in his best John Fogerty growl. Although Chad Allan appeared on only two tracks, the record label saw fit to release his mellow country-flavoured *Dunrobin's Gone* as the first single thus sending out the wrong signals about the album. In many respects, *Dunrobin's Gone* represented the fulfillment of Randy's country rock vision in a finely crafted arrangement. The problem was it was on the wrong album. *BRAVE BELT II* was an attempt at a straightahead rock sound with Fred Turner front and centre. The second single released from the album, Randy's *Never Comin' Home*, was far more representative of the group's new approach but received limited airplay. With sales well below the break-even point, Reprise ultimately determined to cut its losses and jettison Brave Belt.

It was a heartbreaker for me after we did *BRAVE BELT II* and were starting to build a following to be dropped from the label. Don Schmitzerlie called me in and said "I'm sorry, you're just not making the money back we are paying out so we're going to have to let you go." We had just completed sessions for a third album so that was a bitter blow.

. I don't think Reprise ever really got behind the band in terms of promotion. It was one of those situations where they sign ten acts and the one that makes it pays for the other nine. And we weren't that one. My name from the Guess Who helped generate some airplay but not enough to get any momentum going. There wasn't a big push behind us. But to be fair, we were a pale copy of the Buffalo Springfield and Poco. We didn't have the goods. We weren't Neil Young, Stephen Stills, and Richie Furay. And it wasn't truly me; it was only one facet of me that I had a longing to do. We became more honest once I shed that mantle of "country rock wannabe" and we transformed into Bachman-Turner Overdrive.

But maybe I needed to do those two Brave Belt albums to admit to myself what I did best and who I really was. I think going through that struggle was important, that the three of us had to hit bottom and claw our way up. If we had been a success right away we probably would have disintegrated much sooner. You need those strikeouts sometimes to become a better hitter. I've had a few strikeouts in my career that are like cult albums to the real fans, things like *AXE, BRAVE BELT, AND SURVIVOR*, but I needed to have them to get to the next thing. You celebrate your strikeouts along with your home runs. Other people would have given up after Brave Belt. But if I didn't go up to bat and strike out I wouldn't have had that determination to keep going back to the plate and swinging with all my might, energy, and hope to knock that ball clear out of the park. That's what it was like with Brave Belt and BTO, more and more desperate to get that home run. As a result, it made us cast aside some of the frivolities and distractions of the music business and get down to what we did best.

Before any success could be realized, however, several pieces of the puzzle were still not yet in place. On *BRAVE BELT II*, Randy's brother Tim had shared a songwriting credit with Fred Turner. Recognizing the need for another guitar with the band's heavier direction, and to give the group more of a visual appeal onstage to counterbalance two large men, Tim Bachman was approached to join Brave Belt shortly after the album's release.

"It was Gary's idea to have me in the band," acknowledges Tim. "They needed a fourth person for the live show. In the studio, Randy could play anything but live, the trio just wasn't working." For Tim, the offer was the opportunity of a lifetime. "Brave Belt was rehearsing in Randy's basement one day and Randy called me to come down to jam with them. I was surprised but I went down and we played for about half an hour improvising stuff on the spot. Then Randy said, 'Here's something I was thinking about' and we played this new thing he had come up with. Then Fred did the same and we worked out what he had. They turned to me and asked, 'What have you got?' So I showed them a couple of ideas I had. After that Randy said, 'We need to talk about something. Would you go upstairs?' I still didn't know what was going on but I went upstairs anyway. Twenty minutes later they summoned me to come down and they announced, 'We know you're going to college studying business administration and you've got a girlfriend that you're serious about, but we'd like to invite you to join the band. It's a serious decision so we'll give you two weeks to think about it.'

"I was stunned. I walked upstairs and thought for a couple of minutes and realized this was something I had been dreaming of for years, playing with Randy, and immediately ran downstairs and told them, 'I don't need two weeks, I'm in.'

"Our relationship has always been different," muses Tim, on growing up under Randy's shadow. "From the time I was born, all Randy heard was how much I looked like him. Everything was 'Just like Randy when he was a baby' or 'Just like Randy when he was a toddler.' I was always told how much I was like Randy. Randy, Gary, and I look like our Mom. Only Robbie looks like Dad. Randy and I were also alike in another respect. He can be a very thoughtful, soft-spoken individual. I'm often accused by my family of being the same. We both think about things and have a tendency during a conversation to get quiet for a period of time when all we are doing is simply digesting what is being said or going on around us and formulating an intelligent response, rather than just reacting. People often mistake that in Randy for arrogance.

"The band wasn't doing that well but I had faith in Randy. He had done it once and I believed he could do it again. And I heard Fred's voice and thought he had a marvellous style for hard rock, not the country rock they had been doing. That just wasn't happening. I wanted the band to be a combination of Cream, Mountain, Creedence Clearwater, with a dash of Hendrix. Randy had shied away from rock because he wanted to distance himself from the Guess Who. But the Guess Who wasn't Mountain or Cream. And with Fred's voice there were no worries about being compared to Burton Cummings. So I think my joining helped nudge them towards a rockier sound."

Still, the changeover would be slow in coming, with promoters retaining a particular image of Brave Belt in their minds that was not easy to shake. Tim recalls a memorable example of Brave Belt's typecasting. "We were booked into the Saddledome in Calgary for a country music cavalcade with Ferlin Husky and Tommy Hunter. It was a two-day show, sold out. The promoter had heard the first Brave Belt album and hired us on the basis of it being a country rock outfit. We were to be the closing act. This was one of my first times on a huge arena stage. I was backstage hanging around and there was Tommy Hunter. We all grew up watching *The Tommy Hunter Show* on TV so I was thrilled to see him in person. We went on last and did our set and at the end there was dead silence. The lights had been off so we couldn't see the crowd but as we finished they turned them on and the place was empty. Everyone had walked out on us. There was a guy pushing a broom. It was so humiliating.

"The next day the newspaper had paragraph after paragraph about all the other acts, glowing about each one. For us, however, we had two lines at the bottom of the review that said, 'At the end of the show, four Vikings from Winnipeg came out and blew everybody's face off.' We woke up that morning to discover we had been fired. We hadn't been paid for the first night and the promoter informed us that he wasn't going to pay us at all. We couldn't check out of our hotel because we had no money. We were so dejected. Later that day we ran into Tommy Hunter in the hotel lobby. I remember looking up at him because he's so tall. He told us what had been done to us was wrong.

'I've organized the other acts and we're holding a strike unless you guys get paid in full for both nights,' he told us. 'It's not your fault the promoter made a mistake. We may not be into your stuff but we know you're good.'

"In the end, we got paid."

Travel for Brave Belt, to be sure, offered few luxuries. It was a spartan lifestyle borne of the economics of poverty, a far cry from first-class air travel and luxury suites just two years before. "I remember driving out to Ridgetown, Ontario, 1,500 km, playing and driving right back because we couldn't afford to stay over," chuckles Fred. "We had no money. Everything we made we would bring home to pay bills. We would drive to Vancouver to play weekends, two or three nights, and drive back to Winnipeg. It was nuts." When you are only pulling in $600 a night, a hotel room can make or break your trip.

When I was trying to sell the third Brave Belt album to record labels, there was this void in our lives where we couldn't get many gigs. Our prospects were looking pretty lean. We were labelled country rock so we ended up on some shows with the likes of Ian Tyson and Tommy Hunter where I actually shared the stage with my childhood violin idol, King Ganam. These were mostly out west — Calgary, Edmonton, Regina. In-between these weekend gigs there was no point in the band going back to Winnipeg only to head out west on Friday, so they would stay behind as I flew out to Toronto, New York, or LA hustling record labels with the tapes.

The other guys couldn't afford to stay in hotels during the week so they tented. My Dad had a tent we used to take on camping trips as kids, so Robbie and I knew how to camp. The band would drive to Calgary, look for a suitable site to pitch the tent, do the gig, and return to the tent for the night making sure no one was following us to discover our impoverished existence. We had a Coleman stove and we would bring a loaf of peanut butter and jelly sandwiches from home. Or we would cook up some soup. I remember coming back from a trip to Los Angeles trying to sell *BRAVE BELT III* to find the tent covered in frost and snow and inside Robbie and Fred were huddled together trying to keep warm.

In our Econoline van, which was like a sieve on the highway with all these holes and cracks where the wind whistled in, the heater and defroster couldn't keep the windows clear. When it was forty below outside, it was the same temperature inside. So we had a big leather glove-like cover for the front of the van to keep the draft out and some of the heat from the engine in. My father-in-law, Bob Stevenson, would make us large sterno cans from Empress Jam pails. They had a roll of toilet paper soaked in alcohol with a wick in the middle and we would put two of them on our dash to keep the windows clear and a couple on the floor to keep our feet from freezing. We would travel back and forth across western Canada like this in winter, sometimes all the way to Vancouver and back with these burning cans of alcohol all over the van. Ah, the glamourous life of a rock star!

Sure, I could have flown to gigs. I had the money from my Guess Who royalties still coming in. But I didn't, on purpose. I wanted us to be a band. I wanted that bonding that comes with sharing the same goals and experiences. I didn't want to be the

superstar. I went down into the trenches with the other guys.
We went through a baptism of fire together so when the success
came we were already close. I called it Brave Belt boot camp
because it prepared us later for the rigours of BTO.

Once, we were wending our way through the Rockies in
winter when we heard a rumbling outside the car, looked up, and
saw the side of a mountain sliding down toward us. There was no
place to go, no side of the road only a steep drop off. Luckily, the
avalanche stopped just in front of and to the rear of our line of
vehicles, trapping us between these enormous mounds of snow.
The highway was a whiteout on both sides as we sat there shaking,
thanking God, and wondering what to do. Fortunately we had our
peanut butter sandwiches and our sterno cans. A few minutes later,
a helicopter flew low overhead and a voice from a bullhorn shouted, "If you're okay, honk once. If you have any injuries honk twice."

Car one: honk.

Car two: honk. And so on.

"Keep your car running at all times and open your windows to
let fresh air in. Anyone need food? Honk three times."

Honk, honk, honk.

The helicopter returned a half-hour later and dropped buckets
of Kentucky Fried Chicken into the snow as someone from each
vehicle scrambled out to retrieve them. In the morning, snow-
ploughs came and cleared the highway behind us so we were all
able to go back to the nearest town and get a room at the motel
until the highway was completely clear. They then let us
proceed to Vancouver.

On another occasion, we put the van into the ditch in winter
on the way to Grande Prairie, Alberta, north of Edmonton when
Robbie dropped a sandwich he was handing to Fred as he drove.
Fred leaned over to pick it up while still holding the steering
wheel and lost control of the vehicle. The front wheel left the
road and there was no shoulder. He tried to correct the wheel

doing seventy miles an hour as the whole van careened into the ditch and flipped over onto the roof. We suddenly turned from a van into a giant sled, ploughing through the ditch and sinking further and further with the weight of all our Garnet amplifiers. Robbie was in the back on a foam mattress we would lay over a speaker cabinet. So now that we were upside down, the cabinet was on top of him with a three-inch slab of foam keeping him from being crushed.

Eventually, the van came to a halt and Fred and I found ourselves hanging upside down, the seat belts keeping us from falling. Hot oil was spilling from the engine through the vents onto us. In a panic, I tried rolling down the window but it wouldn't budge.

"We're upside down," shouted Fred. "Roll it the other way."

So I did and as I stretched my arm out I found myself up to my shoulder in deep snow. The wheels were still spinning and smoke was coming from the engine.

"We gotta get out."

We managed to free Robbie and crawl out the windows, but the snow in the ditch was so thick that we sank farther with each step. I lay down my coyote fur coat and we leapfrogged like frogs on a lily pad to the highway and headed for the nearest farmhouse to phone for help.

We had to rent cars to get to the gig and ended up driving them back to Winnipeg. The whole round trip cost us a fortune. We lost maybe $1,400. The battered van was shipped back by train where a friend of Fred's with a body shop pounded out the dents. Our former white van now had brown spots where it had been primered so we nicknamed it Scout after Tonto's horse. It became our little in-joke. "I'll pick you up in Scout." When we eventually retired Scout, Robbie put it on his property just to look at it. We were so attached to that van and it carried so many memories.

The trip to Grande Prairie was memorable not merely for the highway accident. It was there that Randy met the next piece necessary to complete the puzzle. As a successful booking agent working out of Vancouver, Bruce Allen carried a lot of clout on the West Coast. By 1972, Randy had come to the realization that Brave Belt was a non-entity in Winnipeg due in large measure to the ominous shadow of the Guess Who that continued to hang over them. Bruce Allen might be able to open doors for the group on the coast, Randy thought, and keep them alive while he continued to hustle the tapes for *BRAVE BELT III*.

Despite our near-death highway experience, we managed to make it to the gig in Grande Prairie. It was an important date because Bruce Allen had booked it for us sight unseen, solely on the basis of my name and reputation with the Guess Who, and he was flying in from Vancouver to check us out. Our gear had survived the accident because it had been so tightly packed that it barely shifted a few inches, so we set up, plugged in, and the crowd loved us. In spite of the limited airplay we had for *Dunrobin's Gone*, we weren't a country rock act any more. The stuff we had put together for that last-ditch effort to save the band in Thunder Bay had transformed us. We were no longer "Brave Belt, country rock group." We opened up with *All Right Now* and into *Brown Sugar*. We even took some of the tunes from the Brave Belt album and played them heavier. We were now a rock 'n' roll dance band.

We were dying in Winnipeg, there was no doubting it. No one would book us. I was like the black sheep that no one wanted. We took a weekend ride to Toronto where we were booked in December and froze. A couple of weeks later we took a trip to Vancouver and it was like seventy and sunny in the middle of winter. As we crossed the Rockies and left all the snow behind, there in front of us it was all green. We thought that was incredible. I called Bruce Allen and asked, "Can you book us for a couple of months?"

"Yeah, I can keep you going and guarantee you $1,200 a week, $800 at a club and $400 every Sunday at the Breakers."

So we decided to make the move to Vancouver.

"We were going bankrupt here in Winnipeg," acknowledges Fred on the group's decision to relocate to Vancouver in the summer of 1972. "It got to the point where we had to decide to either give it up and take day jobs, which Randy wanted nothing to do with, or we could move. Toronto didn't do anything for us. Randy said, 'Let's move west' so the band decided that's where we were going to go. But I didn't. I was very comfortable in my situation in Winnipeg and wasn't going to go. We were just about to have our first child. I wasn't keen on taking that gamble and going to a place where I didn't know anyone, but my wife talked me into it. She said to me, 'You've got to take a chance.' It meant packing up everything and taking a big risk, but she pushed me to it. Otherwise, I probably wouldn't have gone."

On a personal level, it was a difficult decision to leave Winnipeg. It was my home; my parents and relatives were here. But professionally, I had tried everything to make a go of it and met only indifference at best, hostility at worst. People still ostracized me. Only a few friends remained so; others would avoid me. I wasn't one of the boys any more. For my mother, the move was hard because it meant bidding goodbye to three of her four sons and two of her grandchildren.

Gary couldn't go because of his wife's job. He had married a stewardess named Carol who was based in Winnipeg and flew out from there for Air Canada. She had a good job. At the time, I resented Gary's not coming with us because he was leaving me alone. He had been handling our business since quitting his job at my urging to work for us. I felt he had abandoned me. "How dare he defy his older brother!" I was the captain and he was the first mate and here I was in Vancouver without that right-hand man.

"I know Randy expected me to follow him out to Vancouver," admits Gary. "To him there was no choice. He needed me so I had to go. I had just gotten married for the second time, my wife had a good job, and we had just bought a house so I said to her that I was staying here and told Randy that. I had something to stay for and the others didn't. I know I let him down and there were some hurt feelings from him. He was mad at me for a long time because, in his eyes, I let him down. My obligation was supposed to be to him not my new wife and my life here. But I don't have any regrets.

"It's taken Randy a long time to come to accept the decision I made because after the move, he basically said to me 'Okay, screw you. I'm forming a new company.' The company I held shares in with him as Brave Belt was nothing anymore after he left Winnipeg and there was now a new one that got all the money. Not a penny changed hands. And for eleven or twelve years I heard nothing about our company and simply assumed it no longer existed. Then I received a letter from a lawyer in Vancouver asking me to sign off on the company. 'My brother can't even call me and ask me to do this? Forget it.' Years later, I told Randy that story. He said he didn't know anything about it and had he known he would have called me directly. Randy may never admit this, but when he needed me I was there for him. I quit my job for him.

"In many respects, Randy did to me what Burton and the others did to him. 'You won't stick with me? I don't need you.' It was kind of revenge. He could shut you out and give you the silent treatment. But I grew up with him, I knew him no other way, so it didn't bother me."

Bruce Allen filled the managerial void soon enough. "I still believed at the time that Randy Bachman had some hits left in him," stresses Bruce, enthusiastically recalling his first encounter with the ex-Guess Who star. "Randy had called me because he wanted to work in British Columbia and because I had no ties to the Guess Who. I had never booked the Guess Who, never made a nickel off them, so I had no allegiance to them. They were booked by one of my competitors. There was a bit of a triumvirate of agencies that all worked the Guess Who dates across Canada. I think Don Hunter and the band had made it pretty clear that they wanted to make Randy's life a little bit miserable when it came to live work. I figured I could make some money off of Randy no matter what configuration he was in if I brought him into Vancouver and worked him in the bars because I had control of that scene in those days. His name could draw people. In doing so, I took some of the financial pressure off his shoulders because when they were not working or making any money, Randy was keeping the band afloat himself by covering the expenses and paying salaries out of his own pocket. I took some of that weight off of him because they could now live off their gigs. I had enough control out here that I could work them steady."

In Bruce Allen, Randy found the kind of person who would dedicate himself to Randy's cause. Here was a kindred spirit who shared Randy's vision, but more than that, was willing to go to the mats for his client. While some argue that Bruce, much like Don Hunter, merely hitched himself to a train that was about to leave the station, in fact that train, Brave Belt/Bachman-Turner Overdrive, was barely on the rails when Bruce Allen came aboard. His often abrasive chutzpah and brash bravado were just what Randy needed. As BTO began their meteoric rise to the top, Bruce Allen was there every step of the way — at every gig, running the lights, hassling with the promoters, attending all the meetings, rooming with Randy. Randy found his Brian Epstein and Colonel Parker all rolled into one; in return, Bruce received his initiation into the big-time world of the music business and learned valuable lessons he later applied in charting the careers of Loverboy and Bryan Adams. It was a match if not made in heaven then certainly somewhere close by. "There was no question that in that relationship, Bruce Allen was the neophyte," offers journalist Larry LeBlanc. "Randy had all the connections with people like Charlie Fach. Bruce was a local booking agent who didn't have the record company contacts and no dealings with anybody in the States. He grabbed onto Randy's coattails."

"There is no doubt that I aligned myself with Randy," counters Bruce, "but it was mutually beneficial. Those were the cowboy days of rock 'n' roll. Now it's a lot more corporate, but back then you needed to be a maverick. I had a lot of power because of my West Coast dominance. Randy wanted someone to kick ass and I could do that for him.

"I think Randy and I developed a rapport because I was straight with him and worked with him when a lot of people wouldn't touch him," continues Bruce. "Randy knows that the music business is a gamble. I think he has always felt that way so I didn't find any problems with him having been at the top with the Guess Who and now fronting Brave Belt who weren't that big a deal at the time. He looks at some things in a very pragmatic fashion. I never saw him get down about Brave Belt. I think he put out the two albums, gave it a shot and when it didn't work out he just figured, 'Okay, we'll try something else.' I still see that about him. He never sits back and moans over his failures. He learns from them and moves on."

Clearly, the strength of the band from Bruce's perspective was in the two front men, Randy and Fred. The other two Bachmans, in his opinion, were superfluous. "Robbie was still a teenager but he was put in the band because I think Randy believed it would at least eliminate an argument. He didn't need a hotshot in the band who might challenge him and his direction. Randy very much wanted to make it his show. I think Randy's thoughts were along the lines of 'As my kid brother he'll do what I tell him.' Randy wanted control of the band. I think bringing Robbie in was just easier for him."

Dropped by Reprise and with no other labels expressing interest, Randy had financed sessions for *BRAVE BELT III* in Toronto based around the stronger, hard rock sound the group was now favouring. After more than two years, Brave Belt seemed a doomed effort, a ship listing and taking on water. Randy had invested close to $100,000 of his own money — his Guess Who royalties and nest egg — into keeping the band afloat, all in vain. He had a stack of rejection letters from the *BRAVE BELT III* tapes, twenty-six in all. Was there any point in continuing to throw money at a losing cause? Could Randy admit to himself that Brave Belt was a failure?

"We would travel somewhere and play a gig and Randy would fly off to LA or New York for a few days trying to sell the album," recalls Tim. "We would be waiting in our tent keeping ourselves going by saying, 'When Randy gets back we'll be riding in limos and staying in fancy hotels.' That sustained us. But he would come back and tell us it wasn't happening. It came down to the point where we were in Toronto in early 1973 to tape an appearance on *ROQ*, a Canadian television rock show like *Midnight Special*. Afterwards we went back to our hotel and just said to one another, 'I guess this is it.' We were in debt, Randy couldn't float the band any longer, and the well had run dry. We cried, hugged one another, and went back to our rooms to phone our parents, wives, or girlfriends to tell them we would be returning home to sell shoes or whatever. The next day the phone rang in Randy's hotel room. It was Charlie Fach at Mercury Records."

I had met Charlie Fach earlier in New York and he said to me, "I think you're a great songwriter. If you ever do anything on your own, send it to me." So I sent him the two 7-inch reels of *BRAVE BELT III* after we had been dropped by Reprise. I received a form letter back from him saying that he passed on it claiming the music wasn't right for the label at that time. It was very disheartening. So I put it in the file with all my other refusals from labels like Elektra and A&M. I would always read *Billboard* magazine to see who got new jobs at labels and resubmit tapes to the new guys. When you sign on at a label you are always looking for new talent that you can bring in rather than inheriting those acts of your predecessor. I remember saying to the band, "We've got twenty-six refusals. I've sent out four more tape packages. If it doesn't happen I have to stop paying everyone a salary. I've hit $97,000 in expenses financing this band, after this week it'll be $100,000 and I need that money to pay my mortgage and buy food for my family. This Friday is the last pay cheque."

It looked like the end of the band. After that meeting with the guys, my phone rang the next morning and it was Charlie Fach calling from Chicago. I could hear *Gimme Your Money Please* in the background, which was side one, cut one. He was listening to the first tape and had just started the first song.

"Hi Randy, this is Charlie Fach, do you remember me? We met in New York?"

"Yeah, sure."

"Does the whole album sound like this?"

"Yeah, it's a whole album of really rockin' songs."

"I really like it and I'd like to take it to a big A&R meeting we're having in LA this coming Saturday."

So I said, "Just a minute" and I went to my files and pulled out the letter and said, "You passed on this on January 22."

And Charlie replied, "No I didn't, I was at the MIDEM conference in France. Somebody else was running my office and he must have passed on it. I saw your name on it and I'm playing it right now."

Talk about serendipity, fate, or karma!

"What have you put into this album?"

"$97,000."

"I can't pay you that. But I'll make you a two album deal and give you $50,000 per album, that way you'll get your money back. I'll call you on Saturday."

I called the other guys in the band and babbled, "You won't believe this…"

Then on Saturday about two in the afternoon my phone rang. It was Charlie and I could hear *Don't Get Yourself in Trouble* playing in the background so I knew they were deep into the album.

"Everyone loves the album. We've lost Uriah Heep and Rod Stewart and we need a rock band. We're gonna give you guys a shot. But we need two new songs for the album. Go in and record two more tracks." That was it.

One of the truly nicer guys in a notoriously tough business, Charlie Fach was a veteran of several labels including RCA before landing at Mercury in the late sixties. Well respected in the industry, he was looking to establish a footing for Mercury in the white rock market. The label had been a major player on the black music scene with Kool and the Gang and the Ohio Players but needed a white rock presence. "I was working in New York as head of A&R for Mercury even though the label remained based in Chicago," recounts Charlie. "Randy had been recording at RCA's studio in Chicago and someone had passed his number to me. He had left the Guess Who by then. We eventually got together a few weeks later in New York when he was looking to make a deal for a female singer he was trying to do something with. I passed on her but Randy and I went out to dinner and hit it off. He had Brave Belt at the time on Warner Brothers. A couple of months later Randy called me out of the blue and told me Reprise had rejected Brave Belt's third album and would I listen to it. I told him to send it to me and I would tell him what I thought of it. In the meantime, I went off to Europe on business and in my place filling in was a fellow from *Rolling Stone* magazine who I asked to listen to whatever came in and set aside anything that sounded interesting. When I returned a few weeks later, I found Randy's tape box. It had missed being chucked into the garbage can. I recognized his name and listened to it. When I called Randy about it he said, 'Tell me what you didn't like about my album.'

'Randy, I never heard the thing. I've been in Europe and Paul Nelson's been looking after things for me.'

'Yeah, I got a letter from Paul. He rejected it.'

"The album really sounded great to me so I told him 'Randy, forget about the country rock thing. Go remix it and add some heavier guitars.' And that became the first Bachman-Turner Overdrive album, which had been rejected by Warner Brothers. After he redid it, I sent it to label president Irwin Steinberg and he called me back two days later; he had the promotion manager with him, and Irwin says 'Christ, sign this group. This is sensational.' When you can get the salespeople to say an album is great, that's really something. That's how it got started.

"The universal appeal of their music was that it was understandable rock 'n' roll," emphasizes Charlie. "You could hear it one time and it stuck with you. It was workingman's rock 'n' roll. The guy who rejected them, Paul Nelson, signed the New York Dolls around the same time and they were awful. The Dolls got all the press and reviews but didn't sell a damn thing; meanwhile, BTO never got those kinds of reviews but they sold a truckload of records. They worked hard for it, though."

Randy had found the formula for success: a stripped down, no frills, meat and potatoes approach to basic rock 'n' roll — thumping drums, riffy hook-laden guitars, growly vocals, and a chorus everyone could sing along to. Coupled with the music was a work ethic developed from his Brave Belt experience to do whatever it took to make the band a success. "I remember walking my dog around my neighbourhood one day around the time of the second BTO album," reflects Charlie Fach, "and as I passed a garage there were kids in there, a garage band, fourteen, fifteen years old, and they were playing BTO songs. It was music for everyone, simple, understandable rock 'n' roll."

Timing is everything. In the early seventies, the advent of glam rock with its androgynous look and the faceless, manufactured sound of disco had left a large constituency of rock music fans, mostly teenage boys who simply wanted to boogie, disenfranchised. It was to this base that BTO and their contemporaries like ZZ Top and the Doobie Brothers appealed, filling that hard rock void. Their music was the antidote to disco: a hard thumping, pile-driving, no-holds-barred "guys rock."

The final piece to the puzzle was a name change. With a new approach and sound, Brave Belt no longer fit the group's image. Hardly polite country rockers, the group was a powerhouse of thundering rock 'n' roll. Despite two years under that moniker, Brave Belt had to go. "It was real energetic rock 'n' roll," confirms Fred Turner. "But maybe it was the name people didn't like. Charlie Fach at Mercury signed us but told us we couldn't be called Brave Belt because he thought it was an awful name."

Mercury wanted me to use my name Bachman because it had rings of success with the Guess Who. Because the name Brave Belt was so anonymous nobody knew who it was. I told Charlie, "Well, there's three Bachmans and a Turner in this band. We'll just call ourselves Bachman-Turner." But that was the era of Brewer and Shipley or Seals and Crofts and everywhere we went people thought we were two guys with acoustic guitars. It was too folksy sounding. We would arrive and blow the windows out of these little coffeehouses that we were being booked into.

Late one night in Windsor we stopped at a truck stop after a gig and right at the cash register we saw a trucker's magazine called *Overdrive*. I showed it to Fred Turner. We opened it up and there was a centrefold and it was of a guy's truck. I thought this was very cool. I called the record label the next day and said, "How about Bachman-Turner Overdrive?" It was a powerful, driven name that fit the music we were now writing and playing. At that point, no one had used the word *overdrive* to talk about music. It had only been used with cars.

We went to Mushroom studios in Vancouver to record two new tracks and work on the concept and artwork for the band logo. By then, we already had been playing around with the name Bachman-Turner Overdrive. Next to Mushroom studios, which was on a hill around False Creek, was a gas station all greasy with an oil change pit. Behind it was a big empty field. Hans Sipma was our photographer and was taking the band shot with grass behind us, rather than houses and buildings. He kept saying, "Move over a little bit more" and as he told me to back up, I tripped and fell over backwards on something that was all grown over with grass.

"What is this thing?" Fred and I struggled to pull it out of the ground, lifted it up and it was an eight-foot wooden overdrive gear. It had been the mold for a huge metal gear used in the sawmills but looked like a giant zigzaggy overdrive gear.

"Wow, we just picked Overdrive for the band name."

It was like a Chariot of the Gods thing. So we hauled this big gear up and I asked my brother Robbie to design something like it out of tin foil. We took an eagle image from a Titano accordion that Chad Allan used to play. The Titano logo featured an eagle with the T for Titano in its claws along with a lightning bolt. That became the T, Robbie put the B and the O with it and that was our logo. I still have it, black construction paper and aluminum foil. We took it to Mercury Records and they looked at it and said, "This is really cool but what's with this chicken?" Robbie couldn't draw an eagle very well so we dropped the eagle and instead added a little maple leaf. The picture of the wooden gear went on the back of our first album. Mercury thought it was fabulous. Everything just fell into place.

Our image wasn't calculated. It was almost an evolution from living in Winnipeg. We dressed like Neil Young: farmers' flannel or denim shirts, jeans with patches, lumberjack boots. The difference, however, was that Neil was a frail waif with a twenty-eight-inch waist and we were size thirty-eight, soon to become forty-eight. He resembled a young tree while we were mighty oaks. I loved that image on Neil, but Fred and I were much bigger boys. We looked like lumberjacks in fur, fringe, flannel, and long beards. We were the Radisson and Groseilliers of rock, two hearty voyageurs who lived in the woods and never shaved. We were perceived by some as the lumberjack rockers from Canada who'll blow the windshield out of your car. The media picked up on that rustic image and really ran with it.

Fred had what we called the Harley-Davidson voice, like Creedence Clearwater's John Fogerty only bigger, refrigerator size.

He was a big guy like myself and had this flaming orange hair and beard, a stunning visage. People thought we were Canadian loggers from the wilds of northern Canada whose music was for knocking down trees. The legend that surrounded the band in the early days, and I remember actually reading this about us in a magazine, was that we had found guitars abandoned in an old car out in the forest. During the time of glam rock and platform boots we weren't wimps or pretty boys. We looked like mountain men in furs and skins. On some of those early albums Fred looks like Jim Fink, King of the River, right out of Davy Crockett. He even had a coonskin hat and had these big, fringed jackets with beads. I had on leather and moose hide. We were wild men from the northern wilds of Canada.

"These guys didn't eat peanut butter sandwiches, they eat a loaf of peanut butter sandwiches. They eat an apple pie not a piece of apple pie. They don't live in houses, they sleep outdoors in the snow."

Most Americans could relate to this image. We heard all this stuff and it was hilarious, but it spread the name around and created a mystique. The Guess Who never had a mystique about them. True to form, we would come out on stage and the music was full tilt stomping with Fred screaming at the top of his lungs over sledgehammer guitars and drums that sounded like falling trees. So our image matched the sound coming out on the records. We never did a soft ballad in the whole time of BTO. That would be too wimpy for us. We were a guy's band, like a "Tim Allen Tool Time" guys band. Guys loved BTO. I remember on our whole tour of the UK we didn't see one woman at the shows. We appealed to the ordinary Joe kind of guy. At last they could have a band of their own without anyone thinking they were gay. We were heavy rock not heavy metal. We preceded the heavy metal bands in their tights.

When it came time to meet with the head honchos at Mercury to negotiate the terms of their recording contract, Randy was well versed in how to handle such meetings but felt the label expected the group to have a manager. That was de rigeur in the music world; managers represented artists, not artists themselves. With Gary out of the picture and Bruce Allen serving as the group's agent, Randy turned to Bruce. "When Randy asked me to manage the band, I initially wasn't going to do it," maintains Bruce. "I was making a good living in Vancouver. I told him 'Randy, I really don't know how to manage you. You know more about the business than I do.' He responded, 'Don't worry about it. I need someone to say "They want… They need… They have to have…" instead of "I, I, I." So let's make a deal.' We shook hands and that was it. We never had a signed contract."

When I first signed with Mercury and they said, "Come and bring your manager," I didn't have one but I said I did. I wasn't going to say no and jeopardize the deal. I had been serving as our manager but if they wanted me to have a manager, I'd have one.

"Sure, I'll bring him," once again flying by the seat of my pants.

"Great. Bring him to Chicago, we need to meet him."

I then went to Bruce Allen who was working as our agent at the time and asked him to come along as our manager, enticing him with "I'll pay your way to Chicago, buy you a nice rib dinner and we'll see a Cubs game." So Bruce agreed to act as our manager.

We arrived in Irwin Steinberg's office and laid out our demands. I had a list with me.

"We want an announcement ad in *Billboard* magazine after we sign, a billboard on Sunset Strip, posters in the record stores…"

Irwin interrupted me. "You'll get all these things when we feel you deserve them, when you've earned them. Will you earn them? Will you work? Will you get out there and build a following wherever you need to go?"

"Yes, we will."

"When you deserve a poster in the stores and we know they are going to recognize your faces, then you'll get your posters.

There is no sense doing a poster now because no one knows who you are yet and they'll just get thrown in the garbage. When we take full-page ads for you it'll be when people know who you are and know your name. What good is an ad or a t-shirt when no one knows who you are yet? Go out there and work and we'll do our end to get you on the radio. Then the name will mean something."

That was the kind of talk I wanted to hear.

In the end, Mercury came through with everything we had wanted but at the right times — ads, posters, t-shirts. Whenever I thought we should have a full-page ad in *Billboard*, we would get it. Then one day we checked into the Hyatt Regency Hotel on Sunset Strip, looked out the window and across the street — there was our billboard. We got our wish list. They promised, we worked, and they delivered. That kind of relationship is rare in this business. We never had that kind of relationship with RCA in the Guess Who.

"Randy and I were always together," recalls Bruce on the symbiotic relationship the two developed in the early days. "We were a team; we could finish each other's sentences. I believed in Randy Bachman. He had been around and had experience. Once, when I was worried about screwing up or making a mistake, he said to me 'Bruce, don't worry about making a mistake. I've made every mistake there is and I know how to fix them all.' I don't think the other guys in the band ever gave Randy credit for the experience he had. I really valued his know-how." Once again Randy had succeeded in reinventing himself: from pop rocker to country rocker to hard rocker. Signed directly to an American label, BTO set its sights firmly on the more lucrative US market after two years of traipsing back and forth across Canada with nothing to show in return. As a result, BTO's success would be earned in the US; Canada would come onboard after the fact. That success would be due in large part to Randy. "Bachman-Turner Overdrive was Randy Bachman," asserts Charlie Fach. "He wrote the songs, sang the hits, produced the records, and made the money. It was all Randy."

Released in May 1973, *BACHMAN-TURNER OVERDRIVE I* was well received by critics and the public alike and began a slow climb regionally. Wherever the record broke, the band was there. "We were really good at getting AM radio play," admits Charlie Fach, "because the stations were looking for something like BTO. It really fit into AM radio at the time and was easy to get played. The timing was perfect." Various cuts off the album generated airplay including Fred's jazzy *Blue Collar,* *Hold Back the Water*, and *Gimme Your Money Please*. But it was the album itself that propelled sales, unlike in the Guess Who where their singles success moved albums. Within three months, Mercury had recouped its investment and with the album still climbing on the charts without benefit of a hit single, the label clamoured for a second album from the group. The contract had given them eighteen months between releases but here they were six months after the first one gearing up for another BTO album.

"We got a call from a radio station in St. Louis that was putting on a benefit," recalls Fred on a pivotal event in the group's rise. "They wanted a band to headline that nobody had heard of because the head-line acts they had booked had big offers and weren't coming in. We had the BTO I album out by then so they at least had something to play and make it look like we were big. So we said 'Sure, we'll come and play it for nothing.' They started playing us every hour, every cut off the album across six states, 150,000 watts. Within two weeks it was like the Beatles were coming. The record company called and said 'What the hell's happening? We shipped ten thousand albums to St. Louis in one week! Ten thousand units?!' We got there and it was an outdoor drive-in theatre, fifteen to twenty thousand people and we were the headliners. The region had been saturated with our album, all six states. They didn't know we were Canadian, they just knew the songs. It was incredible. We had done some big outdoor gigs, but we were so far down the bill nobody was there by the time we went on. In St. Louis, we were the headliners."

"The master plan for breaking BTO was Randy's plan and it was right

255

and hasn't changed to this day," acknowledges Bruce Allen. "You get out there, you get seen, you get records on the radio, and wherever the record is getting played you get in there and work. Simple. In BTO we worked and worked and worked. We travelled constantly, cutting our costs down so we could keep working. We didn't carry a lot of stuff. We had one guy in a van and the rest of us in a car and away we went. The itinerary didn't make any sense. It could be Seattle on Saturday and Wednesday in Colorado, wherever the record was happening we got there. We couldn't get a major booking agency to book us, they all turned us down, so we had a little booking agent, Paul Smith, who booked us. In those days it was micro management, a scaled-down affair: one manager, me, with one act, BTO; one agent and one crewmember. That was it. And everyone worked a hundred and ten percent to push BTO. Mercury Records really believed in the band. Everyone was working towards one goal and that's pretty rare in this business."

I said to Lorayne that I really wanted to make it. And in those days that meant being out on the road constantly. There was no MTV, Much Music, or rock videos, no easy road, no video that instantly gets you seen by four million people. You had to get out there and play the clubs and work your way up to bigger shows. You had to meet all the deejays to get your record played. There was no other formula for success but work.

In the early months we would play anywhere. We would do drive-in theatres with a stage in front of the screen on a Saturday afternoon. People would sit out on their car hoods like it was a picnic. We did those kinds of gigs with Styx, Peter Frampton, anyone who was trying to get started in the early seventies. We played everywhere — St. Louis today, Boston tomorrow, Buffalo one night, Portland, Oregon two nights later — wherever there was airplay. We did that until Bruce and I maxed out our American Express cards to the tune of $20,000, then we went to Mercury to bail us out.

Charlie Fach had agreed earlier to contribute to our expenses on the road from promotion money. After all, we were doing the promotion at our own expense. Getting the band off the ground meant playing for nothing or close to it, doing radio promotions and interviews, zigzagging across the country wherever the record was breaking. It was very costly. After several months we went back to Charlie and Irwin Steinberg. They had a map of the USA in their office.

"Where you have played, there is a red pin. Wherever you have sold records is a yellow pin. And what we are seeing is that everywhere you go and play, you're winning over people and sales jump."

We were earning a tremendous amount of goodwill with all these radio stations by playing free promotional events they would organize. It benefited them and us and it paid off in airplay and record sales. But it cost us to do it.

"Here's where we want you to go next week," they told us.

"We can't go out any more."

"Why?!"

"We're maxed out on our credit cards. We can't pay our bills. We're looking at $20,000 just on airfare and rooms and we're already getting calls about it. We need you guys to pay this bill so we can get back out there and do what you want."

"What? You expect us to pay this?" came their incredulous response.

"Wait a minute. Charlie, didn't we have this conversation before?"

"Yeah, I promised we'd pay. These are all legitimate expenses."

Irwin Steinberg then ordered the marketing and promotion department to pay our bill. They needed us to get out there again and work the album. We were moving up the bill from fifth or fourth to third or second and starting to earn some money. If we stayed out there we would eventually not require tour support. In that first year we did some three hundred dates. It took its toll on the homefront for each of us but it gave us a foothold into the States.

The impact of the group's relentless touring schedule was felt most at home. "I had a son who was a year old," states Tim, "and I had been home maybe three days. I had heard him talk over the phone but I hadn't seen him take his first steps. I came home and I heard his footsteps coming down the hall and I was thinking 'I'm going to see my son walk for the first time!' He came around the corner and as soon as he saw me he stopped and screamed. He didn't know me. Here I was a strange man in his house. That was hard for me. I remember being in a hotel room in New York watching Fred Turner choking Bruce Allen until he was starting to turn blue on the bed. I wanted to help Fred but then pulled him off realizing it wasn't worth going to jail for. Bruce would tell us we were going home in three weeks, then he would come back with more dates. 'We're getting big. We gotta do these dates.' He kept extending the tour. So we would have to phone our wives and tell them we couldn't come home. This happened several times. 'We'll be home in a month,' we would tell our wives. Then just before the month was up we would have the tour extended another two months. It just kept adding and adding. It was really tough on our families.

"Randy didn't mind this," maintains Tim. "The Mormon Church has always been very family-oriented and there is a lot of support there. I think he felt his marriage was strong enough and the support from the church was strong enough that it could sustain itself in his absence. But you have to go home once in a while and be a husband and father. It was Bruce's choice and Randy's choice to keep going." With infants at home, the pressure of the band's relentless schedule wreaked havoc on Tim's and Fred's marriages.

Lorayne, Tally, Kezia, and I had left Winnipeg in a Starcraft motor home and driven straight to Vancouver. When we arrived we didn't know where to go so we ended up under the Lions Gate Bridge where it lands in West Vancouver at the Capilano Trailer Park. Tally called it Loserville. We lived there for a couple of months and it was really tough. Lorayne got cabin fever. I was away a lot trying to get BTO going and Lorayne was cooped up in this tiny mobile home with two little kids. It rained a lot. I came back from trying to get the group a record deal in LA and Lorayne told me we had to get out of that place. They were all cranky and at each other's throats. We picked up a newspaper and found a house to rent way out in South Surrey, 125 A Street, on a hill looking back over New Westminster. Being from Winnipeg, to us this was like a Hollywood view, because in Winnipeg when you looked out your back window all you saw were other houses. That was it. This was a lovely home but the owner was reluctant to rent it to us because I was a musician and he assumed wild parties, which was ridiculous for us. We had to promise no parties. We stayed there until shortly after Lorelei was born.

Having gazed at New Westminster from our back window all the time, we would often go for drives over there to look at the stately old three-storey homes near City Hall. New Westminster used to be the capital in Vancouver's early years and there were some huge houses that the original city fathers had built. These houses were incredible. We would drive down Queen's Avenue and ogle the beautiful, spacious houses until one day we spotted a "For Sale" sign on a corner lot house at 303 Queen's Avenue. I had always lived on corner lots, with my parents and on our own on Scotia. We bought it for $79,000. It was like *the Leave It to Beaver* dream house, only bigger. It was a great house. It had a cool attic with all these gables and a large basement. We later renovated the attic to put rooms in it and the basement became my studio.

With the birth of Randy and Lorayne's third child, Lorelei Elise, on May 22, 1973, Lorayne would not have it easy on her own in a new city. Randy was away for months at a stretch breaking BTO out on the road, so it was left to Lorayne to turn their new house into a home and raise three pre-school toddlers. There is no doubt that over the next four years she shouldered much of the responsibility for raising all of their children (bearing three more in the process) on her own. With her husband's frequent and lengthy absences, she had to learn to look after herself. In the end, it would exact a heavy toll on both of them.

Out on the road, Randy and Bruce Allen became comrades-in-arms, travelling and rooming together, sharing the same vision and determination. In the music industry, when people recall Bachman-Turner Overdrive today, they most often think of those two. Bruce was a gadfly doing everything necessary to keep the momentum building. "I had to go out on the road with BTO in the early days because I didn't know the business," Bruce admits. "There wasn't a BTO date I missed. I did the lights, I brought the band on every night, I collected the money, drove the car. I drove every single mile crisscrossing the States. Randy wouldn't use a bus for the longest time because he had some bad experiences with the Guess Who bus, so we drove. We put three guys in the back of the car; Randy was in the front with me and we drove and drove. I booked every show, took every record company meeting, roomed with Randy.

"There weren't many times that I was away from Randy Bachman's side and there was a reason for that. I always believed that Randy could turn in a minute. When you have the balls to fire your brother you could turn on anyone. So being young in that business as a manager, I was always going to make sure that the last person Randy Bachman talked to every night was me. I always believed Randy could be swayed. The last person who talks to Randy could win the argument. I thought that if I was that last guy, I could win the argument. Nor was I ever going to allow Randy to accuse me of slacking off, not being around or screwing up because I wasn't there. I just wasn't going to let that happen." Bruce virtually abandoned his thriving Vancouver agency to his partner Sam Feldman in order to devote himself wholly and completely to BTO's cause. This was the kind of dedication Randy could appreciate.

Confirms Charlie Fach, "BTO became one of the premier touring bands during that time. They weren't afraid of work. Bruce Allen did a great job with them. He was a real hands-on manager. While other managers would be sitting in the dressing room cursing, Bruce would be out there manning the lights. He was definitely involved."

The band wrapped up its blitzkrieg assault of 1973 with the release of *BTO II* in December to advance orders of 100,000. By early in the new year, the album had gone gold and platinum soon after, pulling *BTO I* to gold status along with it. The group's concert fees had climbed to $6,000 a night and they were beginning to headline on their own. The touring schedule remained punishing but the rewards were now within their grasp. There was no doubting Randy Bachman was back, this time on his own terms.

The Guess Who and BTO are both very special to me. I often get asked which one I enjoyed more, which one was better, but it's like being asked which one of your children do you like better. It might be one of them on this particular day because he or she was nicer to you at that moment, but tomorrow it might be another one. I feel very fortunate to have been in these two incredible schools because they were an education. The Guess Who was an education in everything to do wrong, except for the music. Business-wise, manager-wise, publishing-wise it was like a textbook on the pitfalls of the music business. We made so many mistakes. With BTO, I got a second chance to do everything right. Not too many musicians get that second chance. So what I didn't make financially in the Guess Who, I did with BTO. I organized and led the band, financed it, produced it, paid the other guys a salary with my own BMI money from the Guess Who million sellers, all until the band was on its feet. I didn't want the other guys to have to work day jobs or play in other bands because it would have diffused the direction and energy. I wanted the four of us to focus on the band only.

Throughout it all I never lost faith in myself or in the group. It was discouraging at times, certainly, and humbling to hit rock bottom, but the climb up is the best part. If we had started at the top there would have been nowhere to go but down. I was driven by a determination to get back up there again, to show all those naysayers who had written me off after the Guess Who that I could still do it. We served our apprenticeship out on the road and it forged a unity between us that became an integral ingredient in BTO's success. The road was our crucible. We earned our success the hard way. It wasn't handed to us on a platter, and that held us together.

But I had to do all of it myself. I had to take the bull by the horns, but it was done purely out of a desire to succeed and out of necessity to get from point A to point B. Someone had to do it; no one else was going to do it or could do it. Therefore, if it was going to get done, it had to be me.

The media embrace that whole Rocky phenomenon. They love it when you're down getting punched and kicked. When you try to stand up and you're still getting punched, they're still yelling, "Yeah, kick him!" They are against you. But when you start hitting back, they begin cheering for you. You're the new Rocky, the new champion and they love you. After the Guess Who, I was the underdog whom they loved to kick until I stood up and started fighting back with BTO and then they loved me. I became the new Rocky.

CHAPTER 7

Takin' Care Of Business

N ineteen seventy-four was the year of Bachman-Turner Overdrive. With Randy at the helm, BTO became one of the biggest selling acts in the world, scoring not only album and concert successes but conquering the pop singles charts as well. BTO became an unstoppable colossus topping the likes of Elton John, Paul McCartney's Wings, the Eagles, Harry Chapin, Paul Anka, and Barry White to rule the rock airwaves that year. "When the second album went gold in the first month of 1974," marvels Fred Turner, "all of a sudden all the rack jobbers across the United States went 'What is this?' and began ordering the album by the hundreds of thousands. By the time we got to our third album later that year it shipped a million and half right out of the chute. It was platinum on release. I think it sold 3.6 million. In 1974, nobody was selling like that. Nobody came near our sales."

On *BTO II*, Randy focused his writing on the singles market and managed to capture that territory for the group with two chart hits and one rock anthem. *Let It Ride*'s melodic chording and sledgehammer verses became synonymous with the Bachman-Turner Overdrive sound and marked a rare collaboration between the two front men.

Somewhere between the release of *BTO I* and recording *BTO II*, Charlie Fach told me we had the album thing down and to now go write some hit singles. He had been bugging us to write more commercial songs for the next album because he wanted a hit single. They had tried editing some of the songs on the first album for singles but it really hadn't worked. Charlie wanted songs that had a verse and chorus everyone could sing. That's when we really hit our stride; we had the albums and the singles, FM and AM play. We got people up to dance, they went out and bought the records, and it snowballed from there. After that, I became almost obsessed with writing commercially hook-laden, singable, good rock songs. Once I realized that's what I do best it became so easy.

We were travelling through Louisiana when a truck cut us off on the highway. When we got to the next truck stop we saw the truck there, and being polite Canadian drivers, we thought we would tell this guy to watch his driving.

"You cut us off back there on the highway."

He looked us up and down and drawled, "Ain't no big deal. Just let it ride buddy, let it ride."

We looked like truckers, we were a truckers' band, so we decided to write a song around that phrase *Let It Ride*. It had a Doobie Brothers feel because we had been touring with them. We were both guitar-based bands.

I found, though, that writing with Fred was difficult. There wasn't the same flow like with Burton. We did write *Let It Ride* together but it wasn't really a collaboration the way it had been with Burton. The song was based around a guitar pattern inspired by Anton Dvorak's *Piano Concerto in D*. I was trying to be influenced by classical writers the way John Lennon had been, so I listened to Stockhausen and found it to be a bunch of noise I just didn't get. I listened to Dvorak's *Piano Concerto*, which is also very boring, but just like when I was about to turn off Bob

Dylan's *Ballad in Plain D* and he says "She's come undone," I was about to turn off Dvorak when I heard this melodic pattern. I thought "Wow, that's not bad." So I figured out chords for it and it became the beginning to *Let It Ride*. It's very memorable, not just vamping on an A chord, more like a melody within the chords. From there it segued into the heavier part. The song really tricks the listener because it opens with a mellower guitar chording figure, then thunders into the ca-chunka chunka rhythm pumping it into a higher gear. That song put us on the singles charts and gained acceptance for us in AM Top Forty radio. It also put us in the forefront of harder rock guitar bands.

The second single culled from the album would go on to become both Randy's and the group's signature song and, years later, take on a life of its own. Much like *American Woman, Takin' Care of Business* was an onstage accident that turned into gold.

I wrote *Takin' Care of Business* about commuters taking trains in New York when I was there recording with the Guess Who back in 1968. In Winnipeg, you drive to work. But these guys would take the 8:15 into the city and at night they would come back. I had seen it in movies, a day in the life of a businessman in New York, and the girls were all trying to look pretty. So it was written about a big city workday under the title *White Collar Worker*. I tried it out in my basement on Luxton Avenue with Burton and Garry but it wasn't much of a song yet. In fact it was pretty terrible. It had the same verses as *Takin' Care of Business*, my Chuck Berry/*Go Johnny Go* lyrics about a day in the life of a working man, played over about seven or eight chord changes. The chorus was a copy of the Beatles' *Paperback Writer* where we stopped and sang in harmonies "White collar worker" just like the Beatles. I kept the verses but couldn't do anything with the chorus. Everyone hated it in the Guess Who.

Fast-forward a couple of years later and now I'm in BTO on the way to a club gig in Vancouver with my radio on, which it always is. I heard a deejay on the radio say, "This is Jimmy Jay on CFOX radio takin' care of business" or something like that. That was his on-air signature. That night, Fred lost his voice after singing several sets all week long. The first set was rough, the second rougher, and by the last set he asked me to take over. So Robbie and I pulled out *Oya Coma Va* from our Brave Belt days, David Crosby's *Long Time Gone*, and ran out of songs. Out of desperation I thought of *White Collar Worker* but I couldn't shout out all the chord changes, so I simply smoothed it out in my head and told the guys to play C Bb and F over and over. That allowed me to sing the lyrics in a more bendy, bluesy manner over a simpler chord progression instead of the Ebm's and G#'s I had in the original. When we got to the chorus the guys kept playing the same chords so I just sang "Takin' care of business" four times. We did another verse and went into the chorus and out of the blue as the others joined in singing "Takin' care of business" I just answered each one with "Every day," "Every way," "It's all mine," "And working over time" followed by "Work out."

When we finished the song that night, people kept clapping, stomping, and shouting "Takin' care of business" over and over. So we picked up the tempo again and reprised the song for another ten minutes. Just like with *American Woman*, we all knew we had something.

We couldn't have a song called *White Collar Worker* in *BTO* when we already had *Blue Collar*, so the title was no good. But I knew the verses were great. "They get up in the mornin' from the alarm clock's warnin', take the 8:15 into the city." Everybody loves those lyrics. It's one of those songs you can't help but sing along to. That was my own kind of Chuck Berry lyric. Chuck always had lyrics that told a story you could sing along.

When we went into the studio to record *BTO II*, I wrote out the lyrics for Fred to sing it.

"Why are you giving this to me?"

"You know the lyrics already?"

"No, I'm not going to sing it. I want you to sing it. You sang it onstage and they loved it. You sing it. It'll give me a break."

Fred was the lead singer, the guy I had specifically brought in to sing in the band. But he didn't want to do it. So I sang the song on the recording.

I still feel very odd about singing. To this day, if someone asks me if I'm a singer I reply, "No, I'm a guitar player who sings." There's a big difference. Neil Young, for example, is a guitar player who sings. So is Bob Dylan, in my opinion. There are some guys who have killer voices but my voice isn't a great voice. People can recognize Neil's voice immediately. It's distinctive. My voice is recognizable too, whatever its timbre or quality.

Singing onstage was no big deal for me because I was used to giving Fred a break and singing things like *Long Time Gone* or *Ohio*, songs that didn't require a whole lot before getting to the guitar solo. But suddenly we were getting positive response to *Takin' Care of Business* and it began sliding backwards in our set to become the closing number because of the tremendous crowd reaction.

In the studio, we simplified the chords like we had done them onstage rather than the eight or nine chord changes in the original version of *White Collar Worker*. It had an incredible number of chords and that's why nobody liked it. Ralph Murphy and I wrote a song in 1967 in London called *A Little Bit of Rain*. I used that riff in the middle of *Takin' Care of Business* just to break the monotony because *Takin' Care of Business* has only three chords played over and over and over. It has no bridge, no hook, no song format other than that, so it was like *Louie Louie*: endless bashing of three chords and it needed a break.

As we were finishing recording it at Kaye-Smith Studios in Seattle, there was a knock at the studio door. I opened it and there stood this guy, six-foot-four, big beard like Fidel Castro, wearing army fatigues.

"Did you order pizza?"

"No, try Steve Miller down the hall."

"Okay."

He headed off down the hall with his pizza and we went back to listening to the playback of *Takin' Care of Business*. It was about one thirty in the morning. Moments later there came another knock at the door. I opened it and there's Fidel again.

"That song sounds like it could really use a piano."

"Yeah, so? We don't play piano."

"I'm a piano player. Give me a shot."

It was two in the morning and we were ready to call it a night.

"Okay, you've got one take. We're putting on our jackets and leaving."

We played him the track, he listened closely, wrote down the chord changes and laid down a terrific piano part in one take. He went home; we went home.

A day or two later Charlie Fach flew in to hear the tracks and flipped out over *Takin' Care of Business*.

"I love the piano. It gives the band a whole new texture. Who played that piano?"

"I don't know. Some Fidel Castro pizza delivery guy."

"Well, you've got to find out his name because we can't release it without paying him and crediting him."

So we went down to Steve Miller's session and asked them if they knew where they ordered the pizza from a couple of nights ago. They had no idea so I started going through the Yellow Pages alphabetically phoning all the pizza joints in town describing this guy to them.

"Do you have a tall delivery guy with a beard like Fidel Castro?"

"No."

Everywhere I phoned I got a no until one place replied, "Yeah, he works once a month for us. He's a musician and only delivers when he doesn't have a gig. His name is Norman Durkee."

So we got a hold of him, paid him double scale, the song came out, and made musical history. And part of its appeal is that piano part. Norman later went on to become the rehearsal pianist for the LA Symphony.

After *Let It Ride* had run its course, suddenly Charlie Fach was on the phone to me.

"Well, Handsome Randsome, you've got it all. The album and the single have charted. This is what we wanted and we're getting it. By the way, the next single is going to be *Takin' Care of Business*."

"What?! How can it be?! I sang it terribly. It's only an album track."

"They're already playing it in St. Louis. It's magic."

The stations that had been behind us early on, the ones we worked hard to win over with promotional gigs and interviews, had jumped on *Let It Ride* right away. So by the time the rest of the country was riding it, these stations were looking for the next single and tagged *Takin' Care of Business* off the album. It became a single as a result of radio demand, not our own design. More than that, *Takin' Care of Business* was becoming an American catchphrase. It had multiple meanings whether for a guy and his girl takin' care of business getting it on, or for someone who just wanted to get the job done. "Okay, let's take care of business." Black people started saying it in sitcoms like Jimmy Walker saying "Dynomite!" Everyone knew what it meant. It quickly became part of the American vernacular. It fit the band as well, these big lumberjack guys who are gonna take care of business, no pussyfooting around. I now hear wrestlers using it in the WWF. The song has more meaning now than it did then. It transcended the charts. It's still a catchphrase today and makes more money now than it did back then.

If I had known it would go on to become such an anthem I would have written better lyrics. I would have sung "If you pass the audition, you can be a musician" rather than "It's as easy as fishin." It sounds corny now but those lyrics were written in 1968. If I had thought that this was an attempt at a hit I would have cleaned it up. But it is what it is.

Takin' Care of Business just keeps on going and, in the nineties, is used in some very respectable commercials like Office Depot, which was the perfect vehicle for me and my song. They provide all the supplies to take care of your business needs. They paid $350,000 for a three-year licence and renewed it for three more years. Burger King paid $150,000 to employ it internally only at their hamburger university. I had previously turned down a lucrative million-dollar offer from an American brewing company who were launching a new nonalcoholic beer. I always said I would never allow my songs to be used to promote cigarettes or alcohol. People told me I was crazy to pass it up but I stuck to my guns. Then Office Depot came along so I was right in holding it back. I'm happier about that association and it's been just as lucrative.

More than merely a concert favourite or chart hit, *Takin' Care of Business* also became the motto of BTO on the road. In an era that measured an artist's success by the size of their entourage or the extravagance of the post-concert soirée, Randy's approach to touring was like his music: "Keep it simple." Why waste your hard-earned money on frivolous expenses? By reducing overhead, travelling frugally, and comfortable if not glamourous accommodations, BTO maximized its bottom line. Some of the most successful artists of that decade lost money on their tours simply because of needless waste flying in Lear Jets accompanied by a retinue of hangers-on all paid for by the artist, carrying massive sets and backdrops, or snorting their profits up their noses. Not BTO. Often ridiculed by the media or the subject of derision by their contemporaries for their spartan touring regimen and focus on profits, BTO simply laughed all the way to the bank.

"We were the only band of the time that was in the black on the road," agrees Fred. "Everybody else was in the red. They had all these big productions and all we took with us were lights, a really good sound system, and we ran our asses off onstage. That was our show. We always made money on the road, tons of money on our tours. Everybody else went out and spent all their money on expenses. None of us was into the raucous rock 'n' roll atmosphere. And we weren't drinking or doing drugs. There were no heavy money demands. We didn't rent the Starship to fly us wherever we had to go. We were flying commercial and getting the best deals we could get. And if we didn't fly commercial, we were taking buses. We just didn't spend the money."

"We stayed at the same hotels, Holiday Inns, because they were always laid out the same, no surprises," states Bruce Allen. "Randy liked that."

Hand in hand with the group's minimalist approach to the road were Randy's rules. Although a hectic touring schedule had been a contributing factor to his discomfort with the Guess Who, this time out it was all on Randy's terms. There were no drugs or partying to contend with. "No drinking, no screwing around with broads, no drugs at all. Those were Randy's rules," outlines Bruce. "He didn't want any of that. I saw Randy sign an autograph on a girl's chest, maybe give someone a peck on the cheek as he said thank you very much, but he always adhered to his rules. There is no dirt on Randy that way. He was a good Mormon. He would go and speak at those fireside talks at these different Mormon places we would go to. He wouldn't drink Coke or coffee, didn't screw around on the road, and didn't drink any alcohol." For BTO, the beverage of choice was Gatorade and their wholesome, clean-cut teetotalling image brought them almost as much attention as their music.

My attitude has always been "Don't waste my time. If you want to goof around go have a good goofy life somewhere else. This is what I am, this is what I do. If you want to get aboard this train we can have a nice ride." That's what I said to the guys in Brave Belt/BTO at the outset. "If you don't like it I can look elsewhere. This is my train, here are my rules: no smoking, drinking, or drugs. Other than that it's lots of hard work, rock 'n' roll, and fun." And that's the way we operated BTO. It was, after all, my band and if they wanted to play with me they had to adhere to my rules. But look what it got them. Not bad.

I was allergic to smoke. Fred smoked before he joined the band but quit; Blair Thornton, who joined later, smoked and quit. Johnny Austin, our road manager, quit too. I just don't like to be around smoke. We didn't travel with a large entourage or stay in lavish suites but we always stayed comfortably. We stayed in Holiday Inns not Marriotts or Four Seasons. It was luxurious compared to the old days in an Econoline van and a tent. Only in the very last days did we end up with semi-trailers. I don't recall us having a big tour bus. Just give us an Econoline van and a station wagon.

How can that be wrong? I'd like you to find whoever said that we were wrong for focusing on the bottom line and see what his station in life is now and how much he has in the bank? How many of those who criticized us for watching our money are now members of Alcoholics Anonymous or Narcotics Anonymous? The trick is no longer how many toys can you get but how long can you stay alive to play with them, to enjoy the fruits of your labours.

"This was Randy's chance and he wanted to take advantage of it," stresses Bruce. "He had all those kids and had to make some money." But for some in the music business, when BTO came through their town it meant no perks and caused a bit of a backlash. "Because of Randy running BTO his style — no alcohol, drugs, or smoking — they didn't cater to the radio and industry types who thought it was their right to party with a band in return for playing their records," muses Gary Bachman. "These people wanted that status and claim to fame. 'Yeah, I partied last night with Randy Bachman,' but the band wouldn't play that game."

After contributing two songs to their latest album, *BTO II*, Tim Bachman was summarily dismissed from the band by his older brother in March 1974 following completion of another tour. That Randy could fire his own sibling just as the group stood poised for the big rewards following the hard years of struggling remains a contentious issue. Certainly Tim's sacking caused a rift between the two brothers that took many years to heal and not before Tim's life bottomed out. Over the years, Randy's detractors often cite what is perceived as a grossly dispassionate action as an example of his cold-blooded nature. From Randy's perspective, however, it was strictly a business decision in consideration for what was best for the group. Tim was not contributing to the level expected of him, and he had transgressed the rules.

Tim was great on stage and great to have in the band, but we had an understanding: when it came time to recording the basic tracks, Tim went out and got everyone lunch. And when he returned, the guitar parts were done. Sometimes he played them, sometimes he didn't. I even replaced some of the bass parts if they weren't as precise as I wanted them. I never told anyone what I did or told anyone they didn't play well enough. I just redid it the way I wanted it. I brought in another sixteen-track machine and copied a song over to it so I could take the first verse and splice it three times so we could have a more precise tempo because Robbie kept speeding up. *Let It Ride* was like the Indianapolis 500 by the time we got to the end. I never told those guys because it would have been ego-shattering and induce infighting. But in my role as producer, I wanted to get the job done right. I think they might have known but didn't want to ask. I would come in an hour earlier or stay later to get it right. I saw BTO as my vehicle to do my songs and I wanted them done right.

When I left home with the Guess Who, Timmy was into the same things a lot of people were into at that time. When I brought him into Brave Belt it was basically for contractual reasons. I was really happy with the band as a three-piece — Fred, Robbie, and I. We had signed contracts for gigs coming up that said the band was a quartet. Some promoters actually came up to the stage and counted the number of players and if you were one short of the contracted number, they would deduct 25 percent, which for us was a killer because we weren't making much money to begin with. That could be the difference between our expenses and any profit to pay salaries.

So I brought Timmy into the band and laid down the rules to him: no drinking, smoking, or drugs. He agreed, then promptly proceeded to break those rules. I would freak out. I would talk to him about it, he would say he wouldn't do it again, then I would hear that he had done it again. This happened another time and he was cautioned not to do it again. His playing wasn't improving by then and he seemed to view the band as a party. I had encouraged him to write some songs to give the band a different personality than just mine. He wrote a couple of tunes on the second album and even sang *I Don't Have to Hide*. But I was under pressure from Robbie, Fred, and Bruce Allen because this was my brother who I had invited into the band and he was jeopardizing the future of the band not only indulging in drugs but creating risky situations for all of us taking them across the border. His actions had the potential to undermine the future of the band and my own personal career future.

We had a meeting where he was told he was out of the band. There were no second chances because it was his third incident and he had been warned of the consequences. That was it. I made sure he received his percentage of royalties and songwriting. It was a tough thing to do for me but I had no choice. He knew the rules and continued to break them. I felt bad because he had a wife and two kids but I knew he had a certain amount of money coming in to get him by for a while until he found something else. Unfortunately, Tim took it quite drastically. It was very tough for me to dismiss Timmy from the band.

Looking back now, I wish I had been more loving with him,

more of a brother, and left it open for him to come back at some point if he got himself together. But at the time, that just wasn't an option. I was influenced by the Bruce Allen mentality: "It's over. He's out. Let's get on with it." Cut and dry. As a band we couldn't stop at that point. Everything was kicking into a higher gear and we had to run with it. To pause could have meant all the momentum we had been working for in the last two years would have been lost. It was almost like my leaving the Guess Who. If they had stopped at that point in the band's career and waited six months for me, who knows what might have happened? You just don't know, so you make decisions at the time and live with them the rest of your life. So we went on without Timmy.

"It was tough on Timmy when he was fired," acknowledges Bruce Allen on Randy's "the band comes before blood" ethos. "I saw the way it was done and it was pretty cold. We got off the road, went to my house in Vancouver for a meeting in my living room, Timmy walked in, and Randy said, 'You're fired.' We hadn't been home more than six hours. Randy thought Timmy wasn't good enough. We used to turn his amp off sometimes onstage."

"It had been hard on my wife when I joined the band," recounts Tim. "We were newly married, we then moved to Vancouver, and we had a child soon after. When our record came out we were on the road all the time and she was alone in a strange city with a baby. So the phone calls home weren't great. It was a very stressful situation for both of us. There were rumours that I was into drugs. I wasn't a Mormon at the time. I did drugs but it was never as bad as they imagined. I think they had an image of me as this incredibly hedonistic drug user. I got like that after I left the band, but I wasn't breaking the rules when I was with the band. I did that stuff on my own time. I went to parties on the road but I didn't participate.

"At the time that Randy confronted me I didn't argue, I didn't resist. I was going through a tough time at home. After Randy told me,

I went home and talked with my wife about it. I told her what had happened but she couldn't comprehend it. My parents were staying with my wife for a few weeks and they talked to her about what had happened and managed to convey the message to her about what had gone down. She then came to me and said, 'It's okay now. I understand what you've been going through.' I went to Randy's house the next day to beg to get back into the band but he said 'No.'

"None of them, neither Randy, Fred, nor Robbie, came to me and offered to help me out. There was no looking at the situation from another perspective. I was having a troubled time but no one ever said anything or was willing to give me the time or the help I needed. It was simply 'We won't put up with this. You're out of here.' Now I can understand Randy's actions. In many ways we are similar. We haven't done the same things but we are similar. In his life, whatever lumps have come along he has taken them. I'm somewhat the same. These are the cards I've been dealt. It hurt, I was sad, but I got over it. But living in Vancouver without the band, I had nothing, so I moved back to Winnipeg. That became the wedge between us. There were no phone calls between Randy and I for quite some time after that."

Contractual obligations once again dictated a fourth member so we grabbed Blair Thornton. We didn't have time to audition, didn't know many other players because we were such an insular group, and didn't want a guy from an existing band that already had a record deal. Bruce recommended Blair with whom he had a booking relationship in a former Vancouver band called Crosstown Bus and, we found out later, also had a relationship with Blair's ex-girlfriend Kim.

"He's a good guy and he can play," Bruce assured us.

Bruce hyped Blair to us as a monster guitar player who could play like Hendrix. He wasn't, but he fit the bill. Bruce felt he owed Blair a favour after he became involved with Blair's ex-girlfriend, so Blair was given our set list and the albums and he showed up at a rehearsal. Tim wasn't a lead player, so Blair gave us a new direction and with him in the lineup we proceeded forward with the *NOT FRAGILE* album.

Blair was a team player who walked into a pretty good situation. He went on salary for a short period then became a full partner. He and I got together and wrote a couple of things like *Four Wheel Drive*. He looked good, played well, and was a good guy. With Blair there was a definite demarcation in the band. Fred and I were the older married guys and Robbie and Blair were the younger, single swinging bachelors.

Blair Thornton's inaugural appearance as a member of BTO came two days later during taping of the American television rock showcase "In Concert." Following that the reconstituted group hit the road once again. Booked by Beaver Production's honcho Don Fox, a New Orleans–based agent and a maverick like Bruce Allen, BTO continued their assault on America, selling out arenas, concert halls, and headlining outdoor festivals across the United States. "Don Fox told me that until New Kids on the Block or Backstreet Boys, one of those bands, BTO sold out concerts faster than any band in history in the US," boasts Bruce Allen. Some 15,000 screaming fans jammed the Long Beach Arena to see rock's newest heroes. Riots outside other venues were commonplace.

"It's funny," muses Fred Turner. "Because I've played so many places all over the US they get wiped out of my memory. Very few places I can remember other than the odd ones, simply because they were big names like Madison Square Gardens, the Spectrum, Cobo Hall in Detroit, or Three Rivers Stadium in Pittsburgh. I remember all those big ones, but there were so many places it just becomes a blur. We played a place in Kansas outdoors where a windstorm came up while we were playing and actually flew the stage right off the ground. That wind kept it right up in the air. Some of the stagehands saw it coming and locked arms and came out and knocked us right off the stage just in time. The equipment was mangled, the drums squashed. We flew helicopters into one concert because we couldn't get in, the highways were all jammed up with people coming to the concert. We played with the Beach Boys and they wouldn't follow us. We really had the crowd going."

Someone who took notice of the BTO juggernaut steamrolling its way across America was Burton Cummings. Having suffered a fallow period following the group's first post-Bachman album, *SHARE THE LAND*, in late 1970, the Guess Who had watched their chart positions plummet with each subsequent single and album release. A revolving door of personnel had seen Jim Kale ousted while several guitar players came and went. By 1974, Burton was both astonished and dismayed to find his nemesis now his chief rival on the charts. Randy Bachman was back on top while Burton languished in the "where are they now" doldrums. Comparing the latest releases by BTO and the Guess Who, one music critic was moved to conclude: "Bachman-Turner Overdrive is like a diesel trailer to the Guess Who's pick-up truck." *Rolling Stone* magazine simply declared: "Make mine BTO, please."

"It was very hard for Burton to swallow BTO's success," acknowledges Jim Martin who had remained with the Guess Who, "because it hadn't ended for Randy. Sure, Randy had a tough time with Brave Belt and took a lot of shit for it but he didn't lie down. Anyone who thought Randy couldn't do it again was fooling themselves. He wasn't ready to give it up."

"It hurt a little bit because of all the past history we had," admits Garry Peterson, "but I admired BTO. Burton and Randy got nasty in the newspapers but you never saw anything from me. But there was a rivalry." So much so that Burton emerged from his self-indulgence long enough to take a run at the pop charts one more time. *Clap for the Wolfman* restored the Guess Who to the Top Ten and the group even discarded their t-shirts and jeans for custom-made suits and leather outfits. When confronted with the inevitable questions about Randy's current success, Burton's defence was to flippantly refer to the group as "Bachman-Turner Overweight" or compare Randy and Fred to the dancing hippos in Fantasia.

In a way it was just another in the endless line of jabs from Burton. That bothered me a little bit, sure. But what's true is true. I've always been a big guy and I have had a weight problem. But you just have to learn to laugh at it. The name I came up with for Fred and I was the "Heavily Brothers" like the Everly Brothers, two guitars and big guys singing. You can't hide it so you might as well laugh at it. When Tim was in the band and had packed on a few pounds like Fred and I, our logo was Half a Ton of Rock 'n' Roll. We even had t-shirts made up with that on it. People loved it. That would have made a great album title.

Bruce Allen never succumbed to the LA thing of crafting an image for us. He didn't tell us to get hairstyles and fancy clothes. He let us be. We had a natural image. It was just us. We looked like a normal band of ordinary guys. A few years later, after we had made it, we toured with ZZ Top and they were into those Nudie cactus suits like the Flying Burrito Brothers used to wear and we got into that a bit but soon discarded them. I had a pink suit with a cactus on it and a gold Elvis suit. But it was a flash in the pan for us. I only wore the gold suit once then went back to jeans and vests.

In August 1974, BTO released their third album, *NOT FRAGILE*, an apt descriptor to their approach to rock and a poke at the recent Yes album, *FRAGILE*. The album turned gold in four days and platinum soon after when it hit the coveted #1 position on the *Billboard* charts. For BTO, the roll seemed unstoppable. In attempting to pinpoint the band's massive appeal, music critic Michael Watts concluded: "They are anybody. Anybody with a little talent and a great capacity for touring and hard work." Often slammed for catering to the lowest common denominator in rock music, Randy responded to such criticisms in a *Rolling*

Stone interview with Cameron Crowe: "They call us a loud, thundering wall of monotony. Well, that's what we are. That's what Deep Purple is. That's what Led Zeppelin is. Everything is monotonous. Who cares what the critics say? Who cares if some turkeys think we're monotonous? There's a million people who happen to like our monotony." But while some critics panned the group's four-to-the-floor approach, BTO's records belied far more subtlety as a result of Randy's studio savvy.

BTO was a blue-collar band; that was its base of appeal. Our songs were about average guys. *Takin' Care of Business* was about the average Joe going to work each day. The Guess Who sang love songs like *These Eyes*. That band was much more emotional, teenage emotions, whereas BTO was more of a guy thing. No love songs.

I always remember something John Fogerty told me. I was in a dressing room in LA when I was still with the Guess Who and I was fooling around with my Lenny Breau stuff. We were playing alongside Creedence Clearwater Revival at the LA Forum and John Fogerty heard me playing around, walked in, and said, "Very cool stuff. Never play it on record." I always play a solo a fourteen-year-old kid thinks he can play when he hears it on the radio. He'll go out and buy it and learn it. If it's to the moon and back, something way out or jazzy, he'll never buy that record. I sing a solo first and then I play it. It's very melodic. If someone else can sing it, they can play it. I always think about that when writing and recording.

Our music *was* geared to a common denominator. It was basic. What's wrong with that? The perception of just four guys playing live underlined everything we recorded. Any embellishments would only be noticed after repeated listenings because they were very subliminal. We didn't have multiple overdubs, synthesizers, and layered voices. If I added bits here and there, they were understated, less obvious but no less important. For example, on

Blue Collar I added a low piano bass note at the beginning of each chord, which enunciated the chord. You don't hear it as a piano part, yet if it weren't there the chords wouldn't be as strong. I'm sure no one hears it when they listen to that song but it is an essential ingredient underpinning the structure and presentation.

My secret BTO weapon, and no one knows this other than the band, was a gallon milk jug turned over and played in a galloping style. It simulated that Beatles bongo sound. Robbie played it and we had two tones, one with the cap off and the other with the cap on. That gallop is in *Let It Ride, Takin' Care of Business* and lots of other songs mixed under the track to give it that galloping effect propelling the song along.

Before I went in to record a BTO album or produce anyone else for that matter, I would listen to Chuck Berry's *A DOZEN BERRIES*, Beatles albums like *RUBBER SOUL* and *REVOLVER*, and listen for the percussion and tempos. The Beatles used a lot of subtle, unobtrusive percussive tricks that weren't always noticeable to the naked ear. Listen to the hand clapping on *Hold Me Tight*, the cowbell on *Drive My Car*, claves, tambourine, cha cha beats in other songs. We used those techniques recording BTO. You didn't really notice it but our music was very rhythmic and subtly percussive. On *Takin' Care of Business*, I had Robbie play a Ringo Starr–style hi-hat at the beginning of each verse, a slightly opened hi-hat, and as the song builds, I had him open it up more as the excitement mounts. It's there if you listen closely. There is tambourine hidden in there, too. I was very conscious of keeping it sounding like four guys but somehow putting in other things to make it more exciting and ear candy for radio. If you took those things out, the songs would sound very empty. You would just hear two guitars, bass, and drums. The Beatles used that lineup but underneath it all there is something more happening. That is subliminally underneath a lot of BTO music. I used a lot of tom toms playing eighth notes like in *Let It Ride, Don't Get Yourself in Trouble, Give It Time.* That tom tom galloping is very primitive — the Indian, tribal, jungle thing that keeps the song thundering along. We even received a disco dance award in Europe for some of our songs.

"Randy is one of the greatest rock 'n' roll guitar players in the world, not so much for his lead playing but for his rhythm playing," suggests Garry Peterson, acknowledging Randy's innate rhythmic sense. "He is one of the greatest rock 'n' roll rhythm players. He has the ability, knowledge, and experience from growing up with rock 'n' roll to know when, where, and what a guitar should play. He knows all the feels of where rock 'n' roll came from. Rock 'n' roll is rhythm and Randy knows those rhythms." That understanding of rock 'n' roll rhythm would be put to effective use on the band's next single, their first #1 on the pop charts. *You Ain't Seen Nothin' Yet* was an afterthought, a song that barely made it onto the *NOT FRAGILE* album.

You Ain't Seen Nothin' Yet began life as a work song destined to be thrown away. We used to do it as a warm up in the studio and I would sing nonsense lyrics. Charlie Fach hauled it out of oblivion in desperation looking for another single to follow *Let It Ride* and *Takin' Care of Business.* He didn't hear a follow-up single on *NOT FRAGILE. Roll On Down the Highway* was a good rocker but Charlie figured it couldn't take us that next level higher than *Takin' Care of Business.* When he heard *You Ain't Seen Nothin' Yet* he declared it magical. And he was right. The jangling guitar reminiscent of *Let It Ride* lures you in, then the delivery of this heavy guitar in the chorus reveals it to be more than a one-level guitar song. By the time the heavy part hits you, you're already rocking and the song's got you. It was perfect for radio, everybody rockin' out in their cars. But here I was again singing on the radio.

The circumstances surrounding that song were equally as weird as *Takin' Care of Business.* It was rather serendipitous that it even made it onto the album at all. In producing the band we would have eight songs that I knew would be on the album and I had them timed out — the song, the lyrics, how many bars before the verse — all written in a notebook. I always preferred to record BTO live in the studio, because playing live in clubs was where we really shone. I would set the band up and run from the studio floor, where I could direct the band through the arrangement, to the control booth to listen to the playback and tell the engineer what needed more or should be brought down. As we worked toward a balance for recording, I didn't want to wear out one of the eight songs we were recording. I wanted each one to retain a freshness to it when we got down to recording the actual tracks. So I had what I called a work song that had a light part to get the rhythm and a heavy riffing part to see the balance. I would listen to it, adjust things, go back into the studio and play it again, then return to the booth to check the balance. Once it was set the way I wanted it, I would discard the track and call out the first song to record. I never liked to wear a song out with umpteen takes and lose the spontaneity of the live feel. If we didn't get it right in the first couple of run-throughs, I would leave it until later and come back to it when no one was expecting it. I wanted to capture the energy, like capturing wild animals. That's how I did the albums.

But when it came to recording the third album, *NOT FRAGILE*, I decided to take the work song, stutter over it, mix it, and send it to my brother Gary as a joke just to scare him that we were going to release it. He had a stuttering problem growing up and I teased him about it. Being older, I guess I had an edge over him when it came to teasing. I don't know if I was really going to send it or not, but I did have that thought. But when it was done the intent changed. I was really fooling around on that song. The slow jangly chord part came from Dave Mason's *Only You Know and I Know*. I don't know where the heavy power chording came from. Out of

the blue I just played this pattern when we got to the studio to
record the album to get into playing and recording mode and I
started singing words. "I met a devil woman, she took my heart
away." I honestly don't know where I got the line "You ain't seen
nothin' yet" or why I stuttered on those particular words, but when
I did on "B-b-b-baby," I noticed everybody in the band perked up.
Robbie instinctively went to his cowbell in the chorus. I thought
the riff was cool and figured I would keep it and work on it for a
later album. The song got recorded but with no intention of using
it and we proceeded to cut the entire *NOT FRAGILE* album forget-
ting about this silly little ditty.

We were recording in Seattle. Charlie Fach came out to hear
the album and declared, "Fabulous album, great sound, congratulations." But he didn't hear a hit single that could top *Takin' Care of
Business* or *Let It Ride* on the charts. Our engineer, Mark Smith,
then suggested we play Charlie the work track, the stuttering
song we cut at the start of the sessions while we were getting
our balance.

"You gotta be kidding? Not the work track."

And Charlie said "What? You mean you've got another song?"

Mark dug up the tape because we had buried it somewhere
and played it for Charlie. The minute he heard those intro chords
he yelled, "This is a radio hit!"

Then the stuttering vocals come in and I started to cringe.

"It's a monster! You've got to put this on the album!" Charlie
was jumping up and down shrieking.

By this time, I had learned to trust Charlie's instincts. But the
album was all done, he had flown up to hear the final mix, and
now he wanted us to add this silly stuttering work track?

"Okay, I'll come in tomorrow morning and try to re-sing it."

We were scheduled to go back out on the road and didn't have
much time. When I tried re-recording the vocal track it just didn't
work. It sounded like Bill Murray doing his lounge lizard routine. It

didn't fit the music but I found I couldn't sing it any other way.

"Just leave it," insisted Charlie. "It's random stuttering and people are going to love it."

Because it had only been a work track, my guitar had not been perfectly in tune when we recorded it. Now I had to overdub my lead guitar. We were heading out on the road so I took the tape with me to a studio in Van Nuys to mix it. This was to be my first mixing job so I was very excited. Mark Smith and I went in and figured we had to disguise my throwaway vocals by putting echo on my vocal track to obscure the variance in pitch. That would steal some of the attention from the ear. The guitar was so out of tune I decided to put a slap echo on it and hook up a Leslie organ speaker cabinet that swirls the sound around and varies the pitch. But we discovered the studio Leslie was blown; the top horn that revolves was shot and had been removed. The bottom speaker had been replaced by a Marshall cabinet. In a flash of inspiration, I took a Coca-Cola paper cup and attached it to the Leslie turntable for a horn and amazingly it worked. It didn't have the Leslie sound and moved slower but it sounded unique. This became my lead guitar sound on *You Ain't Seen Nothin' Yet*. With that I over-dubbed the riff and a Hank Marvin–style solo and it was done. The song became the ninth track on *NOT FRAGILE*. I now had to re-sequence the album from the way I had originally planned it to maintain a balance per side and not lose the fidelity.

When the album came out and that song started getting air-played on radio, Charlie phoned us up.

"The response on this song is unbelievable. Boston, Portland, Texas, all over the country. Everybody's flipping out for this song. It's gotta be a single. It's a monster."

"No way! I do not want this as a single."

I heard it on Seattle radio one day around that time and became so embarrassed I turned it off. My wife and kids were yelling, "Turn it up. Who is that?" and I didn't want them to know it was me.

Three weeks later I received a conference call. It was all the head honchos from Mercury.

"You are insane. This song is the number one phone request in LA, number two in Frisco. People want to buy a single. You're going to kill the album. You could have a million-selling single."

It never entered my mind that BTO could have a million-selling Top Ten single like the Guess Who. I saw us as an albums band. But not willing to fight such an obvious gift horse, I relented.

"Okay, put it out. But it'll be the end of the band," I declared ruefully. I just figured people would hear how bad the vocal was and the out of tune guitar.

You Ain't Seen Nothin' Yet shot to number one in seventeen or eighteen countries. We rode that song for two years as it was released from country to country. It became BTO's only million-selling single.

Our contract with Mercury had only called for one album in the first eighteen months because Charlie wanted to see how we went over. By the end of that year and a half, we had put out three albums all on the charts at the same time. *NOT FRAGILE* was #1, *BTO II* was #18 and the first album was #48. That was momentous. I still have that page from *Billboard*.

"From very early on, Randy had definite goals," cites his brother Gary. "He said to me once that he wanted to play on a number one record and he eventually did. Then he told me he wanted to write a record that would be number one and he did that, too. At the time he expressed those goals, that was unheard of because songs were written by professional songwriters not the artists themselves. So it was quite a dream, far-fetched pie-in-the-sky stuff, but he succeeded. Later he confided in me, in one of the rare times he did such things because Randy doesn't talk a lot, that he wanted to sing on a number one record. I was dubious because he doesn't have a great voice. But he eventually achieved that too. After Fred Turner joined him in Brave

Belt, Randy practised and practised his singing, but he was terrible. Nevertheless, he wanted to sing so much. And he did and made that dream come true."

With Randy's voice gracing BTO's biggest hits, the dynamics within the band began to shift. No longer the lone voice of BTO, Fred Turner was going through a bit of an identity crisis. "Randy wanted to sing the songs he wrote if he could handle them and that was fine with me," states Fred, "because I like to hear a change of texture in the voices in our music, and there were a few of his tunes I would not have wanted to sing." In retrospect, Bruce Allen sees the decision to push Randy's voice to the forefront as a mistake that eventually hurt the group. "The fans loved Fred's singing. Then Randy wanted to be the lead singer. True, Randy had hits like *Takin' Care of Business* and *You Ain't Seen Nothin' Yet* but the fans loved Fred's voice. Fred Turner really sold the power of that band vocally. People loved it when Fred sang. He oozed power stomping across that stage with that powerful voice. It was tough for Fred when Randy began to assert his singing more and he suffered anxiety attacks. It was hard for him and Randy should have deferred to Fred. Fred was valuable."

You Ain't Seen Nothin' Yet found an unlikely booster in Burton Cummings whose schmaltzy lounge lizard take on Randy's song graced the closing track of his debut solo outing in 1976. Though he later claimed his version was a tribute, several members of the Guess Who recall Burton camping up the song in mocking derision during sound checks. Randy simply took it all in stride.

While *You Ain't Seen Nothin' Yet* ruled the North American airwaves, BTO undertook their first European jaunt in the spring of 1975, opening in Copenhagen and winding up with two sold-out performances at London's Hammersmith Odeon Theatre. The tour was filmed for a CTV Canadian television special entitled *Roll On Down the Highway.*

There are two phases of BTO's career in Europe, like BC and

AD: before *YASNY* and after *YASNY, You Ain't Seen Nothin'Yet*. Before that song, the European market didn't know anything about BTO. *Let It Ride* and *Takin' Care of Business* hadn't done that well. But after *You Ain't Seen Nothin'Yet* they knew a lot. We went over to tour Europe and did our big North American anthem *Takin' Care of Business* and nobody knew it. But *You Ain't Seen Nothin'Yet* became a huge hit in just about every country in Europe as did the *NOT FRAGILE* album. We played the UK, Germany, the Netherlands, everywhere. Audiences knew all the songs off *NOT FRAGILE* but little before that. What our record label in Europe should have done after the success of *You Ain't Seen Nothin'Yet* was to back-release *Let It Ride, Takin' Care of Business* and others just like Capitol did in the US with the Beatles after *She Loves You* became a hit. They re-released *Love Me Do, Please Please Me, From Me to You,* and they all charted. We would have had a longer life in Europe had they done that because those songs fit the musical times there — real good party rock records.

To this day, BTO remains best known in Europe for *You Ain't Seen Nothin'Yet*. It's still that way when I go to the UK and all I have to do is mention that song and there is immediate recognition. It was used by a rugby team as well as in a commercial.

Years later a British comedian named Harry Enfield had a television show every Saturday evening that featured a weekly skit, sort of like Dick Clark's *Rate the Record*. In his skit, two deejays, Nicey and Smashy, dressed up like Mods, would play a record, a different one each week, and ask, "Do we like this record? No." Then Smashy would take a hammer and smash it. Then he would say, "Let's play something by Bachman-Turner Overdrive." And they would play *You Ain't Seen Nothin'Yet*. It became a very Monty Pythonesque bit that had everyone rolling on the floor. Each week they would end the skit with *You Ain't Seen Nothin'Yet*. We were always the winners.

I never realized how much that song had become an icon in
the UK until I was flying from Germany to England not long ago.
The British flight attendant knew I was in a band so she asked
who I was. When I said Randy Bachman, it didn't register with her.
"Bachman-Turner Overdrive?"
Nothing.
"What other bands have you been in?"
"The Guess Who?"
A blank stare.
"Any songs I might know?"
"How about *American Woman*?"
"Nope."
"*Undun? These Eyes? Laughing?*"
"Uh uh."
"*Takin' Care of Business? Let It Ride? You Ain't Seen Nothin' Yet?*"
"*You Ain't Seen Nothin' Yet?!*"
She excitedly ran up to the pilot who proceeded to announce
it to the whole plane and everyone fell over laughing. It's like
Monty Python's "nudge nudge wink wink" skit. And that's all
because of Harry Enfield.

"BTO's success was worldwide," Charlie Fach acknowledges. "They
sold in Europe, Japan, Asia, South Africa, South America. The band was
so big at one point, when BTO had a new album coming out, the
German and British companies sent people over to New York to pick
up the masters and take them back and press the albums."
"We were a lucky band," adds Bruce, "because we could have pop
hit singles and AOR, album-oriented rock, album sales. That was amazing in those days. We had credibility in both markets because in those
days hit singles took away your credibility as an AOR act. We had both,
AM pop radio on the one hand and FM rock on the other."
One part of the globe remained largely ignored by the group:
Canada. From the outset, BTO had set its sights exclusively on the

lucrative American market and as a result signed directly to a US label and toured the US relentlessly. The failure of Brave Belt in Canada and the shellacking Randy took from the Canadian music press still hurt, though the sackfuls of money the four brought back to Canada helped salve any wounds. Nevertheless, BTO was a Canadian band at heart, so plans were laid out for the band's conquest of their homeland. True, all their singles and albums had charted well, selling in huge quantities and earning the group several Canadian gold and platinum citations and three Juno awards including Top Producer of 1975 for Randy's work on *NOT FRAGILE*. But they had yet to crisscross the land on a major tour. Nonetheless, their impact had been felt.

"Bachman-Turner Overdrive was the closest thing to a metal band in Canada back then," notes Canadian journalist Larry LeBlanc. "We had hard rock bands here but whenever they went in and recorded, it came out as light sounding. Fludd was incredibly loud live but their recordings were tinky-sounding. April Wine was hard rocking, but recorded things like *Bad Side of the Moon* by Elton John. But here was BTO with these giant guitars revved up. There was nothing like them. I did a piece in *Maclean's* in 1973 or 1974 essentially saying the Stampeders, April Wine, all these bands, their day was over. From now on it was going to be BTO. They were the future of Canadian rock at that time. They swept away all that prissy Canadian pop fluff like *Sweet City Woman* that had come before them."

Like everything BTO did in those days, their first Canadian tour earned the group headlines and healthy returns. BTO's summer 1975 outing became the highest grossing tour in Canadian music history to that point, pulling in $1.5 million in just thirteen days including drawing a record 23,000 to Toronto's CNE bandshell. Retaining their populist appeal, the band always gave their fans what they wanted. "When people go to concerts they want to hear the hits the way they heard them on the radio," notes Charlie Fach, "and BTO gave them what they wanted. They were a band for the people and never gave less than 110 percent."

Though Canadian fans greeted the group like the conquering heroes they were, selling out every stop on the cross-country trek, the four band members and their manager were not prepared for the curious media backlash they encountered. In the eyes of the Canadian press, Bachman-Turner Overdrive had become too big for their britches and had not paid sufficient deference to their Canuck roots, an odd stance given the Canadian media's predilection for embracing our own only after validation by Americans. Accusations of abandoning Canada for greener pastures in the US, then deigning to return for the easy pickin's were levelled at the group at many of the stops along the way. Their decision to let US-based Don Fox book the tour was met with disparaging asides in the music industry. Throughout it all Randy remained steadfast. "We've been down in the United States knocking people dead and only in the last little while have people in Canada realized it," he told one interviewer during the tour. "Canada didn't recognize us when we needed their help. We had to come to the States to get accepted. Why should we care about what happens in Canada now?"

The target of the media assault seemed to be the enormity of the band's financial windfall and the fact that, unlike their contemporaries, they managed to keep most of it. When BTO was mentioned in the media it was generally couched in terms of figures like the band's earning on average $500,000 every ten days. Canadians are supposed to be humble and not talk about money. BTO broke that rule by having the audacity to flaunt their wealth. "It makes me mad when we're attacked for not pretending that money isn't important," Bruce Allen vented to the Halifax media in the midst of the tour. "Sure we're businessmen but, damn it, so is Bob Dylan. Anyone who lasts in rock is a businessman. You have to be. Like anyone else in rock, we're judged by the money we make. I'm not saying we're any better than any band on Yonge Street. But we're richer." Bruce's boasting tended to rub interviewers the wrong way, but no one could argue with his client's accomplishments.

In the face of mounting hostility on the homefront, Bruce determined to fight back. "We made up these passes called 'Flugen Passes' and handed them out to the Canadian press wherever we went across Canada," he chuckles. "It was our own little joke. Flugen was a word we made up and they never knew we were laughing at them. We basically came back and shoved it down the throats of the Canadian press. It was arrogant on our part, on my part, telling them that BTO was the biggest band blah, blah, blah. But we decided to take an aggressive stance. It annoyed other people in the industry but it didn't bother the fans. They loved it. The press would take pretty good shots at us but we would bite back."

"Randy and Bruce became assholes," recalls Larry LeBlanc. "At the opening of their 1975 Canadian tour we were all flown out to Regina, all the music journalists, for a press conference and given press buttons that said 'Flugen.' I don't know what Flugen meant but essentially it was another term for jerk. That was a really bad move because the media then turned on them. That set the band up for a fall. Bruce Allen never learned his lesson about the media. He did the same kind of thing with Loverboy and when the media had its chance to turn on them they did. At that BTO press conference, the whole band were arrogant."

There was a feeling of smugness surrounding the Bachman-Turner Overdrive camp by 1975, confirms Gary Bachman. "There was a period of time when they became rude and cocky. I was appalled at some of the things they did. But they were so huge at one time. For about three years they were outselling everyone. Money changes people. The success really went to their heads. But on the way up the ladder everyone you slap on the head is going to be waiting to stomp you. They thought they would always be up there."

The bloom was already beginning to wilt by the release of *FOUR WHEEL DRIVE* in the spring of 1975, their fourth album in two years. Although the previous two albums had turned platinum (one million units in sales), *NOT FRAGILE* topping out at three and a half million copies, *FOUR WHEEL DRIVE* only earned gold status (500,000 in sales). Clearly the band was going back to the well too often. "I think the band burned itself out, I really do," reflects Fred Turner. "Writing four albums in two years is too much. An album a year, doing a tour for that album, letting that album sell for a period of time, that would have been the smart thing to do. But it was like 'Oh boy, we're making money, everything's happening, let's go for it.' Only we wouldn't do what was necessary to sustain it. Bands like Led Zeppelin would go out for a four-month tour, hit the whole area, then go off the road and spend the rest of the time creatively writing, putting things together and growing. We used ourselves up and never put anything back into it. So there was no momentum to keep it going. We were burning the candle from the opposite ends and when both ends met, there wasn't much there. We got to a point where we had an album that sold over three million copies and then the next album dropped drastically to barely making gold."

FOUR WHEEL DRIVE spawned one hit single that failed to break the Billboard Top 20. *Hey You* once again featured Randy singing lead and packed a veiled message aimed squarely at those who had dismissed him as a spent force in the music business after leaving the Guess Who.

There are some inferences to Burton Cummings in that song, I admit. It was written after hitting number one with *You Ain't Seen Nothing Yet* and *NOT FRAGILE*. "You say you want to change the world, it's all right, with me there's no regrets; it's my turn, the circle game has brought me here." It was my turn to be on top. We all change the world in our own small way and try to feel important and significant. I certainly felt that way after hitting number one again with a band that I had basically salvaged from nothing, a bunch of guys who weren't any better players than were in the Guess Who as far as training and ability. I wasn't picking power players like Domenic Troiano who had just been recruited to the Guess Who. And I did it in a much shorter time with much better contracts and made much more money. So I deserved to gloat a bit after all the mud Burton had slung at me. It was kind of a tongue-in-cheek poke at the Guess Who.

BTO's success was sweet, sure, but I didn't try to rub it in any-one's face. It was all said in the success. I felt a sense of satisfaction on several levels, though. One, knowing that hard work paid off. Another was dispelling the myth from some of my contemporaries in the business that you couldn't make it straight, drug-free. And I showed Burton and company that I was still a force to be reckoned with and could not be stepped on any more. Burton himself said that when he woke up one day to discover that *You Ain't Seen Nothin' Yet* had hit number one it was time to call it quits for the Guess Who. He and the other guys never thought I could do it again.

"When Randy left the Guess Who they were number one with *American Woman* and Burton had a two-and-a-half-year perch to piss all over him," notes journalist Larry LeBlanc. "That was one of the saddest events in Canadian music when Randy left the Guess Who. I don't think Burton ever recovered from it. It was a tremendously fertile period between the two of them. It took Burton years to recover as a songwriter. Every month in the music magazines, Burton would shit all over him. And Randy never fought back. I urged him to but he simply said 'The music will do it.'"

With the victory came the spoils. Always careful with their money on the road, the four members of Bachman-Turner Overdrive applied that same philosophy at home though the millions they were reaping did offer them an opportunity to indulge their fantasies.

We didn't get carried away with excess as a band. On their own, each guy certainly had his moments of what we called "boogalooing" with money, buying Porsches and Ferraris. At one time I had six cars including an Excalibur and a Rolls-Royce. Fred had six Corvettes and six Trans Ams. Fun toys for big boys. It was a lot better than spending it on a rig for smoking crack. And all these toys were appreciable and resaleable; they were investments. Fred has still got one of the first-ever Corvettes, original colour and parts; that's probably worth over a hundred grand today.

While Fred collected cars, Corvettes in particular, I collected children. I was too busy making children. By 1976, Bannatyne Azalea — named after Lorayne's mother's maiden name, not the street in Winnipeg or the Guess Who album — and Brigham Randolph Steel had arrived, expanding the Bachman brood to five, soon to be six with Emilie Lorayne the following year.

Lorayne and I were definitely changed by the success and money, even though we didn't want to admit it at the time. An outing became putting the kids in the car and driving to a mall or Toys-R-Us and giving each of the kids one or two hundred dollars to spend. Give an eight-year-old kid two hundred dollars and he has no idea what to do with it. All he wants is a water pistol or a football. We would go into a store, put something on the counter and say, "I want this" without ever looking at the price. Unfortunately, we became a little obsessed with "I want what I want when I want it" and that carried over to the kids. We lost touch with economic realities because they no longer mattered. Price didn't matter.

"Fred had lots of cars but a lot of cars that never ran," smiles Bruce Allen. "Fred was a dreamer. All Fred had was a lot of stuff. Did he use that stuff? No. But he had a lot of things. Robbie Bachman wanted to be the consummate rock star: blondes, strippers, flashy clothes, jewellery, all the right parties. He wanted to be seen. Still to this day he wants to be thought of as "Robbie Bachman of BTO." He still thinks that has cachet. On the other hand, Blair was smart. He knew he landed in that band by luck, knew he was the chosen one, never blew his money, saved it, and bought smart. He bought in West Vancouver where property always kept its value. Fred went up as high as you can get in North Vancouver; not a smart investment. Blair was the smartest of them all and didn't let it go to his head."

For Robbie Bachman, the fame, wealth, and adulation had a profound impact on his psyche. A teenager plucked from his parents' basement into his brother's band, he now found the world at his feet and indulged his every whim. "I think fame affected Robbie, the youngest one, the most," maintains Gary Bachman. "To be treated like a king, from Japan to Europe, at age nineteen is far more difficult to adjust to than if you had been playing for years and reached success in your late twenties or early thirties. It definitely changed Robbie."

Robbie had been part of our boot camp out on the road in the early years, the endless drives and sleeping in a tent. He was committed to the group and suffered alongside Fred and me. We were the three musketeers together in the early days. He had come right out of high school into the group but it certainly wasn't a glamourous life initially. He could have left but he didn't. He had never really had a normal straight job and I don't think understood fully or can relate to any other life as an adult other than being in a band. Once the rewards came, they came pretty quickly. He came into a band in 1971 having never done anything else other than school, never even played in another band, and three years later he was a millionaire.

A lot of Robbie's personality has been shaped by the fact that he is the youngest of four brothers. He was the baby of the family and treated as such. Whatever your personality traits or character flaws are they become magnified tenfold when you suddenly make a lot of money. If someone isn't a nice person they become *really* not a nice person. Money gives you the freedom to do what you want to do, be who you want to be, and there aren't any real consequences. Everybody puts up with you and hangs around you because of your status and money and will tolerate your tantrums for those reasons. And it's not just in Robbie's case. I saw this with Burton Cummings, too. Success spoiled him even more and exaggerated much of his bad behaviour. I'm sure some of my traits became exaggerated with success as did Bruce Allen's and Fred's. If you like to buy cars, you end up buying dozens of cars. Unfortunately, if you like drugs and drinking, you buy a lot of that. It became the downfall of many bands; there are plenty of casualties in this business. These appetites are limited by your own personal economics. But if you make a lot of money pretty quickly, you can go right off the edge.

Horror stories of squandered fortunes abound in the music business. In fact, tales of artists who actually managed to hold onto their earnings and invest wisely are rare indeed. Upon dissolution in 1975, the Guess Who soon found themselves broke. Garry Peterson lost his luxury home in the exclusive Tuxedo neighbourhood, along with his Mercedes and art collection and was forced to take a job as a night clerk at a suburban Winnipeg hotel. Faced with gigantic tax audits, other latter-day members simply handed over the keys to their homes and walked away. Only Burton was able to weather the storm because of his songwriting royalties. A lawsuit against the group's former management and accountants was eventually settled out of court for a pittance of what the group had lost, a sad legacy for such a groundbreaking band. But the fact remains that with so much money coming in so fast, few artists or managers are equipped to make astute financial decisions for the long haul. It still goes on today. Just ask the Bay City Rollers, MC Hammer, or Vanilla Ice. In the Guess Who's case, they entrusted their financial affairs to a reputable accounting firm who proceeded to lose it all in bad investments.

Never one to make the same mistakes twice, Randy was determined to prevent BTO's money from disappearing into a series of ill-advised investments. Success in the music business is fleeting; you have to grab the money now because it may not be there tomorrow. He had certainly experienced that with the Guess Who. As well, Randy had taken his cue from Jack Richardson's Nimbus Productions, which had staked their future on the Guess Who in 1968 and in return took a significant portion of the band's income as well as their publishing. Randy had invested his own Guess Who nest egg in keeping Brave Belt/BTO afloat, and he expected to be compensated. Bachman-Turner Overdrive was, after all, Randy Bachman's band.

Because I staked the band — my own financial commitment and nobody else's to the tune of $97,000 by the time Charlie Fach called us, I produced and financed the album, paid everyone a salary, paid all the fees, copyrighted the name — I was operating like a production company. In the music industry, a production company signs a band, feeds and clothes them, keeps them afloat on salary, pays the bills and then when the band finally signs a record deal, the production company gets 50 percent or more and the band the rest. That's standard in this business. But I did not do that with BTO. Out of the 12 percent we got from Mercury I could have rightfully taken 6 percent, with the band dividing up the rest, which would have also given me one-quarter. I chose not to do that. I sat the band down and told them I wouldn't do that because I would be cheating my brothers. A normal producer takes at least 3 percent. I wouldn't do that. I took 2 percent and the rest went to the band.

If you add the 2 percent I took off the top for my producer credits to my one-quarter take from the band royalties, it adds up to a greater share. But not half of which I could have been fully justified in taking. If I had taken 6 percent for the production company and given 6 percent to the band, one-quarter of which I would have received , I would have had almost eight points and the guys would have had less than 2 percent each. And that would have been too imbalanced and unfair to them.

I was in control of the money and contracts because I produced the records and published the songs. But on the other hand, I hadn't risked all my own money for nothing, so in return I took the song publishing. No one was paying me interest on that money I invested in keeping the group alive. After all, I was the principal writer and BTO was a vehicle for me to get my songs played. But I also knew I couldn't write a whole album and needed that diversity to show we were a band. I was encouraging Fred and the others to write and giving them suggestions. *Roll On Down the Highway* was a twelve-bar blues progression until I suggested the Led Zeppelin/*Walk Don't Run* solo and guitar riff. I didn't take any credit. They had the gist of the song in the lyrics and basic structure. I also told them that in case it became a turntable hit I needed to have the publishing. That was my payback. And I didn't take full publishing. I gave them 20 percent of the publishing income, which they still get today. I think I was very fair.

I could have rightfully demanded my investment back from the band's revenues off the top, but instead of doing that I got it back in time. If I had done that we would have had nothing. All I wanted to do was keep my bank happy. I had a mortgage to pay. I knew I would get my $97,000 back from two albums, $50,000 per album, and it was to my great joy that instead of waiting eighteen months to renew our option and ask for another album they asked for it in the first six months. I had laid out almost $100,000 and got that back and the guys in the band still got their salary every week, $175 a week. Two years later they were millionaires.

"Randy was much more knowledgeable about the music business than we were and had far more experience," admits Tim Bachman. "The rest of us were pretty much in the dark business-wise. We were happy to be doing what we were doing and trusted him to look after everything. That was a mistake because it taught me that you shouldn't suppose someone will do things the way you think they will. And I think that contributed to the rift between Robbie and Randy that still exists today."

Fred Turner has no regrets about the business arrangements in BTO. "Randy had taken the real gamble with the band so he had the major control of the band," he acknowledges. "There was a lot of animosity from the younger guys especially over why he was reaping so much money. We were signed to Randy and he was signed to the record company. He was, in fact, selling the band to the record company and we were getting a piece. Randy was getting the same share that we would get as a band member, then he was reaping the rest of it as producer, publisher, and things like that. Myself, I could see nothing wrong with that because I would never have taken the gamble he took. It was an unreal gamble so he deserved to get back a real big piece of the pie. But the younger guys couldn't see that, especially after he had been paid back such a big piece of the pie. It caused resentment."

With the money rolling in faster than the band knew what to do with it, Bruce Allen brought in Graeme Waymark to act as financial adviser. "Randy and I were from the same place," states Bruce, "two kids with a limited education, so we got an accountant and believed in him as a professional that he knows what he is doing. We really believed in him like we would believe in a doctor as a professional. What do we know what to do with our money? That's why we leaned on these guys to help us."

Graeme Waymark made a very astute business decision that not only set the four members up literally for life but also remains the envy of their contemporaries. By investing in guaranteed income annuities, the four band members avoided a crippling tax bill in the short term by deferring their taxes on the income to a later date. Today, some twenty-five years after BTO's heyday, each member continues to receive a monthly five-figure cheque and will do so until death.

We had tried other investments like fishing boats and apartment buildings early on but they all went awry. The government wouldn't allow depreciation deductions because they viewed these as tax dodges. At the time in 1976, Revenue Canada was closing the tax loophole for forwarded averaging income annuities so our business manager, Graeme Waymark, suggested we take advantage of this window of opportunity before it closed and tie up as much money as we could. I thought it would be a wise decision to take our recording profits which we only saw every six months anyway and sock them away where they were a guaranteed payback for a reduced tax load. Back then, if you made a million bucks you paid $900,000 in taxes that year. The annuities allowed us to put that million away and not pay any tax on it and if you took out $100,000 a year you paid far less taxes. We took what we had, asked Mercury Records for an advance, I got what I could get from my publishing and we even borrowed money from the bank after providing royalty statements and projected earnings. As the royalties came in, we paid off the bank. We invested several million dollars with the principal paid back in fifteen years. In 1991, I was having heart attacks thinking the annuities would end once they had matured but my accountant assured me they were for life. So what we have been receiving since 1991 is interest on the investment. It has had its ups and downs over the years. Confederation Life went through some rocky times so we received notice that all annuities were being reduced 15 percent. I ran into Fred Turner at that time and asked him, "Are you getting 15 percent less on your annuities?"

"Yeah, but at least we're still getting them. We surpassed our payback."

Since that time I have been notified that they are up 10 percent. So it was a wise, secure investment that I hope the other guys in the band are grateful for. I wish I could take credit for it but I can't. It set us all up for life. From 1976 on, we enjoyed millionaire status. Most bands of our vintage have little to show now for all their hard work. Look at the guys in the latter versions of Guess Who. They lost everything. At the time, some of our contemporaries scoffed at what they perceived as our focus on the bottom line. But I am thankful we made the right decisions. When you're getting five figures a month for life that's a pretty comfy blanket.

"I figured it was a great idea," recounts Fred Turner "because I have never been a money manager. When I get money in my hands I tend to spend it. So I told the accountants to take everything they could get their hands on that I hadn't spent and buy these annuities. That gave me a salary every month for the rest of my life. So that's what we did. It allows me to write my music and do what I want to do without having to go out and work. And if it dwindles, I'll adjust my lifestyle accordingly as long as I don't get crazy and think that I have to buy a bunch of elaborate things."

Mercury Records showed its support for the group by coming through with their royalties early allowing the four members to take advantage of the tax loophole before the end of the tax year. As Charlie Fach remembers it, "Near the end of 1975, Randy or Bruce Allen called me and asked 'Christmas is coming and the guys would like to have some money.' Their royalties weren't due until ninety days after the end of the year. Regardless, I called Irwin Steinberg and said 'Let's send these guys some money.' Irwin called me back and said, 'They have about $925,000 coming to them. I'll cut a cheque for a million dollars and you fly it up to Canada for them.' So I flew up and on the plane I was showing everyone that cheque. A million dollars. It was a nice Christmas present. We overpaid them but the way the product was selling it was no problem." Randy still possesses a Xerox of that million-dollar cheque.

Record companies are notorious for screwing their artists out of their money, siphoning it off here and there. It's almost a given in the music industry. But Mercury was different. We had an extraordinary relationship with them when it came to money, which is rare in this business. I've envied it ever since. It was a personal relationship as opposed to strictly business. When we heard that the Canadian government was closing the loophole on forward averaging annuities, we called Mercury and asked how much money was in the pipeline for us from all our foreign sales.

They told us and when we explained the situation to them we got a couple of million dollars that wasn't owing for at least six months. They did that for us.

We did an audit of Mercury's books expecting hundreds of thousands of dollars to be owing to us and instead we discovered to our chagrin that they had overpaid us by about $26,000. We were disappointed. So I called up Bruce Allen and told him, "Well, I guess we have to give it back."

"Are you crazy?!"

"No, no. If the situation were reversed we would be screaming for it, throw ourselves a big party, and split it up."

So we gave it back with one caveat: the lady who made the mistake on our behalf not be fired. A couple of years later we were in Chicago for a party to receive some gold records and we discovered that same woman had been promoted to manager of business affairs.

By now a millionaire several times over, Randy decided it was time to live the life of a wealthy rock star with Lorayne in their own palatial manor. What began as a weekend retreat just across the border in Lynden, Washington, would rapidly expand to become the couple's dream home with a three-million-dollar price tag.

We were living in New Westminster and thought it would be fun to go down to Lynden and Bellingham on weekends and maybe have a couple of horses the kids could ride on our own land. All we intended to have was a simple Lindal-style pre-designed cedar house, the kind with several plans and you choose one. Just a house for weekends. But we had a couple of frights involving our kids where we were living in New Westminster, me being so successful and the kids being accessible, that caused us great trepidation. With me travelling all the time, it was a bit unnerving for Lorayne. I even took out kidnapping insurance. We wanted a greater sense of security for the kids and had purchased this property down there already so we decided to build a large family home and relocate. We pulled up stakes and set up outside Lynden.

We had initially looked further inland in British Columbia, around Abbotsford and Langley, but found property values too expensive. Someone suggested we take a drive just across the border and we discovered the property values really cheap. We bought twenty acres in 1976, the year I got my green card, and expanded it to thirty when we started building the house the following year. Our property was like an island in an ocean of wheat. I found out later that the photo of the Guess Who that accompanied a cover story in the *Weekend* magazine back in 1968 about our sound being "wheatfield soul" was actually shot in that same field.

I figured if I lived in Lynden it wouldn't make much difference because it was only a seventy-five-minute drive to Vancouver, so I could make our meetings with Bruce Allen or Graeme Waymark. Other than that, we were simply flying in and out anyway to tour. It didn't seem like a problem to relocate to Lynden so the house plans kept expanding from a weekend retreat to a permanent residence. We adapted the original blueprint from wood to stone all round, added more bedrooms in case we had more kids, a gym, an office for me, and suddenly it was becoming an expensive house. But I didn't mind because I saw this as our dream house where we would live happily ever after. I had money in the bank, the group was still successful, and my future looked secure.

The 16,000-square-foot house had literally everything: family room with indoor swimming pool, twelve-man hot tub, elevator, triple attached garage, stables for horses and a barn that I converted into a state-of-the-art recording studio. Resembling an old abbey or castle, the house featured three full floors and a fully completed basement. The second floor included the master bedroom with walk-in closets and a huge bathroom and tub that could hold four people. Down the hall were six bedrooms, one for each child, and a large double kid's bathroom. On the main floor I had a spacious office with a quadraphonic stereo system mounted on the walls. The room had a twenty-foot ceiling and skylight and in the middle I hung the original wooden gear that we had tripped over in the field out back of Mushroom Studios. I had lights on it and it looked impressive. Also on that same floor was the entranceway and foyer, kitchen, dining room, a library with a television, and living room. When the house was being built, it was the talk of the community.

The barn became my playroom where I built my studio and filled it with my dream equipment. It allowed me to write, record, and produce while still being at home each night. The downfall of this business was having to be away from home and the ones you love so much.

"I wasn't privy to the conversation where they decided to build the giant house on that lot so I don't know what the reasoning was," offers Tal Bachman, by then nine years old. "I've heard they were concerned for our security but the weird thing is when you drive down to that property, it is completely conspicuous. If you said to someone 'Do you want to know where Randy Bachman lives?' all you had to do was drive the twenty miles down H Street Road and there it was, this gigantic house sitting all alone in the middle of a field. We didn't have a lot of neighbours, just cows, so I spent a lot of time by myself in the woods with my BB gun. I have no idea what they were thinking but they were young, had a bunch of money, and one thing led to another and it just got out of hand.

"For that period of three or four years, Dad was gone an awful lot," remembers Tal, "but I think he felt he had a job to do mainly feeding his ever-increasing family. It was just one of those things that was a given, his being away a lot. I don't really remember feeling neglected or anything. My Dad was just on another trip. I was sort of emotionally and intellectually self-sufficient anyway. I didn't need someone to always be there to tell me what to do or think of a game for me to play. I had my own little thing going on and would spend most of my time by myself. Plus, I had a bunch of sisters who I didn't really want to be around because they played with dolls and teased me.

"I don't really remember there ever being some epiphany where all of a sudden it clicked 'Hey, my Dad is a rock star.' By the time I was conscious of the world around me he had already been in the Guess Who and had a bunch of hits and was a figure of note. From the earliest age, I was hearing his music on the radio. So it wasn't like I walked out of a cocoon and saw him from a different perspective. I remember one time when I was still a kid the family, my Mom and the kids, went down to the Vancouver Coliseum to see BTO play a soldout show at the height of their popularity. That was a big deal because it was the first time we had seen him in a giant arena in full rock regalia with a light show and everything. But even so, it was still in line with what I perceived of him anyway so it wasn't any great revelation."

Nevertheless, the fame and wealth did have an impact on the children. "We would go to Southgate Mall in Seattle," Tal continues, "and each kid would be handed a hundred bucks and let loose in a toy store and go cuckoo."

"When I was five and we were living on Queen's Avenue in New Westminster," recalls Kezia, on her first awareness of her father's profile, "I had a lemonade stand outside. But no one was buying my lemonade and I was quite upset. So instead of a sign saying simply 'Lemonade 25 cents' I wrote 'Rock Star Lemonade' and as every car passed by I yelled out 'Rock star lemonade for sale! Come get your lemonade from the famous home of Randy Bachman.' I think my Mom put a stop to that pretty quickly but I have photos of the whole band coming over to buy lemonade from my stand to appease me. I think that was the first realization that my Dad was famous and I was going to use it to my advantage. But the reality was it all seemed like quite a normal life to me. I didn't know any better. Both my parents were adamant that our lives seem as normal as possible. We all did chores around the house. My mother was quite heavily invested in the idea that we worked hard for what we got instead of having it handed to us. I remember clearly my Dad saying, 'Our kids don't have to work but they need to learn how.'"

Kezia attributes the Bachman siblings' strong sense of proper values and morality to their mother. "She worked very hard to instill good values in us all at an early age. Since my Dad was gone all the time when we were growing up, it's a good thing we had a mother who was so dedicated to being a good mom, because we all turned out to be quite respectable people as adults. Every morning we got up and read the Scriptures; we had family home evenings every Monday night; and there was always a chart on the wall prompting us to be a good person like 'Be honest' and 'Get along with one another.' All the kids were at a crucial age where if she hadn't inculcated any values in us we wouldn't ever have them. Every meal was a family meal with a well-balanced diet — breakfast, lunch and dinner — not just grabbing a piece of toast on the way out. And besides that she had responsibilities in the church as well. We never missed church. We had a stable life, which was pretty amazing considering what the circumstances were. She had everything regimented and whipped into shape. There was always a project for us. I was never bored. There was always something to be done."

Nevertheless, when he was home, Randy always had a special time for his kids. "We used to have this thing every night when we were little called a snuggle," smiles Kezia. "We used to look forward to getting our snuggle when we went to bed each night. 'Who's giving me my snuggle tonight?' And it would be either Mom or Dad. All it meant was one of them would come into our room, lay on the floor at the bottom of the bed, and sing us a song or tell us a story. My Mom's snuggles consisted of petting our head and singing opera arias while my Dad's would be crazy stories or songs that made us laugh so hard we would fall out of bed. He always sang this silly little song about walking over a bridge and there was a giant under the bed who gruffly yelled out, 'Who's walking across my bridge?' And you'd sing 'It's me, it's Kezia!'

And you would have to tell what you brought the giant to eat and he would either let you pass or eat you. Dad used to come up with those little things that you knew were just for you and your brothers and sisters and nobody else."

BTO closed out 1975 with the release of its fifth album, *HEAD ON.* With pressure from Mercury Records for more BTO product, the album was recorded in a rush and suffered from weaker material. The BTO formula was being stretched too thin. Critics were not as kind as in the past and *HEAD ON* barely turned gold. "Looking back, we shouldn't have put out so much product so fast," admits Charlie Fach. "*FOUR WHEEL DRIVE* and *HEAD ON* came out in close succession and we should have spaced it out for more longevity. But that's the way it was back then. When an artist is hot you just run with it as fast as you can before it slows down."

As if to underscore Randy's stewardship of the group, *HEAD ON* featured a photo of Randy front and centre. Though not intentional, the cover nonetheless portrayed the growing division within BTO and the feeling that the other three were merely serving Randy.

The original cover concept for the *HEAD ON* album was two semi-trailers smashing head on, but the label thought it was too grotesque and might imply the band was smashing and burning. Instead they put the head shots of each of us on it and as it folded up mine ended up on the front. It became horrific for me for the next two years because my face was the one shown in the record racks so in airports I was constantly being spotted. "Hey, aren't you Randy Bachman?"

The *HEAD ON* album featured an unlikely guest appearance by one of the founders of rock 'n' roll and an early hero of Randy's.

I had gone to LA to mix the *HEAD ON* album and discovered that a couple of tracks needed a piano. I called Bruce Allen in Vancouver.

"I need someone who can play rock 'n' roll piano like Little Richard." "What about Elton John?"

Elton was busy recording at Caribou Studios and wasn't about to be pried away. Bruce mentioned a couple of other players but they were all too young.

"I need somebody who can do that primal, jungle rock 'n' roll piano pounding like Little Richard." There are only a few players who can really do that style justice.

"Well, why don't you ask Little Richard?" Bruce suggested.

"Yeah, sure," I replied, facetiously.

"No, really. He just played a club here in Vancouver. I've got his number. His brother Payton is his manager. I'll give him a call."

I was beside myself at the thought of playing with Little Richard, the black Elvis.

A couple of hours later, my phone rang and it was Bruce.

"I got a hold of Payton. Little Richard thinks BTO are great. He'll play on your album."

"Fabulous!"

So we set it up for the following Monday at noon. I continued mixing the album but saved the two songs, *Take It Like a Man* and *Stay Alive*, until the end, once Little Richard had laid down his piano parts.

Sunday afternoon the phone rang at the studio. It was Payton, Richard's brother.

"Hi. I'm looking forward to Richard coming down tomorrow. Do you need anything?"

"Richard wants to practise the songs."

"There's not enough time to get a cassette together and get it to you. The session is tomorrow. They're really easy rhythm and blues rock 'n' roll songs like he's done in the past."

"What key are they in?"

"The key of A."

"Oh. Are you sure they're in A?"

"Yeah. They're already recorded."

"Okay." And he hung up.

An hour later Payton called back.

"Can you change the keys?"

"No, they're already recorded. Richard's just playing to the tape."

"Okay. Bye."

The next day, noon rolls around and Little Richard doesn't show. Two-thirty, still no show. I'm sitting in the studio killing time playing guitar when I hear a commotion at the door. I had seen Little Richard several times onstage with a big band — this row of saxophones, two drummers, and two bass players, and every time he stepped out onstage, the band was playing the riff to *Lucille*. So as Richard walks through the door, I started playing *Lucille*.

Dum dum da da dut dut da da, dum dum da da dut dut da da.

There he was, the Man himself, decked out to the nines in a white ermine coat over a cape and an orange jumpsuit with a silver R on it and carrying a travelling make-up case. He had on the eyeliner and mascara and was every inch Mr. Rock 'n' Roll, the epitome of cool.

Suddenly he stopped.

"That's it! I'm not playin' on no white boys' version of *Lucille* making 'em money off *my* record. I'm leavin'!"

I jumped up, ran over to him, and exclaimed, "No, I was just playing your entrance. This isn't the song you're playing on."

I played the tape of the first song for him in the control booth and told him the chord changes. It was a simple number.

"What key's it in?" asked Richard.

"A"

"Are you sure?"

"Yes. It's just A, D, A, E, and an F#m." As he looks at me, Richard spaces out when I say F#m like I'm speaking in another language.

I had him try playing to the tape, but he couldn't do it. He couldn't follow a simple chart.

Payton called me aside and said, "Richard's really embarrassed."

So I figured I would try one more thing. I picked up my guitar and went into the studio, plugged into a little Fender amp, and sat beside him at the piano.

"Let's warm up a bit and just jam." So I played some of his songs and he started wailing away. They're all in G, C, or D. But the minute I said A or F#m he was lost.

Before I went out to join Richard I told my engineer, Mark Smith, to vary the speed of the tape, which slows it down and alters the pitch. Mark took a tuner and got the speed of the song a tone lower to G.

"When I give you the signal, start rolling the tape," I told him.

With Richard thinking he's only playing along with me on guitar, we tried *Take It Like a Man* in G. Unbeknownst to Richard, I give Mark the signal to roll tape and Richard takes off, totally rockin'. He's going crazy pounding out 16th notes, 32nd notes, 64th notes as I yell, "Play it Richard!" You can actually hear that on the track. Afterwards Mark gives me the okay sign. He got it all on tape.

"Richard, come into the control room and listen."

"What are you talkin' about?"

Mark brought the song back up to normal speed and Richard's looking at Payton.

"Who's that playin' piano?"

"You are!"

"Really?! What key's it in?"

"A."

"A? Hallelujah! Praise the Lord! I can play in A! Randy's taught me to play in the key of A!" And he fell to his knees.

I was stunned.

"Play it again. Play it again. Lord, I'm playing in A!"

We did the same thing for *Stay Alive* with Richard nailing it on the slower speed. Here he was one of the original rockers and he only knew a few chords. He was the master of three-chord rock 'n' roll. And he had been recording for twenty-five years and never knew about variable speed on tapes. The poor guy had been wailing away at the top of his lungs without realizing he could have the pitch lowered by the tape speed.

When Little Richard came through Vancouver again a few months later, we all went to see him and presented him with a crown as the king of rock 'n' roll.

Despite the presence of Little Richard, *HEAD ON* failed to make much headway beyond the group's loyal fan base and the single culled from the album, *Looking Out for #1*, offered a radical departure from the group's hard-rockin' sound. It did, however, signal that Randy was looking to expand BTO's range of styles and grow beyond their stereotype. Featuring a lengthy jazz-flavoured guitar break demonstrating Randy's virtuosity, *Looking Out for #1* also became a personal statement by the guitarist.

That chord progression was from the *Mickey Baker Guitar Book* Lenny Breau had told me about when I was a teenager. All the jazz stuff I've played in my career including *Undun* and *Looking Out for #1* is from either Lenny or that Mickey Baker book. I was very thrilled to play that song for Lenny much later. I hadn't seen him in years. My verses on that song are the endings to just about every third jazz song. Lenny had shown it to me from an old jazz standard called *Mean to Me*. The downward-dropping bass line chords are from that song and my chorus tag is from Ray Charles's *This Little Girl of Mine*, which the Everly Brothers had cut.

Not a lot of deep thought went into the lyrics, though so many people have attached it to me and my career. I was just looking for something to sing over these chords and someone had mentioned something to me about sticking to your goals and following your dreams and that sparked it. I felt a little awkward at the end saying "I mean me," but it's true that you can't look after others if you can't take care of yourself. The song has become associated with me but not intentionally on my part. Strangely enough, it is the opening track on a *BTO GREATEST HITS* CD, so when people buy that album expecting thumping, smashing rock they hear this soft jazz number.

In a move that generally signifies a loss of faith in an artist's future earning potential, Mercury Records rushed out *THE BEST OF BTO (SO FAR)* in 1976 as if to milk the cash cow before putting it out to pasture. Although the album ultimately went triple platinum and remains their most consistent seller, all was not well between the label and band. The freefall in sales following *NOT FRAGILE* sent a clear message: BTO's time just might be up. As well, the group and label had been the victim of its own success. The marketing and promotion team had launched BTO so effectively that it had been lured away to other labels seeking the same for their artists. Their replacements did not share a history with the group. As a result, BTO began to feel alienated from the label.

More than that, there was a growing dissension festering between the four members themselves and the focus of that frustration was on what was perceived as Randy's greed. Bruce Allen sums up those feelings: "After a while Randy started saying 'It doesn't matter what it sounds like, we're BTO and it'll be a smash.' And that's when Randy made mistakes. It was expedient, it was money, but it was short-term money. He didn't think long term. He didn't think about getting better songs, taking more time between albums, waiting to get better material. Instead he wanted to rush, rush, rush — get the advance, get the song publishing money, get the new record out there, get another tour — and finally he killed it. In those days I didn't have the strength to stop him. I wish I could have stopped him. He didn't need to put out a record all the time. He needed to take some time off, let the American public wait, go work more overseas. But no, Randy wanted to make more money.

"Every time Randy walked into a studio he was making money as a producer and a publisher and the other guys didn't share in that. They thought it was unfair and when they started protesting against material because Randy was knocking it off, you could see the group falling apart. The boys fought him on it, I've got to give them credit for that, but they couldn't stop it, nor could I. Randy had the contracts signed, Randy was BTO. The record company was pushing him for more product and Randy complied. He knew better. You can make it last. Sure there was pressure from the record label, but Randy had been around long enough to know that he could say to them 'We can't write right now. We're taking some time off.' We could have claimed writers' block, anything, but no, the band continued to put out product. Randy was the voice now and he wanted the hits. The prevailing attitude was that BTO could fart and it would sell a million."

CHAPTER 8

Everything Is Grey

Following Bachman-Turner Overdrive's remarkable rise in the mid-seventies, record labels came knocking on Randy's door to see if a little of his own brand of magic could work for their artists. As a producer with a proven track record, Randy soon found himself in demand and as a result formed his own record label for his side projects. With his knack for catchy radio fodder, Randy would go on to score an impressive string of AM chart hits in Canada for one of his protegés, Trooper. *Two for the Show, Round Round We Go, Oh Pretty Lady, General Hand Grenade, Santa Maria, The Boys in the Bright White Sports Car,* and the ultimate party songs *We're Here for a Good Time* and *Raise a Little Hell* all possess Randy's distinctive commercial touch. They remain rock classics alongside the Guess Who and BTO catalogues. In the process, Trooper would learn valuable lessons in the Randy Bachman school of hit songwriting and production that would serve them well.

As my experience and confidence grew from *AXE* through Brave Belt to BTO, I became a record producer. After writing and creating a song, as producer I could then direct the vision of how that song should ultimately be, the soundscape. The success I accrued with BTO elevated me into a role as a bankable producer who could possibly deliver hits for other artists. I received dozens of offers to produce bands like 38 Special and an Australian outfit called the Dingoes, among others. As soon as you hit #1, people assume you can impart that same formula on them. It's a naïve assumption. Parachuting me into a whole new environment was not necessarily going to be the ticket to success. The artist had to have some talent and potential.

Following the success of *You Ain't Seen Nothin' Yet* and *NOT FRAGILE*, I was offered my own label by several companies eager to ride my gravy train by allowing me to produce new artists. These are known in the business as vanity labels. MCA made me the best offer so I proceeded to open my own label. All I needed was a name and an act. I had an old 1959 Fender Stratocaster that I had christened my Legend guitar. It had been through so much it was rather legendary to everyone around the Guess Who and BTO. Also, after BTO's success, deejays on the West Coast would play a Guess Who song and a BTO song back to back then announce, "This guy lives around here and he's a legend." So when it came time to create a name for my label, Legend Records seemed a natural choice.

Running a record label can be a time-consuming endeavour, especially for someone like me who already had a full-time job with BTO. Rather than turn to Bruce Allen to act as label manager, because he was already overworked managing BTO and his growing stable of other artists, instead I approached Graeme Waymark, my financial adviser. I also felt it would be a smart move to keep BTO separate from the acts on my label. But I think it alienated Bruce, who took it as a snub. As for a recording act, I found Trooper and a friend of Bruce Allen's, Bill Wray. In the end I was forced to farm out Bill Wray's album production to someone else because of time constraints on me. Trooper was a different story.

Bruce Allen and his partner Sam Feldman had a pet band they had been working with in the local clubs around Vancouver by the name of Applejack. Sam called me one day and asked if I would give the band some tips on writing and perhaps produce them. They had reached a level where their next step was to record. BTO had some time off the road where we were at home ostensibly writing new material for our next album. However, because I tend to write all the time, not specifically for one album project, I had a backlog already. At that moment, Sam called me again to convince me to check out Applejack who, as it turned out, were playing a couple of blocks from my house at the Royal Arms Hotel in New Westminster. It was an easy stroll from my place. I went in, met the group, caught a few numbers, and thought they were a decent band. I went again the next day and asked them if they had any original material, which they did, one or two numbers; but once I heard what they had I realized the songs weren't very strong. Over several weeks in-between my BTO commitments, I began the process of teaching them how to develop their own material.

The method I employed with the group was fairly rudimentary. First, I suggested they list their ten favourite songs. Their list was typical of the time with *Brown Sugar, Jumpin' Jack Flash, All Right Now* — all the best-known hard rock hits. I then told them to pick one song from the list, keep the whole song and chorus, but sing a different melody over it using the same lyrics. Add a new guitar solo as well. Once they had a new melody, I told them to change the lyrics. For example, if it was about a girl, make it about a car. Then change the phrasing and breaths. Finally, take the chord progression they had been using from the song and alter the tempo. Now they had a new song derived from their influences. They did this with three songs over two weeks while I was away. When I came back and asked them to play their songs, I couldn't recognize the originals they had adapted. They were that good. From that experience, the group began writing songs in earnest in preparation for their first album. Around this time, I suggested they drop the Applejack moniker because I remembered a British Merseybeat group of the same name. They eventually came up with Trooper.

The guys were easy to work with, well rehearsed and soon ready to go into the studio for their first album. By that time, we had run through their original numbers so often I knew them backwards and forwards. I took them down to Kaye-Smith Studios in Seattle where I knew everybody from recording there with BTO. We banged out the tracks over a week, only to discover the tape operator had altered the tape heads, rendering a week's worth of work unusable. I was under the gun for time because I was due on tour with BTO so, in apologizing for the screw up, the manager at Kaye-Smith gave us free time to complete the album. I said to the guys in Trooper: "Remember how you used to run through all your tunes back to back for me in rehearsals?"

"Yeah?"

"Guess what we're doing Monday?"

"What?"

"Monday we're doing the album. Tuesday, overdubs; Wednesday, mixing. That's it."

We did the whole album's band tracks in one day with vocals and overdubbing the following day. We delivered the debut Trooper album to MCA free. It got a lot of airplay and the band took off.

Trooper became an instant success across Canada because their singles were radio-friendly and their albums and live shows really rocked. They later brought Frank Ludwig in on keyboards from another Vancouver band and he expanded their sound and writing. I was determined at the outset that Trooper not be just another BTO. I wanted to make sure they had a different sound and I was able to apply my experience at crafting good AM pop songs with them. I always had my ear in tune with radio. I think one of the reasons Trooper sounded different from BTO was the absence of a rhythm guitar. BTO always had a strong heavy rhythm sound that I took from early rock 'n' roll. I added chunky rhythm guitar to BTO tracks almost like the horn section riffs in those old Fats Domino/Little Richard recordings. A song like *Gimme Your Money Please* simulates horn parts on the rhythm guitar using heavy-gauge strings. That was an essential ingredient in BTO that wasn't in Trooper. Trooper also had a more vocal sound than BTO.

"Randy has an incredibly commercial ear," states Trooper singer/songwriter Ra McGuire. "He absolutely knew the things that would work and those that wouldn't. He was amazing like that. He would listen to our material and immediately be able to say 'This song works. That song doesn't. This other song would work if that part weren't in it.' It must have been kind of fun for him. And we would slavishly work toward what he said. There were occasions too, when he would strap on a guitar and play with us. He came up with the guitar solo and the little turnaround in *Two for the Show*."

Ra remembers working with Randy as a very positive and fun experience. "A key element of our time with Randy was the enormous amount of respect we had for him on a number of levels, not just musical. It wasn't a dictatorial situation. What he offered in the way of guidance was always welcomed. There were lots of downtime moments where we would all be sitting around and Randy would get out his guitar. Once, we went through every Beatles song we could think of, Randy playing and us singing, until we exhausted our own memories. We had to phone Brian Smith's wife in Vancouver to ask her to dig out her Beatles albums and read out song titles to us so we could play some more."

Guitarist Brian Smith found a mentor in Randy. "Randy gave me a sense of my own worth as a guitar player. I developed a lot of confidence working with him. I remember he told me that we needed some solo guitar at the end of *Raise a Little Hell* so I went in and played a solo. When I was finished, he came running out of the booth jumping up and down saying, 'That's the best thing I ever heard!' That's the kind of support you want from your producer. I can still see the grin on his face. He would do some very kind things, too. I remember he called me up once. 'Chet Atkins is playing the Queen Elizabeth Theatre in Vancouver. You and I are going down there and you're going to meet him.' He picked me up, we went to the show, and it was just awesome. Afterwards, he had it all arranged for us to go backstage and he introduced me to Chet Atkins. Then Chet made a short speech on behalf of himself and Gretsch guitars and presented Randy with a Chet Atkins Gretsch guitar. Randy hadn't said a word to me about this but I was very honoured to be there with him. And at the same time he was also introducing me to a different kind of music I probably wouldn't have listened to on my own."

Randy's knack for finding just the right nuance to enhance a recording found full flight with Trooper. "On *General Hand Grenade*, right towards the end of recording it," recalls Ra with a chuckle, "Randy told us all to go into the vocal booth and sound like we were having a party. All the way through the song we were whooping and yelling, hollering out words that didn't make sense and when you hear the song it really makes the record jump. It was a brilliant idea. Another thing he did was on *We're Here for a Good Time*. While we were tracking that one, our drummer started hitting his cheeks making that tick-tock kind of sound so Randy told him to do it on the track. That's the sound that most people think is a metronome. He had to do it over so many times to get it in pitch that his face was like hamburger by the time we finished. That was just Randy hearing something that worked." On another occasion, Ra and Randy disagreed over a song title only to have Randy acquiesce. "Randy wanted to change *Raise a Little Hell* to *Raise a Little Howl*," he laughs, "but I prevailed on him and I'm glad I did."

Between 1975 and 1978 Randy Bachman and Trooper were a winning combination notching up more than a half-dozen Canadian hits.

But if Randy's talent for crafting hit songs found favour with Trooper, his hard-nosed business savvy took them by surprise. "Randy is a tough businessman," notes Brian Smith. "He never came across to us as being that brutal, but we would hear all these stories. Then we started hearing things to do with ourselves that we had been kind of shielded from, but we would simply think 'Well that's okay. He's just looking after his best interests.'" Indeed, Randy owned the group's publishing and as producer took points on each album and single. But neither Ra nor Brian, who wrote most of the hits, harbour any regrets. "I look at our publishing deal today and think 'I would have signed anything.' He could have asked for more and I would have signed it. In retrospect, it was the standard of the day anyway. I don't begrudge it."

Adds Ra, "I don't think we were that critical of the business arrangements. We were so pleased to be working with him. He was Randy Bachman and how he did things was just how he did things. It never really occurred to us. He was extremely successful, extremely prolific, and had written some of the greatest songs ever written and he was our producer!"

Randy's relationship with Trooper ended during recording of their *THICK AS THIEVES* album. Facing family pressures on the home front, Randy wasn't able to devote as much time to the project. The two writers shouldered a portion of the responsibility in his absence. Having recorded four albums with Randy, Ra and Brian had learned their lessons from the master and now felt comfortable in the producer's role. "Randy had limited the amount of time he would come into the studio to work with us on that album," recalls Ra. "Prior to that, we had all gone in together and all left together. Now he was setting times for himself. I can only speculate it was a family issue for him. We never talked about it but he would leave at ten or twelve at night. As friendly and talkative as he sometimes is, he would never talk about his private life. He is a very private person. But a lot of the creativity comes after ten o'clock once you've got everything set up and rolling. It usually doesn't start to take shape until after midnight. After working with

Randy for several years we had the sense of how to make a record."
Expecting to see a co-production credit when the album was released,
Ra and Brian were dismayed to see their names omitted. "I don't think
it was Randy that did it," suggests Ra, "I think it was the manager of the
record label, Legend, but we were really hurt by it. After that we sev-
ered our relationship. It was an unfortunate thing. But we had learned
a lot from him and were now able to go out on our own after that.
There is a song on our next album called *Go Ahead and Sue Me* that
nobody realizes is about our split with Randy."

BTO took Trooper along as opening act on tour in the States a
few times to try to break them south of the border but the group
didn't want to be there. They preferred to stay in Canada where
they were already big as opposed to working for less and trying to
crack the US market, which they never did. It was safer to play in
Canada. I'm not putting them down, that's the road they chose to
follow and have achieved the level of success they wanted. Rather
than open for $1,500 with the hope of building a market and
working towards $100,000 they would rather play for $5.000 in
Canada. Trooper chose the security.

I did five albums with the group including a greatest hits album
called *HOT SHOTS* that represents Canadian seventies radio rock at
its finest because Trooper captured that sound and enjoyed so
many hits. But after that the band changed. Ra came and thanked
me for guiding them to the success they enjoyed, then announced
that the group felt they were now ready to produce themselves.

The success of BTO became mind boggling by 1975. The
momentum we had built in North America spread around the
world from Asia to Europe with gold and platinum records coming in from all corners of the world along with offers to tour.
Trooper and my Legend Records label were merely diversions during my downtime with BTO, and it became increasingly difficult
to find enough time to allocate to their needs. I love to be

involved in music and Trooper offered a different direction than BTO. From that experience, we managed to create a body of music that remains timeless and still plays on radio across Canada every day. Trooper has become Canada's fun party band. Their songs have that joie de vivre that makes them infectious.

Scoring hits for Trooper led to more offers to produce other artists, one being Hollywood Starz. I listened to their tape and thought they were great but I had to call them and pass on it because I simply had no free time at that point. Unfortunately, one of the songs I heard on that tape came back to haunt me. A little later, Charlie Fach called to say BTO were off the charts and needed a single between albums to keep the name in the public eye. Head On was done its chart run and the next album wasn't ready yet. All we needed were a couple of songs to choose for a single. I came up with *Down to the Line*, which was selected as the single. It was released, and four months later I received a letter from one of the guys who wrote for Hollywood Starz, Mark Anthony. He had written a song for that group entitled *Escape* that ended up on an Alice Cooper album. Cooper had contributed to it along with Kim Fowley. In the letter he pointed out that the two songs, *Escape* and *Down to the Line*, bore the same chording riff. He was correct, it was identical, only the lyrics were different. In my rush to come up with a new song, the riff I had heard months before had stuck in my head and emerged in *Down to the Line*. There was no contest. I ordered all the writer royalties be directed to Mark and amended the credit to read Bachman, Anthony, Cooper, and Fowley. So I wrote a song with Alice Cooper and never met him.

The release of *THE BEST OF BTO (SO FAR)* in 1976 had bought the group some much-needed time to catch their breath and reassess their position following three years of solid work. The rewards had been beyond anyone's wildest expectations, but the costs in terms of personal lives and the dynamics within the group were beginning to take their toll. In early 1977, Randy once again took the group into the studio but this time he had an agenda in mind: it was time to rock the boat, to tinker with the formula and try moving BTO ahead. But even he was tiring of the race and his contributions were nowhere near his usual standards. The results would be devastating for the group. The *FREEWAYS* album would become the BTO's crucible.

When you become a successful band there is always this dichotomy within your fan base and within the media. There are those who don't want you to change, who don't want you to move away from what they love about you, from the formula that brought you success. . But the other faction criticizes you for not changing, accusing you of being stuck in a rut or playing it too safe. You can never please both factions. By the latter seventies, I sensed a change in the music. It was happening everywhere. The Doobie Brothers recruited Michael McDonald and reinvented themselves on *TAKIN' IT TO THE STREET*; the Stones did a disco song; dance music was becoming increasingly popular, and live bands weren't getting booked. The two guitars, bass, and drums lineup just wasn't cutting it. I brought in strings on the next album, *FREEWAYS*, and used horns. This wasn't anything that revolutionary for me, I had worked with strings and horns in the Guess Who. But I was trying to push a few boundaries with BTO. I was looking for a transition to something new. My thinking was, "It might not be successful with this album but it could open some doors on the next one." Had we stuck it out, the next one might have been the solidifying album. Who knows? You go up to bat and take three big strikes as hard as you can and if you get a hit, great; if you strike out, you go back to the dugout and try again.

We were fighting a revolutionary change in rock music worldwide. Disco was flourishing and artists were spreading out, mixing more influences into their sound and reinventing themselves. I tried to change with the *FREEWAYS* album. It might have worked, but the dissension within the band and management got back to the label who weren't about to go out on a limb to pump a lot of money into something that some members believed wasn't our strongest effort. There was rebellion from within the ranks. I was no longer getting the same level of cooperation from the other guys who would always chip in their parts. I even felt that part of the reticence and lack of cooperation manifested itself in some of the playing, which I believed was not up to par on purpose. I sensed a withdrawal by the others in being a creative unit. I found out later that if I had sought more creative input from them, Robbie would have insisted on a share of the publishing of our songs.

As in the Guess Who or any band there are usually one or two creative people who write the songs and thus, directly or indirectly, shape the sound, vision, and direction of the band. To radically alter that relationship or to give away a piece of that to someone who could not further advance those songs, I just wasn't prepared to do that. I resisted a demand for group publishing of our songs. As a result, I ended up having a lot of songs on that *FREEWAYS* album because the others didn't offer up anything.

I think part of the problem stemmed from sibling rivalry, the younger brother wanting to achieve what the older brother has done. It exists not just in my family but other families. There were jealousies and resentments directed at me by Robbie. I was the big brother who wrote, produced, played, and therefore achieved more and received more attention. He figured he could do it, too. It happens when one brother is more successful than the other is. Neil Young's brother had difficulty living under the shadow of Neil's success; Tom Fogerty was overshadowed by his brother John. It's tough. You can't always accomplish what your sibling has done, especially if they have been at it longer. It can cause frustration. Even in marriages, if one spouse becomes more successful than the other it can tear the relationship apart.

I believe the other members were attempting to subvert the album to force me to relent and say, "Okay guys, I give in. Let's do it your way with the publishing." It was like blackmail and I wasn't about to do that for people who were, in my opinion, less creative. The album came out and got some mild airplay on some songs but it just didn't happen.

Opinions remain varied and positions entrenched over the *FREEWAYS* debacle and Randy's decision to forge on with it in the face of mounting opposition from the others in the group. Once again, Randy would find himself facing a bitter confrontation that would result in his exiting another group.

"To be honest, I thought we had run out of steam and our writing was not good enough to push through another album," maintains Fred Turner. "Randy didn't agree. I started seeing that we were writing songs too fast and they weren't good enough. Something should have been done two albums before this but we got to *FREEWAYS* and Randy had a whole bunch of songs. Because he had control over the product, he said he was going to go ahead with the album as a BTO album because his songs were good enough, but it would look funny if the album only contained his songs. I gave him a song that I considered filler and it got added. Had we been a little smarter and thought things through, we would have suggested to Randy that he do a solo album with us supporting him but we were all tired and burned out. He thought he had written a collection of gems. We had a standing joke in the rest of the band that this was going to be the first album to be returned platinum. The rest of us were not going along with his plans for the band.

"Because we had all this animosity going on, instead of saying 'Do a solo album, we'll support you,' I got my back up and said, 'I don't like what you're doing so you're not going to get much of a performance from me on it.' And when the photographer came to shoot the album cover I told him not to take a picture of me straight on. 'You take a picture of me from the side. I'm a sideman on this album.' What a stupid thing to do, but that's what it had gotten to. After that, we left Randy to finish off the album by himself."

Bruce Allen offers his spin on the FREEWAYS fiasco. "Randy wasn't listening to the others. He started to listen only to himself. I think what Randy wanted to do with FREEWAYS was to launch or set up his own career. I really believe that. I don't think he wanted to pound it out on the road anymore. I think he was getting tired by then of Robbie's shenanigans, and tired of dealing with all these other issues that had nothing to do with the music. Randy would put his family second. He didn't care if he wasn't home. Randy wanted to do stuff and the band wanted to stay home and Randy just figured, 'Screw it, I'm going to take it in a direction I want to go.' But the audience that we had wanted the group to rock and to rock hard and there still was a market for that. It was obvious the guys weren't into it. Something had to give. I tried to keep it together but I couldn't."

In May 1977, the group held a meeting to listen to a playback of Randy's final mix of the album before its release. When it was over, Randy walked out alone.

The demise of BTO creatively can be put down to too much, too fast, too soon. Maybe if we had spaced the albums out more but instead in a matter of a couple of years, the albums were coming out boom boom boom, one right after the other. It became a big flash and it was over. There was no other place to go but down after we had hit #1. You can't be popular forever. It's nice looking at #2 but then you go down to #200 from there. I knew there would be an inevitable decline after our peak and I accepted that. I almost looked forward to starting over, searching for the things that inspired me in the first place and excited me now. After a while it got boring doing the same thing but you get caught in a straightjacket. And when you have too much product coming out too quickly, you don't have a chance to sit back and take stock of what you are doing. We were on the treadmill and the pressure mounted to get more product out. We started copying ourselves and our stuff became redundant. We didn't have anything to say any more.

I didn't quit the band. It was my band, my ship. But the crew was becoming a little restless onboard. I played back the album at Bruce Allen's house as we did with all the albums after I had mixed and sequenced it all. The others hadn't been there during that process. When it was over, there was silence in the room. Then Fred said, "'This doesn't sound like BTO. It seems like we're not the same band."

"I agree," I replied.

"I think we're going in different directions and want different things."

"You're right."

"So what's the point in carrying on?" asked Fred.

"I agree."

It was so hard doing that album largely alone. Whatever their contributions were on other albums, there wasn't a whole lot on this one. The band had reached the end of its run but none of us would admit it until after the album was done. It had been a really great ride right to the top, but it was time to get off. It couldn't last forever. I didn't need it anymore so I jumped off and they attempted to carry on.

The end of BTO came as a relief for me. We were dragging something out that should have stopped.

With Randy out of the lineup by mutual consent, the other three determined to soldier on without their leader, producer, and principal writer. It was doomed to failure. After recruiting bass player Jim Clench from April Wine, Fred moved over to guitar and the reconstituted group recorded two albums before calling it a day. "I didn't want to go on with BTO after Randy left," admits Fred. "The other guys, Blair and

Robbie, really wanted to keep going. That was very tough because I knew that the band was not the same as what people had come to expect. I was carrying the whole thing. I had seen what happened to the Guess Who after Randy left. It wasn't that the Guess Who wasn't any good after that but in the public's eye, and especially in the critics' eyes, it was like someone had yanked an arm off and it would never be the same again. I thought the same about BTO. I felt I owed it to Robbie and Blair to give it a shot but I really lost interest during that period."

In the ensuing clash, Bruce Allen chose to stick with the group. "I didn't think Randy was worth anything by himself," he asserts today. "I believed Fred Turner was the voice of BTO, the signature of that band. I figured that if I kept Fred going maybe he could be better without Randy around. He still was the image of the band. What I misjudged, though, was just how important Randy was. Fred tried to play guitar and Fred didn't look like he should play guitar. He was this lumberjack bass player stomping about the stage. He should have been playing bass."

Graeme Waymark represented me as an artist when I left the band. Bruce Allen was angry with this but he wasn't my manager anymore. In my opinion, Bruce made a mistake by choosing sides. When Peter Gabriel left Genesis, he retained the same manager as the group so there was no conflict between them. Bruce is a real warrior and takes sides. Instead of continuing to represent me, he put his eggs in BTO's basket and didn't want to work with me and I think that situation contributed to some of the friction that followed between us for several years.

Bruce had become a very powerful guy and harboured resentment toward me for some time afterwards. He had literally lived with me for two years on the road as BTO built its audience and learned the ropes at my feet. He then applied that experience to Loverboy, Bryan Adams, Anne Murray, Kim Stockwood, and Martina McBride. We talk occasionally now, but it's just one of those things. When you are not in Bruce's camp, you are not in Bruce's camp. You are either for him or against him, no grey area. And for several years I was out of favour with him.

With Randy giving his notice and the others choosing to carry on, the question of the group's name and logo immediately arose.

At that playback meeting it became acrimonious. Robbie and Fred indicated they wanted to go on.

"So, go ahead."

"What about the name? What about the logo?"

"I own that," I informed them to looks of surprise.

"No, what do you mean? We all own that."

"No you don't. I own it."

"When did that happen?"

"Four years ago. No one had a cent. I was paying you a weekly salary. The label told us to get this trademarked worldwide or someone else might use it. I was the only one with the money to get it done, so I did. You guys couldn't do it."

"What did it cost?"

"Twenty grand."

"Well, we need to be able to use the name."

"You can't use Bachman because I'm going to do a solo thing and if you do, that it will be confusing."

So we agreed that they could use "BTO" and the wheel logo and I could have Bachman-Turner Overdrive. I agreed not to go out and perform as Bachman-Turner Overdrive because I didn't want to make a sham of the band and its legacy by floating two competing groups on the market like when there were two Fleetwood Macs out on the road or three Platters touring. That's where we left it as far as I was concerned and we agreed to go our separate ways.

Do you walk out a champ? Do you quit when you're world heavyweight champ? Or do you wait until you're beaten into a pulp by a twenty-two-year-old kid? I think I walked away from BTO at the right time. I walked away from it saying, "I've done it all. I've done it again. I've done it twice." I wanted to leave with my reputation because I had built it up all these years. I looked at my career as "Book I: The Guess Who and Book II: BTO" and I wanted to go on and try to do it again. The successful guys in this business, when you look at them, the Neil Youngs and the Bob Dylans, keep doing it and trying to reinvent themselves.

When I left BTO, just like with Brave Belt after the Guess Who, I wanted a fresh start; I wanted to do something different from what I had been doing. I wanted a different manager to represent me and my solo contract on a different label so that Mercury could continue with BTO. I wanted to protect myself since BTO were carrying on and I didn't want to appear to be competing with them.

Never one to remain idle for any lengthy period, Randy wasted little time in jumping headfirst into a solo career with the writing of his most ambitious work to date, a concept album based loosely on his own rise to fame entitled, appropriately enough, Survivor. Signed to Polydor Records, Randy set about developing the autobiographical concept and recording it in Los Angeles with help from an old friend.

Burton Cummings hadn't talked to me in seven years but when he played in Vancouver, he stopped in the middle of the show and apologized in front of five or six thousand people for the bad stuff he had said about me over the years. He dedicated the next part of the show to my wife and me and started out with about twelve bars of Streisand's *The Way We Were* and then segued into *These Eyes, Laughing, Undun, No Time*, and *American Woman*. I was sitting there in tears; everyone else was up screaming, going nuts.

Backstage, the two hugged one another and posed together for photographers. Having disbanded the Guess Who in 1975 to launch his own solo career, Burton was riding high with his million-selling debut single *Stand Tall*. The very public reconciliation resulted in the two former writing partners recording together again, Randy guesting on Burton's second solo album *MY OWN WAY TO ROCK*, and Burton returning the favour by appearing on Randy's *SURVIVOR* album. Randy even showed up as special guest on Burton's first CBC television special.

I had met a playwright in New York who wanted to mount a Broadway production. I wrote *SURVIVOR* after meeting him because I conceived it as a concept. On the album sleeve are the lyrics and all these narrative segues to tie together the theme of someone climbing the ladder of success — sixteen years of Canadian dreams and playing in a band riding the highs and lows concluding with the song *Survivor*. Maybe it was my story subconsciously. I had Burton playing and singing on it, Tom Scott contributed sax, and the Pointer Sisters are on it. Once it was completed, I felt pleased with it, not as a commercial entity to compete with BTO on the charts, but a new direction that could be a stage play or television concept. There was a story line, character development, and different life transitions throughout. It had a sense of wholeness to it as opposed to random songs geared for the pop charts. So I contacted Polydor.

"Remember that guy I met at Sardi's who had this idea for a play?"

"He passed away."

So much for my big plans. *Is the Night Too Cold for Dancing* came out as a pretty cool single from the album but didn't burn up the charts. I guested on *American Bandstand* playing it. The guy who had signed me at Polydor was solidly behind the album but not long after it came out, he was transferred to their branch in Europe. His replacement had no connection to the album or me and swept me aside. As a result, the Survivor album was left to twist in the wind.

Released in 1978, *SURVIVOR* was one of Randy's most elaborate works, a personal reflection on his career and a heartfelt and revealing labour of love that was largely misunderstood by fans and maligned by critics. Yet the concept holds together well, offering some of Randy's finest lyric writing to that point. Produced by Randy, it was recorded simultaneously with Burton's third album, *DREAM OF A CHILD*. Using many of the same personnel, the cream of LA's session players who would go on to form the group Toto, and with Burton himself on most tracks, *SURVIVOR* is a departure from the grinding guitar riffs of BTO. *Is the Night Too Cold for Dancing* even found Randy mining some of Burton's soft rock territory. The song themes throughout mirror Randy's own career: growing up in Canada, ear glued to a radio; playing barn dances in the early days; the one-hit wonder status after *Shakin' All Over*; meeting Lorayne and finding a higher purpose in his life; the bright lights of the Guess Who's success; the inevitable decline and his rise once again with BTO as a survivor. Had it been a success, *SURVIVOR* might have offered an intriguing new direction in Randy's career; however, the album hit the delete bins almost as fast as BTO's first post-Randy album. Rather than an attempt at a blockbuster chart album, *SURVIVOR* was a personal triumph for Randy whether anybody else bought it or not, something he needed to do for himself at that point in his career.

While Randy enjoyed the comforts of his three-million-dollar home and launched his solo career, his brother Tim had bottomed out. Moving back to Winnipeg following his dismissal from Bachman-Turner Overdrive, Tim had become involved in concert promotion, living life in the fast lane on a path of destruction. The two brothers had not spoken in several years when Tim called Randy for help. "I was living the rock 'n' roll lifestyle," reflects Tim. "I had regressed, drinking a lot and doing drugs. I had whatever I wanted, a huge house in Southdale with a pool, a Jaguar, a Maseratti. My house was party central every weekend. I ran my own company, Audience Concerts, and was doing concert promotions. I was the first to break Supertramp in North America. Then all of a sudden the rug was pulled out from under me. I had Supertramp booked for the next year along with acts like

Montrose and Shawn Phillips, but I needed cash flow to keep going. I had dates booked and holds on venues but I needed cash to keep the business operating until those dates. I had two brothers who were millionaires so I phoned Robbie first and told him all I needed was a hundred thousand to get me out of the hole and keep operating. I would be able to pay him back in two years. Well, I don't anymore use the expletives Robbie said to me, so I can't relate to you directly what he said before he hung up on me. So I phoned Randy.

"Randy's response wasn't 'I won't do it' but instead 'I can't do it.' Now I knew from BTO that he had publishing rights, producing rights, and he basically owned everything. So I thought to myself 'Are you kidding? You've got the money.' So I asked him again and he repeated, 'No, I can't.' I was so angry I hung up on him.

"About a month later the phone rang and it was Lorayne. She said 'Your brother wants to talk to you.' Randy came on the phone and asked me how things were going. I told him. 'The same as a month ago.' I kept thinking 'What is this all about?' Then he said 'Lorayne and I have been talking and praying about this and we have decided to help you out.' I cupped my hand over the phone and screamed to my wife 'This is it!'

'I don't know how to thank you,' I told Randy.

'We're going to send you something that will be the answer to all your problems.'

'Thank you, thank you so much.'

'We'll be praying for you.'

"I hung up the phone and my wife and I were dancing around the living room. We weren't going to lose our house or anything else. Every day we checked the mail, anxiously awaiting the arrival of the letter from Randy. Then one day a box arrived. My first response was it was a hundred thousand dollars in cash all stuffed into this box which would explode all over the room. Years earlier, we had done something like that for my Mom and Dad. So we tore open the box and there was all this packing paper. I started throwing paper all over the floor. My wife was yelling, 'Where's the money?!' I dug deeper and there were some sleeves and material with a note from Lorayne to sew together a Ukrainian shirt for my mother. I kept digging, figuring maybe he sent a cheque. Next thing I pulled out was a Ukrainian cookbook from Lorayne to my wife. That got thrown across the room. 'Where's the money?!' I picked the box up, turned it over, and shook it. A thud hit the floor. I looked down and there was a pocket-sized Book of Mormon. All I could think of was 'You big jerk! How could you do this to me? How could you get me excited for this?'

"Stunned, I picked up the book and opened it up. On the inside cover Randy had printed 'Dear Timmy, this is the most precious gift that I can ever give you. On its pages are the answers to all the problems you have. With love, your brother Randy.'

"I was so angry I threw it in a drawer and left it there. 'How dare you abandon me when I need you.' A thousand thoughts crowded my head. Here I was getting kicked in the head by him once again.

"I wasn't attending a church at that time but each night I would go out onto my back patio, look up at the stars and talk to God asking him to please help me. I went through a really tough time and my brother Gary and my Dad stopped me from doing some foolish things and helped me keep my family. Those last few years, my life had been all about money. Now I didn't have any and all I could think of was 'What good am I?' I felt no sense of self-worth."

Being a promoter in Winnipeg, you are at the mercy of Jack Frost for several months of the year. The weather can suddenly change all your well-planned bookings. Timmy had organized some tours and received deposits for English bands who had never driven that many miles in the UK to be faced with thousand-mile treks across Canada in the middle of winter with blinding snowstorms and icy roads. For us it's nothing. "Oh, the roads are closed? Good there won't be any traffic," and proceed around the barricades and drive in the centre of the highway to the gig. But these English guys were terrified of Canadian winters and

Timmy lost big money on one of these tours when the group refused to travel under these conditions.

He phoned me and asked if I could loan him six figures to bail him out of this loss. At the time, I had to turn him down because we were building our house in Lynden. Timmy was in the riskiest end of the entertainment business, even riskier than being in a band, and he had no means of paying me back. Instead, I sent him the Book of Mormon. His life was in shambles at that point and he was still doing drugs. In the end, he left the promotion business and took a job with my Dad as an optician, riding the bus to work each day just as my Dad had done.

I must confess to feeling a sense of envy for the relationship Tim developed working with my father. They became extremely close during that period and I was jealous of that relationship. Tim was the only son to follow in my Dad's footsteps and the two of them ran Shopper's Optical together in Winnipeg until my Dad decided to retire.

"When I was sixteen, I suffered a head injury and had seizures from time to time," continues Tim. "I had one that summer and had my driver's license revoked for a while which left me riding the bus. During that time, my father and I began working together at Shopper's Optical. He managed a franchise and I had taken the optician's course, so everyday I would ride the bus downtown to work. I was still floundering, but I started to think about the book Randy sent me and decided to take it as a challenge to read it. Every day on my way to and from work I read the Book of Mormon on the bus. I soon began reading it on coffee breaks and lunch breaks. I started to pray, asking God to have my questions answered but I was still focused on my own problem. 'Okay I'm doing what you ask, now how can I get the hundred grand?'

"I started to change as I became more concerned about what was happening in the book. Then one day sitting in my office, I had a spiritual experience that changed my life. The question that came into my

mind at the moment, the most terrifying question that I had ever con-
templated in my life, was 'What if this isn't true?' That was the most
awful thing I could consider. How could everything in that book be
untrue? Then there was no God, no Jesus Christ. That was terrifying to
me. After that, my prayers changed from 'Give me a hundred grand' to
'I want to know if this is true. Please tell me.' And I received a very personal, spiritual experience that revealed to me the truth and from that
point on my life changed forever.

"So, in the end, Randy did give me the best possible gift he could.
If he had given me the hundred thousand dollars I would probably
have signed my death warrant. Not only would I have blown the
money, I probably would have blown me. I joined the Mormon Church
in 1978 and I have been there ever since."

Smarting from the failure of his first solo project, in a reflex action
Randy returned to the security of a band. BTO road manager John
Austin had continued on with Randy as his home studio engineer.
Randy and John were very close and Randy had even paid for John's
training at engineering school. John had a friend named Tom Sparks
from Seattle who wrote and sang so John suggested Randy meet Tom.
The two hit it off and decided to build a band around their songwriting. Out of that emerged Ironhorse. Signed to the fledgling Scotti
Brothers record label, Ironhorse released their self-titled debut album
in 1979. With a sound derivative of BTO's heavier, riff-oriented guitars,
the album spawned a hit single with *Sweet Lui-Louise* featuring Randy
on lead vocals. *Stateline Blues* also received considerable airplay, so
Ironhorse took to the road to promote the album. A brief trip to Italy
where *Sweet Lui-Louise* had topped the charts was followed by the
offer of a coveted spot opening for the Beach Boys on their summer
1979 North American tour.

Around 1978, during the *SURVIVOR* album sessions I finally
had the opportunity to slow down a bit and take stock of the last
seven or eight years. As I looked at my life I thought I had it all:

beautiful wife, wonderful children, great family life, gorgeous house all paid for, money securely invested forever, everything I wanted was at my fingertips. Life seemed perfect. But on the heels of *SURVIVOR*, things fell apart personally for me. The roller-coaster ride that had taken me to the top with BTO was about to take a nosedive.

The Scotti brothers, two independent record promoters, had been hired to promote *SURVIVOR*. They were riding a wave in the business at that point promoting hit albums by Barbra Streisand, Foreigner, the Osmonds, and Debby Boone, among others, so they were on a roll. Once *SURVIVOR* had run its limited course on the charts, the Scotti brothers approached me regarding my signing as the first rock act for a new label they were launching. Great! These guys were hot at that point so I went home and formed Ironhorse, recorded an album, and took it to them. They liked it, put it out, and the single *Sweet Lui-Louise* rose to #16 on *Billboard* and #1 in Italy. So off we went to tour Italy. On our return, I received a phone call from Carl Wilson of the Beach Boys.

"I'm hearing Ironhorse played all the time in LA. Would you consider coming along to open for us on our summer tour?"

"Would I! Yes!" This was the Beach Boys. I was as giddy as a teenybopper.

"There is a three-day trial run on the East Coast — Boston and Philadelphia and one other date. Would you do it and we'll see how it goes?"

"Sure."

I kissed my wife and kids goodbye, told them I would be back in four days, packed up, and took Ironhorse out to join the Beach Boys.

The first gig went fine. The second was a sold-out gig in Philadelphia at the Spectrum. I went to the sound check and had just returned to my hotel room when the phone rang.

"Hello?"

"Hello. This is Lorayne."

"Oh, hi. I just did the sound check and I'm getting ready to go back for the performance."

"When were you planning on coming home?"

"Well, today's Philadelphia and tomorrow there is one more gig then I'll be flying home the next day."

Then, out of left field, Lorayne blindsided me with, "Do us all a favour. Don't bother coming home." Click.

"What?!" I was stunned. What just happened? I dialed the number and called her back.

"Hello?"

"Is this Lorayne?"

"Yes."

"What just happened? What did you just tell me?"

"You heard me. Don't come back." Click.

At that moment, there was a knock at the door.

"It's time to go to the show."

I was completely dazed. I got to the Spectrum and promptly threw up in the dressing room. I have no idea what my performance was like that night because I wasn't there. Physically, I was onstage but mentally I was somewhere else. I returned to my room after our set and called our bishop in Bellingham and explained the bizarre circumstances to him.

"I'm stuck here. I have to play one more date with the Beach Boys. Lorayne just told me I couldn't come home. Can you check on this for me?"

He called Lorayne and after a lengthy discussion with her he suggested that I not come home, but instead come to his house the following day and she would be there. He would act as a mediator. I arrived still reeling from all this to find her sitting in his counselling room. She looked at me and calmly announced, "I never want to see you again."

The bishop then said, "Why don't you go out on the Beach Boys tour for the summer and give Lorayne some space and time to work things out. You can still stay in touch with your children. But let's have the summer go by and meet again at the end of the tour and see where things are by then."

Reluctantly I agreed. I didn't have much choice. I was still holding out hope that this could be worked out with time.

So I went out and buried myself in that Beach Boys tour. It was an interesting time to be along with them because Brian Wilson was just starting to come out with them again, accompanied by his full-time psychiatrist Dr. Eugene Landy. Brian appeared off and on throughout the tour.

Growing up, the Beach Boys had been North America's answer to the Beatles. I loved their records. They epitomized America and California to us kids growing up in Canada. When we played Beach Boys songs in the Guess Who, I sang the high parts. Every night after Ironhorse's set I would change my clothes and sit in the wings and sing along with them. I would sing all my old parts in *I Get Around* and *California Girls*. I was reliving my youth. It was a dream come true for me in the midst of a personal nightmare.

Despite being preoccupied with my domestic dilemma, I had a wonderful time on that tour and got to know the Beach Boys' Carl Wilson very well, so much so that we wrote some songs together including *Keep the Summer Alive*, which they recorded. We would be sitting around by a pool on a day off with acoustic guitars writing songs when "The Man" himself, Brian Wilson, would come down accompanied by the ever-present Dr. Landy. The group was trying to get Brian into writing again, so Carl would say, "Hey Brian, Randy and I wrote some songs." And we would sheepishly play our songs for "The Man." Brian would nod along and try to sing a part. It was a tremendous thrill for me.

Meanwhile, despite outward appearances to the contrary, I remained heartbroken inside. I was aching so much I stopped eating and took to jogging every day because with all the sweat pouring down no one could see me crying. I was the slimmest I had been since a teenager. The situation was gut wrenching. I agonized over what I had done wrong and what the outcome of all this could mean, but I put on a brave face every night and went onstage and performed with Ironhorse. It was a huge break for the band that was completely lost on me because I was adrift in my own world.

I decided it was important to maintain a dialogue with my children, so every second day I wrote each one of them. I would put in little things like a package of Dentyne gum, hockey cards, a balloon, or some little trinket just to show I was thinking of them and making contact.

Somehow I made it through the tour and when it ended I accompanied Carl to Caribou Studios in Colorado to complete songs for the next Beach Boys album. The songs were really strong and I left for home rejuvenated, ready to get things straightened out with Lorayne. I returned to our house outside Lynden. Lorayne had moved out to her mother's place in the town of Lynden with the kids after I left for the tour, and I called the bishop. A meeting was then arranged for the end of the week. I was excited. Summer was gone and things could now get back on an even keel I told myself.

The next day I was in my barn studio with Johnny Austin when we heard a beep at the front gate. We went out to see whom it was only to find a state trooper car, lights flashing on top. As I opened the gate, a man in a suit stepped out carrying a suitcase, walked up to me and handed me some papers.

"What's this?"

"I'm serving you notice of your wife's intent to sue you for divorce."

I guess the trooper was there because the lawyer thought I might punch him out. How could I? I was in a state of shock.

What followed over the next two years would tear Randy's life apart, leaving him heartbroken and bitter but determined to fight on. The divorce and subsequent custody battle would turn ugly and sap him both emotionally and financially. In the ensuing row, Randy would sideline his music career and turn down lucrative and personally satisfying offers to focus all his attention on getting custody of his children and rebuilding their shattered lives.

Recalls journalist Larry LeBlanc, "I ran into Randy during the divorce, he was in Toronto to do Ronnie Hawkins' show, and it was the most dejected I had ever seen him. It was very sad. He was sitting in the cafeteria all by himself. It was quite a contrast after seeing him in the heyday of the Guess Who and BTO playing huge shows and being big stars to be sitting there alone, head hung low."

Were there warning signs I could have perceived leading up to this? Perhaps. I was aware that things seemed different after the birth of our last child, Emilie, our sixth. But I wasn't certain if I was changing or Lorayne. Or were we going through our midlife crisis? I never ever imagined it would affect us the way it did, to have such finality. Was I surprised? Yes. Could I have seen it coming? Maybe.

Did my lengthy absence from home contribute to the split with Lorayne? Definitely. After leaving the Guess Who, I became so driven, so obsessed by all the bad press that followed me, claiming I was all washed up and could never make it straight nothing was going to stop me from proving them wrong. I didn't realize at the time, not until much later, that I was sacrificing what was the most important thing to me, my family. That's why I had left the Guess Who. I wanted to be with my family. I didn't want to be on the road so long. Yet in breaking BTO there was no other way to do it. I jammed five or six years of Guess Who touring into two years with BTO. And it took its toll.

I said to Lorayne at the outset, "If you can handle my absence and look after the house and the kids, here's our opportunity to

maybe make millions of dollars and finance our dreams: a beautiful house and money in the bank for the kids' education and
future. It might take a few years though. Can we do this?" And she
said, "Yes, we can do this." But the amount of heartache, homesick-
ness, and loneliness that I experienced was gut wrenching. I
missed so much. To go home and the child that was crawling
when I left is now walking or to pick up your new baby and have
her cry because she doesn't know who you are, that was heartbreaking. When I hooked up with Bruce Allen who was as driven
as I was, we became relentless. He was my co-pilot. We got in that
truck called BTO and drove it non-stop for three years right to the
top. I saw Bruce Allen more in those three years than my wife and
kids.

I knew I had to devote all my energy and time into making the
band a go, so when BTO did finally hit it big, we continued to be
one of the hardest-working bands in the business. Out on the road
— the US, Canada, Europe, Japan — recording, touring again. It
was a constant cycle. During those years, Lorayne basically held
down the fort at home. She had to learn to do everything that
needed to be done around the house and in raising the kids, and
she did all that extremely well in my absence. There was just no
other way. But it was hard on her and I guess I never realized it.
Here she was in this huge house out in the middle of nowhere
with all these kids by herself. I thought everything was fine.
However, once I left the band I was around home more often and,
unbeknownst to me, I was treading on her turf. I was getting in
the way of her smooth running machine, the home front, and dis-
rupting her routine.

"I hardly remember my Dad being around from the time I was
three to about seven," confirms Kezia. "He was never there. He would
come home from the road and we would get to dig through his suitcase for all the change that had fallen out of his pockets. That was like

buried treasure for us. But in every memory I have of birthdays or Christmases in the big house, he's not a part of them. He wasn't there. Maybe that's why that house feels so unhappy to me because it wasn't like a family anymore. He was away so much. I'm sure it was hard on him as well. The sacrifice he made was his family. The family fell apart. He lost the family bond."

Suggests one close friend, "I think Randy liked to keep Lorayne pregnant. She was a stunningly attractive woman and as long as he kept her pregnant and at home with the kids he didn't have to worry about her. I also don't think Randy particularly liked being at home."

"Obviously there were serious problems in the marriage," reflects Tal, "but I have always had the impression that Dad was very much devastated and shocked by the split." Pondering the portent of their dream house in Lynden, he muses, "My Mom always talks about how terrifically depressed the kids were living out in the country, how morose we all were. But for the life of me, I don't know why she thinks that. I can't account for the difference in recollections. I don't remember walking around crying. I had a good time. For her to have felt morose makes a lot more sense but me or the other kids? We were just little. I don't remember that. I think she felt very isolated and lonely and I think changed her mind about the whole project of building the dream house in that location. We moved in when I was seven and were gone before I was ten."

"I remember feeling incredibly isolated there," counters Kezia, "because we were in the middle of absolutely nowhere. Everybody assumed we would be stuck up before we even moved in and I was treated accordingly in school. I don't have many happy memories of living in that house. My happiness ends in New Westminster. I can remember that carefree, childish, not-a-care-in-the-world feeling in New West that I never had in the big house. I just remember feeling a lot of unhappiness. We went from playing in a neighbourhood where I could go outside and play with other kids to this gated acreage and all I had were my brothers and sisters. Everything changed. I didn't really have any friends. It was incredibly isolating. When my parents split up, we moved back to a neighbourhood where I could ride my bike with other kids and I remember feeling happy again despite all the stuff going on with the divorce."

"My parents seemed like they really had something special going," Tal continues, "some real understanding. They started out with rags and went through that whole process together as husband and wife, step by step building a family and their little empire. Even though there was a division of labour there was still a partnership between them.

"Dad once said to me, and I've never forgotten this, that all of a sudden they had the means to make all of their dreams come true and did make them come true. But as soon as they made that last dream real, the big house, it turned into a nightmare. And then he said, 'There are some dreams you should just never attempt to realize.'"

With the papers in hand, I immediately called the bishop who was surprised at this turn of events. He had believed Lorayne would attend the meeting and accept his efforts at mediation. Obviously, the time for talking was over. I was then advised to consult an attorney, which I failed to do because I still believed that it would all blow over. "Just give it time" I kept thinking. I had waited two months; I'll wait a bit longer. That was my mistake. It wasn't happening. I just wasn't prepared to accept the reality of the situation.

I am still guessing about the motivations behind Lorayne's actions. There was no adultery on either side — no big proof of any misdemeanor on my part. It remains to this day a mystery to me. It boiled down in the legal documentation to simple incompatibility. What made the whole thing even more astonishing to me at the time was that our marriage had been sealed in the Mormon Church.

In the Mormon faith there exists something beyond normal civil marriages. If one of you is a new convert, after about a year you prove your commitment to obey the commandments you have been given to be good people, good Christians, honest with each other and to obey the word of wisdom — namely no drugs, no drinking. You then go to the temple and are sealed to each other for time and eternity. Back in the late sixties, Lorayne and I went through the interview with the bishop who asked all these questions about us meeting our obligations to each other and our faith. Following that we were sealed in Cardston Temple in Alberta.

Mormons believe that your life on earth is only one of your experiences. You pre-exist as a spirit in heaven and your time on earth is a journey where you prove our faith. We really don't know what kind of life we will have but it is all to test us. And when we die we go back to heaven forever. So the concept of sealing a marriage is to bond together for time and all eternity. It is a complete picture without an end. When we go to heaven we will be together there. It's a very comforting feeling to know that my kids who are sealed to me will join me in heaven.

Having gone through all that with Lorayne, the divorce seemed all that more unreal to me. Weren't we supposed to be together for eternity? We had made a far greater commitment than simply a church wedding; we had entered into a covenant with God. I think that's why I kept holding out hope that it would all pass and we would get back together. I resisted facing the reality of the situation for some time.

After a couple of months, I finally got to see my children. I was granted one hour on a Saturday. I arrived at the door and as I bent down to hug them individually and collectively, Kezia who was eight by then, came over and tentatively touched my face. It was very strange. I knew I had physically changed because I had lost so much weight over the last few stressful months, but her action was very disconcerting. There was nowhere to go in Lynden so I took them to a little roadside chapel along the highway in order to just talk to them, to explain what had happened as best I could understand it.

"Sometimes there is a really great thing that happens in this world. Two people meet each other and fall in love. And sometimes one or both of them fall out of love. And I think that is what has happened with your mother and me. I still love her and you kids but she has fallen out of love with me and doesn't want to be with me any more. So I think we are going to be apart from this point on."

I moved out of our luxurious home outside Lynden and took a small, unassuming house just two blocks from where Lorayne and the kids were living, just so I could see them on their way to school and be a part of their lives in some small way. They were thrilled to see me every day on the way to and from school. It made the world of difference to them and me. I had no furniture at first but I invited Tally and Kezia to come over and share some pizza with me. They simply walked the two blocks to my house. We turned over a garbage can, placed the pizza box on it and sat on the floor.

I've tried to erase most of that period from my mind. It isn't something I want to relive. But what started to happen after I moved into my little house was truly special. I got to see the kids more often and they would help me decorate and furnish my place. The house had a basement, and being a Winnipeg kid I loved basements. Everybody lives in the basement in Winnipeg. So I turned it into a playroom with an old jukebox and a rocking horse you could ride. I hung swings, ropes, and tires from the ceiling and put foam rubber on the floor so they could swing from the stairs and fall on the floor. I put up a basketball net over the garage. I wanted to create an escape zone for them from the reality of the situation so we didn't just sit and brood about it.

On his way home from school, Tally began stopping by to shoot hoops. When he started little league I put a mattress against the garage door and I would pitch to him for batting practice. I didn't know until years later that he was telling his mother that he was hanging out at a friend's house after school. Kezia started coming over then, too. The younger ones could see the pattern of things and followed along. Slowly, the other kids began coming to see me.

Things continued to improve between me and the kids, and then one day I received a phone call.

"He's yours. Come and get him."

I drove to Lorayne's house, it was drizzling out, and there was Tally sitting outside under the mailbox in the rain beside two garbage bags. In them were all his possessions. His mother had discovered that the friend he was hanging out with after school was, in fact, me.

So Tally moved in with me.

What gradually emerged was the Randy Bachman Clubhouse where the kids could take refuge from all the tensions and heartache with their Dad. "My Mom made it clear to my Dad that he wasn't welcome around the house and that we weren't to visit Dad," recalls Tal Bachman. "But I would go over there nonetheless and hang out shooting baskets with him. It just seemed like a natural thing for me, but I came to realize later how much it meant to him. I wasn't thinking 'Gee I think I'll go over and cheer up my Dad because he's depressed and upset about the breakup.' It was me coming home and my Mom would be baking and my sisters would be playing with dolls. That's why I went over to his house. Then something happened and I was no longer welcome at my mother's house, so I went to live with my Dad and stayed there. I became the only kid that was there with him until adulthood.

"At Dad's little house it was like that TV show *The Courtship of Eddie's Father* for a year and a half, him and me, just two guys.

'Hey, what's for dinner?'

'A bag of Cheeto's.'

"It was 'guy living.' There was an element of crudity about the situation, two males living together.

'Maybe we need to vacuum the living room?'

'Nah, it's not that bad. Just let the dog in and he'll eat some of these popcorn twists on the floor.' The refining hand of womanhood hadn't touched this house.

"Dad lost about a hundred pounds during that time and I'm not sure if it was an effort to make himself more attractive to Mom or what. He ate nothing but fruit for four months."

Nonetheless, the two found a common bond. "When I was living with Dad, everything was all about music. We played records all the time. I would come home from school and listen to my ELO records and play the drums. I was really into drums at the time and hadn't picked up the guitar yet. Dad would be trying to write a song. We'd have dinner and play some more tunes.

"Even though we have different personalities, I think there is some understanding there between him and me that may be from the fact that we spent more time together that may not be as extensive between him and the other kids because he didn't spend as much time with them. And the musical connections are a part of it. We obviously had that in common. We like a lot of the same music. He played a lot of his favourite music in the house when I was growing up and that music was great, so at an early age I came to appreciate and admire the Beatles and British Invasion stuff. When I was seven or eight I loved Herman's Hermits."

In the middle of all this, as I gradually rebuilt my relationship with my children as someone important in their lives while at the same time dealing with the lawyers — Carl Wilson phoned me. Up to this point, my career had taken a backseat to my kids. Ironhorse was on hold. I was simply living off my reserves.

"Hi Randy, it's Carl. Will you come to Los Angeles and produce the next Beach Boys album?"

"I can't come." It broke my heart to say those words.

"Something's wrong."

"I know something's wrong," Carl replied.

"How do you know?"

"I was with you all summer. I could see you were going through something."

At the same time I was dealing with my problems, Carl, too, was going through his own marital difficulties and saw the signs. Maybe that's why we got along so well together that summer. We both were unknowingly sharing the same heartache.

Carl needed me to be there to help him turn the songs we had written into reality. When you write songs you have a conception in your head of how they should sound and he had difficulty conveying that to the other Beach Boys. *Keep the Summer Alive* and *Living With a Heartache* made it onto the album but two or three songs we also wrote at that time didn't, simply because Carl couldn't force them all on the band. I have those tapes, the great lost Carl Wilson–Randy Bachman songs.

So I had to pass up a dream project for the reality of a bitter battle of wills.

In the meantime, news of Randy and Lorayne's separation was received with shocked disbelief by family and associates. Though Randy had failed to read the signals, some saw flaws in their marriage. For many, Randy's years away from home had taken their toll. "I was devastated when Lorayne and Randy split up," recalls Gary Bachman. "She had been like the sister I never had. There was a real warmth to her in those early years. When they split up I thought it was the end of the world. How could this happen? They were like the perfect couple together."

"There were those who were surprised it ended," suggests Tim Bachman. "To everyone they were the perfect couple. But there were also those who were equally surprised it had lasted that long. It wasn't an easy marriage. Randy was away a lot when his kids were growing up." Former manager and confidante Bruce Allen drove down to see his old friend when he heard about the split. "There was nothing in the house. All I remember seeing is a light bulb, a Boy Scout kit, a lamp, and a bed or sleeping bag. I would never have known it was coming. He never said anything about any problems at home. And I would have known because I was always with him."

Adds Garry Peterson, "Randy left Lorayne alone with six kids in this big house while he was away on the road a lot. It must have been tough for her. Did it make her different than when they were first married? Probably. I've heard Randy's version but I've never talked to Lorayne about it. In a marriage, if it breaks up it isn't just one person."

Jim Martin had known the couple from their first date together. "I never thought it would happen but in many respects it was a tough marriage. She was on her own much of the time and had to go through a lot raising all those kids alone in this little town in Washington. I think she got tired of being the one taking care of everything. There was a lot put on that lady. I don't know what happened but I know Randy loved that woman. With Lorayne there was something special there. If Randy could have saved it he would have."

The one constant in Randy's life since his early teens had always been music. Faced with a devastating marital crisis and preoccupied with the ensuing legal wrangling, he turned to music for solace. With the original lineup of Ironhorse in limbo following the Beach Boys tour, Randy set about retooling the group bringing in singer/song-writer/keyboard player Frank Ludwig from Trooper who had written and sung the marvellous *Round Round We Go*. Frank brought a more melodic touch to Ironhorse's sound eschewing the harder edge of the debut album. Tom Sparks bowed out soon after allowing Randy and Frank to redefine Ironhorse with a more contemporary eighties approach involving less emphasis on guitar riffs and more on synthe-sizers and melodies. The two began writing together in a collaboration reminiscent of the Bachman-Cummings relationship. What emerged would be an album, *EVERYTHING IS GREY*, whose upbeat, appealing pop sound belied a more morose lyrical theme as Randy poured out his feelings on several tracks colouring the album's overall tone with a tinge of sadness. The title seemed more than appropriate.

"Writing with Randy was such a neat experience for me," recalls Frank Ludwig, "I was quite amazed at how prolific he was. We would get together in an afternoon and we could put together ten or twelve songs." But Frank also saw the residue of the divorce hanging like a dark cloud over his new partner. "He definitely had distractions and could get pretty down about it. I would arrive and he would be talking about it and trying to deal with it. The saddest thing for me was on a few occasions I had to stay overnight at his huge house in Lynden because we were using his studio and I would be in a room with children's prints on the wall. It seemed so empty and depressing, this big house meant for a family and there wasn't one there any more. It was tough on Randy. Johnny Austin and I kind of nurse-maided Randy through a difficult time. We were his support group. And Randy gave back to us too in the music. It wasn't that he lacked focus. When we got down to work, we worked."

When someone is hurting inside and looking to find music that reflects that heartache, they turn to Roy Orbison. Nobody hurts like the Big O. With the pain of the split up Randy found both consolation and inspiration in Orbison's music. "Randy and I had a real affinity for Roy Orbison's work and that sort of became a bond between us," notes Frank. "On the album there is a song called *I'm Hurting Inside* where I keep going higher and higher at the end like Roy Orbison's *It's Over*. We were directly influenced by Roy on that."

I'm Hurting Inside is one of my greatest songs. When I am writing a song, at the time I'm not conscious of sitting down and writing about what's going on in my life because it's too personal. I've never been one to write personal songs. But it does come out subconsciously and I guess it did in that song.

EVERYTHING IS GREY was my therapeutic divorce album. Some of that stuff was written with Carl Wilson who was going through a divorce at the same time. My therapy was to keep working. I had realized on the first Ironhorse album that I wasn't Burton Cummings or Fred Turner. It is so comforting to be on stage with Burton Cummings, who is a guy who sings his buns off. All I had to do was be Eric Clapton and play guitar. It was the same with Frank Ludwig who was a guy with a great voice who was in total control out front. I don't mind singing the odd song but I never really thought of myself as a front man.

Frank points to several incidents where Randy's experienced ear and recording expertise astounded him. "Here's one lesson I learned from Randy. I had done a vocal for a song and my voice cracked. So I told him I had to do it again. Instead he said 'Come in and listen to it.'

'No, my voice cracked. I have to do it again.'

'Come in and listen.'

"So I came in and listened to the playback but still insisted on doing it again. Randy said, 'Listen to it once more. It sounds like your heart is breaking.' I listened once more and sure enough he was right. From that I learned that it doesn't matter whether you sing a hundred percent in pitch and sing the note you intended to sing or not. What matters is the emotion. If the emotion is there, that's the power. That knocked me out. Randy was right."

Having passed up the opportunity to produce the Beach Boys, Randy and Carl Wilson nevertheless remained in contact, with the result being Carl coming up to Randy's studio in Lynden to work on several songs, one of which became Ironhorse's next single *What's Your Hurry Darlin'*. "That song was very autobiographical," states Frank, "a product of Randy's situation and his hurting and sadness." Released as a single, the radio-friendly song with its Beach Boys–style harmony and catchy chorus was the antithesis of the BTO sound and quickly began climbing the charts, particularly in Western Canada where it hit the Top Ten in several cities. Unfortunately at the same time, Scotti Brothers Records shut down operations, thereby dooming the single and album's chances of success. As a result, we were left in the lurch, which killed any chances for the album in the States. A lot of the songs on that album had chartability because they were more melodic, so it was frustrating that nothing happened with it."

When Ironhorse's second album hit the skids due to factors beyond the group's control, Randy once again took the group back to the drawing board. It was 1980 and his relationship with Fred Turner had come full circle to the point where they were once again communicating. Fred's fronting BTO had been short-lived and he wasn't doing much of anything. Perhaps it was an attempt to rekindle some of the old magic or merely the comfort and security of a formerly close musical alliance, but gradually Fred was integrated into sessions for the next Ironhorse album. As those sessions proceeded, the band transformed into Union and in 1981 released an album, *ON STRIKE*, on Portrait Records, the label that had just dropped Burton Cummings.

"Because of his ongoing custody battle, Randy wouldn't tour, so Ironhorse was kind of in limbo," states Frank Ludwig. "Fred had been out of BTO long enough to maybe start thinking it might be a good idea for him to get back together with Randy. It almost seemed simultaneous, the two of them reconnecting. I was still working with Randy but all of a sudden Fred was involved with us. It was a very positive situation. As a matter of fact we considered calling ourselves BLT — Bachman, Ludwig, Turner — which had a clever ring to it. In retrospect, I think we should have done that. It said more about who we were than Union.

"When Randy signed the group with Portrait, they were keen to get BTO happening," claims Frank. "Their thinking was 'Ironhorse didn't do anything with that soft, melodic sound. Your thing is BTO.' So they were nudging Randy in that direction." Fred Turner's booming voice and heavier bass playing brought a beefier edge to the group, in some instances reminiscent of BTO but in a more contemporary context. Randy's *Mainstreet USA* was almost rap-like and Steely Dan–influenced, whereas the Randy Bachman-Carl Wilson composition *Keep the Summer Alive* received a tougher treatment on the Union album than the Beach Boys version. But Union was fated to be a brief liaison.

Following the second Ironhorse album, Fred and I were speaking to each other again. When Ron Foos, our bass player, received an offer to join Paul Revere and the Raiders it left a hole in the band for a bass player. Ironhorse was pretty much done by then so I called Fred and asked if he was interested. We exchanged tapes of our songs and liked what we both had. I had written a mini musical suite called *Mainstreet USA* that he liked. He had written a song called *On Strike*, I thought of the name Union, and it just seemed to come together with Chris Leighton and Frank Ludwig.

When the album came out, the baseball strike was on so Portrait figured they would get lots of attention with the *ON STRIKE* title. *Mainstreet USA* was picked as the first A side but somehow it was shipped out over a long weekend and radio program directors usually meet every Monday to decide what to pick to debut. When the deejays received the record, it hadn't been cleared by the program directors. They saw my name and Fred's together so they started playing *Mainstreet USA* and the phone response was fantastic. We were picked up by dozens of stations including New York. I flew to New York for interviews and everyone was excited about the album. A week later the record went flat. The independent promo men were miffed that they had been bypassed as the record went straight to the stations, and they were now trying to bury the album unless we funded them. As a result of this little power play, *ON STRIKE* lost its momentum.

The Union project died soon after, scuttled by a corrupt industry and Randy's own personal problems. "In Union we felt we needed to get out and let people see us," surmises Frank. "We were a band and could play and put on a show. We started gearing up to do a tour, we had dates booked, did a handful of gigs around Vancouver and Seattle, then Randy was informed by his lawyer that if he went out on the road he would clearly lose the custody battle. So he shut it down. It was tough for him and for all of us. We understood his situation, but we realized it would impede any chance for success for the band."

Concludes Fred Turner, "Union could have been very good, but Randy was in the throes of his divorce and he couldn't get things together. He had so much stress and pressure on him from lawyers. And he could not talk to Lorayne; she was gone and all there was were lawyers. Once the lawyers get hold of a situation where there is money like that, man, they're like vultures. The bills were incredible. I saw Randy develop a really bad eye twitch during that time, obviously because of the stress. The Union album was okay; it had some good things in it. But it had something there that if it could have gone on further, I think it would have been very good. Everybody just realized there was no way that Randy was going to get it together to put what he had to into it. I moved back to Winnipeg after that. I just felt it was time to go home."

Throughout all this, the divorce and custody battle continued.

The only communication I had with Lorayne during this whole period was in regard to the visitations, phoning to arrange to pick up the kids or to notify her if I was going to be delayed crossing the border back into Washington. I never wanted the perception that I was abusing my visitation rights because I didn't want to lose them. On one occasion I went over there and her mother and brother answered the door. Lorayne was elsewhere in the house. I took the chance of asking them.

"What is all this about? What is really going on? If it's money, I'll give you a million dollars."

Soon after, Kezia came to live with Tally and I for a trial period. Then Lorelei, my third oldest, came to stay for a couple of days while Lorayne was away. I seemed to be rebuilding my relation-

ship with those kids, except with Lorelei who was extremely
attached to her mother. When Lorayne returned, I took Lorelei
back to her mother's. She had cried much of the time Lorayne
was away.

Meanwhile, the battle of wills continued. Then came the court
battle over custody of the children.

By now the media had picked up on the story and were having a
field day with it. "The millionaire rock star and his costly divorce" was
the slant of most stories. With so much at stake financially, the
Bachman divorce became big news.

At the depositions, friends, associates, and acquaintances were
summoned to testify as to the fitness of either spouse for custody.
I discovered that most of our friends had already been lined up in
Lorayne's corner. As a couple, we had shared the same circle of
acquaintances, but when I approached these same people they
had already committed to Lorayne. I had Johnny Austin and a couple of other associates from the music business on my side. On
the day of the depositions, you each sit in a room, both spouses
and their attorneys facing each other as your friends come in one
by one, swear on the Bible, testify before a court stenographer for
the record and answer questions. It is very uncomfortable because
each side can challenge the friends. It's easy to say someone is a
jerk behind his or her back, but when it's face to face and on the
record it can be extremely intimidating.

Not surprisingly, what came out of all these testimonies was
that we used to be the ideal couple held up by others as a model
marriage. They all had wanted to be like us — successful, happy,
nice house, cars, love, and wonderful children. No one knew what
went wrong, but none of them considered me a bad person
despite being in an evil business, rock 'n' roll. On the contrary, I
was presented as a beacon of virtue in a world of drugs. When all

this was completed, four or five psychologists and psychiatrists who we had been seeing by order of the court were summoned to give their opinions on both Lorayne and me. Following this, the process moved to a court in Bellingham, Washington.

The week-long case became almost surreal for me. It was like standing naked at Portage and Main. Once again the friends were called in to testify as were the various analysts, only this time it was before a judge and an audience that included reporters. This was major news in that area, the local rock star's court appearance. And again the comments were consistent with the depositions: I'm not a bad person; we don't know what went wrong in this perfect relationship. At the end of this week from hell, the judge banged his gavel and declared to the hushed courtroom:

"On the basis of the evidence presented I award custody of the children to the father, Mr. Bachman."

Whoa! Elation! I won.

Prior to the conclusion of the two year long, bitter custody battle, Randy had met another woman and would soon embark on a new life with her.

It was just before Christmas of 1981 when I was approached to play a benefit, Blues For Christmas, for the homeless. It was organized annually at Vancouver's Commodore Ballroom by Gail Bowen, an ex-Winnipegger who used to play in the Feminine Touch. God bless her for doing that every year. But you don't play as a band, you get together with other musicians in different configurations and jam. The lineups were fairly loose. It's a wonderful way for musicians to get together and catch up on each other's lives over the past year because we are all so busy with our own projects.

I did my set, three or four songs, and while I was back in the dressing room chatting with some players, I heard *Respect* coming from the stage. "My God, Aretha Franklin's onstage!" So I looked out the dressing room door and all I could see was the back of this girl with a nice figure and knee-high boots belting out *Respect* backed by a rhythm and blues all-star band with horns and a female chorus. They were really rocking.

"Who's that?"

"Oh, that's Denise McCann."

"Wow. Who is she?"

"Haven't you heard *Tattoo Man*?"

I thought back briefly but it didn't ring any bells. I was living down in Lynden, Washington in the latter seventies and didn't hear a lot of Canadian radio so I missed that one. Then she did another Aretha song, *You Make Me Feel Like a Natural Woman*, and it was unbelievable. What a voice! As she came offstage I was introduced to her briefly with a simple "This is Randy Bachman" and at that moment there was an instant reaction in me, a spark or a chemistry that had been missing for several years.

Born in Clinton, Iowa, Denise McCann's family originally hailed from Louisiana. At age eleven she moved from Iowa to San Francisco where she spent her adolescent years, receiving her initiation into music on the thriving San Francisco scene. In the fall of 1973, Denise relocated to Vancouver after being captivated during an earlier visit. "One of the things I loved about Vancouver," she recalls, "was that I could just walk into a recording studio, say 'Hi, I'm a singer' and have them reply 'Great, we need a singer on this tape. Come right in.' In San Francisco, you had to have an in, you had to know somebody, whereas in Vancouver I would be judged on what I could do not who I knew. In Vancouver, I could make a living in music performing in clubs and work a full week. I couldn't make a living in California. My first band was called Hot Crackers, two girls and a rock lineup, and we did a Dan Hicks and his Hot Licks kind of act." Soon after, Denise met Guy Sobel and the two managed to land a Canadian recording contract with

Polydor Records. In 1977, *Tattoo Man* became her first hit transforming her into Canada's disco queen. Following that, she briefly worked around Vancouver as Denise McCann and the Dead Marines, a punk band. "I was wearing lingerie onstage before Madonna, really wild outfits and hair," she laughs. Denise later worked with Brian McLeod in the original Headpins before hooking up with the Night Train Revue.

I wasn't on the rebound when I met Denise. It wasn't like that at all. My breakup with Lorayne and divorce proceedings began in 1979 and from that point until I met Denise two years later I had nothing to do with other women. No interest. I was totally consumed by the circumstances of the divorce, the court battles and the welfare of my children. I was walking through life like a zombie. Outside of that, what kept me going was music. I was pretty much stripped down to nothing. Going to my studio with Johnny Austin and recording became my healing and kept me from brooding constantly over my predicament.

I hated the process of dating, but occasionally friends from church would arrange a double date with their cousin or someone. I was lonely, but it wasn't the same. I was simply going through the motions of dating, but the dates were faceless to me. I was waiting for the same thing to happen to me that had happened when I first met Lorayne: fireworks, stars, and explosions. I was blinded when Lorayne first walked into that Regina coffeehouse in 1966. I believe in acting on impulses like that because if you don't then it's gone and may never happen again. That person will be gone. And if the same impulse is returned, then time means nothing. It doesn't matter whether you knew each other an hour, a week, or a month. You just know it's right; she is the person for you. I had felt that way with Lorayne and that's why I was so heartbroken when it ended because the dream was suddenly over. And I felt that way with Denise that first night. She was surrounded by her friends and had a boyfriend who was in the band, but we managed to exchange pleasantries and she moved on.

I was then invited to play another charity gig out in Langley a week later — just throw together a band and play a few numbers. I called Lindsay Mitchell from Prism who had been doing a few things with me already, Frank Ludwig from Union, and Garry Peterson who had been working with Burton's band. I found out Denise's number and called her to join us along with a sax player from the show. This was a thrown together thing so in the dressing room we were all deciding on the songs to do like *Kansas City, Takin' Care of Business, Respect, Whole Lotta Shakin' Goin' On*. It was like a Delaney and Bonnie and Friends thing, fairly loose but fun. During the show, I started talking to Denise and in our conversations throughout the evening found out she was divorced, had a son named Demian about the same age as Tally, was in a relationship at the moment and was going away in a few days to San Francisco to visit her mother.

After the gig I still felt a tug at my heartstrings and wanted to talk to her again. She was living in a house with several other divorced women, some of whom had children. They were looking after Demian while she was away. Demian lived on the computer twenty-four hours a day anyway so he probably never even noticed his Mom was away. I phoned looking for Denise and ended up talking with him.

During the time Denise was away, I had two disturbing dreams. At the time, I was living in my little house I rented in Lynden to be near my children during the custody battle. The first dream was that water was pouring from the ceiling down the walls. It was so real to my subconscious that as I was waking up I looked down to see if I was ankle deep in water. I woke up actually feeling wet. The next dream was a vision of a woman in a particular outfit, like a woman's suit, standing by a wall of windows looking out over a cityscape of lights. I thought nothing of these at the time.

A couple of days later I felt some strange compulsion to go out to the big house in Lynden. I arrived and checked the barn. Everything was okay. As I approached the house I could hear an alarm. It wasn't the burglar alarm so as I entered, I followed the ringing down to the basement, opened the door where we had a generator in case the power ever went out and I stepped in water. Water was pouring from the ceiling. The sump pump was full and the alarm was sounding to warn us that there was a problem. It was eerie. The dream I had just days earlier was a premonition. It really rattled me.

A day or so after that, Denise returned from San Francisco and Demian informed her I had called and left my number. She called me and asked what was up. We chatted back and forth and then she told me she was flying out to New York for New Year's Eve to do *Tattoo Man* at Studio 54. She had been sent a plane ticket. We agreed to get together before then and when I came over to see her, she showed me some photos of her trip to see her mother. One of them was of Denise in a purple suit standing by a series of windows looking out over San Francisco Bay. It was taken at her mother's house. I was stupefied. This was my other dream image come to life. Now here she was about to go away again.

Denise called me the next day crying because a blizzard had snowed in Vancouver airport and she couldn't get a flight out to New York. It was such a major event for her and she was devastated that she might have to miss it. So I inquired "Are there any flights going out of Seattle?" She contacted the airlines and found out they were still flying from there.

"Great. I'll pick you up and take you to Seattle."

I had a big GMC four-wheel drive Suburban wagon that ploughs through snow like confetti so I rolled up to her place, picked her up, and took her to Seattle. Driving in snowy conditions was nothing for me. I later picked her up on her return and brought her back to Vancouver. At that point I asked if I could take her out sometime. She balked because of her ongoing relationship with another guy, so I suggested something safe. Foreigner was coming to town and I really liked that band so I proposed something that might placate her boyfriend. Denise and I would take our respective kids, Demian, Tally, and Kezia, to the show, go to dinner together first, and then take in the concert. That's what we did. We looked like a family, a couple and their three kids. The children hit it off fairly easily as kids do discovering common ground in sports, music, and computer games. Afterwards, I took her home and gave her a hug as she was leaving. Once again the electricity was there. I knew she was the one meant for me and so I began pursuing her, despite her boyfriend.

Denise was going away again for a gig somewhere, but before she left I confronted her. By then I had been buying her flowers and writing poetry about her, all the "goo goo fourteen year old falling in love" stuff. I wasn't sure I would ever feel that way again, but here I was preoccupied with thoughts of her. I sort of proposed to her at that point before she was leaving, pouring forth my feelings about her since we first met a few months earlier. It certainly wasn't a very long period of time. I seem to have a track record for that. I left her with the question: do you want to marry me? It was a bold move after such a whirlwind romance but I knew my own feelings. The uncertainty was whether those feelings were reciprocated.

She went off, did the gig, and returned. I received a call from her a day or two later and I asked how the gig went. She replied, "Everything went fine and my answer is yes."

"Yes what?"

"Don't you remember before I left you asked if I would marry you?"

"Yeah?"

"Have you changed your mind?"

"No."

"Well my answer is yes."

I had originally posed the question without even considering the response. I was elated but it was like "Be careful what you wish for because you might get it." Had I asked too soon? My life had been put on hold for two years and now I was about to jump into a marriage situation again with someone I barely knew. But in my heart, I felt she was the one. Now came the dilemma of announcing this to my children and ex-wife. This would mean the breakup was irrevocable. How would my kids respond? Would they embrace Denise and accept her? Would it cause more conflict with Lorayne?

Denise had met my children a few times while I was living in Lynden. I would bring her down to my little house, we would all go out to dinner together, then I would drive her back to Vancouver for her gig. She was a working musician and played most nights. She got to know the kids and they, in turn, took to her. We were married March 27, 1982, in my big house that I no longer lived in but I maintained as lodging for musicians who were recording at my studio. All my children were present. It was wonderful.

Our honeymoon was a true adventure. I am the kind of person who likes to have everything arranged and booked before I leave. I am fastidious that way, but one of Denise's endearing qualities is her carefree spirit of adventure and joie de vivre. Her idea of a honeymoon was simply "Let's go to Mexico." So off we went with no hotel reservations or accommodations. We would do everything on the spur of the moment. When we needed a room for the night we simply looked for one. It was marvellous fun and I was feeling twenty-four all over again. We were in love, having fun, travelling this carefree path and suddenly life was worth living again.

When we returned, we set up house in my little Lynden abode. The big house was seized by the lawyers soon after anyway but I had no desire to reside there given the memories attached to it. It was time for a fresh start. Denise didn't like to be in that house. It was Lorayne's house, not hers. We were married there because of the size, which accommodated the wedding party, but I never lived in the dream house again.

CHAPTER 9

Looking Out for '1

If the seventies had been a time for Randy to explore new directions in his music and reap success on his own terms, the eighties would find him retracing his former steps through a series of reunions in an attempt to recapture some old glory. It would not be a decade of new music but instead of consolidating his personal life and family, of rebuilding in preparation for a rejuvenated career in the nineties. The end of the seventies had left him emotionally and financially drained. Now he had to pick up and start over.

When Randy walked away from Bachman-Turner Overdrive in 1977 life seemed sweet. He had a loving wife, six wonderful children, a palatial home, and financial security. His accountant had pegged his net worth at roughly $10 million. Randy was among the elite of Canadian musicians, having garnered an enormous windfall without forsaking Canada for the US. But that idyllic life with all its luxuries, along with all the sweat equity logged in turning Bachman-Turner Overdrive into a phenomenon, was rocked to its very foundation. Within a few short years, that same accountant would inform Randy that he was now a "red millionaire." In other words, by the early eighties instead of having $10 million in assets he was now $1 million in the hole. Astronomical legal bills and a minefield of sealed accounts and frozen assets was a bitter pill to swallow. But as he did with everything else in his life, Randy drew strength from his setback, determined to reverse his fortunes and get back on course.

In the legal disbursement of assets, things were equally bitter. Lorayne receives a healthy portion of my BTO annuity income, the nest egg that was supposed to set us all up for life, which has allowed her to live comfortably. My studio equipment and all the state of the art gear I had purchased was sold. I retained some of my outboard gear, but in order to do so I had to pay for half its assessed value. I had to pay for half the assessed value of my publishing company, too, which included my BTO and Trooper songs.

One morning while I was at my barn studio, another state trooper arrived at my gate with a lawyer who I didn't know and insisted on entry. You can't say no to a state trooper. They demanded to see my collection of guitars — instruments I had acquired throughout my career — some Stratocasters for stage use, old Gibsons including my original 1959 Les Paul, Martin acoustics, and my Legend guitar. Unbeknownst to me, the lawyer had been in touch with George Gruhn of Gruhn Vintage Guitars in Nashville and he had George on hold ready to offer appraisal value.

"Show us all your guitars."

As I did so, the lawyer wrote down the make, model, vintage, and any other distinguishing characteristics. He then went away to phone George. Later that day, the same lawyer returned accompanied by the trooper.

"I need a cheque for $40,000 right now."

I had to come up with the money, half the appraised value I guess George had provided, or he would seize all the guitars for auction.

This also happened with my cars, including my rare Excalibur that I had to sell. My 1954 Rolls-Royce Silver Dawn, totally rebuilt, was sold at auction but I did something to trace where it went. I kept the beautiful leather-bound Rolls-Royce handbook from the glove compartment and left a note instead with my name and address:"If you want the manual, please call me." I wanted to find out what it was purchased for.The car was ultimately auctioned off in Seattle for a mere $19,500. It was worth twice that.

Our $3-million dream home on thirty acres outside Lynden was held by the lawyers in a deed of trust against legal fees owing and was eventually seized by them. Over the years, they have tried to sell it but it is still unsold as far as I know.The most recent asking price was $7.5 million US. If it sells, we won't see anything from it though. I turned over the keys and walked away from it. It was almost like the minute we built our dream home the dream was over.

When Denise and I married, we had Tally and Denise's son Demian living with us.We envisioned a life with two teenage boys and my other children remaining close through visitations.They had all met Denise and seemed to get along well with her, but she could never replace Mom in their eyes. Suddenly Denise became the mom. I had been awarded custody of all six children. Following adjournment, however, the judge took me aside and suggested that because the youngest, Emilie, was so young and had been with her Mom virtually throughout the entire melee, she should stay with Lorayne for the time being. Kezia also wanted to be with her Mom. I agreed to that for their sake. Lorayne ultimately relocated to Logan, Utah, living in a Mormon community.

"Having Demian around was great,"Tal enthuses. "We had a great time.We were about the same age and had similar interests. Both of us were from dysfunctional family situations. That was a very positive period for me. It was the four of us for a while, then the custody situation got settled and the rest came to live with us, some unwillingly.Two stayed with my Mom and the rest came with us, but desperately want-

Randy and
Blair Thornton,
1975

Randy with his Legend guitar, 1974

BTO – Fred, Robbie, Randy, Blair, 1975

BTO – with a few gold records

ndy with Trooper, 1976

Randy with Little Richard on
the *HEAD ON* album, 1976

TO's elaborate stage setup, 1975

Randy, 1976

The "Big House," Lynden, Washington, 1977

RICHARD CREAMER

Randy recording with Burton for his *MY OWN WAY TO ROCK* album (producer Richard Perry looking on) – 1978

DEE LIPPINGWELL

Tom Sparks with Randy and his 1954 Silv Dawn Rolls-Royce, Lynden, Washington, 19

Randy and Burton on Midnight Speci when Randy was promoting *SURVIVO* – the two reprised *American Woma*

Randy with Prime Minister Trudeau at the Juno Awards, Toronto 1979

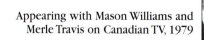

Appearing with Mason Williams and Merle Travis on Canadian TV, 1979

Randy with reunited Guess Who, July 1983

onhorse, 1979

Randy with writing partner, Beach Boy Carl Wilson, 1979

The reunited Guess Who, 1983

Ad for Guess Who reunion tour, 1983

BTO, 1984 – left to right: Garry Peterson, Randy, Timmy Bachman, Fred Turner

Randy with BTO, 1984

With Mountain's Lesl
West backstage durin
the Van Halen tou
where West gueste
on several show

With guitar legend Chet Atkins
(Chet presenting Randy with a
Super Chet model guitar)

MERRY GRETSCHMAS
1992

Randy Bachman

Randy's Gretsch
Christmas card, 1992

Randy with the Stray Cats' Brian Setzer on
the Gretsch stage at the NAMM show, 1996

Randy amongst a few of hi
over 300 Gretsch guitars i
his basement in White Rock, B

CAREY LAUDER

Randy jams with Neil Young for the
first time – Winnipeg, June 28, 1987

Gretsch ad featuring Randy – mid-80s

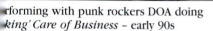

...rforming with punk rockers DOA doing
...kin' Care of Business – early 90s

...Bachman joins Randy's band on drums, 1994

Randy and Neil Young recording
the video for *Prairie Town*
at Neil's ranch, 1992

Randy and Neil rockin' out, 1992

Ringo Starr tour, 1995

Randy and Denise on their wedding (
in the "Big House," March 27, 19

Randy, Denise and all the kids at their weddi

The arrival of Callianne (on Randy's knee)
expands the family - fall 1984

The proud father - Randy
Lorelei's wedding, 19

Singer George Michael,
Callianne and Randy, 1989

JOHN EINARSON

...mily portrait, 1986.
...ockwise from left:
...nnatyne, Denise, Callianne, Randy,
...relei, Brigham, Demian, Tal, Emilie, Kezia

The Guess Who reunite for the
Pan Am Games – rehearsals at the
Walker Theater, August 5, 1999 –
left to right: Randy, Burton,
writer John Einarson, Jim, Garry

...nning Back Thru Canada tour June,
...00 – Randy, Burton, Bill Wallace and
...nnie McDougall rock out

Ad for surprise gig
at Crescentwood
Community
Center, Winnipeg –
Runnin' Back
Across Canada
reunion tour

RUNNIN' BACK TO...
CRESCENTWOOD
COMMUNITY CENTRE
with
THE
GUESS
WHO
THE "CLUB" SHOW
SATURDAY MAY 20TH

CRESCENTWOOD COMMUNITY CENTRE

BARRY RODEN

At the Family Farm Benefit – January 16, 2000

"Have guitar, will travel."
– RANDY BACHMAN

ed to live with my Mom. It was tough for Dad and for the kids. He had spent quite a bit of time away from the little ones and hadn't spent all that much time in childrearing and wasn't used to that routine, nor was Denise.

"Denise was a person that none of us had ever really met or seen before. She was like full-on bohemian. We had never seen anything like her. When a man and a woman marry and have kids, that family unit develops its own culture, a set of expectations and behaviours in the way they function and exist. You don't question them when you are in that environment, but when someone who doesn't really share those beliefs or attitudes moves in, it's perhaps similar to an organ transplant. It's a foreign body and as a kid you don't really know how to respond to it. Children being innately conservative will think 'This is foreign to me.' And this person is making rules for you and is in a position of authority over you. So I think it was a struggle for everyone involved, though I think less so for me because I was in my own world in my room with my records, books, and guitars. Dad and Denise struggled to keep order in this house full of rambunctious and sometimes uncooperative kids. I hear all these stories from my siblings and from Denise about that time, but I guess I missed a lot of it. I was in the house, but I was out of the loop. Dad and I talked about guitars and music and Denise dealt with the little kids."

"It was a big change for me coming up to live with my Dad and Denise," states Brigham Bachman who was only two when his parents split up and had remained with Lorayne until the custody issue was settled three years later. "My two sisters Lorelei and Bannatyne and I really wanted to live with my Mom. So there was this immediate sting of missing her, especially for me being the youngest of the three and leaving my sister Emilie behind with Mom. Moving in with this new pseudo-Mom was a shock for me. I got along with Demian because I think we both were feeling the same things about this whole new family situation. That was the hardest part of my childhood and I think Lorelei and Bannatyne's as well. I'm closer to Lorelei because she was older and took Banna and me under her wing when we were taken from our Mom. She was a comforting force in my life at that time. There are always scars no matter what, but I think I've managed to put a lot of it behind me.

"From about age five to age eleven we all wanted to live with our mother and it was a constant fight to do so. We were like confused children. We certainly didn't make it easy for my Dad or Denise, and I think Denise became fairly fed up with us. I was the most problematic of all the children, not necessarily rebellious as devious, wild, full of all this energy. I guess I qualified as having Attention Deficit Disorder and was diagnosed as hyperactive. At age eleven, I moved back to Utah but I didn't like it so I came back to live with my Dad at fourteen or fifteen. I had always wanted to get closer to my Dad and I certainly am more now, but we had to go through a lot to get there. He had a lot of kids and there wasn't always the attention given out to each, so there was some reaching out and trying to grab some of his attention. A lot of the times he wasn't there or wasn't as interested in some of the family things. I look back on times in my childhood and wonder 'Why wasn't he there for me?' Most children go through that, but as an adult I understand more now his professional duties intertwined with his family life. We were always well aware of our Dad's status, but we purposely never focused on 'Dad the rock star.' My father was quite adamant about the value of privacy. We were just another family. It was an unspoken rule that we didn't divulge anything and kept to ourselves about his life. We didn't really see the rock star side of him. All my friends used to bug me about who my Dad was and how much I must get because of him but in reality I got less than they did. I used to say, 'If only you guys knew.' Everybody assumes a lot when your Dad is famous."

During this period, I was still working in my barn studio and would drive over each day to work with Johnny Austin. Denise would come on occasion and contribute some vocals. One day I returned from the studio to find a strange car outside our house and two strange men standing in the living room.

"What's going on?"

As they turned around I saw name tags on them. "Who are you?"

"They're Mormon Missionaries," Denise replied. "I've been taking the lessons. I want to join the church and I'd like you to baptize me."

I had tears in my eyes. I had not tried to force her to join my church. She was a free spirit in the fullest sense of that phrase, having lived in California in the sixties. The choice was completely her own. I never really thought she would fall into this life of mine and that was okay with me. She respected my religion and I respected her own free will. At the time we were married, she simply said politely, "Just leave me alone about it." There was no pressure from me. Making this decision on her own brought such joy to me. A couple of years later, we were sealed in the Mormon Temple in Seattle and our own daughter Callianne was sealed to us there.

For Denise, marrying me came with a lot of extra baggage. Not long after we wed, we went from a family of four or five to nine as my other kids came to live with us, some permanently, others temporarily. And she had to manage this mostly on her own because I was away much of the time on the road. She was wonderful under these circumstances, but it had to have been difficult for her. Some of the kids gave her a rough time, not because they didn't like her or that she mistreated them, which she never did, but just because she wasn't their mother yet had to act like their mother. There was some resistance at first. But Callianne's birth was the catalyst to bring us all together. It was no longer simply your kids and mine, it was now our kids.

"I was unprepared for how intense and bitter Randy's divorce was and how present it remained in our lives," recalls Denise. "The amount of nastiness astounded me. In my previous relationships and my marriage, when we broke up we all remained friends. To me, Randy's divorce was like a war. It has been so rough on Randy's kids because they adore their father and adore their mother too. But he has been very determined to maintain his presence in their lives and it hasn't always been easy. He is crazy about his kids; he lives for them. I'm almost jealous of it sometimes, the kind of feeling he has for his kids. It's unprecedented in my experience. Those kids come first. So we ended up with four of them. We would have had all six, but the oldest girl, Kezia, said she wouldn't come with us and the youngest, Emilie, was so completely bonded to her mother that to take her away would not have done her any good. Demian thought it was going to be perfect because he had always wanted a brother and he and Tally were only one year apart. Suddenly there are eight kids. I wasn't quite prepared for that. It was like being thrown into the deep end. Then two years later we had our own daughter, Callianne.

"People ask me, 'How did you manage that?'" smiles Denise. "How? I focused totally on the kids. My life stopped. I put my career on hold, which is something I look back on with a little regret. Randy and I sat down at that point and came to the conclusion that he could earn more money than I could, so if one of us had to go out and one stayed home the logical one to go out was him."

During the divorce and custody battle, my money was frozen until everything was settled. I came back to Canada after the settlement in the early eighties and my accountant at the time laid out my financial state of affairs. With all the money I owed the IRS and Revenue Canada during that period when everything was frozen, along with astronomical legal and accounting bills, I was broke and deep in debt. It had taken me four years with BTO to become a millionaire and just four short years to lose it all plus more. I was devastated.

We had moved back to Canada because Denise wanted to live here. One day, I was walking along Granville Street in Vancouver feeling very depressed at my recent circumstance and I stopped to sit on a bench where hobos beg for spare change. I guess the setting seemed fitting. There was a McDonald's across the street so I was absentmindedly picking at an order of fries, slouched on the bench, head hanging low when I heard a voice above me.

"Hey, aren't you Randy Bachman?"

I've heard this a zillion times in my life, but the last thing I needed right then was a fan hovering over me.

"Yes I am," I moaned disconsolately, hoping he would go away and leave me wallowing in my misery.

"You played at my high school graduation in Winnipeg, Melrose School in East Kildonan."

"Yeah, okay, great." Still hoping he'd go away.

"*These Eyes* is our song. My wife and I were engaged to that song and play it every year on our anniversary."

"Yeah, yeah, fine," still not looking up.

"My name is John, by the way."

"Yeah, hi."

"I'm the new loans officer at the Canadian Imperial Bank of Commerce over there. Do you need a loan?"

"Loan?" I looked up.

"Yeah."

"Wow, do I need a loan! But I've just gone through a divorce and all my money is frozen, I owe money to everyone."

"I know. I've been reading about it in the papers. I'll give you a loan. Come to my office."

I followed him to his office. He asked me what my sources of income were and I explained to him how record royalties, touring income, songwriting and publishing income worked. By that point I had bought back my one-half of the publishing from the divorce, using money I was anticipating receiving. So I told him I had that income in the pipeline that would be coming from BMI Canada.

"Is there any way you can verify that flow of income?"

"Sure, I can phone them."

I called Toronto from his office right then and BMI confirmed it. Bang. That was all he needed. John loaned me $30,000 that day. As a musician, all your life you can never get credit. Nobody will give you credit because they consider your income source unreliable. You have to save up and pay cash. But because I now had this loan, I could get credit. And when I paid it off in a year and a half, I had more credit.

I went home and told Denise. "Guess what? I got $30,000!" We put some of it as a down payment on a house we wanted and I was then able to secure a mortgage and have some money left over for odds and ends. We were on our feet again. With a larger household to manage, Denise and I set up home in a big house on Marine Drive in White Rock. Then in January of 1983 I received a phone call asking if I would be interested in a Guess Who reunion later that year. "Sure." That became a guaranteed income I could count on, so I was able to make lump sum payments of $50,000 on the mortgage. From there our financial situation progressively improved.

The offer of a Guess Who reunion could not have come at a better time for Randy. He needed financial stability and cash flow as well as to re-establish his name and reputation in the music industry. A lot of water had gone under the bridge in the intervening thirteen years since he had left the group, but in recent years the four original members had all made efforts to mend fences. Garry Peterson had been working in Burton's touring band, while Jim Kale had gone back out on the road in 1978 with other players under the Guess Who banner with Randy and Burton's blessing. Granting Jim rights to use the name, however, still haunts them to this day.

I did a stupid thing when I left Bachman-Turner Overdrive. I let the others have the logo, which was worth probably millions of dollars. No licensing — I just let them have it. I did that twice in my career. The second time was in the late seventies. I was in a studio in LA working with Burton on his album at the same time I was doing my *SURVIVOR* album. The phone rang in the studio one Saturday and it was Jim Kale.

"I'm in trouble with the IRS and Revenue Canada and they're going to take my house and car. I have one chance to work."

"Yeah? So?"

"I need the name. Can I use the Guess Who name?"

Burton and I both had our solo careers going and didn't figure we needed it so we said, "Yeah, go ahead." In reality Jim was like the true inheritor of that name anyway because he was the only guy from the original Silvertones. So he took the name out on the road and has been using it ever since. But, unbeknownst to Burton and me, Jim went and trademarked it, and now we can't get near it. Neither of us wanted it then, but now I'd love to have it. But you live with your mistakes.

Since that time, Jim Kale has toured relentlessly throughout the US under the Guess Who banner with varying lineups. At times these have included ex-latter-day Guess Who members Kurt Winter and Don McDougall. More recently Garry Peterson has fronted the group. "Kale's Klones" as Burton derisively labels them are part and parcel of the clone band phenomenon that has sprung up in the last two decades to feed the insatiable demand by baby boomers for the music of their glory days. There are dozens of these nostalgia acts plying the state fair circuit; some illegally pilfer a well-known name, others hold a tenuous connection to an original lineup. Indeed, Mike Love tours with a roster of sidemen as The Beach Boys while Diana Ross resurrected the Supremes name in the company of two singers who never shared a stage with her in the past, despite original member Mary Wilson's protests. Others, like the Lovin' Spoonful minus lead singer and principal writer John Sebastian or a Herman-less Herman's Hermits continue to find work. In that context, a Guess Who without Burton Cummings and Randy Bachman seems plausible. What has allowed Jim and Garry to earn a decent living flogging the hits is the fact that in the United States, the original Guess Who members were largely anonymous. This ersatz Guess Who has rarely ventured north of the border.

By 1983, nostalgia for the Guess Who in Canada had grown exponentially. Their songs remained staples on the radio and their albums, both the originals and various hit compilations, continued to sell in impressive numbers. With a one-time reunion offer on the table, phone calls were exchanged and the four agreed to meet face to face in Winnipeg in January to talk over the proposition.

The spark initially came from the Nederlander family who owned a number of major theatres and halls in the US. The son was a big Guess Who fan, and when the family was about to open a new amusement park, Canada's Wonderland outside Toronto, he floated the idea of a Guess Who reunion to inaugurate the entertainment venue of this new facility. Initially, it was to be a one-off performance, but once the word got out among the industry people, Michael Cohl of CPI, Concert Promotions International, entered the bidding, offering more dates at larger venues. Instead of Canada's Wonderland, CPI was pitching the CNE, two nights, videotaped for First Choice Pay TV and home video release, the whole nine yards. So the project turned in that direction.

When we got together in Winnipeg to discuss the offers, it was like four guys who had been through boot camp and battles together and hadn't seen each other in years sharing old war stories. "Hi, how are you doing?" and backslapping all round. Sure there were things we didn't like about each other or what each of us had done or said in the intervening years, but that was all set aside. In spite of all the acrimony and legal entanglements, when we are together there is a special camaraderie between us. We're like old friends — the team that shared the same dreams and managed to achieve them.

Dollars were placed on the table, $250,000 for two shows ini-
tially, and we all agreed to do it. That ante soon upped as more
dates were presented. The reunion came at a fortuitous time for
me because I was just getting my new life together with Denise
and had won custody of my children. Once the reunion was made
public, it was "Oh you can't not play Winnipeg." "You can't leave
out Calgary and Edmonton." Because we were rehearsing in
Vancouver we were offered the opportunity to perform at the
opening of the new BC Place domed stadium at the BC Lions season opener for $50,000. What had started out as a one-off show
turned into a mini-tour and the pot kept getting bigger. I think we
each took home around $200,000 in the end.

Rehearsals were great and we even came up with five new
songs, one of which was from Jim. We opened at the inauguration
of BC Place in Vancouver and it was wonderful. We did a really
long set, thirty to thirty-two songs, two and a half hours, with not
only Guess Who tunes but BTO and Cummings' solo hits plus the
new numbers.

Once we arrived in Toronto, however, the old habits resurfaced
when friends showed up with various substances and the whole
positive atmosphere was thrown off kilter. From that point on the
dynamics were irrevocably altered. It was 1970 all over again. All I
wanted to do was get out. I couldn't wait for the tour to end so I
could go home to peace and quiet.

I think some of us believed this was going to be a long-term
thing. We would stay together, do an album, tour again. "The Guess
Who was back." I sincerely wanted to believe it at that time. Once
the tour was done though, we simply went our separate ways.
Mercifully, there was no more talk of taking it any further. Burton
and I resumed our separate careers, Garry continued to back
Burton, and Jim returned to his Guess Who clone band. What had
started out on such a high ended with a bad taste.

But I came away from that reunion with a new level of what

they call in the business "phone acceptance" where I could phone someone and say "It's Randy Bachman" and actually get through rather than get "Oh I'm sorry, he's busy." And I also received a boost in personal ego and self-confidence at a time in my life when I desperately needed it, as well as the realization that this music really does mean something to people and I can get together with these three guys and make that magic again.

"When I did the 1983 *TOGETHER AGAIN* reunion live album," recalls producer Jack Richardson, "by the time we finished the last date that we were recording I recall Burton going right up the wall in the dressing room. I just figured it was certainly a short-lived affair. Burton and Randy seem like matter and anti-matter when they get together for any length of time. As co-writers, they were an amazing team. It's just too bad that their personalities create a schism that prevents them from continuing on with that greatness. I find it very unfortunate that they can't seem to cage the personality differences to a degree that would allow them to get together and be a good writing team again."

Attempts at moving the reunion tour to the more lucrative United States fell apart early on, compounding the frustration. "During rehearsals, Randy came to me to ask if I would get Bruce Allen involved," recalls Jim Martin, who returned as road manager for the reunion. "There was a bad vibe happening between Randy and Bruce over the BTO thing when he left and he wasn't sure Bruce would speak with him. Bruce was now the kingpin in the States with Bryan Adams and Loverboy, a heavy hitter. Randy figured Bruce could make it happen in the US and keep the reunion going. I knew Bruce well, so I went to him and asked him to come out to a rehearsal and maybe get involved. Bruce was a Guess Who fan from day one and a Randy Bachman fan, still is to this day. So Bruce checked it out with US promoters and came back to the band before they left Vancouver to head out across Canada and told them it wouldn't work. He surveyed his connections across the border and what came back to him was, "Why the hell do I want to book this band called the Guess Who when I've got them down the street at a bar for two grand?" Kale's clone band hurt the name in the States. That hit Cummings heavy and he went nuts. I remember sitting at a table with Randy, Burton, and Jim, and Burton looking at Jim and asking, "What's it going to take to get the name back?" Kale replied in that slow, deliberate manner of his, "One million dollars." I was on the floor pissing myself. I couldn't believe Kale's nerve."

Swept along with the tide of nostalgia, Randy followed up the Guess Who jaunt with a Bachman-Turner Overdrive reunion in 1984 but with a revamped lineup.

At every single place we played on the Guess Who reunion I was asked, "Are you going to do this with BTO?" True to form, a phone call came soon after offering us a tour for the original BTO. It had a couple of false starts and wasn't as momentous an occasion as the Guess Who because the backers had money problems, but it got the four of us together again. We signed with Charlie Fach who was working at a new label, Compleat Records.

The offer to re-form was for the original lineup that included my brother Tim on guitar, Fred, Robbie, and me. But when we all met to talk about the reunion, Robbie came out with his old gripe: "I want a share of the publishing and your songwriting."

"No, that's for me and my wife and kids. That's their future. When you write a song it's yours. But you're free to write and pitch songs to the group."

"Those are my terms. Take it or leave it. I either get a share in the publishing or not be the drummer in the reunion."

"Fine. I won't accept those terms."

Robbie walked out and I immediately phoned Garry Peterson and explained the situation to him.

"I'm in," replied Garry without hesitation, leaving Burton's touring group to join me.

Fred had no desire to share his songs with Robbie either, so we were in agreement.

That evening Robbie called me.

"I've changed my mind. I've reconsidered. I want in."

"You're too late. I called Garry Peterson. He's in. We needed to know that day for the backers."

"Well, change your mind."

"I can't. You gave us your ultimatum. Fred sided with me. Tim was in, so we got Garry. That's all there is to it."

Maybe that was the fuel on the fire for Robbie's later feud with me; I don't know.

We proceeded to do an album for Charlie at Little Mountain studios and it had *For the Weekend*, which had hit potential. I looked at that album as a first step and the next one would be the one to get things flying again. But Charlie just didn't have the manpower or the deep pockets to get behind the album enough. Compleat Records was a small independent operation. We went on tour and couldn't find our album in the stores. We would do an in-store album signing and there would be no albums there. But the live shows were well received because we did all the hits that everyone loved.

With Fred living in Winnipeg and the other three out on the West Coast, rehearsing new material was problematic. Nevertheless, the quartet managed to stay together over the next two years playing an increasing number of dates and re-establishing the BTO franchise. While most observers assumed Randy was simply along for the ego stroking, the reality was he needed the income to sustain his family. As far as he was concerned, this was a long-term decision. "It was never a temporary thing when we got back together in '84," confirms Fred Turner. "A lot of people thought that, but we had actually talked about it before the Guess Who reunion. When the Guess Who played in Winnipeg, I talked with Randy after the show and he told me that the

Guess Who had a tremendous amount of offers to keep it together. So I told Randy that was okay, we'd put our thing on the back burner while he went out and did the Guess Who thing. But as it turned out, Burton decided he didn't want any part of it after the tour, so the Guess Who thing was gone and we went back to putting BTO back together. Tim Bachman was instrumental in getting BTO going again, so he was a part of this, not Blair. Robbie had a lot of demands we couldn't meet. Garry Peterson wanted to do it so that's how it came together. There was some talk at one point of getting Burton in the band. There were two people, promoters in New York, who wanted to get the original or as much of the original Guess Who and BTO together and call it Merger. I think they put it to Burton but nothing came of it."

While we were getting BTO off the ground again working constantly out on the road, Sammy Hagar called me out of the blue. He and I had written some songs together in Lynden for one of his solo albums and had recorded the demos at my studio.

"I've just joined Van Halen. We're going out on the road and really need a strong opening act. Will you open for us?"

"For how long?"

"Well, let's road test it for a week and see how it works out."

"Okay." This was a terrific opportunity to gain some high-profile exposure.

But by now Fred had dropped out of the group. We had been slugging it out on the road travelling in two vans on the cheap for two years and Fred needed to be at home with his wife and teenage sons at that point. We had agreed to temporarily disband for six months to sort out all our personal problems, then the phone call came from Sammy on a Friday. He needed an answer by Monday morning. The four members of Van Halen had unanimously chosen BTO as their choice for opening act.

Sammy had said, "We need an opening act that will be so powerful that no one will be screaming, "Where's David?" [former singer David Lee Roth]. "You guys will get them rocking doing all your hits, bam bam bam, we'll do a quick turnover and come out swinging and hit 'em hard so that no one will even remember David Lee Roth. But we've gotta have an answer by Monday."

I hung up the phone and immediately dialed Fred Turner. No answer. I called back a few hours later. Still no answer. I learned from one of his kids that he had taken his wife on a short vacation, but no one had a contact number and he wouldn't be back until Monday or Tuesday.

Monday morning arrived and I had to call Sammy back. I discussed it with Denise and she agreed that it was a chance of a lifetime. Tally was flipping out because he loved Van Halen's music. He was seventeen, and Eddie Van Halen was his personal idol. More than the career opportunity and financial gain involved, I wanted to do this tour just to show my son his Dad was hip. "My Dad knows Van Halen!" At this point it was only for a week, so I called Sammy that Monday.

"Some of us are in, some of us aren't."

"What do you mean?"

"I can't get hold of Fred Turner."

"Who have you got?"

"Me, my brother Tim who can play bass, and Garry Peterson. But basically our lead singer is gone."

So Sammy replied, "Who sings *Takin' Care of Business?*"

"I do."

"Who sings *You Ain't Seen Nothin' Yet?*"

"I do."

"Who sings *Hey You?*"

"I do."

"Who sings *Let It Ride?*"

"Fred."

"Okay, we'll take you. Van Halen is coming without its old lead singer so you guys can come without your lead singer.

Let's give it a shot."

With Tim switching to bass and Garry Peterson on drums, BTO hit the road as a trio opening for Van Halen.

"A few years earlier I had been writing for one of my albums during my Geffen Records period," relates Sammy Hagar on first meeting Randy, "and John Kalodner suggested that I write a song with Randy Bachman. I thought 'Great!' I'm a big fan and always dug those songs, great simple rock 'n' roll tunes, my kind of stuff. So I flew up to Washington and Randy picked me up at the airport, but at that time he was in a pretty bad frame of mind. He was going through his divorce and was about to lose the house. But we managed to write three songs, never used them on the record, but I really liked Randy. It was wonderful getting to meet him, a real down home human being. I thought he was totally cool and completely talented. It was just that at that moment he wasn't focused.

"When the time came for our 5150 tour with Van Halen, we tried to get James Brown to open for us. It was before he went to jail and had just had a big hit with *Living in America*. But he wanted even more money than we did, so it didn't work. He thought we should be opening for him! It was crazy, so we went back to the drawing board and put our thinking caps on. I just said 'BTO' — the name just popped out of nowhere. We all loved BTO and figured every song the fans will love. So we just went for it. Who knows how many tickets they moved but you always knew that every person in the building got off on what they did. It was great. They got encores every night! They were the kind of band we could cheer on because we knew they weren't trying to compete with us. They were just going out and doing what they do and doing it well. Some bands go out and try to blow off the headliners. It was so comfortable having a band like BTO. They did every show on that tour, 110 shows. I used to watch them every night. They were the best band Van Halen ever took out on tour."

Metal guitar guru Eddie Van Halen confirms the esteem his band held for BTO. "It was a great run with BTO on the 5150 tour," he offered recently while recuperating from hip surgery. "We had a good time and every night they took care of business." Adds Sammy, "It was never a competitive vibe between Eddie and Randy, just a mutual respect. In fact, there was never an argument or bad vibe between anyone on that 5150 tour. We all got along great. Never an incident and that's rare on such a lengthy tour. It was wonderful working with those guys."

Sammy adds a twist to his connection to Randy. "When I was growing up around 1969-70 in San Francisco, Denise, who is now Randy's wife, used to know my drummer David Lauser, who is still in my band today. I used to see Denise all the time and she was a good singer. Then in the early eighties when I went up to see Randy, Denise was his wife. They had just gotten married. It was so weird. I hadn't seen her in fifteen years and to discover she was Randy's wife blew me away."

The first gig with Van Halen was in Shreveport, Louisiana, which was Mrs. Eddie Van Halen, actress Valerie Bertinelli's, hometown. Huge arena, sold out, twenty thousand people. We were in our dressing room nervously waiting to go on when the door suddenly kicked open. In came the whole Van Halen gang huggin' and backslapping. "We just want you guys to know we think you're great!" They wanted to hype us up. They were also very anxious because this was the first tour with Sammy Hagar up front singing and they were nervous about how the fans would take to not seeing flamboyant front man David Lee Roth. So we both went out and rocked the joint. Just before the week was done, they came to us and said, "We want to do this with you guys for three months." It wasn't gigantic money but was a smooth deal, our gear could go in their truck, and all we needed was to transport ourselves. It was guaranteed work every day for three months.

I called Denise and she was on side with it. My only stipulation to the Van Halen team was that I wanted a guarantee of family access throughout the tour because I was giving up that precious time with my family at a critical juncture in order to be out on the road. No problem. Van Halen were bringing their families on the road, too. Wives and kids were welcome they reassured me.

Tim Bachman vividly recalls that first night. "At 7:30 the arena doors opened. Five minutes later the chanting started. 'BTO! BTO! BTO!' Louder and louder. 'BTO! BTO! BTO!' We weren't slated to go on until 8:00. I looked over at Randy and he gave me the Randy Bachman look: 'Go do something about this.' We figured we were toast because the opening act isn't supposed to upstage the headliners. But what could we do? Go onstage and tell them to stop? 'Excuse me, it's not our show?' The chanting continued.

"Suddenly there was a pounding on our dressing room door. I was scared to answer because I figured it was Van Halen's manager Ed Leffler in a rage. The pounding continued. Finally I got up the courage to open the door and it was Valerie Bertinelli, Eddie's wife. She grabbed me by my collar and dragged me down the hall, up the stairs, and into the hall where she screamed over the din 'Can you hear that?!' Of course I could hear it.

'What do you think?' she asked over this deafening chanting.

'More importantly, what do Edward and the rest of the band think?'

'They think it's incredible. They've never had this happen to any of their opening acts before. They love it.'

'Well, if they think it's great, then so do we.'

"We still figured we were going to get dumped from the tour after this anyway, but we determined to do our best to pull back and direct the audience as often as we could to the headliners. After our set, we were promptly summoned to Ed Leffler's office and fired. As I left his office, I passed the guys in Van Halen. I stopped, shook their hands, and told them, 'Thanks for a wonderful experience and good luck with the tour.' They were bewildered and asked me why they wouldn't be seeing us tomorrow night. So I told them we had just been fired. Without a word, the four of them marched into Leffler's office and

demanded we remain on the tour or else the whole thing was over. We
ended up doing a hundred and ten shows with Van Halen."

I wasn't going to be around for the next three months, so as
an incentive for the kids to get along and do their chores around
the house and help out Denise, I arranged a little contract with
them. They could each pick a week and come and join me on the
Van Halen tour. So the kids each chose a week and we had a
wonderful time.

Near the end of the three-month odyssey across America with
Van Halen, the group came into our dressing room on one of the
last dates and presented us with a $10,000 bonus.

"We want you to do another seven months with us."

It had become almost like a family situation; everyone had grown
close and would continue to be so over the next leg of the tour. It
was like a travelling gypsy caravan of a hundred and fifty people.

On a couple of occasions, I was really surprised as I warmed up
in the dressing room playing my Lenny Breau/Chet Atkins stuff
when Eddie Van Halen would pop his head in and ask, "How do you
do that?" I, in turn, would ask him how he did all his guitar tricks.
We found we had much in common and it became a mutual admiration society sharing many special moments together.

But the greatest thrill was when Tally joined me on the tour. He
was the biggest Van Halen fan and he showed up in the identical
clothes Eddie had been wearing in a recent teen magazine feature.
As a result, Eddie took an instant liking to Tally. They kibitzed around
together and played practical jokes on each other. Eddie let Tally
play his guitars and sit in on drums with them during sound
checks. We had some really great jams at sound checks playing
Crossroads, which is Eddie's favourite song. And Tally got to sit in.

As Tally's week was nearing its end, Eddie came to him and told
him what a great buddy he had been. He hugged Tally and told
him it was great having him around. Then he asked for Tally's hat.

It was an old Ed Norton–style fedora that my Dad had given him. Without hesitation, Tally took it off and handed it to his hero.

On Tally's last concert date, he went in to say goodbye to Eddie. Eddie then turned to Zeke his guitar tech.

"Go get number 2."

Zeke looked incredulous. "What!?"

"Go get number 2."

"Not number 2?"

"Zeke, go get number 2!"

So Zeke went up onstage and picked up Eddie's number 2 custom-made Kramer guitar with the characteristic red, white, and black stripes, brought it backstage, and handed it to Eddie. Eddie signed it "To Tal, my buddy, love Edward Van Halen, 5150 tour" and handed it to Tally. Tally had tears streaming down his face.

"Oh thank you, thank you." Tally still has that guitar. It's priceless.

A few years ago when Tally needed money to finance his recordings he called me to say he had an offer to sell that guitar to a collector. I told him to bring the guitar over. We took off the neck and looked at the end of it. There, written in the wood, was the signature of the luthier and the number 2. I told Tally, "You can't sell this guitar, it's an original, one of a kind." Instead, I offered to loan him the money and hold onto the guitar until he could pay it back, kind of like collateral.

"My son Paxton came to join me for a few days on the tour," relates Tim. "He was a teenager and it was a big thrill for him to meet the guys in Van Halen. After one of the shows, Paxton was in their dressing room gushing over how great they had been. Michael Anthony, Van Halen's bass player, responded, 'Yeah, well, your Dad was pretty good tonight too.' And Paxton replied, 'Oh those guys are so old. I don't know how you guys could even have them with you.' The four members of Van Halen suddenly stopped everything, sat Paxton down, and told him in no uncertain terms why it was an honour to have us on the same show as them.

'When I was passing out pamphlets on a street corner begging people to come see my band,' Eddie pointed out, 'your Dad's band was breaking the all-time attendance record at the Los Angeles Forum. Having your father's band open for us is like having the Beatles or Led Zeppelin open for us. We worship them.'

"When Paxton came back and told me that, I was three feet off the ground."

In the midst of the Van Halen tour at the annual Texas Jam in Dallas, the day before the concert, the local deejays play the performers in a charity baseball game. We had two days off prior to the gig so I used that time to fly home and see Denise and the kids. On my return to Dallas on Saturday morning for the concert, the driver who picked me up asked, "What band are you in?"

"Bachman-Turner Overdrive."

"Are you the new drummer?"

I froze. "No, I'm the guitar player. What are you talking about?"

"Oh, your drummer spent the night in the hospital."

"What?!"

"You didn't know about that?"

The day before, during the Texas Jam baseball game, Garry Peterson hit the ball, ran to first base, tripped, did a flip in the air, ripped his hamstring and smashed his Achilles tendon. His whole right leg was in ice and they had him on painkillers so he was numb from head to toe. I went straight to the hospital and when I arrived he was babbling, "I'm okay. I'm okay. I'll play with my left leg." I had never seen Garry like this, all doped up.

Somehow he made it to the sound check, but his playing was terrible. He kept slowing down and was in obvious discomfort. We stopped playing and he slumped over on his kit. Loverboy was also on the bill so I thought of having their drummer, Matt Frenette, come out and play *Takin' Care of Business*, then explaining the situation to the crowd hoping they would understand. But if we did that we still wouldn't have a drummer for the next dates and would have to forfeit the Van Halen tour. Our drum tech was Billy Chapman, a good friend of Garry's who set up the drums. Billy would often play the drums at sound check. So I grabbed him and asked, "Billy, do you think you can play drums tonight?"

"Well it's been awhile. I used to play drums in a Led Zeppelin clone band."

"Perfect. You're in."

It was a multiband bill so we only needed to play a couple of songs. We had Garry taken back to the hospital and ultimately sent him home to recuperate. Timmy, Billy, and I went on as Bachman-Turner Overdrive. Billy had a sampler and sampled Fred's vocals for *Let It Ride, Roll On Down the Highway*, and *Four Wheel Drive*. We put in a click track and onstage Billy would discreetly turn on the sampler, follow the click track, and we would do those songs. Sammy and Eddie were amazed at the powerful sound we had from a trio, meanwhile we had the vocals sampled from the original recordings. So we finished the rest of the tour that way.

For Garry, the decision to proceed without him following his recovery several weeks later was a bitter pill to swallow. "I was thrown out of BTO. I received a call from Timmy saying, 'We no longer require you in the band.' How do you think that made me feel? Here I was with a broken ankle and I lost my house because I didn't have any income. I had to sell it and move. I left Burton to join BTO and Burton never forgave me for that."

To capitalize on the higher profile the group enjoyed with Van Halen, Randy felt they should have an album on the market. A hasty deal was negotiated with Curb Records in California to rush release a live album cobbled together from previously recorded dates when Fred Turner was still in the lineup though his picture and name were excised from the final product. *LIVE LIVE LIVE* was a half-hearted effort that received scant promotion but did include one curious track, a cover version of the old Mountain hit *Mississippi Queen*.

> We were recording the *LIVE LIVE LIVE* album in Florida and we wanted to include a cover tune so we all wrote a few song titles on a napkin or piece of paper and turned them over. One by one as we revealed our favourites, one tune came up several times: *Mississippi Queen*. So we recorded it and subsequently played it on the Van Halen tour. Leslie West, the massive guitarist and singer from Mountain, somehow heard about us doing his song so he contacted us and asked to come out on tour as special guest for *Mississippi Queen*. We thought it was a cool idea but said. "Look Leslie, we know you've had a problem in the past with heroin and other drugs and we're totally clean. There's no place for that in our organization." He replied, "Yeah, sure, fine, everything's fine."
>
> He came out to our sound check and we ran through *Mississippi Queen* and *Roll On Down the Highway*. Fine. But that night when we went onstage, it had only been about two hours since the sound check, and he forgot everything. He couldn't even remember that *Mississippi Queen* starts on the five chord and it's his own song! I had to go over in *Roll On Down the Highway* and sing the riff to him in his ear and tell him the notes because he had completely forgotten it. Afterwards we figured maybe it was just opening night jitters. The next day we had a longer sound check and went over the songs again with him. That night we went onstage, forget it, he couldn't remember again.
>
> The following day we were driving along to the next gig and pulled into a McDonald's to eat. Leslie told us, "I gotta have a cigarette." So we told him he couldn't smoke in the car or inside the restaurant because the smoke would stick to his clothes and make me sick. Fine, he took his lunch outside. As we sat in the restau-

rant we looked outside and there was Leslie pulling out a plastic bag and rolling a joint! Cops are pulling in for lunch, families, kids everywhere, and he's rolling this huge joint. Tim went out and told him that he couldn't do this because we couldn't jeopardize our work permits and besides, we weren't into that. So he said okay. To him, grass and heroin were different things. Grass was okay. Anyway, he went off into the bushes; we looked over and there was this smoke signal emitting like a chimney from behind the bushes.

We had to find a way to ease him out of the tour. We got to New Jersey, his home turf, and politely told him, "It's been great Leslie, but you're home now so why don't you stay home." And he did.

During the Van Halen tour, Randy acquired a prized guitar, one he had coveted since his teens.

We were playing Detroit. Ed Dupas, my Dad's cousin's son from La Broquiere, Manitoba, who gave me my first lessons on guitar back in the fifties, was now living in the Detroit area and heard I was coming through. He called my Mom and she got a message to me to phone him. I called Ed and he wanted to bring his son to the show. He said his son played guitar. Cool.

"Do you still want my blond Gibson?"

"Yeah!" I would call him every four or five years and ask to buy that guitar. He would never sell it. They had worked hard to buy that guitar back in the fifties.

"Why do you want to sell it now?"

"My son wants an Eddie Van Halen-style guitar. He doesn't want this big old Gibson. He wants a hotshot guitar."

"How much do you want?"

"He's picked out a guitar in a music shop. All I want is what that guitar cost."

"Bring the Gibson to the show."

Backstage, Eddie Van Halen spotted this gorgeous, mint guitar unchanged from the fifties and flipped out. I plugged it in and it was Chuck Berry, the authentic sound. Playing Chuck Berry on a Fender or Gretsch just doesn't sound the same. I paid Ed the price of the new guitar and everyone went home happy.

As the Van Halen tour wound its way across America, Randy learned that celebrity does have its drawbacks. After the tour had made a swing through the southern US, he received word that someone in Little Rock, Arkansas, was running up some serious bills in his name. Posing as "Randy Bachman of BTO fame," a man looking nothing like Randy had conned his way onto a local noon-hour television show and promised that BTO would headline an upcoming charity concert. Apparently no one bothered to check his credentials, or lack thereof, and instead began trumpeting the imminent BTO appearance. The poseur managed to persuade a five-star hotel that he was the BTO leader. He also convinced a music store, which fronted him a pile of musical instruments and equipment ostensibly for the charity do, and a truck rental firm that provided a half-ton for his use. And use it he did, carting the instruments and equipment across the state line and selling them, plus the truck. When the hotel bills went unpaid, the real Randy was somehow traced to Vancouver and confronted. It took the efforts of the RCMP in Vancouver and Arkansas State authorities to verify that an imposter had scammed thousands of dollars from local merchants. Still, the charity gig remained. When Randy learned that tickets had been sold for a bogus BTO engagement, he and Tim arranged for the group to fly in at their own expense and perform for the fundraiser.

This guy kept it up, impersonating me again in Texas. I received a call from someone who knew me and needed me to verify that the person who was having an affair with his friend's wife was not, in fact, the real Randy Bachman. Again, I was required to go to the local Vancouver RCMP detachment and provide evidence of my identity. The imposter was milking a wealthy woman, claiming he was me. She had a tough time accepting that he was a phony. This happened a third time, again involving band equipment. He would be arrested, serve his time, get released, and do it again. Why he picked me I'll never know.

I ended up on Sally Jessy Raphael's afternoon talk show with Peter Criss, the original drummer from KISS, along with my imposter and Peter's. His guy had been going around claiming to be Peter for quite some time. When Sally asked my imposter why he did it, he casually replied, "Because I can." He didn't even look much like me. He then proceeded to reveal how he had bilked Sally's producers into paying for a luxury suite, room service for his friends, and a Rolls-Royce rental car without them even realizing it. It proved the power of celebrity and just how much people want to believe they are in the presence of someone famous.

On a brief respite from the lengthy tour commitments, Randy received an honour from BMI acknowledging over one million airplays of *These Eyes*. He and Burton were invited to attend the awards ceremony in New York in the fall of 1986. From that meeting, the two determined to test the waters and see if that old magic might still be there. With Burton's solo career on the skids and Randy's current BTO seeing nothing looming on the horizon following the Van Halen trek, the timing seemed right. But a much larger issue was pressing on Randy's agenda, one that had been festering with him for several years and that Burton had hoped to keep hidden from his former partner.

After I left the Guess Who in 1970, I went to Jack Richardson to ask for my songs back. He said they had to stay with the band because they were still releasing records. There was a five-year waiting clause in the contract preventing anyone from re-recording the songs. So in 1975 I contacted Jack again for my songs.

Once again he said I would have to wait another five years. In the meantime, the Guess Who broke up that year. At the time the songs were worth nothing. There were no CDs, classic rock, oldies radio, or nostalgia movies. The records were all sitting in delete bins. During that time my career had grown as had Burton's. By the late seventies, Burton and I were guesting on each other's records. Burton was touring with Garry Peterson on drums and I ran into them in December 1981 at a Christmas party hosted by Garry. Prior to the party I learned that Ben McPeek was ill and Nimbus 9 had gone into receivership. Offhandedly, I said to Burton 'I hear Nimbus is going bankrupt.'

"Yeah."

"Great. We can get our publishing back."

"I've already got them back."

"What? How could you do that?" I asked, incredulously.

"Uh, my lawyer worked out a deal."

"What about my songs? My half of our songs and my own songs like *Undun* and *A Wednesday in Your Garden*?"

"Don't worry about it. Just have your lawyer call my lawyer, Abe Somer in LA."

"Okay, I will."

In January, my lawyer contacted Abe Somer and was rebuffed. At one point he turned nasty and used language unbecoming of most lawyers. I tried throughout much of that year to get Burton on the phone to no avail. He wasn't responding to my calls either.

Later in the year, Burton went on the road with Garry again and in a repeat of the previous Christmas, I found myself at Garry's Christmas party with Burton. Everyone was there: Ian Gardner, Burton's bass player from Winnipeg, Jim Martin, Marty Kramer. Ben McPeek had died earlier that year. Burton and I discussed his passing. 'Isn't it too bad. I hope his kids are okay.' I then confronted Burton again.

"I tried all year to get my songs from Abe Somer, but you didn't give him any instructions. He was belligerent about it and kept stonewalling me. What's going on? I want my songs."

"Oh yeah, okay. I'll tell Abe for sure. Have your lawyer call him again. Merry Christmas and goodbye." He clearly wanted to avoid the issue.

Again nothing happened.

Before long it was January 1983 and the Guess Who reunion was in its formative stages. Do I bring up the publishing issue and risk bringing the reunion to a crashing halt or wait until afterwards and raise it? I figured there had to be some residual good feelings on the heels of the reunion that would allow me to settle the issue once and for all. Meanwhile, our catalogue was revived and back on the shelves. The tour would raise our profile and move product again. The songs had viability again and were earning money. I brought it up near the end of the tour and was told, "Yeah, I'll look into it. Let's not mix business with pleasure."

"Okay. We'll take care of it later."

Nothing.

In 1986 I joined Burton at the BMI presentation in New York where we sat at a table with Yoko Ono, who was there to accept a similar award for John Lennon. Songwriters we admired, like Lieber and Stoller, were there, too. Burton and I were called up for our award and as we received it we shook hands. At that moment, Burton turned to me and asked, "Do you think we could ever do it again if we tried?"

"Let's try," I replied.

At the end of January 1987, I was in LA for the NAMM (National Association of Music Merchants) show and arranged to spend a couple of extra days there at Burton's house where we sat down with guitar and piano and attempted to write some songs. Over two days the muse was there again; absolute magic, monster songs. It was just like old times. All that was missing was Granny Kirkpatrick's cookies. A couple of weeks later, Burton came up to my studio and we demoed ten songs. Just the two of us and a drum machine. Not all the tunes were great, but enough were that we could pull off a couple of hits and an album. In many ways, the songs were the logical follow-up to *American Woman* and *No Time*, what might have been had we stayed together.

Suddenly the phone started ringing with offers for a Bachman–Cummings tour. We went out that summer playing a two-and-a-half-hour show of our greatest hits from the Guess Who, BTO, and solo careers plus a sampling of the new material that received a tremendous response despite never being heard before. The two of us even played on the *Joan Rivers Show* with the house band. I knew the band leader Mark Hudson and had asked him for tickets for Denise and I to attend the show.

"Why don't you come and play on the show and sit in with the band?"

"I'm working with Burton Cummings now."

"Great! How about the two of you come on and play your hits as we go to commercials?"

"Fabulous."

The Bachman–Cummings tour across Canada, with sporadic forays across the border into the northern states, was a smashing success drawing huge crowds wherever the tour touched down. Optimism ran high that something big would emerge, an album of all new material. Indeed the demos were strong, revealing the two still had the chemistry to conjure up hit songs. Beneath the surface however, the tour turned ugly with the two leaders no longer speaking directly with one another.

Capitol and Polydor record labels both expressed interest in our demos as did IRS Records. With momentum for Bachman–Cummings growing, I decided to once again raise the issue of my songs with Burton. His reaction was to avoid me personally unless we were onstage together. Suddenly I couldn't find him until show time. He wouldn't be caught sitting alone with me for fear that the issue might be brought up. As a result, the final leg of our tour in the fall of 1987 was strained. There was a distance between us that, although never showing onstage, was apparent to everyone involved in the tour.

In response, I wrote Burton a letter and slid it under his hotel room door on the last date of the tour. The letter outlined my disappointment with him as an old colleague and friend for the way he had mishandled the issue and my frustration that the publishing question remained unresolved in my eyes now for several years. I informed him that I would once again approach Abe Somer on the issue of my share of the publishing and requested that he intercede with Abe on my behalf as he repeatedly said he would. If the matter remained unsettled, I stated emphatically, I would have no recourse but to take legal action.

Following the final date of what had become a tense touring situation, with everyone on pins and needles and Burton continuing to avoid me, I received a call from Polydor offering Bachman-Cummings a recording contract. But in our conversation, the Polydor rep asked me, "What's going on between you and Burton?"

"What are you talking about?"

"Well, I received a call from Burton's manager that if there is a contract offer to present it to him alone in LA for Burton, not Bachman-Cummings."

I figured "Oh brother, here we go. I'm out of this thing because I asked for my songs."

I sent another letter to Abe Somer and received a rude reply. After almost seven years, I finally took the legal route and had my lawyer serve Burton with a summons demanding my share of the publishing.

Back in 1981, Burton had acquired the publishing rights to the

Nimbus 9 period Guess Who catalogue (including all the big hits from *These Eyes* onward) serendipitously, but nonetheless legally. Nimbus, namely Richardson, McPeek, MacMillan and Clayton, had sold the company in 1979 and the new owners sold the publishing to Burton. The intermediary was none other than Jim "Jumbo" Martin, former Guess Who road manager, at the time serving in a similar capacity for Burton Cummings' solo career. It is left to Jim, in his own unassuming and unbiased fashion, to explain the strange circumstances that set up potentially one of the largest and most contentious cases of its kind in Canadian music history, the court case surrounding ownership of the Guess Who songs: Bachman versus Cummings.

"I'm the guy who got it for Burton," attests Jim. "If I had known what publishing was back then I would have bought it myself. I could have. Anyone could have. But the fact is nobody in the Guess Who would have gotten it if it wasn't for me. Nobody knew that the publishing was available or the company was going down, not Cummings or Bachman.

"We were filming the movie *Melanie* in Toronto. I had some time off and wanted to go over to the Nimbus building on Hazelton in Yorkville just for old time's sake because we made a lot of records there and had a lot of great times. I walked into the building and there wasn't a soul around. The place was deserted. I was looking around when for some reason a guy came walking out of the back.

'Can I help you?'

'Not really. I just came by to look around the building. I used to be with the Guess Who and we recorded here. I was in town and wanted to drop by.' I thought the studio was still working. I didn't know Jack and everyone was gone.

"We stood in the front and talked for about half an hour and I told him what records were recorded here. Then, out of the blue, he says to me, 'You wouldn't happen to know anybody who would want to buy the Guess Who publishing do you?'

'Excuse me?' A light bulb went off in my head. I didn't know much about publishing but I was smart enough to know it was something. Obviously I knew more than he did.

'I've got this publishing I'm trying to sell.' He was trying to get out of the business. This guy had no idea he was sitting on a gold mine.

'You mean Cirrus Music?' That was Nimbus's publishing company.

'Yeah, that's it.'

'What do you want for it?'

'I'm looking for maybe $35,000 to $45,000 for it.'

"My mind was going a hundred miles a second. So I said to him, 'I think I can help you out. Don't do anything with it for twenty-four hours. I'll be back.'

"I came out of there and went 'Holy shit!' It was already evening by then and I had to get back to the hotel, Sutton Place, to wake up Cummings. 'He isn't going to believe this.' I worked for Cummings and at that time I was dedicated to him. We had been together since 1966 and I was the only guy he had kept on when he went solo and moved to LA after the Guess Who so I had a loyalty to him. I woke him up and he was pissed off.

'What the hell do you want Jumbo? I'm sleeping for Christ sakes! This better be good.'

"So I told him about the deal. As I did so, he sat straight up in bed and said 'What?! Are you serious?' He thought I was joking. He didn't believe me at first.

'Burton, I got better things to do than make this up out of the blue.'

"Finally it hit him and he said, 'I gotta get a hold of Abe.' Right then and there he called his lawyer Abe Somer in LA and laid it all out for him. Abe got the guy's name, looked into it, and the next day they did the deal for $35,000 US. Abe moved quickly. It was legally sold to Cummings by this guy. I just happened to be the one at the right place and the right time. Randy didn't know about the deal until months later. I didn't realize at the time that he wanted it. I could have flipped a coin. If I had been working for Randy maybe he would have gotten it. Who knows? The only reason Burton got it was because of me. That's the only reason."

What is at stake in this? Just what does the publishing issue mean in terms of dollars and cents? Hundreds of thousands of dollars since the Guess Who broke up and with the use of a number of their songs in recent hit movies, soundtrack albums, and re-recordings, considerably more. This is the way a song makes money. Fifty percent of what a song earns is for publishing purposes. Whoever owns the publishing receives half of the income from four sources: performance income including radio, television, film; synchronized licensing with film, television, or movies; print — sheet music; and mechanicals — record sales. Randy's legal claim was based on a handshake agreement between him and Burton to share publishing of their joint songs and complete control of individually composed songs once Nimbus relinquished its control of the Guess Who catalogue. Besides Randy's songs, Burton also owns the publishing for the other Guess Who composers.

In June 1987, before the Bachman–Cummings tour got underway, Randy and Burton returned to Winnipeg to appear at the Variety Club sponsored Shakin' All Over Bands and Fans Reunion charity concert where Randy and Neil Young played together for the first time. The two, plus Burton, ran through *American Woman, Just Like Tom Thumb's Blues, Down by the River* and a raucous *Takin' Care of Business* before some 3,000 ecstatic fans. Later Randy proclaimed, "Jamming with Neil was like going to heaven. Honestly it's one of the highlights of my life. He and I had never played together so it was an affectionate, joyous occasion for me."

On the heels of the ill-fated Bachman–Cummings tour, the Canadian Music Hall of Fame, an honorary roll call of Canada's greatest musical contributors, announced that the Guess Who was to be inducted at the annual Juno Awards in Toronto in November 1987. On the appointed evening, the four members arrived separately and took their seats as Jack Richardson offered his personal perspective of the groundbreaking group's achievements accompanied by a brief video retrospective. Then the members themselves were called up collectively to receive their award and say a few words of gratitude. As those at home and in the hall watched in astonishment, the telecast abruptly cut to a commercial as the four moved en masse towards the microphone. Having heard rumours of a potential fracas on camera, an overly anxious stage director panicked. Backstage, it had been tipped that Burton intended to use his microphone moment to assail Jim Kale. The slight was a national disgrace that was later rectified with a half-hour CBC special on the group the following month.

We didn't know we were going to be cut off. When we were first approached about the induction, the various factions within the Guess Who responded in kind. "If that so and so is going to be there, I'm going to be choking him on national television." "I'll come but I don't want to stand beside him." These sentiments were expressed by certain members toward others several times. The offer first came through when I was on tour with Bachman–Cummings and we were aware this stuff was being said. "When I see so and so I'm going to kill him." It was one guy making these statements, but there were ill feelings between others as well. Burton resented Jim using our original records in radio ads promoting his Guess Who and making a living with that name when it was him, Burton, who sang the songs. He still feels that way. The animosity was between those two.

Apparently this got back to the producers of the Juno Awards show and they got jumpy. This was pre–Jerry Springer so nothing like this had ever been shown on television. Some letters were exchanged back and forth in which these sentiments had been openly expressed. I know for a fact that Burton wrote a draft of an acceptance speech that was scathing, scorching in its indictment of Jim Kale and his Guess Who. Burton can be the master of words and language when he gets sarcastic. He can shut anybody down without being able to rebut what he is saying about you, your mother, your dog, and your personality. He has an incredibly barbed tongue. He was writing this speech on the road and showing Marty Kramer and me the various drafts of it. "Hey guys, check this out." It was directed at Jim doing his thing with a bunch of clones.

There was a fear that at any moment all hell would break loose. In the end, the producers didn't cut us off because they were rude or inconsiderate; they panicked that a full-scale war was about to erupt with the cameras on. It was like a gas in the air and if we hit a spark it would all blow up. To spoil the moment with an inappropriate statement would have fouled the whole induction and the producers did not want that to happen. They had received word that a disaster was impending. Knowing those two guys, I can sympathize with the producers' dilemma.

We got up onstage after Jack Richardson's speech and when no one made a beeline to the mike and there was an appearance of hesitancy, they cut to commercial. I honestly did not know for sure if Burton was going to give that speech or not. I didn't prepare a speech myself but was prepared to run through the obligatory thank-yous: parents, Gar Gillies, Don Burkhimer, Jack Richardson, the unsung people who were behind us. But I didn't get my chance. Other guys had other agendas. Had they let us speak, who knows what might have happened?

We stood there together, shook hands with Jack, and had no idea what to do next. We figured that following the commercial break we would each have our fifteen seconds at the mike. We anticipated someone ushering us to the podium but nothing happened. The floor director who you never see on camera instead motioned us offstage. The show came back from commercial and, butta boom, they introduced the next Juno Award presenters and we were standing backstage in shock wondering what just happened.

The CBC tried to placate us with a half-hour retrospective special. At the taping of the show we all sat together but there was a lot of ill will. We were not on the best of terms. Jim was mad that Burton and I were out there doing our Guess Who songs as Bachman–Cummings. We felt we deserved to do them, we wrote them. Burton was mad at Jim, and I shared that sentiment, that he was performing our songs and when people came out to see the group he and I weren't there. There was serious animosity hanging in the air when we came to do that special and it showed.

Back in 1977, while mixing the *FREEWAYS* album in Toronto, Randy's prized 1955 orange Gretsch 6120 Chet Atkins guitar — the one he bought with his savings from a variety of part-time jobs after seeing his hero Lenny Breau with the same model, and the guitar that had inspired Neil Young — was stolen. Heartbroken, he issued a reward but despaired of ever getting back his cherished possession. What resulted instead became a routine for him in every city or town: scouring the pawnshops and vintage guitar collectors in search of his beloved guitar. But a funny thing happened along the way. Though he never did locate his lost guitar, Randy began to acquire other Gretsch models and what began as a mere hobby to pass the time on the road turned into another Randy Bachman obsession: to own as many of the no longer manufactured guitars as possible. At last count his collection numbered close to three hundred and ranked as the largest Gretsch collection in the world.

When men go through their midlife crisis, some get a girlfriend or buy a fancy sports car. My midlife crisis diversion was collecting guitars. And I approached it with a zeal bordering on fixation. It began with a dream of mine to get my original orange Gretsch back, which I never did. I was on the road in 1987 with Bachman–Cummings and Burton and Marty Kramer would disappear in every city looking for comic books or records and I would be left alone. They would fight over who found what first and who should own what. "I found it first." "You work for me so I get it first." They would fight and not speak to each other, then at the next stop off they would go again. I felt left out so I told Burton I was going to collect comic books too and he said, "Please don't. You'll be fighting with me and Marty. Collect something else, something you know, like guitars." It became the thrill of the hunt for me and gave me a great deal of pleasure and fun.

Wherever I went I searched out guitars. I had contacts notifying me if a particular guitar came across their counter or if they heard about someone with a rare model. Initially it was just if they found my original orange Gretsch to notify me immediately but they started calling if any Gretsch came their way. It piqued my curiosity and I would go see what they had and more often than not buy it. I became known as "the Gretsch guy" — they would call whenever they found one. I wasn't spending my mortgage money or my investment money; this was my per diems I'd saved over the years or extra money I received that was unplanned, small royalty cheques that weren't my normal income flow. I wasn't a "Gretsch-aholic" with a family waiting for me to come home with money for food and instead I've spent it on a guitar.

Denise got into it as well. She would be in San Francisco visiting family, make a detour to a second-hand guitar shop, and call me if they had any interesting Gretsch models. She even dickered with store clerks and felt elated when she could acquire one at a great price.

I would receive monthly mailouts from Gruhn Guitars in Nashville and Deitz Guitars in Minneapolis that kept me abreast of current market prices as dealers called me with their finds.

"Wow, this model's worth $2,500 and I can get it for $150."

In the process I became something of a Gretsch authority and suddenly people were calling me up not just to sell but to inquire about particular models.

"What's a 1960 White Falcon single cutaway in its original condition supposed to look like?"

"Just a minute." And I would look on my wall or open a case and describe it to them.

"Thanks." Someone was selling them one and they wanted to make sure it was an original.

When the *Gretsch Book* came out documenting the history of Gretsch guitars I was honoured to be invited to write a foreword alongside George Harrison, Brian Setzer, and Duane Eddy. There I was in there with these guys like one of their peers. It gave me real credibility as a Gretsch man. The book had pictures of my Gretsch walls in my house.

There was a guy named Dean Turner in Dallas/Fort Worth who was a Chet Atkins player who had been collecting Gretsches for years. His collection was informally known as the Gretsch museum. I received a call from him one day and he announced he was retiring and selling his museum. He had a lot of rare prototypes. I didn't want the whole collection because I already had some of those models but I negotiated with him to acquire some of his rarest pieces. As a result, I became the Gretsch museum. I still go to gigs and have players or dealers show up backstage with rare guitars for me. I just don't buy Gretsches; I collect Gibsons and Fenders, too. On the Van Halen tour, Eddie and I would be playfully fighting over these guitars that dealers brought in.

I now have about two hundred and seventy Gretsch models worth between one and two million dollars. Soon to be sold though. I don't see them anymore. When I lived in White Rock, I had them all on the walls of my big basement room and it was stunning to walk into that room. I remember taking Fred Gretsch there just to see the look on his face. It was unbelievable. I had a white wall of all white Gretsch Penguins and Falcons, an orange wall of Duane Eddy 6120's, a coloured wall of Sparkle Jet models, a blond wall. It was insanely over the top, but I loved it. When I moved though, I put them all in cases and they are now stored in shelves. I have maybe ten that I keep in my studio that I use for their variety of sound, but the rest remain stored. When I have the time I plan to document my collection for a book and have a huge guitar sale. *Vintage Guitar* magazine has offered me the cover story with a special spread on all my guitars. It was a shrewd investment because they have all appreciated in value. I'll make more than I paid for them. If I don't I'm in deep, deep trouble.

The fact is you can only play one guitar at a time. It will be tough to part with them, though. When I moved I didn't want just moving guys to pack them up. I had Marty Kramer rent a truck and I hired Brigham and my nephew Paxton, Timmy's son, to pack each one individually in its case. We had hundreds of cases spread out on the driveway and the boys matched guitar to case. They would look at a closed case and say "What's in that one?" and open it to find some exotic, one of a kind rare guitar, a Black Falcon or a Penguin. If I don't get the price I want I'll probably keep them, but regardless I'll keep a few like a Penguin just because it is so rare. I might let my kids pick out one guitar each not to be sold unless they are in dire circumstances.

Over the years, Randy developed a close personal relationship with another of his early heroes, Chet Atkins. The appreciation was reciprocated by the "Country Gentleman," one of music's best-loved and most respected players.

When we did our first Guess Who album with *Shakin' All Over* and had to do those silly promo sheets about what your favourite food was and favourite band, when I was asked who my influences were I put down "Chet Atkins, Lenny Breau, and Hank Marvin." Nobody knew who they were. Years later when we were with RCA I received a message via Don Burkhimer from Chet Atkins who had heard that I acknowledged him and Lenny Breau as my mentors and how I had learned to play Chet Atkins–style

from Lenny. Apparently someone had told him I had lost many of
my Chet Atkins records over the years lending them out to other
guitar players or students. I guess I had mentioned that casually in
passing during an interview. Chet was, of course, an executive at
RCA. About a month later I started to received three or four Chet
Atkins records in the mail every week or so. He told someone at
RCA to send them to me. It was about fifty or sixty of them in all.
I still have them, still sealed, never opened. And they all have
Gretsch guitars on the covers so I was ga ga over these albums. It
was really a very thoughtful gesture. When I finally met him, he
was the epitome of southern gentility.

When I lost my Gretsch guitar, I was living in Lynden,
Washington, at the time and I was out in the backyard with Tally
and Kezia trying to build a tree house for my kids. I was balancing
plywood sheets on my head trying to hold onto everything and
build a platform when the phone rang in the house.

"Kezia, please answer the phone."

She went inside, then came to the patio door and hollered "It's
Chad."

Here I am with nails in my mouth, and Tally's up in the tree
with a rope holding these 2x4s in place. I think it's Chad Allan.

"Tell him I'm busy. I'll call him later."

Kezia hung up the phone, came back outside, and a few minutes later it rang again.

"Kezia, go get the phone again."

"It's this guy again. It's Ned."

I knew a guy from Winnipeg named Ned.

"Tell Ned I can't come to the phone." Meantime, I'm still balancing all these boards and trying to secure the platform.

The phone rang a third time.

"Dad, it's this same guy again. He has a funny accent." Throughout
all this, the person on the phone had been hearing Kezia and I
yelling back and forth and knew I was building something.

"He says his name is Chet."

I immediately dropped the boards and rushed in to pick up the phone.

"I've built a few tree houses in my time and you really need a couple of construction workers," came the slow southern drawl on the other end of the phone. It was Chet Atkins. He heard I had lost my Gretsch and was calling to offer to help out.

"Is it true you lost your Gretsch?"

"Yeah, it was stolen. It broke my heart. It was like having your dog run over."

"I'm going to do something special for you. What's your address?"

So I told him my address and a week later what arrived at my door was the prototype of the Super Chet guitar. It had custom modifications by Chet himself. There were only three of these in the world, one of them he had made left-handed for Paul McCartney. Later on, when he played with the Vancouver Symphony, I took that guitar and had him sign the pick guard.

That's my favourite guitar story.

CHAPTER 10

Any Road

Though Randy had spent much of the eighties treading musical water in various revivals of former associations all the while putting his family, personal life, and finances back on an even keel, he had not stopped writing throughout that period. Now, as the nineties arrived, back on his feet again, he looked for an opportunity to present his new material and launch his comeback as a musical leader and innovator, not a follower.

Randy had closed out the eighties in yet another reunion. In 1987, he had walked away from the Randy, Tim, and Billy Chapman version of BTO to take a flyer with Burton, leaving Tim to carry on with the group. This time out it was a uniting of the hit-making lineup — Randy, Fred, Robbie, and Blair Thornton — brokered by none other than Bruce Allen. Initially, with no album deal on the cards, just tour dates, Robbie Bachman temporarily set aside his publishing demands to join the others.

Contrary to agreements the four made back in 1977, for a time there were two competing entities out on the road: BTO, fronted by Tim Bachman, and the reunited Bachman-Turner Overdrive. Just as Randy had done during the Van Halen tour, Tim paid Robbie, Fred, and Blair 2 1/2 percent of his gross in order to use the BTO name. But with two groups vying for the same ticket-buyers and trying to run the other off the road it was a situation fraught with tension and family discord that brought father Charles Bachman into the fray demanding that his sons settle their differences. In the end, Tim relented and folded his version of BTO while his brothers continued on. "I've learned over the years not to argue with Randy," concludes Tim who left music behind for a career in real estate.

I had spent the better part of five years touring with various configurations of BTO as a golden oldies band and I was feeling discouraged. It was starting to become like a job and that's not for me. Nobody wanted to hear a new song and I was dying to play my new songs. If BTO was to survive, we needed to take it forward, not be just a classic rock nostalgia act. I write songs all the time and had a backlog of new material. I wanted to record a new album. Fred and I both were exchanging tapes with the idea that if we heard something magical we would convene the band and lay down some tracks. I encouraged the other guys to write as well.

One of the constant problems in any band, though, is the division of songs among its members. In the Beatles, Lennon and McCartney were the principal songwriters, with George Harrison contributing maybe one song per album. If it had been three or four or if Ringo contributed more than the occasional number, it wouldn't have sounded like the Beatles. In The Who, Pete Townshend wrote the bulk of the material while John Entwistle came up with maybe one or two songs that added a further dimension to the group without altering the quality or character of the group's overall sound. For me, I was always writing. If I had to come up with four or five songs for an album, I would come in with forty and work from that. I might collaborate with Fred, Robbie, or Blair on a couple more. Fred would have his own songs that fit the band sound.

As we looked toward recording a new album as BTO, Robbie began demanding that if there were twelve cuts on an album he be given three of those. But he just wasn't an experienced writer nor as prolific. He might come with one or two and the third would be a slap-together job from a jam. But that doesn't mean they are strong songs. Robbie was pushing for equality and it just couldn't work.

When John Fogerty caved in to his fellow Creedence Clearwater Revival members and gave them an equal number of tracks, the resulting album was a disaster that hastened the group's early demise. Randy wasn't about to do that. He felt confident his current collection of songs was worthy enough for a BTO album or, if not, then his own project.

In late 1991, he and Fred agreed to set aside the next year to write and record demos of possible songs. The intended goal was to release a new BTO album in 1993 to coincide with the band's twentieth anniversary and the release of a commemorative BTO box set anthology. In the interim, however, Fred decided that going out on a summer 1992 tour was more expedient in terms of cash flow than sitting on the sidelines. When Randy balked the others soldiered on without their leader leaving Randy and his parcel of recently completed demos free to shop them for a solo deal. It was a move that left him feeling liberated from the shackles of the BTO legacy and able to pursue some personal goals that had been placed on the back burner over the previous years as the BTO nostalgia machine rolled on down the highway. Recruiting Randy Murray from Tim's former BTO lineup, Fred, Robbie, and Blair hit the road again where they remain to this day working the classic rock circuit. Unfortunately, the decision to abandon his band mates for a solo career once again set the stage for a nasty row that pit brother against brother and left a rift still gaping to this day.

Invigorated by the positive response to his demos, Randy set about recording what many would term his comeback album, *ANY ROAD*. The album found Randy in a reflective mood with the *pièce de résistance* a poignant paean to his hometown roots. Along the way, he enlisted the support of a couple of high-profile friends.

Frustrated at this turn of events but still confident I had some quality material to offer, I pitched my batch of songs, my own demos, to labels and publishers on my own to get some feedback. What I got back was quite encouraging.

"These songs are good. Who's singing them?"

"Me."

"This is a new voice for you, lower in register and stronger. You've kind of reinvented your voice."

The result was that Paul Berger at Sony Records offered me my own album deal. Bruce Allen couldn't even get BTO a record deal, then I go out on my own and "bang" I get offers and a deal for myself.

Normally I'm spinning the radio dial tuning into all sorts of stations in the car, but Denise had previously been listening to CBC. I started listening to this literary critic talking about Lewis Carroll, author of *Alice in Wonderland*, and he mentioned a line from the book: "If you don't know where you're going, any road will take you there." Brakes squeal as I instantly stop the car.

"Wow, what a great idea for a song!"

As I pulled off the road, I scrambled to find a piece of paper in the car and began scribbling some lyrics. I had the basic idea down in twenty minutes.

Another song, *Prairie Town*, literally took on a life of its own. All these thoughts and recollections of my childhood just fell into place. It is an honest reflection of my roots and I don't normally do that. I try not to make my songs too personal.

Neil Young's participation on the album was rather serendipitous, as is often the case with Neil. I sent the words to *Prairie Town* to his guitar tech who was looking for a part to a Gretsch guitar and he then showed the lyrics to his boss. Neil called me up and declared, "That song is so honest. I want to play and sing on this, the lyrics are so great." He hadn't even heard the music, he had only read the lyrics.

I took the tapes down to his ranch and he overdubbed his parts. It was truly one of those moments you never forget: Neil Young playing like a man possessed on my track and singing "Portage and Main fifty below" alongside me. I stayed over at the ranch and the next day at breakfast Neil announced, "Of course I want to be in the video." There were no plans for a video at that point but I said, "Oh yeah, you're in the video." I rushed home and put a video concept together. We almost won Much Music's video of the year, too, losing out by a mere three votes.

I had recorded two takes of *Prairie Town*, a mellower acoustic country version and a pounding rocker. I couldn't decide which one to include. In the end someone suggested I bookend the album with both versions like Neil had done on *RUST NEVER SLEEPS*. I thought it was a great idea. So Neil ended up adding his voice and guitar to both, a country folk version and a grunge rock take. It was marvellous. Having Neil play on my album was such a thrill.

Neil's manager told me later, "I don't know how you got Neil to do this. He gets a dozen calls a week to guest on records. He doesn't have the time." Neil just wanted to be a part of *Prairie Town* because it represented his roots, too.

Neil Young remains a continued source of inspiration for me. Here is a guy who takes risks, doesn't play by any rules but his own, yet still remains on the cutting edge. I feel a kindred spirit in Neil — we share a restlessness to pursue many different facets of music without being pigeonholed. What he has had the benefit of that I have lacked in my career, however, is the continuity of management and record label support willing to indulge his diversions without giving up on him. He has always enjoyed that solid foundation and I envy his situation.

I had wanted to ask Joni Mitchell to sing on the acoustic version of *Prairie Town* with me because she was from the prairies too but I couldn't get to her. I sent a tape of the acoustic version of Neil and I doing the song to my lawyer Graham Henderson in Toronto and one night he phoned me and said, "Listen to this." And as he played the tape, I heard this other voice coming over the phone. It was his wife Margo Timmins of the Cowboy Junkies duetting with Neil and me. I was knocked out. I was in the process of mixing the album tracks, so I told them I would hold off mixing that track until Margo could fly out to Vancouver. She flew in the next day and recorded her harmony, I mixed it the following day, and it was on the album.

Margo's voice added an ethereal prairie lilt to the track, a Joni Mitchell quality but in Margo's own distinctive style. In many ways it presented a coming home, family sentiment — a small circle of friends making music. Three Canadians singing about growing up in Canada. I felt really good about that song. When we filmed the video she appeared on it along with Neil. At Neil's Governor-General's Awards ceremony, my band and hers, The Cowboy Junkies, performed before I gave a little speech about Neil.

Originally slated for release in July of 1992, the album's deadline was postponed to accommodate Neil's busy schedule allowing him to add his own personal touch to *Prairie Town*. Neil was finally available in September and Randy flew down to Broken Arrow Ranch, Neil's sprawling 2,000-acre spread nestled amid the giant Redwoods of Northern California, to allow his old friend to lay down his parts. Another delay was the result of Neil's insistence on appearing in the video for *Prairie Town*, which once again necessitated accommodating his scheduling. With a one-day window of opportunity, Randy and his backing musicians made a hasty return trip to Neil's ranch to shoot the video. Neil filmed his part in a degree of discomfort having suffered a fall while hang gliding a few days earlier. He arrived in his rehearsal barn with the aid of a cane, showing his bruises proudly like some war wound.

Neil came into the studio with a baseball cap on backwards, wearing an old t-shirt and ripped pants, and hobbling on a cane. The bruises on his leg were wicked. His response to my concern over his obvious pain was "Man, I'm playing on pure adrenaline right now but it's going to hurt like hell later." We got all the gear and crew together in Neil's barn where his *RAGGED GLORY* video was shot and Neil strapped on his guitar. Once he had that guitar on you couldn't tell he was in any pain. He just rocked out and it was terrific. Once the shoot was completed, Neil said to me, "Let's do something together next year as a band once I'm done the *HARVEST MOON* thing and you're done your *ANY ROAD* tour. Let's record and do a tour together." But unfortunately nothing came of it. I would have loved that.

With the final touches to the album and video completed, Randy sent off the master tapes and artwork to Sony in anticipation of an imminent release. Confident that *ANY ROAD* was the strongest effort he had mounted in more than a decade, he prepared himself for a heavy round of promotion and publicity only to be cut down at the knees by his former BTO cohorts.

In the interim, Randy was served notice by his brother Robbie in collaboration with Fred Turner and Blair Thornton over the album's use of a stylized Bachman gear wheel logo claiming copyright infringement on the BTO logo which the band continued to use. The album was ultimately delayed until March 1993 after several months of redrawing the logo and redoing the cover art and video. The long wait did not sit well with Randy. The initial momentum and enthusiasm of the label had soured by the time *ANY ROAD* hit the store shelves and Randy found himself with a solid effort that was floundering from a lack of promotion. Label politics played a part in that frustration as well. Like he had often done throughout his career, Randy took the bull by the horns himself.

In the midst of completing the album, Paul Berger was promoted to head of Sony UK and the manager of promotions and marketing left as well. The new label head had no stake in my project so as a result there was little behind it. That's when I learned the notion of a key man clause. When you sign a contract, include a key man clause that states that you are signing to this label because of this particular person and if he goes, you have the right to discuss your relationship with the new head. If that relationship proves unsatisfactory you can terminate the contract. That kind of thing happens to artists all the time. The executive that signs them has a personal commitment at stake with them. But when he or she moves on, the next in line has his or her own agenda and wants to make their own mark with their own signings. So you find yourself ignored or dropped.

Having Neil play on *Prairie Town* made it an obvious single. It almost broke through, but I think the problem was that it might have been too personal and Winnipeg-oriented. "Portage and Main fifty below." Many people didn't know what it meant. It received some airplay in Winnipeg because of the Portage and Main reference but little anywhere else. Here was this wonderful opportunity to do something with this great song featuring Neil Young and Margo Timmins and nothing was happening for the first month. It was frustrating for me personally because no one was getting to hear the sentiments I felt in writing the songs on the album. I cried when I finished writing *Prairie Town*. I played it for my brother Tim and he was equally moved.

"You've captured the era in that song," he told me.

Neil Young and Margo Timmins had done a wonderful job adding a surprise element to the album, but there was no marketing or promotion to support it. The album was quickly going nowhere.

Bobby Gale called me up out of the blue to tell me how much he loved *ANY ROAD*. He had been working with Polygram when I was promoting my *SURVIVOR* album in the late seventies and was now an independent promotion man in Toronto. Bobby was deeply moved by *Prairie Town* and how honest a picture it presented of Neil and I growing up in Winnipeg.

"I want to promote that album." He believed in the album and in me.

The problem was I didn't have a cent because I had to pay for the revised artwork and my deal with Sony was for distribution with a little kicked in for promotion. The rest had to come from me. I had spent the budget already.

"I'll work for half my fee."

"Great."

I could afford a month of his time. In that month I was literally on every major radio station, Much Music, television; I went across Canada doing interviews and promotion. I had a very high visibility and it felt like I was back. Gigs started pouring in. At the end of the month, I paid Bobby his full fee for all the work he had done. He really worked that album. *ANY ROAD* raised my profile, thanks in large measure to Bobby Gale's efforts.

Chris Wardman, fresh from his production chores with ultrahip new acts the Leslie Spit Treeo, Sons of Freedom, and the Watchmen, had been enlisted to co-produce *ANY ROAD*. Randy took a further leap into the nineties by signing on with a new manager, Jeff Rogers, whose roster of clients included The Pursuit of Happiness and Winnipeg's own Crash Test Dummies.

Reviewers fell over themselves in praise of Randy's return to the charts with *ANY ROAD*. Rodney Marsh in SoundCan declared, "*ANY ROAD* comes across as a current, meaningful, and at times quite powerful effort." *Backwoods* magazine wrote, "At his best a working-class dog playing working-class songs for working-class audiences, Bachman reminds us of past glories with *ANY ROAD* and proves that there is still life in Rover yet," while *RPM* magazine proclaimed, "*ANY ROAD* should have plenty of pick-up trucks blasting this album out from their stereos this summer." In the eyes of the Canadian music industry and critics alike, Randy Bachman was back, stronger than ever.

In the midst of the fraternal fracas over the BTO logo, Charles Bachman was diagnosed with cancer of the pancreas. Fiercely self-reliant, healthy and strong as an ox all his life, it was a bitter blow to the man who had given so much of his life to serving others. In 1985, Charles had retired and he and Anne decided to move to British Columbia. At the time, they were living on Bachman Bay, named in his honour for his years of civic duty, in Mandalay West, a recent subdivision of West Kildonan. Behind Charles and Anne lived Tim and his family. When his parents announced their intention to pull up stakes and head west, Tim decided to do the same. "My Dad told me they moved out to British Columbia to try to show my brothers what a family was again," states Tim. "They felt Randy and Robbie needed them there." Charles and Anne stayed with Robbie outside of Vancouver until they purchased a parcel of land for a house.

A lot of my relatives would make the pilgrimage to Vancouver, usually in winter, and would return to Winnipeg, sell their house, and move out. Every time I would go through Vancouver on tour with the Guess Who I would look up my relatives. Then I moved out with Robbie and Tim and our kids. My parents would come for visits but have to go home. My Dad had family out there as well. As more grandkids were born, they were coming out more and more. Finally they simply came to the conclusion that what is life for if you can't live close to your loved ones, the most important things in your life? Go live where they live. I'm starting to feel that now as my own kids are moving away. So they sold their house in Winnipeg and moved out to British Columbia.

My Dad bought a piece of land in Surrey and built a West Kildonan-style house complete with a full basement. A whole band could practise there. He was used to that kind of a house. I lived very near them so we all would come over and spend Christmases with them just like back in Winnipeg. A few years later he became restless and, lo and behold, he went out and bought another parcel of land and built another house. This was his life. He was always working around the house. When he came out to British Columbia he continued doing that.

"When my Dad became ill, the doctors gave him thirty to sixty days," recalls Tim Bachman. "He lasted eleven months. But near the end, he was really going downhill. By then he couldn't look after himself and my Mom was considering hiring a male nurse to look after his personal needs. For a guy like my father, the pain of the cancer was nothing compared to the humiliation of having to be dependent on someone for his needs. He was the proverbial self-made man; his own father had died when he was a kid, and now he couldn't look after himself. That was really paining him. I went home and told my wife I couldn't let someone else do that for my Dad. 'I have to look after him.' She understood and told me not to worry about her and the kids. I told my manager I would carry my pager and look after my real estate clients when I could, but I couldn't always be there. He understood and let me go. I dropped everything to move in and take care of my Dad for his last two and a half months. I bathed him, carried him to the washroom, and did everything that he needed. For me, it was a privilege and a blessing to look after him. When we were growing up, he was never Mr. Compliments but we always knew he loved us. He and I had a different kind of relationship because we had worked together."

For Randy and Gary, the news of their father's ailment was a crushing blow compounded only by their own circumstances at that moment. With Randy on the road or recording and Gary back in Winnipeg running a thriving real estate business, the two welcomed Tim's decision and helped out when they could. "When my Dad was dying I went out to Vancouver every month for a week to be with him," states Gary. "During that time, Randy was extremely generous toward me. He would come to me and shove $500 in my pocket saying, 'I know you're losing money coming out here and being away from work. Here's some money for your next flight.' He really appreciated the fact that I was coming out because it was important to my Dad and also because Randy couldn't always be there. He would almost be embarrassed as he did it, not begrudging the money, but because he didn't know how to do it. It wasn't easy for him, but he appreciated it and I understood."

Charles Bachman passed away on January 24, 1993. "My Dad's passing was like the final blow of the hammer for Randy," muses Tim. "It had a powerful impact on him. Being the oldest son, he was now the head of the family. It made him realize the importance of his own family, his children, as well as the rest of his family, his brothers."

Tal Bachman offers an insight into the hierarchical nature of the Bachman clan and Charles Bachman's role as head of a large extended brood: "My grandpa always struck me as a sturdy, reliable character who could be stern but fair. He could be a tough cookie. That's how I saw him growing up. But even though he wasn't intimately involved in everyone's lives all the time, in a subconscious way the Bachman family was like some sort of pyramid with him always the eye at the top, kind of like the patriarch. This has been a real source of wonderment to me. I wasn't really conscious of it until he passed away. The family seemed to be this cohesive set or unit just by virtue of my Grandpa, even though there were these internecine, interclan rivalries occasionally. It was still this stable unit because of him. That, in itself, is quite remarkable. Nobody talked about it. It was just always there."

It was devastating to see my Dad vulnerable. He was such a

strong man all his life, always working. His circumstance was very tough because once he was diagnosed with cancer it moved quickly. My brother Tim did a wonderful thing. When Dad became ill, Tim stopped working and was there to care for my Dad all the time. It was an incredibly loving thing to do. Tim and my Dad were very close after he took Tim into the business with him. At the time he became ill I couldn't look after him. I had too many things going and Tim lived nearby. We were further away in White Rock. But the kids and I would go over to see him as much as possible. Tally wrote about that in *If You Sleep*, which I didn't realize until he mentioned in an article how that song touched so many people and was the song that got him his deal. I listened to it again and realized the song was about my Dad's passing. It's very moving.

I learned a wonderful lesson from my Dad when he was ill and dying. He called the four brothers together and gave each of us an envelope with some money in it. It was then that I discovered my Dad's greatest secret. Years ago when we lived on Hartford and Airlies, he had bought a plot of land further down toward McPhillips way. It was his dream that we as a family all build houses and live in this crescent on eight acres of land he had purchased and held for years, never telling any of us. He never sat us down and told us of his dream. When I moved away from Winnipeg taking two of my brothers with me that must have devastated him. I felt the same pain when Tally moved away to Maui and later LA and took away my grandson. I thought I would never see them again. I asked my Mom, "Was that what it was like for you?" and she replied, "Oh yes!" She was glad I didn't take Gary too. And at the time I was taking her grandchildren away as well, Tally and Kezia.

My Dad wanted us to have our inheritance now before he passed away. So on his deathbed he handed each of us these envelopes with cheques in them.

"How did you get this money?"

"I sold the property I had for us in West Kildonan."

He then told us of his dream and it broke my heart.

He told me something else, as well. Back in the seventies when BTO became successful I had purchased a car for Lorayne's parents and one for my parents and, although I wasn't able to pay off my parents' house, I did give them a lump sum to put down on the mortgage, a lump sum payment. I found out on his deathbed that he never used that money on his mortgage. Instead he put it in the bank and left it to collect interest. Here he was giving me back my money I had given him. I was broken up. I knew he was struggling to hang on.

The next day I came to visit him and gave him back his cheque.

"This meant so much to me, where you got this from. But I have had such a great life because of what you provided for me — the violin lessons, buying me a guitar, supporting me — I don't need this right now in my life. I would rather see you have it to maybe make your time a little easier or to give it to someone else who really needs it more."

I told him to give it to Tim because he wasn't working and had sacrificed so much for my Dad.

My Dad gave his children their inheritance while he was still alive to enjoy some of the fruits of it, and I have applied this lesson with my own children. Every Christmas, besides the usual presents, I give them each a little dividend on their future inheritance. I really enjoy sharing that money with my kids and seeing them use it rather than having a great party and dancing on my grave when I'm gone.

Anne Bachman now lives with Tim and his family in Abbotsford, B.C. "My boys have all been very good to me," she concludes. "I have no complaints about them."

In 1994, Randy made two shrewd business deals that once again set him up comfortably for the rest of his life. Both came up rather by chance, but never one to miss an opportunity, Randy grabbed hold and took care of business.

Sometime in the late eighties I received a letter on very official Government of Canada letterhead from the curator of the National Library of Canada in Ottawa. The library had recently acquired Glenn Gould's personal collection of memorabilia, transcriptions, and mementos from his illustrious career that would not only preserve these artifacts for posterity, but also allow people to research Gould's life or simply enjoy and appreciate his work. The curator, Tim Maloney, wanted to do the same with Canada's pop successes to demonstrate its legitimacy as an important contribution to Canada's cultural endeavours. Ottawa tends to be stuffy, so while the Gould collection was embraced, Tim was fighting an uphill battle gaining acceptance for a pop archives. Even Oscar Peterson was deemed a bit risqué. Undaunted, Tim had written to me to inquire if I would be willing to donate my collection. My initial response was, "What collection? It's just my stuff." So I ignored the request.

A few years later I received another letter again accompanied by the same request. This time I simply set it aside without giving it much more thought. Not long after, Denise and I were flying out to Toronto, a nonstop flight from Vancouver, but ironically as I looked in the pouch in front of my seat there was a Winnipeg newspaper. It was such a blast for me after so many years to read the Winnipeg paper with all its local references. It was comfort food for my brain and I devoured every article. As I was working my way through the paper, I came across an article about two Manitoba Metis artists who had donated their early works to the National Gallery and received a tax credit. Tax credit? I turned to Denise.

"They're asking me for my stuff but no one's mentioned anything about a tax credit."

When we land, I tucked the newspaper under my arm as I exited the plane. I brought it to the attention of my lawyer Graham Henderson. Two days later Graham called me back.

"Yes, you can earn a tax credit on the assessed value of your collection and 51 percent of it can apply to your taxes and you can carry it forward over five years."

When we moved from Lynden to White Rock in the early eighties, the accumulated debris of twenty-five years of rock 'n' roll had been stored in dozens and dozens of boxes never unpacked. Contracts, photographs, tapes, posters, original song sheets, tour itineraries, stage clothes, even my gold and platinum records, a hundred and twenty of them, were all in storage going on eight or nine years. I never saw this stuff. The gold albums were not on the walls because I didn't want to draw attention to myself. In Lynden, I had walls covered in gold albums; but in White Rock we lived in a neighbourhood and when people came to the door or the kids brought their friends over I didn't want to alert anyone as to who lived there. So the bottom line was I might as well donate my "archives" for want of a better word.

Meantime, my accountant informed me that the government was closing a capital gains loophole. I could take advantage of it before the following February if I could find something to sell and claim the exemption from a small business as well as a personal exemption. My publishing company qualified as a small business, so if I sold something through it I could also declare myself a half-million-dollar salary tax-free. "What have I got to sell?" I like my house and don't want to move. Graham suggested "How about your publishing?" I put everything together, my list of titles, my awards, had printouts of statements from BMI as well as a ten-year projection given the increasing demand for classic rock and CD repackaging. When seen in this light it had a definite value. So I ended up selling it to Sony Music in New York for a seven-figure offer. When I brought that back to Canada, the exchange rate added even more to it and I took the capital gains exemption.

The reality was I couldn't handle my publishing catalogue effectively any more. It had become just too big for me to manage. Actually, all they wanted were two songs, *Takin' Care of Business* and *You Ain't Seen Nothin' Yet*. The rest of the catalogue was just gravy. According to Sony, those two songs alone receive between ten to a hundred requests a week for use in ads, movies, promotions, you name it. So many people around the world were recording those songs that I couldn't keep track of it all. I needed a whole army, the machinery of a giant collection agency, so I had to sell it to a larger entity that could manage it better. I still receive my writing royalties, and the other band members get their percentage of the publishing that I gave them.

Simultaneous to this, I made the donation to the National Library for a tax credit well into seven figures. When word of my tax credit hit the news there was a slight furor from a few people who protested that their tax dollars were being squandered on a bunch of junk. It took nine or ten months for Billy Chapman and me to catalogue everything I had. With this astute bit of high finance complete, I paid off my house and all my debts and bought another house; life from that point on has been sweet.

"The value of the Randy Bachman Collection," confirms National Library curator Tim Maloney, "is that it contains pretty much the complete documentary record of his professional activities, anything and everything from the Guess Who and BTO to his solo career, including legal and financial documents, records of tours, promotional items, original songs, photographs, plus physical items like guitars, stage clothes, albums, Juno Awards, and gold records. Randy also kept a tremendous amount of video that offers a rich opportunity to glimpse his concerts over many years. He has the greatest number of film materials of any archive held by the music division of the National Library. The collection runs the gamut of his entire career. It is a one of a kind collection because we don't have anything else from someone who has covered the same territory.

"Randy offered us a big leg up in the pop domain. I have a feeling that the word got out through him and others came forward. His donation showed others that we were interested and serious about this. Being so visible in the Canadian music industry, Randy offered a tremendous boost for us." Since then, Bruce Allen and his agency partner Sam Feldman have donated their corporate records as has producer Bruce Fairbairn and songwriter Jim Vallance. And Bryan Adams has begun donating his materials.

Notes Tim Maloney with amazement, "I recall being incredibly impressed with Randy's encyclopedic knowledge of his career down to the minute details of tours, recording sessions, gigs, which guitars were played on which sessions. And he very astutely kept a lot of material over the years as well." Being a packrat certainly paid dividends.

Again taking my cues from my Dad, I set aside a chunk of money for each of my children to be used for their education, furthering their career, getting married or if they were already married, for buying a house. Not to buy a car or have a two-year long party. Those already established with a family and house, Tally and Kezia, simply got their money. Others, like Brigham who was younger and a little more reckless, didn't get the money right away. They had to come and say they wanted to go to college and I would pay for college, but only if they went and passed. Ownership of songs go to your heirs for eighty years after your death so I asked them all to sign an agreement that the songs will go to them upon my death. In return, they got their little bonus.

With his financial needs securely squared away, a proposition came through the following year that, though not a bonus payday, nevertheless was an offer Randy could hardly refuse. Initially, though, he did just that. But the chance to play alongside a real live Beatle was just too much for Randy, the eternal fan, to pass up.

Each summer for several years, former Beatles drummer Ringo Starr assembled what he called his All-Starr band, a different configuration of name players who went out on tour with him and his drummer son Zak Starkey for a little money and a lot of fun. Such well-known musicians as Joe Walsh, Dave Edmunds, Todd Rundgren, the Eagles' Tim Schmit and Burton Cummings had served time in previous All-Starr lineups. In the 1995 edition, Grand Funk Railroad's Mark Farner, Felix Cavaliere from the Rascals, The Who's John Entwistle, and keyboard player and Beatles supporter Billy Preston were invited to participate. Randy also received the call.

The offer had been mentioned to me a few years before, but I was too busy with other things. It had only been mentioned in passing and never pursued at that point. Then I heard Burton was doing it and I heard what each guy was getting paid. Everyone was making the same pay and the money wasn't bad, not great but not bad. A couple of years later, I was officially approached by David Fishof who was promoting the tour for Ringo but the money was about half what Burton's lineup had received. So I told David I wasn't interested. I felt there must be an inequity somewhere.

Fishof kept at me saying that Ringo loved *Takin' Care of Business* and really wanted me to come onboard. He thought my songs would be a perfect fit for the band. All the guys were getting the same pay, he assured me, but I remained adamant that I wanted more money. I also wanted my manager, Marty Kramer, along on the tour in various capacities because he had experience in every aspect of touring from road managing to merchandising.

Eventually, I was shown the books and was told that Ringo had lost money on previous tours so they had to scale down. This was the bottom line offer. The clincher was when David Fishof said to me, "I guarantee you that when it's all done you will come to me and say this has been the most fun in your life and that you would have done it for nothing."

"No way."

But in the end I took up his challenge and agreed to do it.

While I was holding out though, I mentioned the tour to Denise and that I had turned it down. She sat me down and told me straight to my face, "Are you insane? Who is your favourite band of all time?"

"The Beatles."

"And who is your favourite drummer of all time?"

"Ringo Starr."

"On every recording you've ever done, what have you told every drummer to do?"

"Play like Ringo." It's true. I have always said to play like Ringo Starr.

"Who have you always dreamed of playing with?"

"One of the Beatles."

"Okay then, this is your opportunity."

So I caved in on the pay issue and signed on.

The night I agreed to join the tour, PBS happened to show *A Hard Day's Night* on television followed by *The Making of A Hard Day's Night*. As I watched, I was in my glory. I had sat through that movie a half-dozen times at the Garrick Theatre back in 1964 until my father had called the police to find me and now I was going to play with a real live Beatle! The next morning the phone rang at my house.

"Hello, this is Ringo."

I couldn't move. I was numb. There was that voice, that name, that Scouse accent.

"I'm just calling from Monaco to say how happy I am that you're going to be in my band. I'm looking forward to having a

rockin' summer. I'll see you soon in Vancouver for rehearsals. Ta."
Click.

I could barely breathe. When I regained my composure I
hollered to Denise.

"Guess who called me?!"

I called up Marty Kramer.

"Guess who I just talked to?!"

I was like that same kid at the Garrick Theatre.

Because I was the last one to sign on and had a bit of a bargaining position holding out, I wanted the rehearsals convened in
Vancouver so I wouldn't be away from my family. Also, Marty had
certain tasks to take care of in his capacity as road manager for the
tour and couldn't do them in a strange town. In Vancouver he was
able to arrange to get us a hotel, sound, and lights, and the New
York Theatre for rehearsals. Prior to rehearsals, we were all sent a
tape of everyone's songs to become familiar with so that when we
got together nothing would be brand new and we could move
along smoothly. Each of us learned each other's songs.

The night before rehearsals were to begin, we had a get
acquainted dinner at an Italian restaurant where the wives were
all invited. Ringo and his lovely wife Barbara Bach were present
and were extremely gracious and charming.

The next day, May 28, we arrived at the first rehearsal, met one
another, and we're all jamming a bit until we heard a little tap on
a mike.

"Gentleman, attention. Let's get it started. You all got your tapes.
My first song is *Yellow Submarine*. Mr. Bachman?"

I strummed the opening chord and we were off.

"In the town, where I was born…" It's Ringo Starr singing
behind me! I was in seventh heaven!

It was just like any other band rehearsing. Someone makes a
mistake, we stop, sort out the right note or chord, jot down some
notes on cheat sheets, count it in, and proceed through the set. It

was tough to learn so many different songs because they ran the gamut of classic rock in a myriad of styles from Mark Farner's Grand Funk hard rockers like *Locomotion* and *Some Kind of Wonderful* and John Entwistle's *Boris the Spider* to Felix Cavaliere's slower *Rascals* soul groove. Billy Preston's *Will It Go Round in Circles* must have had four thousand chords. It was like learning a Lenny Breau song. We ran through all the songs, took a break for a catered lunch, then carried on in the afternoon, broke for dinner, and met up the next day to do the same. It was all so civilized.

Everyone became more familiar with each other as the rehearsals progressed, but the ice was really broken once we started sharing "You think you got screwed? This is what happened to me!" stories. Everybody had something in common, even Ringo.

"You know what Brian Epstein did? He sold our merchandise for 10 percent."

All these kinds of stories told with a chuckle brought us together as a unit.

It wasn't long before we were onstage in Japan in early June and discovered we were a real band. We played throughout the country with stops at places like Nagada, Osaka, Nagoya, and two nights at the famed Budokan. It was magical standing there playing those Beatles songs. And it wasn't just me feeling that way. All of us had grown up on the Beatles and felt that same exhilaration. I had played those Beatles songs decades before in the Reflections, but to listen and actually hear behind you the drummer play that exact part was mind-boggling. To be playing *Boys* or *With a Little Help from My Friends* like the record was so exciting. It made us all want to play our songs like the records instead of the interpretations we may have developed over the years. For example, in *Groovin'* I turned my guitar off because there isn't any guitar in the original version. I stepped back when Mark Farner did his numbers and he did the same when I came forward to do mine. We all respected one another and played like a unit rather than six or seven solo artists.

Each of us had our own distinctive sound; however, the one consistent problem throughout the tour was John Entwistle's bass rig, his amplifier, and speaker cabinets, which vastly overwhelmed our amps. When Mark Farner and I showed up with 100-watt amps, you couldn't hear us because Entwistle had a 3,000-watt amp and two huge cabinets on either side of the drum rostrum. He had an active bass, which means the pickups are like pre-amplifiers themselves powered by batteries, only John had a pick-up for each string with a separate volume control for each. He would literally touch a string like you would tickle your own fin-ger or flick a hair off your sweater, just barely caressing the strings, and it would go "BOOOOOOM Budda BOOOOOM Budda BOOOOOM!" Thunderous. He was a wonderful guy, very nice, polite and gracious, a true British gentleman, but he is pretty much hearing impaired from years of playing in The Who and had to have his bass that loud just to hear it. He had to feel the pres-sure against his back as the air moved his speakers. So it was an ongoing problem Mark Farner and I had to deal with throughout the tour. On either side of us were keyboard players Felix and Billy who weren't even amped. They went directly through the PA. And we didn't play consistently sized theaters, so sound checks would be one thing and the live performances something else entirely. John would sound check fairly quietly then turn up for the gig and keep turning up throughout the set. There were times when Mark was literally rolling on the floor in pain, holding his ears after our performance.

But despite that, all the songs were fun, the audiences loved the shows, we all got along fabulously and had a ball. I started out with four songs: *No Sugar Tonight, Takin' Care of Business, You Ain't Seen Nothin' Yet*, and *Looking Out for #1*. Sometimes the shows were longer and I would do all four, but most nights I did

the first three. We did *No Sugar Tonight* with more of a driving
Buddy Holly/Bo Diddley beat. Having Mark Farner and Felix
Cavaliere singing harmony was marvellous. We had Mark Rivera
from Billy Joel's band as a utility man on sax, percussion, acoustic
guitar, and backing vocals to give the band a more studio sound.
When we did *Takin' Care of Business*, I gave everyone in the
band a solo and we would stop for the audience singalong bit.

I was totally ga ga the whole tour. Ringo knew I was a true fan,
not merely one of the musicians in the band. I would look over
my shoulder in *Takin' Care of Business* and grin from ear to ear
because there was Ringo Starr backing me up on my own song.

Ringo Starr rarely deigns to be quoted for a book on anyone, even
fellow Beatles or close associates, but he offered this affectionate epithet about Randy when approached regarding this book. Asked to
comment on his time with Randy, in his own characteristic sense of
humour, Ringo had this to say with great affection: "Yes Randy is a big,
fat guy and I love him." Ringo always referred to Randy as the Big Guy.

"Deep down, Randy is still a fan and always will be," smiles brother
Gary. "And I think that's what makes him pure. He's not saying he is bigger than or better than anyone. He respects other artists and is in awe
meeting them." Indeed, Randy often speaks in the superlatives of a life-
long fan such as "incredible," "unbelievable," and "Wow" when describing encounters with his heroes, without realizing his own status as a
hero to many and as someone respected as an equal by his peers. He
has never lost that naïve enthusiasm and appreciation of music and the
artists who create it. It is an endearing quality about him. "Randy still
catches himself in the middle of his life," notes Claudia Senton
Anderson, "and steps back and says 'Who is this? My god it's me. Me?!'"

Chuckles Marty Kramer, "When Ringo would say 'Take it away,
Randy' for Randy's numbers he would be beside himself. He would
play his songs and take that ship to the moon he was so exhilarated at
being onstage with Ringo Starr. He was just a salaried player in the

band like the others, but he played his buns off every night. The other guys would be looking at Randy and wondering 'What's this guy doing?!'"

"Dad seemed totally excited about playing on the Ringo tour," adds Tal Bachman. After Tal, an avowed Beatles fanatic himself, suggested to his Dad that the All-Starrs consider pulling out *I Wanna Be Your Man* from the Beatles back catalogue, Randy brought up the idea with his new boss who thought it a wonderful suggestion. He hadn't sung it since the earliest days of the Beatles. The group ended up performing the number throughout the duration of the tour.

Ringo was so much fun to be around. Me being a Beatlemaniac and avid collector, I brought a stack of things to the first rehearsal for Ringo to sign — albums, singles, books. As he walked in he looked at the pile and simply said, "Pick two." I had him sign my copy of the *Abbey Road Sessions* book and another for Tal. He just couldn't sign everything for everyone or he would have been there all day. But a couple of days later he did sign a few more things for me.

Once we started the actual tour, we could see how normal he was. Everyone called him Richie. No star trips, no tantrums, no power plays, and everyone treated equally. When he travelled first class, we all travelled first class. If he had a private plane, we all took it. If it was on a bus sweating with no air conditioning, he was there with everyone. And he continually acknowledged how lucky he was to have been the right guy at the right time to end up being the timekeeper in the greatest group in the world. He was so humble and down-to-earth.

Ringo travelled with his own minder, a very British, Rutles-like "Leggy Mountbatten" type named Hilary Gerrard — Ringo's confidante from Apple. He was an eighty-year-old tax expert dressed in a striped button-down shirt, vest, tweed suit, cane, breeches. He was a very cool guy, a proper English gentleman, who advised

Ringo when to move from house to house around the world to avoid heavy taxes.

The American leg of the tour began in St. Louis on July 2. Over the next seven weeks, it wound its way across country with dates at Caesar's Palace in Atlantic City and Radio City Music Hall in New York. I recall we had a day off in Rhode Island and Ringo asked, "Who's up for a movie?" No one replied.

"Well, I'll be here in the lobby at 1 p.m. if you want to come along."

I wasn't about to miss an opportunity to go out with Ringo Starr, so I got down to the lobby early with Felix. Ringo and Barbara arrived and we waited a few minutes to see if anyone else would be joining us. I leaned over to Felix and whispered, "I wonder if this will be an Elvis thing."

"Where the whole theatre is ours?"

"Yeah, this guy can't go to a regular showing. He'll get mobbed."

Just then a big van pulled up and took just the four of us to the theatre to watch a movie all by ourselves. We arrived and it was this enormous elegant old-fashioned theatre. And there we were, the only ones there. We strolled in, selected seats, and plunked ourselves down in these plush old chairs. Twenty-two hundred seats and as Ringo and Barbara sat down, for fun I plunked myself immediately in front of them. Ringo is five-foot-six and I'm six-three; he's thin and I'm wide. Ringo leaned over, tapped me on the shoulder, and in his best upper-crust British accent intoned, "Excuse me sir, you forgot to wear your ten-gallon hat." We laughed, I moved behind them, and we proceeded to enjoy Mel Gibson's *Braveheart* in a theatre all to ourselves.

We celebrated Ringo's birthday when we were playing in Chicago and for the occasion we rented a big restaurant for a party. Beforehand I had called Denise at home.

"What do I give a guy who has everything?"

She came up with a novel idea.

"Why don't you buy Ringo his own star?"

Some astronomers in an observatory near Chicago had discovered a cluster of new stars in the galaxy and you could name one of them for a nominal fee. Denise took care of the details and a certificate arrived at the hotel from this famous observatory, along with a star chart identifying and circling the star you had named. The certificate proclaimed that from henceforth this star would be known as Ringo Star. What a great present! Ringo was knocked out. This is what you get a guy who has everything — you get him his own celestial body.

The tour made its way across the US to the Greek Theatre in Los Angeles. Following our two-night stand, we were all invited to a lavish party in Beverly Hills hosted by the former lawyer for the Beatles who still handled a lot of celebrities. The house was incredible. The guest list included a who's who of Hollywood. You would turn around and there would be Tom Petty or Pee Wee Herman or Katey Sagal or Jeff Lynne. I received a tap on the shoulder and someone whispered to me, "There's someone who would like to meet you." And there standing before me was Phil Spector. What do you say to Phil Spector? "Hi, I like your wall of sound"?

The Electric Light Orchestra had opened for us years earlier in St. Louis, so I took the opportunity to reintroduce myself to leader Jeff Lynne by reminding him of that gig.

"Oh yes, I remember that," he replied.

I reminded him as well of a very touching personal incident.

"A couple of years ago I wrote you a letter that was sent to your record label informing you that my son Tal was a huge fan of ELO. A few weeks later a giant spaceship mobile was delivered to our house with the ELO logo and medallion. Tal hung it from the ceiling in his room. In the package along with that came an entire ELO catalogue plus photos. It was such a thrill for him at the time because we were going through a family breakup and your music was something he could find a sense of security in. Now he has recorded his own demo tape that sounds very much like the Beatles and ELO."

"I wouldn't mind hearing it," Jeff responded genuinely.

"Really? I have one down in the car."

"Well now's your chance. Go get it."

This is the kind of party that had valet parking and because the house was on a winding hill, all the cars were parked in and around the adjacent streets. They actually had a map to indicate where everyone's car had been parked. My car ended up several blocks away. I returned after having run up and down these hills to retrieve the tape and I was all sweaty. I came up to Jeff.

"Here's the tape."

Four or five days later I received a breathless call from Tally.

"What's the matter?"

"Dad, I can't talk."

"What's wrong?"

"Jeff Lynne just phoned me! I can't believe it. He likes some of my songs."

"I told him how ELO were a big influence on you and about the spaceship."

It was such a wonderful gesture from Jeff.

When the tour hit Seattle for two nights in late August, Tal got to come down and meet Ringo, which was a big thrill for him. Some of my other children were there too, and Ringo went above and beyond the call of duty to meet them and even my Mom who came down for the show.

There was one gig left in Reno, Nevada, on August 24, which was slated to be taped for an HBO special. On the last day in Seattle during the downtime, and because there was no set up or sound check, I took the opportunity to get everyone on the tour including Ringo to sign two dozen tour programs, like an end of school yearbook. Everybody thought that was a terrific idea so they decided to do the same in Reno. Unfortunately, they didn't get the chance. We touched down in Reno the next day and as the equipment was being set up we all received an emergency call to meet in the hotel lobby immediately. Someone called my room as I was getting ready to head downstairs.

"Do you know anything about Ringo leaving?"

After we assembled in the foyer, we were told that Ringo's daughter Lee had been rushed to the hospital in London diagnosed with a tumour and was scheduled for an operation the following morning. With that announcement, the final night was cancelled and the tour disbanded then and there. Everyone received plane tickets to wherever they needed to go. It was a sad denouement to such a memorable experience. In the end Lee came through just fine.

A month later, I received in the mail an expensive designer-style watch with the inscription "To Randy Bachman, Ringo Starr's All-Starr Tour, thank you."

True to his prediction, I did go back to David Fishof at the completion of the tour and told him he had been right, it was the most fun I had had in many years and I would have done it for nothing. It was incredible.

Randy and Denise were later invited to Barbara Bach's extravagant fiftieth birthday party in Los Angeles, along with a star-studded guest list. At the conclusion to the evening, Randy ended up onstage jamming on *Takin' Care of Business* with the likes of Stevie Nicks, James Burton, and Don Was. Tally and Callianne attended as well.

"I was over at Dad's house when the letter arrived," recalls Tal with a chuckle, relating the story of his father's elation. "He looked through his stack of mail and came upon this invitation. All of a sudden he rolled into one of his characteristic boisterous exclamations.

'Wow! Rock! Unbelievable!'

'Dad, what's going on?'

'Birthday with a Beatle!' and he's screaming it through the house.

"Then he loudly reads out the invitation. 'You are cordially invited to attend the fiftieth birthday of Barbara Bach. This is going to be great!'

"A month later they came over to pick me up, I was staying at my manager's house in Los Angeles, to go to the party. Dad and Denise went into a back room while I was waiting in the living room. It was a little before seven and the party was starting at 7:30. Five minutes go by, they're still in there. Ten minutes. Twenty minutes. So I figured 'What's going on?' Finally I walked into the back room and there is this awful, terrible tension in the air. My Dad looks like he wants to kill himself. Denise is about to slay a dragon, totally peeved off.

'What's happening?'

'What's happening is your father doesn't have the right address. This address doesn't exist!'

"He hadn't brought the actual invitation. He had scribbled the address down on a scrap of paper and the address he wrote down didn't exist. They couldn't find it on any map of Beverly Hills. They called various people, the Beverly Hills Police Department, the chamber of commerce, my manager's Dad who grew up in Beverly Hills. They couldn't find it anywhere. The big moment of my Dad's life is slipping through his fingers and he looks like Charlie Brown who's missed the football. He looks sick. They've come all the way down here and now they are about to miss it. Then my manager suggests that maybe it's not Hillcrest Street but Crescent or Boulevard. So we all piled into the car — dead silence as we drive around looking for this road or boulevard and, miracle of miracles, we found it, went in, and had a great time.

Following his Beatles experience, once again like a rolling stone, Neil Young crossed paths with Randy. This time it was to honour their own early mentor, Shadows guitarist Hank B. Marvin, by appearing on a tribute album to the British guitar great. But like everything these two seem to tackle together, there is always an element of kismet involved and the Hank Marvin tribute was no exception.

Recalls Tal, "When this thing with the Shadows came up, Dad faxed Neil and he responded. I received this excited phone call from Dad.

'We're going to Broken Arrow! We're going to Broken Arrow! This ROCKS! This is amazing!' He totally idolizes Neil Young and was so excited. We got down there and Neil walks in and he's a cross between Jim from Taxi, Yoda, and Jack Nicholson from *The Shining*. In all his Neilness, he nonchalantly announces, 'Hey man, let's rock.'"

I had heard about a tribute album to Hank Marvin spearheaded by Sting and his management for his own record label. So I sent Sting's management a fax. I wasn't sure if they would know who I was.

"I grew up with Neil Young, and Hank Marvin was our greatest influence. Neil Young went on to find fame with Buffalo Springfield, Crosby, Stills, Nash, and Young, and on his own. I was a member of the Guess Who and Bachman-Turner Overdrive. Most of our solos are Hank Marvin–based. I would love to do a track on the album and I will try to talk Neil into it as well."

The next day I received a fax from Sting's manager assuring me I need not explain who I was, they certainly knew of me, and directing me to the tribute album's producer in LA. When I contacted the project producer, Stevo Glyndenning, he told me there was only room for one more track. Peter Green, Brian May, all these great guitar players had already picked all the best Hank Marvin songs.

"I want to play *Man of Mystery*."

"It's gone. Pick another song. Can you get Neil involved?"

I faxed Neil and laid out the details of the album for him and who was involved.

"Are you interested?"

I received a faxed reply.

"Yes, here's an open time. Come on down. Just bring your guitar, a drummer, and a bass player, all the gear is here."

He was recording with Crazy Horse at that time.

So Tally and I and Richard Cochrane, my bass player, flew down to Broken Arrow Ranch in Northern California. Tally would play drums as he had been doing in my band recently. Just before we left, Neil and I talked on the phone about which song we would like to record.

"Do you remember *Spring Is Nearly Here?*" he asked me. "I'd like to play that."

"Yeah, I think Doc Steen used to play it on CKRC back in Winnipeg in 1963."

But for the life of me I couldn't find it on any Shadows albums I had. I barely remembered it. When I arrived at Neil's I had told him the two songs I had in mind, one being *Shindig*.

"I told you I don't want to do these songs. I want to do *Spring Is Nearly Here.*"

"I don't have it. Do you have it?"

"No. Let's try it from memory."

It was over thirty years later. Neil closed his eyes and a few seconds later he started playing the melody.

"Oh yeah!" And I joined in on the rhythm and we got through the verses.

"I forget the bridge," sighed Neil as we came to a sudden halt.

"Well, it's in C so I'll go to C7 and into F."

Shadows stuff was very predictable. We went through it again and as I hit the C7, Neil went right into the actual bridge. He remembered it! We were pulling these notes from each other's brains. Neither of us had a record of this song back in the sixties and we only knew it from the few times Doc Steen played it on CKRC. It was one of those rare moments, two minds becoming like one.

We had the verse and chorus, but we were stumped on the intro and outro. Neither of us could pull that one from our cob-webbed memories, so we decided to make up an intro that we both liked.

"Hank Marvin's not going to care," commented Neil.

We recorded the whole thing in one or two takes. Neil doesn't like to lose the spontaneity of the moment. He is a one- or two-take guy. There were a couple of odd notes where he hit harmonics that were not exactly in the same key but gave the track a funny tension where he's playing a B harmonic and I'm playing a C chord.

"Neil, should we correct it?"

"No, it happened. Pretend we're the Shadows playing live at some seaside resort in Brighton just like in those Cliff Richard movies."

So I left it alone figuring that when I got back to my studio in Vancouver I would tweak it.

Following the session, we had dinner at Neil's ranch with the guys from Crazy Horse and his steel player Ben Keith. During dinner, I told Neil about my idea for a song entitled *Made in Canada*. We had talked during the overdubbing for *Prairie Town* about actually recording live together, two guitars wailing away. Suddenly Neil announced "Let's go back and try it."

"When Neil replied to Dad, 'Why don't we go record it, man?' I couldn't believe Dad's face," chuckles Tal. "I thought he was going to jump on the table and do a Chris Farley cartwheel. It was wild. His eyes bulged out like Buckwheat on *Little Rascals*. 'That would be great!' he shouted. So we recorded it in a barn surrounded by farm animals, and before each take the engineer had to go out and shoo away the chickens and goats because of potential leakage onto the microphones."

I ran through the song once as he listened to the arrangement and picked up the chords.

"Go through it one more time."

He then nodded to his engineer and picked up his guitar. We played it again, Tally, Richard, and I, and this time Neil was into it. As we got to the end of the song where he is supposed to solo the track out, he became transfixed like he was in a trance. His hair fell over his face as he kept going on and on soloing like a maniac. The three of us just kept following him. It was like when he plays *Like a Hurricane* with Crazy Horse soloing with wild abandon as the wind from a giant fan tries to blow him over. Unbelievable. He went from a double to a triple solo, stomping on his big red foot pedal board as the sound suddenly swirled and swooped around us. He kicked his reverb unit and it exploded in noise as he soloed on and on, higher and higher, eight, nine, ten solos. It was like playing with Jimi Hendrix. The end of the song is simply incredible.

"That's it. We got it. Good night guys, I'm going to spend some time with my wife, Pegi."

I was under the impression we were just doing a run through and was freaking out at the thought of losing this incredible once-in-a-lifetime take. But he had his engineer rolling the tape. That was it, the recording of *Made in Canada*.

The next day as I was leaving, Neil's manager, Elliot Roberts, came up to me and laid the heavy speech on me.

"Neil feels strongly that this was a moment captured in time and nothing should alter it. We know you have plans to take the tape of *Spring Is Nearly Here* home and fix it up but we urge you not to. If you want to stay another day, we'll mix it right here."

So I stayed over and Neil and I did a rough mix to DAT and HDCD, high definition CD format. I took it home and fixed it up anyway. I sent him a copy with me correcting the B to C mistake. I then received a phone call from Elliot, the gist of which was "Don't mess with it."

So I didn't. I put it out the way we originally recorded it. When the Hank Marvin tribute album came out, Stevo called me to tell me how much Sting enjoyed our track. Sting said we sounded like the Shadows live.

Before the album came out though, I was still perplexed about the origins of that song. Did the Shadows actually record *Spring Is Nearly Here*? Did Neil and I remember it correctly or had we recorded a Santo and Johnny song by mistake? I was wracked with anxiety fearing I had blown $10,000 on the session. I scoured my record collection, checked biographies I had of Cliff Richard, as well as Bruce Welch's book on the Shadows. Nothing. In desperation, I called a Shadows expert, Richard Patterson who had been the drummer in an Ottawa Shadows-style band The Esquires back in the mid-sixties. He had actually encouraged me early on to be included on the tribute album. He wasn't in, so I left a frantic message on his answering machine.

"Richard, you have to help me. I can't find a Shadows song called *Spring Is Nearly Here* anywhere! I think we recorded the wrong song. Can you help me?"

I took Callianne to school and as I came back in the door I could hear *Spring Is Nearly Here* coming over my answering machine. Richard had found the track and was playing it to me over the phone. It turned out to be on a British album not released in Canada and we pretty much had it right pulling it from our collective memories, having never owned the actual record thirty years ago.

When the album was finally released, one thing came out loud and clear: no one can come close to playing like Hank Marvin. The song he played on it, *The Rise and Fall of Flingel Bunt*, was one hundred percent Hank Marvin. The tone, the phrasing, the playing was his thing, and we all sounded like the fans and imitators we were. We had all thought we were getting the sound, but we weren't. No one gets that sound like Hank. I even played a white 1964 Burns model guitar like Hank's. I showed up with that at Neil's place and he freaked out. I wanted to be authentic. I didn't even come close. There is only one Hank Marvin.

Randy was invited to speak at Neil's induction into the Order of Canada in 1996 at Rideau Hall before the Governor-General. He spoke of the common bond they both shared growing up in Winnipeg and of

Neil's courage and determination in the face of daunting odds to become successful in music. Both had managed to turn their dreams into reality.

One cannot help but feel that Randy's achievements have been woefully neglected when these kind of honours are meted out. While Neil left Canada in 1966 to find fame in Los Angeles, Randy stayed behind to achieve success from a much tougher vantage point here in Canada. Notes son Tal with rightful indignation, "What about Dad? With the exception of a couple of years a few thousand feet from the Canadian border, Dad has lived his entire life and based his entire career from Canada. Making it from Winnipeg was against so many odds and far more difficult. Weren't the Guess Who the first pop rock act to break out of Canada and BTO the second? Yet BTO haven't even been inducted into the Canadian music Hall of Fame. I just don't get it. He has been totally ignored. Every single guy in Canada knows who he is. Everybody knows at least one or two of his songs. I get it every single day of my life. He is a prime mover in Canadian music. He has certainly inspired hundreds and hundreds of Canadians to write songs and play music."

In 1996, Randy released his next solo album, *MERGE*, featuring him and Neil burning up the frets on the grunge-inspired pile-driving rocker *Made in Canada*. With Neil's characteristic shrill guitar wailing away throughout, the track sounds not unlike his finest work with Crazy Horse on albums like *RAGGED GLORY* or *SLEEPS WITH ANGELS*. Once again, Randy had reinvented himself showing he was capable of grunging with the best of them. Son Tal co-produced the album with his father, as well as playing throughout. Tal had placed one of his own songs on the previous *ANY ROAD* album marking his emergence from behind his father's shadow as an artist in his own right.

Working alongside his father, Tal noticed something about Randy's vocal delivery during the *ANY ROAD* sessions that was rectified on *MERGE*. "I think Dad lost his confidence after the divorce," he postulates. "That fact manifested itself in his vocal performances. He seemed defensive about his voice and I had never encountered him being so self-deprecating. He hadn't really been doing any serious recording in the eighties but to hear him say around the time of *ANY ROAD* that he had a new vocal persona because he couldn't sing or carry a tune, I was incredulous. What was *Looking Out for #1* or *Takin' Care of Business*? When he played me his songs for *MERGE*, I told him he had a lot of good ideas but the melodies were non-melodies. He had adopted that talking style that he referred to as a Mark Knopfler/Bob Dylan kind of thing. For it to be a struggle for him to sing after songs like *Hey You* and *Looking Out for #1*, I couldn't understand. Finally I raised the issue.

'Dad, you already *have* a vocal persona. It was established twenty-five years ago. What were the two biggest hits BTO ever had? Who sang them? Everybody knows you're not Pavarotti. It doesn't matter. The vocal performance on *Takin' Care of Business* is perfect for what it is. It's a flawless vocal performance for what it is. People can sing along to it. You can't sing along to a rap song. That's not what you've been all about nor is it what you should try to be.'

"So he gave it a go and came up with some legitimate melodies and a sequence of pitches and sang them on *MERGE*. Unfortunately, that album didn't really do anything but I thought there was some good stuff on it."

MERGE represented Randy's synthesis of his early influences; it was an assimilation of all the sounds and styles from his younger years into his own writing. Like its predecessor, *MERGE* was recorded for Randy's own label with distribution, this time by True North Records. A worthy follow-up to the stalwart *ANY ROAD*, it too suffered from a lack of marketing and promotion.

That same year saw the launching of the Guitarchives label, a personal project owned and operated by Randy. Guitarchives was created with the express mandate to re-master and re-release the long-lost recordings of Lenny Breau. Randy's meticulous work in uncovering these recordings and offering younger audiences the opportunity to enjoy and appreciate the genius of Lenny's music has been hailed far and wide. The recordings reveal the timelessness of Lenny's playing and his innovative approach, still unrivalled today. For Randy, the eager pupil, the circle was now complete. Guitarchives and Randy's other label, Legend, would further offer him the opportunity to restore the early Guess Who catalogue to the public and set their legacy straight.

The Guitarchives label was never approached as a money-making venture. It was the proverbial labour of love for me. When CDs and classic rock turned my life around with all the re-releases, I thought I could now replace my old worn-out or lost Lenny Breau vinyl albums with CDs. But no one was bothering to re-release them. No one was interested, which was such a shame given the body of work he left behind. It needed to be heard by a whole new generation of guitar players.

Through an attorney I knew who was negotiating a contract for another artist at RCA-BMG, I inquired about the possibility of them releasing Lenny's catalogue. The word came back to me that they weren't interested because they saw little revenue potential in the recordings. So I asked to lease the tapes. But in the meantime, a Connecticut label named One Way nabbed the rights and put them out.

I missed the boat with those, but what transpired afterwards was that when people back in Winnipeg heard I had been looking to release Lenny's work, they came out of the woodwork with all sorts of tapes. Breau was best live; everyone who ever saw him will attest to that, myself included. The albums were wonderful but they never fully captured his magic. I received word via the grapevine that there were tapes lying in people's basements of Lenny at places like the old Paddock Restaurant, the Ting coffeehouse, the Royal Alexander Hotel, the Cellar Door. Did I want them? Absolutely! Suddenly there was a wealth of Breau tapes available.

I have always acknowledged Lenny Breau as my mentor.

Certainly, people in Winnipeg knew that. I was never a student of his in the formal sense but everything I needed to know about guitar came in those eighteen months or so I spent hanging out with him. It has served me well and I felt I owed him something. So when these tapes emerged, I also understood how precious they were to those who possessed them for so many years. They, too, had been touched by Lenny. These people had taped Lenny on their own little machines in some dark club just to have a piece of his special gift. Rather than keep the tapes, I took them to Finucan Studios in Winnipeg and transferred them to DAT, Digital Audio Tape, and promptly returned the originals to their owners.

With my usual obsessive zeal, the unearthing of these tapes kindled a desire in me to search out more tapes of Breau and before long other sources contacted me with their own archives. More and more tapes surfaced and, along with the four CDs I have put out so far on Guitarchives, I am hoping to release even more of Lenny. I have some two hundred hours of tape to choose from. One of our releases that is very special to me is *BOY WONDER*, tapes of Lenny at age fifteen recorded in Maine by a friend just before he moved to Winnipeg and I met him.

The reviews for the Breau releases have been wonderful. Critics love this stuff. I set up an artist fund for Lenny's children to receive the royalties from the releases. I feel very humbled to be the informal caretaker of the Breau musical archives. I have recently spoken to American guitarist Steve Vai about having his own Favored Nations Records, a guitar specialty label, distribute the catalogue in the United States.

Lenny Breau died tragically under mysterious circumstances in Los Angeles in 1984. His body was found floating in the swimming pool of his apartment complex. No one has ever been charged and the case remains open. Regrettably, Lenny was not able to shake off his personal demons and was plagued by drug abuse to the end. A recent Canadian documentary *The Genius of Lenny* cast further light not only on his remarkable career, but also on his unsolved murder. Randy appeared in the film reminiscing about his time with Lenny as he stood in front of the house on Airlies in West Kildonan where Lenny lived in the mid-fifties and where Randy would skip school to bask in Lenny Breau's brilliance.

To me, Lenny Breau was the Johnny Appleseed of the guitar. Every place I go in the world today I can find a guitar player who either saw Lenny play, hung out with him, or had a lesson from him. Anything you asked Lenny to show you he freely gave. There is an unspoken division and a bond, the Lenny guitarists and the non-Lenny guitarists, and you just know when you hear someone play that they listened to Lenny.

"Lenny Breau?"

"Yeah, how'd you know?"

He gave us more than just notes; he imparted a style that is recognizable no matter in what genre. Rock players like Steve Vai revere him. He planted his seed in all these guitar players, generations of them, because young players are again discovering his genius from the re-released recordings. That's why it is so important for me to be releasing that music.

It was a strong message for me a few years after our lessons together when we were teenagers to see Lenny deteriorate as he became increasingly involved with drugs, moving from marijuana eventually to heroin. I don't know how it affected his music, but his life fell apart as he became more reliant on drugs. It took its toll. No one could depend on him and he could not function as a human being. He was consumed by drugs. I was determined never to let that happen to me. Drugs are the scourge of the earth. It takes people and robs them of their soul, their talent, their families and relationships, and ultimately their life. Drugs did that to Lenny.

In 1997 Randy's Legend Records release the long since deleted and highly collectable first three Canadian Guess Who Quality Records albums, *SHAKIN' ALL OVER, HEY HO,* and *IT'S TIME.* With these releases, Randy has assumed the role of archivist for the Guess Who and plans further releases including a compilation that covers the quartet's pre-*These Eyes* years from 1966 to -1968. It will feature almost a dozen tracks from the CBC television series *Let's Go,* illustrating the embryonic stages of the Bachman–Cummings songwriting partnership. "Randy told me he wanted to be the caretaker of all the Guess Who stuff," notes Garry Peterson, "and I replied that it should be no one else."

With the early Quality tapes of the Guess Who, I envisioned myself in the same role as with the Breau tapes — the caretaker when no one else wanted them. It all came about after I received a phone call inquiring if I wanted to buy the "Selkirk Tapes." I thought "Selkirk Tapes? Selkirk, Manitoba, the town north of Winnipeg? They must be live tapes from one of our old shows at the Selkirk mental institution back in the early sixties." I offered $500 for them and was told, "Are you crazy?" They wanted $100,000. We finally agreed on a price and when I received the box and opened it, I discovered all our old recordings — the Quality Records masters and all the artwork. I thought someone had made a mistake. Then I looked at the box and saw "Selkirk Communications" and it hit me: Boing! The Selkirk Tapes. Quality Records had been owned by Selkirk Communications.

They had been offered to the other guys in the band who weren't interested, so I took them on. The risk was that these recordings could have been acquired easily by noncaring individuals who could put them out without much care in packaging and pay no one for them. We never saw a cent from those Quality recordings anyway, but maybe we could if they were re-released properly. So I took the same attitude I applied to Breau's long lost catalogue.

To leave Quality Records in 1968 and go with Jack Richardson at Nimbus, we relinquished all future royalties on those tracks. We never received a penny after that, even though the tracks were reissued in various compilations after the success of *These Eyes*. I could be selling these all over and licensing those songs to anybody and making a lot of money, but I would not feel right doing that. We were all there in the trenches together in the early days so I don't feel right reaping the benefits of it.

Jim and Garry were always on side with me re-releasing the early stuff, but there had been some hesitation from Burton and his manager Lorne Saifer questioning my right to re-release these tracks. They are on side now after the Pan Am reunion. We will split the money four ways; each guy can have his own publishing on the songs he wrote so it is not complicated. But it is important that this legacy not be lost. What I am working toward is to have every track out for the public. I don't care whether it sells or not; it matters to me to have that music preserved for my kids, and Garry's kids and Jim's kids, the next generation.

CHAPTER 11

Survivor

A re there still musical frontiers left for Randy Bachman to conquer? Having done it all not once but twice, what's left for him? At fifty-six, what keeps him out on the road several months of the year or toiling away in his home studio the remainder of the time? Never one to slow down for very long, Randy has turned his focus in the latter nineties toward songwriting exclusively. He is carving out a new career for himself, plugging his songs to other artists in a variety of genres from traditional country to "new country" and pop/dance music. And he approaches his latest goal with the same passion and determination that has marked both his career and his whole life.

In addition, Randy has turned his experienced hand to producing, recording, and assisting other artists to achieve their dreams. In recent years, he has appeared on albums by such diverse artists as punk rockers DOA, folk rock duo Lava Hay, and country group Prairie Oyster (as well as appearing with them onstage at the Canadian Country Music Awards). He has recorded with Farmer's Daughter, written songs and performed with Big Sugar's Gordie Johnson, produced up and comer Colin Arthur's debut album, and posted songs on Donnie Osmond's next release.

Jetting between Nashville, Los Angeles, and London, England, Randy has forged songwriting partnerships with some of the finest young songwriters in the business. One would think his tag as a seventies classic rock dinosaur a hindrance. Quite the contrary, Randy has discovered to his eternal delight that record executives and song publishers today grew up on his music, the songs of the Guess Who and BTO. Rock 'n' roll is no longer a liability in Nashville nowadays, it's an asset. Randy has, in the vernacular of the music industry "phone acceptance," instant name recognition that gets him ushered into the exclusive inner sanctums of the songwriting and publishing world. In Nashville, the song is king, and a successful songwriter will have artists seeking him or her out for material tailored directly to their sound, style, and image. This is the goal Randy has set for himself as the new millennium unfolds.

"Randy is a very driven writer, extremely determined, and single-minded," points out ASCAP's (the American Society of Composers, Authors, and Publishers) Nashville head Ralph Murphy, a long-time friend and collaborator of Randy's from the sixties. "He is totally committed to his craft and that's the kind of writer that publishers want. Randy is pursuing songwriting first and foremost, and he is the kind of guy who will do whatever it takes to be successful. He's proven that many times as an artist. Nashville is a story town; the songs have to tell a story and a convincing one, and one of Randy's strengths is his ability to frame a story and set it up in a song. Randy will never write a bad song; they will always be good."

I love writing songs and recording. If all I could do were touring, playing classic rock, it would only offer a limited satisfaction. It would be a job, and one thing I have never wanted is to make music a job. Going out on the road with my band is a fun thing to do and it generates income flow, but the creative side is really what keeps me going and stimulates me. I am using the road to finance my songwriting career. I have been in Nashville pitching songs to the likes of Wynonna Judd, Reba McIntyre, and George Strait. People have no idea when I walk into an office what I'm going to play them. They expect to hear *Let It Ride* or *No Sugar Tonight* and I play them great country songs. When I go to LA, I play them great pop/dance songs because I have learned to do that. I enjoy working within all the genres. I could not just be a country writer or a pop writer. I love to get a song idea and wherever it intuitively takes me, that's the demo I'll do first. If that doesn't work, I'll rework the song in another genre. If nobody likes it, I'll rework it and present it again. Sometimes the song is right, but it's just been dressed up in the wrong clothes. I might have been in a Beach Boys mood when I wrote it, then my teenage daughter will bring home a tape by Garbage or the Smashing Pumpkins and I'll think "I can do that" and go redo the demo in that style and resubmit it.

Everyone in Nashville is very conscious of my rock 'n' roll background. I will phone around and introduce myself by saying "I'm Randy Bachman and I used to play in..." and they invariably interrupt me with "Come on down. You don't need to tell us who you are. We all know who you are." You see all these country artists in Stetsons and you assume they were all weaned on Hank Williams and Tammy Wynette, but they grew up on rock 'n' roll. When they were kids they were screaming to all the hard rock bands and now they are Mr. Middle of the Road. Look at Garth Brooks growing up on KISS. Alabama have used *Takin' Care of Business* as their encore. I listen to Restless Heart, Travis Tritt, and Alabama and they are all using that distorted guitar sound that I used in BTO. I think my songs fit in with that country rock groove just fine.

I first started coming to Nashville at the urging of Ron Irving, a songwriter I met in White Rock. He told me about Tin Pan South, where writers from all over the world come to Nashville to present their songs in clubs for publishers, artists, and other writers. Every club was booked for the event. Over here it's Radney Foster and Rodney Crowell, and just down the street it's John Hiatt and Jim Messina, rocking kind of country guys.

Ron got me on a showcase, just me and an acoustic guitar. I'm brave. I like those kinds of challenges. Well, this turned out to be a very scary situation for me. I'm used to playing in a rock band with an electric guitar and here I was playing acoustically at The Ryman Auditorium, home of the original Grand Ole Opry with the ghosts of Hank Williams, Patsy Cline, everybody who has played there, and it's Legends Night. The Ryman is an old church with stained glass windows and everyone seated in pews. It's a tabernacle, not a comfortable place, but the sound is wonderful. The program runs in alphabetical order, so I opened the show. Following me were the likes of Alan and Marilyn Bergman who wrote *The Way We Were* and *You Don't Send Me Flowers* for Barbra Streisand, Justin Haywood of The Moody Blues, Michael McDonald from the Doobie Brothers, Joe South, Paul Williams, Steve Winwood. Just a fantastic show.

As I looked at the list of illustrious performers, all I could think of was "I can't really sing like these guys. Not like Michael McDonald or Steve Winwood. I'm a guitar player."

Before going on I was told, "Start at the beginning. Do a verse and a chorus of each of your songs. You've got fifteen minutes."

When you get up there onstage you have to tell the audience how you wrote the song. Nashville people like the folklore, the background, and motivation behind the song. Why did you write it? What woman broke your heart? They really don't care about your voice — it's the songs that count. I started to tell them the story of how I wrote *These Eyes*. I then started singing it and I'm no Burton Cummings. I can't sing it; my delivery was more like Randy Newman's talk/singing. I did a verse and a chorus of *These Eyes*, but as I was doing so I thought I heard feedback so I pulled back from the mike and I sang softer. Then I realized they were all singing my song with me. "They know my song! They know me!

They like me!" I felt like Sally Field at the Oscars. It was an incredible evening. I was hooked.

The next night I did another showcase at a smaller club and performed a song I had written that day. Afterwards I had people coming up to me and reacting to the song.

"I'm from the Kentucky Headhunters. I like that song *Can't Go Back to Memphis*. Can you do me a demo and bring it to the studio tomorrow?"

I thought "Wow, this is incredible."

Prairie Oyster pianist/songwriter Joan Besen was in Nashville for Tin Pan South and caught Randy's club appearance. "I remember being at the Bluebird Café in Nashville for a Canadian night during Tin Pan South. They even had little Canadian flags on the tables. Shirley Eikhard was there, Marc Jordan, Eddie Schwartz, Randy, and a few others. Here were all these Americans there all looking for the next hit song and they had no idea who these people onstage were. We all knew, but they didn't have a clue. Then they each started singing their best-known songs — Eddie doing *Hit Me with Your Best Shot*, Shirley singing *Something to Talk About*, Marc doing *Rhythm of the Heart*, and Randy playing Guess Who and BTO hits — and the attitude among all the non-Canadians was total bewilderment. "Who are these people we've never heard of singing these other people's famous songs?" When it hit them, it was like an epiphany. By the end of the evening the audience was going wild with all these hit songs being played by the actual writers. Randy was playing hit after hit after hit that everyone was singing along with and going crazy."

On that same trip I attended the Songwriters' Hall of Fame induction ceremony. I was seated beside Buddy Holly's widow Maria Elena because Buddy was being inducted. Barbara Orbison, Roy's widow, was there, and the Crickets played Buddy Holly songs. Sitting at my table, this gentleman leans over and introduces himself.

"Hi, I'm Woody Bomar."

Ralph Murphy had told me I should meet Woody. He is the kingpin song publisher in Nashville.

"I asked to be seated near you," Woody says. "I love your songs with the Guess Who and BTO. I think you could make it in Nashville. Come to Little Big Town, my publishing company, and I'll put you with my best writers."

When I asked around, everyone confirmed that Little Big Town was the best with dozens of hit songs to their credit. On my first writing trip, Woody lined me up with the hottest writers who all proceeded to tell me how they grew up on my songs. One of them was Sharon Vaughn who has scored several top ten country hits. She is an amazing lyricist. Many of these writers are booked up six months in advance but Sharon had a cancellation and agreed to fit me in on short notice. We met at the brand new MCA building where we sat in an empty room to begin creating a song out of thin air. Despite having never met her before I immediately felt an empathy with her, a connection.

"What have you got?" she asked.

"Well, I've got a couple of chord progressions I think no one's used before." I played them on acoustic guitar for her. At that moment there was a knock at the door and when Sharon opened it there stood Joan Baez.

"Sharon, aren't we supposed to be writing today?"

"Oh yeah, I did tell you that didn't I."

Sharon got up, walked toward the door, and whispered to Joan, "Just give me fifteen minutes with Randy."

Okay, so I knew I had fifteen minutes to prove myself.

Sharon turned to me and said, "I gotta go tell some guys where to put some furniture. What can you do with this title *Looking Forward to Looking Back*?"

When she came back I had a whole chorus.

"I've told that title to eight or ten writers and no one could do anything with it. You've got a chorus so let's do some verses."

In fifteen minutes the song was done. We shook hands, then both signed the rough copy of the song, and dated it. That's a traditional thing between songwriters in Nashville. Later I played the song for Woody Bomar and he exclaimed, "Killer song, fabulous!" Woody had a demo made and hustled it around. I played the song for George Strait's people and I told them, "Here's the title of George's Greatest Hits album, *LOOKING FORWARD TO LOOKING BACK*." The main line of the song is "If we treat today like the only one we have, then we can look forward to looking back." The guy was in tears.

"This is a great song for George."

If my phone rings and they want more country songs, I have a hundred more ready to go. I've got maybe fifty demoed already, professional quality demo recordings from my studio. If it happens, I'm ready. I have my own little arsenal of songs just waiting for the right artists.

Landing a song on a George Strait album would mean everything to me. It would be the result of four years of coming to Nashville and trying to play their ballgame. Many artists would have given up facing what I had to, trying to reinvent myself as a songwriter pitching my songs.

What do I want from a songwriting career? I want to be accepted as a songwriter, someone who has a talent and knows his craft. My dream is to play my songs to people and have them say, "Wow, we're discovering a whole new Randy Bachman sound." That's what I've been working for.

Randy is a member of Songlink, an Internet songwriters' organization with ties to all the major record labels. Producers e-mail songwriters, alerting them to the style of song they are looking for and for which artists. Writers who have contacts at a label or publisher will be notified in advance what they are looking for, whether it's a ballad or a rocker, for a particular performer. On a recent sojourn in Nashville, Randy met with Byron Hill who writes at Reba McIntyre's Starstruck Productions. He also pitched songs for Tony Brown, the hottest producer in Nashville handling the recording careers of Vince Gill, Reba McIntyre, Wynonna, and George Strait.

"Randy is a true writer and a true musician," attests former Van Halen singer Sammy Hagar. "He has remained true to what he is and what he does. Randy is one of those guys who will be a writer his whole life. It's him; it's what he does. When I heard he was writing in Nashville, I thought that was great. You have to find other avenues if you are a true writer and musician and that's Randy. I love that about him. I wouldn't be surprised if in the next ten years all of a sudden there is this #1 song on the radio, a song I just love to hear, and I come to find out it's a Randy Bachman song. He definitely has that talent and ear for a hook."

I don't take no for an answer. Never give up, that's my philosophy. I know I'm good. I'm not the greatest but I'm not the worst. I believe in myself and my songs. If I get a refusal I analyze it. "Why did this song not work? What has this other writer got that I haven't? How can I take this and use it?" It's a slow learning process, but I think I am writing the best songs of my life right now. There is so much living and life, my own life, in them. I'm writing about realism, my own realism. Before I was writing about other things. Writing with these people all round the world who are pretty much the best in their profession has been an incredible learning experience. Much different than when I wrote songs with Burton Cummings because we wrote separately, then would get together, play each other our songs, pick the best pieces, and stitch them together. It was our own formula and it was unique, but now when I write with someone, we go into a room and they say, "I want to write a song about this," a situation or circumstance and I'll say, "Wow, this happened to me and my wife." Then it

becomes "That's the right sentiment, now let's find the right words to say it like Celine Dion or Boyz 2 Men might say it." I'm writing more intuitively now. I feel I'm a far better writer now and I'm proving it with the material.

"There is an assumption that all this just sort of happens for Randy out of the blue," offers Denise Bachman. "That's certainly not the case. Randy works incredibly hard. He's kicking at those doors and for every one that opens, fifty more don't. He never stops writing songs, never stops recording songs, never stops getting on planes and flying to any place that might offer him an in to have his songs heard. He sends out dozens and dozens of demo CDs. Anyone who thinks once you have made it you can stop doing that is naïve. He's doing as much work to get his music out now as he ever did.

"Randy has complete confidence in his abilities in the areas where he knows he is strong. But he was also able to realize that some of his musical ideas and lyrics were dated, he was starting to repeat himself, so he sought out every young, current songwriter he could find to write with them and learn from them. As a result, his new material is amazing. It's so unlike the old Randy Bachman stuff. When people see Randy's name on the credits they won't believe he wrote them. They are very modern, lyrically adroit, and musically complex. That's because he is humble enough to admit he doesn't have all the answers and accepts that he can learn from others. He never feels 'I'm too good for this.' And that's why he continues to find it exciting."

But while his rock pedigree and solid gold credentials have opened doors in the country market, the notoriety Randy accrued in the seventies can be a double-edged sword when it comes to the current rock scene and the movers and shakers in the industry who shape the latest trends. To them, Randy Bachman is a name from the dusty past in a business that has a very short memory. "Randy is well aware of his reputation and the respect he has earned," maintains Denise, "but he is also acutely conscious of the fact that it doesn't necessarily help or open doors when he is trying to get his new stuff out. He'll encounter 'You're Randy Bachman. You're BTO, power rock, seventies music' and slam goes another door. So he knows it isn't always helpful, especially with younger guys in the business who want to make their own mark as a new executive looking for the latest, hippest thing, to hear about this old guy, old enough to be their father, saying, 'I've got this great new song, can you give it a listen?' He is aware that his reputation can help and it can hinder. It's great to be respected and to be able to go out and still play BTO and Guess Who songs to thousands of people. But it has to be frustrating when you are writing some of the best material you have ever done and trying to open those doors when all people want from you is classic rock."

Still, being a respected rock 'n' roll songwriter does have its perks.

A few years ago I was in London and Tony Hiller, on old friend from Mills Music and our trip to England in 1967, called and asked me, "Would you like to go to a SODS meeting?"

"What's that?"

"The Society of Distinguished Songwriters. All the rich old songwriters from the sixties. We dress up in tuxedos, have a fancy dinner, sit around, and sing our old songs and pat each other on the back. It's quite a party."

"I'm in! I want to experience this."

I rented a tuxedo and as I arrived at this posh restaurant, I discovered I had been seated next to Bruce Welch. Bruce Welch of the Shadows! I couldn't eat. We started talking and he knew who I was. Incredible. I asked him about all my favourite Shadows songs, how they wrote them and recorded them. I was amazed that a lot of what they did was purely accidental, just trying things out in the studio. He gave me his phone number and told me to stay in touch.

At the end of the evening everyone was at the piano; some had acoustic guitars, and they were singing old American rock 'n' roll songs. *Be Bop A Lula, Bye Bye Love*, old Everly Brothers songs, Ricky Nelson stuff. And there I am alongside Bruce Welch, both of us on acoustic guitars, singing the songs we all grew up on. That was the common denominator between a kid from Winnipeg and a kid from Newcastle, England — American rock 'n' roll. I was playing the leads and Bruce was on rhythm. I was playing Hank Marvin to Bruce Welch. We must have gone on for two or three hours until we were all hoarse.

On the evening of May 18, 1997, Randy returned to Winnipeg to take the stage at the Forks, the park at the junction of the Red and Assiniboine Rivers, to join two old friends in a benefit concert televised nationally by CBC. Organized by local actor/singer Tom Jackson, The Red River Relief Concert included a star-studded cast assembled to raise funds for beleaguered rural Manitobans who had suffered damage or loss during what came to be known as The Flood of the Century, surpassing the notorious 1950 flood. Late in the concert, Randy came out onstage with Fred Turner for a three-song mini BTO concert. The two were then joined by Burton Cummings to close the show with an emotionally charged Guess Who set that brought the capacity crowd to its feet.

I know about floods in Winnipeg. Everybody in Winnipeg does. I can recall being let out of school to fill sandbags with my Dad in 1950. I remember floating in a boat down Inkster Boulevard to the front porch of my grandmother's house. Much of West Kildonan was under water up to Main Street. I have photos of that in the video of *Prairie Town* because those are very precious childhood memories for me. Because we lived further west on Seven Oaks and Powers, we didn't have to evacuate but we had sewer backup in the basement.

When I received a call to participate in a flood relief concert, I had no hesitations. But it was a peculiar situation, though, because they asked me who else to contact and Marty Kramer and I suggested Fred Turner.

"How do we get a hold of him? Where does he live?"

"Try the Winnipeg phone book. He lives there."

"Oh really?" They didn't have a clue.

Fred has lived in Winnipeg since the early eighties and they didn't know that? They had to ask two guys out in Vancouver how to find someone living right under their noses. He was being excluded simply because these organizers didn't know Fred was already in the city and I felt badly about that. Fred Turner is an important Winnipegger who helped put the city on the musical map. So I personally invited Fred to join me in my set and he came out and we really rocked. I'm sure his presence helped touch some people to phone in a pledge. Then I performed with Burton and Fred and it was great. We could see the emotion on the faces of the crowd when we played those BTO and Guess Who songs. It obviously meant something special to them. There were tears being shed in the crowd. It made me feel good to give something back to Winnipeg.

Backstage it was good see to Burton and Fred again. It's a little uneasy when you haven't seen people for a long time and things have gone down between you or someone has been quoted in a newspaper saying something that might be hurtful. But when you get together, all that no longer matters and you set that aside for the sake of camaraderie. Fred and I had dinner together the night before the concert and enjoyed each other's company. I still feel a little disjointed at how that whole BTO thing went down. Even though there is still this legal issue hanging over us, we were able to put it aside as adults to play the music again.

Although Randy has never wavered in acknowledging Winnipeg as his hometown, both in interviews and in song, and has willingly given his time to a variety of local causes, the city that gave him his start in music has never reciprocated in kind. Though the latter-day members of the Guess Who were honoured with a hastily organized luncheon and presented with the key to the city mere weeks before breaking up in late 1975, Randy was long gone from that lineup. Always far more vocal in his opinions and never reluctant in expressing them to all and sundry, Burton Cummings has frequently taken umbrage with his hometown for failing to properly fête him or the Guess Who. One of his typical rants in the local media in the early nineties was directed at what he dubbed "Negativapeg" and caused a furor of public indignation that found the singer lampooned in a political cartoon crying over his lack of recognition at home. In the midst of the tumult, a proposed community club named in Burton's honour was submitted as a sort of sacrificial offering to placate his fit of pique. Though the debacle left a bitter taste in many mouths, West End Memorial Community Club, where as a teen Burton's Beatles boots had scuffed its plywood stage with the Deverons and Guess Who, became the Burton Cummings Community Centre.

During the uproar, Randy was solicited for his opinion on the apparent lack of suitable local appreciation for the Guess Who. He respectfully responded, "What does it matter whether they name streets or community clubs after us. It's the music that counts." He stills feels that way.

Someone recently asked me what I thought of naming a new hospital in West Kildonan "The Randy Bachman Memorial Hospital" and I said no. If they want to name it after someone who contributed to the community of West Kildonan or to Winnipeg, name it the Charles Bachman Memorial Hospital. I did nothing for Winnipeg. By the time of my success I was spending more time away from the city. My Dad was dedicated to the community and felt a civic responsibility to serve and get things done that needed doing. Because of him, hospitals and seniors homes were built and new housing developments as well as community centres. Guys like that are the ones who should have things named after them, not Burton and me. Just because we had hit records is hardly sufficient justification for naming something in our honour. There are far more deserving individuals in the city who gave so much more than we ever did. Those people do not receive any awards or gold records or million-dollar cheques, but the least the city can do while they are still alive is to have something commemorative done for them. They deserve the recognition more than I do.

Since his father's passing, Randy has gone out of his way to mend fences within his family. The harsh reality of his own mortality, his role as the new patriarch of the Bachman clan, and the realization that after decades of pursuing his dreams out on the road, there were more important things in his life back home have all impacted on his change in attitude and demeanour. For someone so singularly focused on music since his teen years, it was as if the blinders had been lifted and he could finally see the bigger picture. Reconciliation with brother Tim has resulted in the two forging a partnership in a new, nonmusic-related business venture that holds much promise. Gary, too, has noticed a change in his big brother. Rarely one to participate in family events, Randy last year flew to Winnipeg with Denise and Callianne to attend Gary's son Max's bar mitzvah. Randy was the hit of the party when he got up to play *Takin' Care of Business* with the band and brought Max and his friends up to join him.

For a long time I resented the fact that Gary chose not to follow me to Vancouver. For me the band came first. I eventually got over it. But as I look back I see that if I hadn't met Bruce Allen and instead had given Gary another chance, called him back to join me in Chicago to meet the heads of Mercury Records when the contract was offered, Gary would be a millionaire several times over now. He would have become a successful rock manager.

Gary floundered around for a few years in various sales jobs before landing on his feet in real estate. He found something he was very good at and has built a successful real estate empire in Winnipeg where he is well respected. In latter years he has branched out into pieces of car dealerships and restaurants.

A few years ago, in the early nineties when I was in the process of selling my publishing to Sony and donating my memorabilia to the National Archives and had a hefty chunk of money coming my way, Gary called me. He had a problem with his bank calling in their markers and one of his businesses was in jeopardy. He needed some money to get past this rough spot and knew I was about to come into several million dollars. That money was pretty much spoken for with renovations and expansion to our house in White Rock, putting some away for each of the kids' futures, financing Tal's demos, and purchasing another house for investment. But when he called, I felt I owed him something for missing out on the BTO windfall. He had a piece of the little company we had with Brave Belt back in Winnipeg, but was cut out when he chose not to come with us. Here I was, his big brother, and I felt not only a filial obligation but also a sense of payback to him in some way for the time he put in on our behalf with Brave Belt. There couldn't have been a BTO without Brave Belt coming first and Gary was a part of it. So I lent him the amount he needed. And Gary paid it all off on schedule and it was over.

In the end, I felt a real sense of satisfaction at being in a position to be able to help out my brother. That money should first be for the good of my immediate family, then after that is taken care of my next priority is my other family, my brothers and parents.

"It was *my* brother who helped us out, my partners and I, and I felt good about that," acknowledges Gary. "And I think Randy felt good about it too. It was his way of offering a back door apology to me. It has come full circle. We are closer now than we have been in years. Age will do that to people. Family is family. Whenever he comes through town now, he calls me and we get together. We e-mail each other several times a month. It's terrific. We talk like we are still fifteen and sixteen. When he was in town for the Pan Am Games reunion, we got together and yakked until the wee hours of the morning. It was wonderful. I got to meet his grandchildren for the first time then. It had gotten to a point where his kids were asking him, 'What's Uncle Gary like? What's Max like?' I knew his children, but not well. I never attended any of his children's weddings. There wasn't that closeness of family to warrant going then. But this is a real transition. I think maybe he is coming around to realizing there are more important things in life than music and money. Family is important. The closeness he admired in Lorayne's family years ago he didn't have for so long in his own family. He had distanced himself from us.

"Randy's way of dealing with things, his way of survival, may appear callous to others," Gary surmises, "but over the years he has had to build up a shell around him because of the fame and the money. He had a huge responsibility with all those kids. I don't envy him or his life. It's difficult being Randy Bachman sometimes. I love him, I'm proud of him, he's one of the best guitar players in the world, but I wouldn't want to be him for one minute."

Reconciliation with youngest brother Robbie appears remote at this point in time. With litigation still ongoing, Randy and Robbie remain estranged. The boys' mother still holds out hope though. "For a while there was friction between all four boys," sighs Anne Bachman. "I didn't intervene because they had to work it out themselves. There was no sense me trying to force it. Now Tim and Randy are close, and Randy and Gary too. But Randy and Robbie aren't close. Robbie didn't talk to me for a good five years after my husband died. I would send him birthday cards and Christmas cards and now he is in touch with me and we are pretty close. He has a nice wife now, a very nice girl, which, I think, has changed him a bit." None of his three brothers was invited to Robbie's wedding. Tim was asked to drive his parents to and from the reception but not to attend.

"You would think those two could get past all this," suggests former BTO manager Bruce Allen. "But somehow they haven't been able to. And it's between blood, which is sadder. Even Burton and Randy seem to have gotten past their problems better than Robbie and Randy. Robbie thinks Randy screwed him but if it wasn't for Randy, Robbie Bachman might never have drummed in a rock 'n' roll band in his entire life. He didn't get a job in another band when he left. No one ever called Robbie up to do a session or join a band, ever. BTO was his one and only band."

Despite years of residue from a bitter divorce and custody battle, Randy has worked hard to be a factor in his children's lives. It hasn't always been easy. While several stayed with him and Denise, others eventually ended up returning to their mother and as a result remain closer to her than their father. "It's kind of a shame the kids aren't really united like we would be had we all grown up in the same house," laments eldest son Tal Bachman. "We, my siblings and I, are all close to each other and close to my Dad," offers Brigham, "but there are degrees of closeness. Some are closer than others. We all love each other and love him, but there is a rocky past behind us and some issues that still aren't resolved." Nevertheless, Tal acknowledges his father's affection for his children. That love has now extended to the next generation of Bachman, Randy's ten grandchildren. "He is very tender-hearted. He really has a soft spot for the grandchildren and has been generous to them over the years for sure."

True to the patterns of life, kids grow up and leave the nest. We went through some really happy and some pretty tough times together, and there was a difficult transitional period. But through it all, my children have managed to maintain a healthy relationship with both me and their mother. That is to be commended. Many have gone on to college, most served their missions for the Mormon Church, have gotten married, and have come back home bringing the greatest gift of all, grandchildren.

Tally lives fairly close by — not as close as I would like — in the Vancouver vicinity so I see him and his children whenever I am coming or going through the area. He is doing very well with his career.

Kezia has two children and lived in Utah for many years. Lorelei served her mission in France and now lives in Alberta with her husband and two children. Her husband is a very brilliant man who has helped me with my web sites. She has a very happy life. Bannatyne is in college in Utah studying languages and is fluent in Spanish. Like Tally, she served her mission in Argentina.

Emilie spent most of her life with her mother because she was the youngest and stayed with her mother after the divorce. She never lived with me. Emilie and I have a long distance relationship and I would see her during limited visitation periods, which unfortunately are false living circumstances at the best of times. But I can't change it, that's life. We stay in touch and she is coming up to stay with us this summer. Brigham came to live with me later and Kezia went back and forth between Lorayne and me during her rebellious years.

All my kids are very musical and have incredible singing voices. Kezia had the opportunity to study opera in New York at the Metropolitan Opera on a scholarship, but chose modelling instead. Lorelei has a beautiful voice, more like a Karen Carpenter voice, and writes songs, and Bannatyne also has a great voice. When my five daughters get together and sing, you cannot believe it. It's like the Lennon Sisters or McGuire Sisters, that natural family harmony. They do Mamas and Papas or Andrews Sisters and it's incredibly angelic and glorious, whether it's a Beach Boys song or a carol. But I can never get them together long enough.

When you have a large household, six or eight kids, you need almost a military-like structure and routine to maintain any semblance of order. Otherwise it becomes chaos. Brigham fought that system as did Demian. It's tough enough trying to maintain a regimen with a large brood but to have two kids going against the grain all the time, continuously, is extremely stressful. Kids thrive on attention, even negative attention, just for the sheer joy of getting us riled up. That happened with both Brigham and Demian. But after coming through a particularly difficult time, Demian has come round and is now a brilliant computer whiz in Los Angeles working in graphics and motion capture.

Brigham fought every rule we had. It got to a point where we had to go through that tough love thing with him. He ended up going to live with his mother and after running into trouble down in Utah was sent to Guam to stay for a time on a military base there. That became a turning point in his life. He couldn't rebel against the strict military structure and came out of it with a sense of self-discipline and training in swimming instruction as a lifeguard.

After we received custody of this large clan, it was tough for each of them to find their place in this new family structure with a new mother figure. They didn't want a new mother; they had their own mother who was just fine with them and that's who they wanted. It was difficult and awkward. Denise thought that before we got too old it was important that we have a child of our own. That child would be someone we could all belong to, the other kids, hers and mine, and be something to bring us all together as a unit. So when Callianne was born it was a joyous moment for all of us. She did bring us all together. She has made us a family again.

For most of my children, I was away out on the road much of their early lives and I missed those important moments seeing their development day by day. I was in and out of their lives and their mother raised them. When Callianne was born, I was in a lull in my career and was able to be home for her and to take a direct hand in raising her. Denise had decided to earn her university degree so I made Callianne breakfast, took her to pre-school and school every day, picked her up, and read to her each night. As a result, we really bonded. We had all these books from the other kids who had grown up, and each night I would lie down beside her and read to her. It progressed from the Richard Scary children's stories to more complex books like the Hardy Boys until one day she started bringing home books in French because she was in French immersion. The first ones were easy for me "le chien et la chat" which I could handle, but before long I couldn't read them. Callianne then said the most incredible thing to me: "I'll read them to *you*, Dad." I sat there with tears streaming down my face as she read the story in French then translated it for me.

From the age of nineteen, I never had a birthday at home until I was thirty-eight. So on my thirty-eighth birthday, I celebrated my twentieth birthday. As a travelling musician you learn to adjust, to celebrate those kinds of events on days off, to have a birthday party on the next available night off. Now, with so many children and grandchildren, I try to at least call on their birthdays, if not be there.

I recently received a card from my daughter Emilie who is on her mission and it said, "The best things in life aren't things." How true. No matter how many guitars I have or what kind of car I drive or house I live in, they don't mean anything. They are just things; they don't matter. What does matter is your family.

"Some of the kids are still working through issues," admits Kezia, "but we love our Mom and Dad whether we agree with the decisions they made or not. Each of us has worked through the divorce in his or her own way. I don't know if we ever really felt like a family at my Dad's house after the divorce. I would come back to my Mom's in Utah and say, 'It's just like a bunch of people living in the same house together but it's not a family.' But that family bond exists now. We've grown closer now as adults than we were when we were younger. Back then it was everyone for him- or herself."

"He's a far better granddad than I ever remember him being a dad," laughs Kezia. "I've never seen him in a temper with the grandkids. He is always kind and loving and understanding. When I was growing up he sometimes was quick to temper and I was never sure if he was going to be angry or not. But he had a lot more stress back then. He missed us growing up and doesn't want to do that with the grandkids. He's pretty good at it now."

In 1993, Tal joined his father's road band on drums, ultimately co-producing Randy's *MERGE* album. "It wasn't like employer-employee," he admits, "never hierarchical. I had a good time on the road and it wasn't awkward at all." Having spent the most time living with his father, the two enjoy a close personal relationship with Randy encouraging his eldest son's musical ambitions.

Although Kezia majored in opera at college ("This is a rockin', pickin' family and I was the black sheep opera girl," she laughs), it comes as no surprise that one of Randy's offspring would choose a career in rock 'n' roll. Yet for Tal, the route was somewhat circuitous. "Dad was never really overt about me following him in music until I went to college years later," he relates. "Then he would call me up and tell me 'What are you doing wasting your time? Why don't you quit and form a rock 'n' roll band?' That may seem contrary for most parents but that's kind of typical for Dad. When I was younger he didn't consciously leave records out for me to follow a trail. It was never a pushy thing like, 'Did you practise your guitar today?' Instead it was more like two guys who played guitar that happened to live in the same house. I guess we had a bond that most teenagers don't have with their father."

Following his stint in Randy's band, Tal determined to pursue his own musical ambitions with the full support, encouragement, and financial resources of his father. "Dad has helped me," he acknowledges. "He loaned me money; I used his studio and engineer. My Mom and my sisters thought I was really making a mistake going through a period of dependence on my Dad, using his studio, and playing for him. But how many Dads and sons work together? Millions. Who cares? I was going to roll the dice and go for it. So far it's been working out." It seems the dice have turned up sevens for Tal Bachman whose self-titled debut album on Sony, released in the spring of 1999, garnered rave reviews around the world and spawned a hit single with *She's So High*. By all industry predictions, Tal Bachman's career appears set for a long and healthy run. Two recent Juno Awards served to underscore his recent success. His Dad is justifiably proud.

I helped finance Tal's demos and gave him the use of my new studio. I tried engineering, but ended up accidentally erasing a guitar track. I was just learning. When it's your own track that's okay, but when it's someone else giving their all you can't make that kind of mistake and say "Oops." There were a few jokes back and forth about that one.

I am very proud of him. He has a great career ahead of him. We're just seeing step one on his ladder to success. What I'm proudest of is how hard he worked, and that he didn't give up and persevered. There were times when he felt like throwing in the towel, but then he would receive a phone call from Jeff Lynne or words of encouragement from Ringo Starr or Neil Young liking his tape. Those moments kept him going. When he landed his record deal, he didn't slack off. He worked even harder. He isn't just talking the talk — he's walking the walk as well.

What did he learn from me? Probably the same thing I learned from my Dad and that was a strong work ethic. We were both fortunate that our vocations happened to be our passions. So that makes it a lot easier to do. Tally has that same work ethic. I have to assume he indirectly learned something about music from me, though I didn't give him any directions and he never really took any formal lessons. Music was just always around from the time he was born. I have seen him mention in interviews that when I went away on the road he had this incredible record collection from Chopin to the Beatles to Keith Jarrett to Van Halen and that became his library, his place of discovery.

I recall coming back from a tour when he was about fourteen and seeing all my Beatles albums scattered over the floor. Not just the legitimate pressings but my rare Japanese releases and German pressings, my entire collection was in disarray. I found myself welling up with anger because they had been left out where the littler kids could have stepped on them. That was sacrilege to me, the original Beatles fan par excellence. I knew it was Tally, so I went to find him and give him a piece of my mind.

"Have you been playing my Beatles albums?!"

"Yeah Dad, and they're so incredible. They mean the world to me to listen to them."

I had to bite my tongue and couldn't say anything other than to sheepishly suggest, "Could you at least put them away when you're done?"

If they meant that much to him how could I get angry? They meant the same to me, too.

Tally's songs are extremely literate and intelligent. Mine are more "cave man club 'em over the head" songs, whereas his are well thought out and everything means something. One of the things I admire about him is that he is writing from personal experience. He is baring his soul and that's why his music is connecting with kids. When you put your heart on your sleeve and write about your grandfather dying like he did in *If You Sleep* and someone tells you they don't like the song, it's like a personal stab in your heart. It wounds you. For most of my early writing, I was afraid to do that. It takes a very special person to be able to write those kinds of songs.

It is inevitable that Tal gets asked about me in interviews and he handles it very well. It's been tough trying to break out from under my shadow, but I think he has managed to do it on his own terms without riding on the Bachman name. Maybe in a few years

I'll be asked "Are you related to Tal Bachman?"

"Yeah, I'm his older brother."

"Dad can be reluctant to share his inner most feelings in his writing," muses Tal. "Although he generally doesn't write personal songs, Dad does have a few songs that have never made it onto any album that even he has a tough time getting through playing the song. He has played these for me. He doesn't say anything and he doesn't need to say anything. I just know what they are about."

Regarding the constant questions about his famous father, Tal confesses, "It comes up first in every single interview. 'What was it like growing up with a rock star as your father?' You just have to accept it as a given." Nevertheless, the persistent references to Randy's musical legacy underscore to his son the role his father has played in shaping the lives of so many people and perhaps the weight of carrying the Bachman name to a new generation. "I recently did a US tour and at every stop I would get these guys, forty-five years old, come up to me and say with complete sincerity, 'Hey man, I don't want to bug you but I still love your Dad's music.' For all these hardworking guys, Dad's music has become the soundtrack to a portion of their lives. They fell in love and got married or got divorced to his music, to those songs. I hear that every day. Every kid in Canada grew up to his music."

While Tal has enjoyed success in the family business, Brigham has yet to make his mark. As a guitar player and writer, he finds it far more difficult saddled with a famous father. "The Bachman name offers tremendous advantages in terms of the connections my father has," notes Brigham, who has recorded some demos at his father's studio and served as his guitar tech on the road. "But it can also be a liability in terms of people's expectations. If my Dad was an optician maybe I might have a better chance. It can offer a little sunshine or a rain cloud but it is always hanging over me. Every young man seeks the approval of his father and Tal and I have sought that from him. It hasn't always been easy. Dad and I have played together on the road and he and Tal have worked together, but I think it would be great for the three of us to play together some time. I would like to see that happen someday. I admire both my Dad and Tal as my role models and mentors."

Randy and Denise recently built their own dream house in the Gulf Islands in the Strait of Georgia between the British Columbia mainland and Vancouver Island, where they took up residence in the late 1990s. "One of the things I found charming about the island community," notes Denise, "is its post-hippie ethos and lifestyle. For me it was like being back in San Francisco's Haight-Ashbury in the sixties. It's not quite Randy's thing because he is very conservative, the prairie boy from the fifties, but he gets along fine with everyone there."

At home on the island, Randy spends his time in his recording studio, writing and recording demos of his new songs. Music remains his focus. "Randy doesn't have downtime," smiles Denise. "If you want to find him, he's up in his studio, conducting business, or out on the road. He has always had a recording studio in his house so that he is never away from work. The minute he gets a thought he's off to the studio to lay it down. He watches a little television; his favourite show is *Jeopardy*. He answers all the music questions and I answer the rest. But we don't share a lot of common activities outside the home other than vacations. I have my own diversions — I play in a local Celtic/Irish group, tend my lovely garden, and study the art of basket weaving, which sounds funny but it is quite complex to become a master weaver.

"Sometimes I think Randy tends to forget that I was a singer and had a career," offers Denise with a shrug. "He sees me as his wife not someone who can sing or write. We collaborated early on but he doesn't like to work with me. He once told me how every other rock 'n' roll relationship where the couple work together and live together has never worked out. They always end up splitting up. He doesn't want that to happen to us. Our marriage is so important to him that he does not want to jeopardize it with a working relationship. But every once in a while he will ask me to contribute some vocals to his demos."

I find that playing with Denise's Celtic band once in a while is the most soothing, wonderful experience. I just play rhythm guitar while they bang their bodhrans and play accordion, mandolin, and tin whistle singing all their Irish songs in Gaelic. I don't even know what they are singing but I sit there and play this stuff and it's just for fun. It brings a simple joy back to me that I can't get any other way. My life now is geared toward writing songs, so my fun is on weekends playing the open mike at the local inn and things like that, where nobody cares what you are wearing or what you look like. I'm lucky I have that balance.

"He's fun," adds Denise, "he'll do pretty much whatever anyone wants him to do because he doesn't have a lot of interests outside of music so everything else is new and different and he'll go along with it. None of us is much interested in sports or athletics so we don't do much of that. I do have trouble forcing him on a boat though. He doesn't like boats and we live on an island! He'll take the ferry but forget sailing or canoeing. He likes to go sightseeing and he loves to do things with the children and grandchildren."

One of Randy's diversions is calligraphy. Each year he personalizes his Christmas cards to close friends in his own hand-drawn calligraphy. He has recently been approached by Graham Nash of the Hollies and Crosby, Stills, and Nash to write out the lyrics to several of his best-known songs in calligraphic form for a series of limited edition lithographs to be marketed by Nash's company Manuscript Originals through Niemann Marcus.

He also had an original handwritten copy of the lyrics to *You Ain't Seen Nothin' Yet* auctioned off for charity in the UK for Hits under the Hammer, in the company of the likes of the Beatles and David Bowie. Though the charity auction focused on British artists, Randy was asked to contribute *You Ain't Seen Nothin' Yet* given its continuing appeal in the UK. A British group named Bus Stop recently recorded a dance/rap version of *You Ain't Seen Nothin' Yet* released in the UK. Randy's voice was sampled in the song and he was flown to London to appear in the video that recreated the popular Nicey and Smashy skit. The record reached #12.

The respect and esteem Randy is accorded in the Canadian music community has led to several unique alliances. When country trio Farmer's Daughter cut a version of *Let It Ride*, they invited Randy to play on the track. Guitarist/singer Gordie Johnson of Toronto-based blues rock group Big Sugar sought Randy out as a collaborator. "It's easy to work with Randy because there is no pretentiousness about him," notes Gordie, a respected guitar player in his own right. "He is just a guy who is happy to make music. People always talk about his songs but I think his ability on the guitar is highly underrated. He'll sit all afternoon with you playing guitar and he can play every style of music imaginable — Chet Atkins finger picking, Lenny Breau jazz, Link Wray–style rock, blues, surf, you name it. He can play like Neil Young, but Neil can't play like Randy. Any music that has passed through the guitar, Randy can play it."

Award-winning Canadian group Prairie Oyster even conceived a song with Randy in mind before asking him to grace the recording with his patented sound. "I absolutely had Randy in mind when I wrote *Canadian Sunrise*," admits the Oyster's Joan Besen. "I had always loved him as a player and writer. We all loved the Guess Who and BTO in Canada. Randy has that great balance between power and sweetness in his playing. It always struck me how he could come up with the big power-chord, goofy rock anthems at the same time as having this jazz-ier style with things like *Undun* and *Looking Out for #1*.

"We were halfway through recording our album when we decided to do the old song *Canadian Sunset* as an instrumental just for fun. As I was driving back from the studio one night I thought to myself 'Wouldn't it be neat to have the album go from sunrise to sunset, book-ending the album?' So my challenge was to write a song about a Canadian sunrise. Since we were mining Canadian influences I imme-diately thought of the Guess Who, the imagery of wheatfield soul. And

I thought 'If I were Randy Bachman, what kind of power chords would I play?' and the chords came to me right away. I literally wrote the song while driving home. I phoned up Randy and asked if he would like to play on it and he, of course, said 'Yes.' The wonderful thing about Randy is he loves to play. I didn't have to sell him on it.

"All I did was sketch out roughly what I wanted him to do but I didn't want to direct him. I wanted him to put his trademark sound and style on the track, the classic Randy Bachman thing. Randy recorded his part at his studio and when it came back we were all so excited. It was like a Christmas present from Randy. We put on the tape and there it all was — the power chords, the hook line, the melodic solo played with an octave climb, the ride out with the hook line, and throughout it all the whole Randy Bachman tone. It couldn't have been more perfect. It was so unmistakably Randy. It was such a thrill." Randy later appeared in the video and sat in with the group for several performances.

Over the winter of 1998–99, Randy produced band member Colin Arthur's marvellous debut album *LIVING ON DREAMS* at his home studio. Joining Randy and Colin on the sessions were latter-day Guess Who member Don McDougall, now a member of Randy's touring band, and an old and dear friend, Garry Peterson. "During the course of recording Colin Arthur's album, Randy was very kind to me," offers Garry, "and I said a lot of emotional things to him. I said to him 'Wouldn't this be something if this could have been the original band doing this?' and he agreed. Something I have seen in the last few years, especially since making that album with Colin, is a great change in Randy. It's like he is trying to make amends for what he did back then. I think he realizes he was wrong. I don't feel I need the satisfaction of having him tell me he was wrong, it's more for him a healing process. The truth is the truth. God, family, and friends are the most important thing in life. Hopefully Randy sees that now. It isn't all about money."

Throughout much of his adult life Randy has battled his weight problem. Although he has never indulged in drugs and he gave up alcohol some thirty-five years ago, he understands the power of addiction. Randy's addiction is eating. "One of the things we had to do during the custody wrangling," Denise points out, "was take a battery of personality tests including the MMPI which has hundreds and hundreds of questions that inventory your personality and chart it. Randy scored right off the charts on the addiction quotient, which made us realize it was a good thing he never did get involved in drugs because he probably couldn't have stopped. But the one thing that gets expressed in his addictive behaviour is food. He does have a hard time stopping when certain foods are involved. He is aware of his predilection to compulsive eating, especially his weakness for baked foods. If he stays away from those things he is okay, but in his business you go to all these events where food is spread out for free everywhere and it is tough to turn away. He is a compulsive person especially when it comes to music, but on the other hand that's what made him so successful. But even though he has that side to his personality he does possess a very strong will."

Kezia has suffered weight problems like me. When we were in Winnipeg recently, she and I underwent a blood analysis which tells you what foods you should and shouldn't eat, what is good for you and not good for you. We found out we were both addicted to carbohydrates. To that point in my life no matter what I did, no matter what I ate or didn't eat, I endlessly gained weight. I've been on every diet there is and they never worked. I continued to gain weight. I couldn't do it on my own. Denise would try diet after diet and I would last a couple of days then "screw it" and eat an entire pie. I was a carbohydrates junkie. It was no different than heroin. I would go fill up my gas tank at a gas station and go in and fill up my own tank with twelve chocolate bars. I was out of control and could never go more than a few days before breaking down.

I think that is why I am more sympathetic now toward anyone

with substance abuse problems. I understand what it is like. And as a result, I am more patient about it now.

"When I saw my Dad at the Pan Am Games," Kezia recalls, "and they started playing *No Time*, the words to that song hit me. My reaction was so different from everyone around me. I looked up at my Dad onstage and thought he wouldn't be around much longer on this earth if he didn't do something about his health. There was no time left for him. Everyone thought I was crying because the old band was together again, but I was really crying thinking I was going to lose my Dad if something didn't happen. I wanted to save his life."

Kezia has taken it upon herself to get me in shape by becoming my own personal trainer. We joined a gym and she started cooking for me. Since we started together I have lost forty-five pounds. I feel so blessed that she is sacrificing her life to get me healthy and keep me alive. To be three pant sizes smaller now is quite an accomplishment, and every day I look forward to working out. When I look in the mirror I still see a big fat guy but I know I'm getting better and have a pattern that I am sticking to. It's been a life-changing experience for me and given me a whole new lease on life.

Every book I read about overeating over the years claimed it was attributed to some deep dark secret in your psyche. I would be searching my brain trying to figure out "Did I steal an O Henry bar when I was six? Did I break a window with a baseball? What have I done?" Nothing. There is no mystery; it is just the way my body is. I am addicted to carbohydrates.

The first day I went to the gym it was like that old seventies expression "Boogie 'til you puke." After just a few minutes I felt like throwing up. It was such a violent attack on my body that it tried to reject it. Lifting the weights and riding the stationary bicycle just about killed me, but it began to get easier and I am into a pattern now.

"This is the most positive, exciting development in his personal life in years," maintains Tal, who echoes the resounding support from Randy's family for his recent health regimen. "He goes every day and works out and is really serious about it. He told me it has been a life-changing experience for him. Already he is noticeably healthier-looking and feeling much better. This is a big deal for him."

Having conquered the real music world, Randy set his sights on the imaginary world. On February 6, 2000, he and Fred Turner became the first Canadian rock stars to be immortalized in cartoon form, making their debut as animated characters on an episode of the popular television series *The Simpsons*. It seems that BTO was Homer Simpson's favourite band. The group was scheduled to make an appearance in his fictitious hometown of Springfield. The experience was great fun for Randy.

I came home from a tour in mid-1999 and there was a fax waiting for me from Sony Music asking if I knew anything about The Simpsons television show wanting to license *Takin' Care of Business* and *You Ain't Seen Nothin' Yet*. I faxed them back saying, "Great, let them use them." I figured maybe they were going to have the songs playing in the background in Moe's bar. The next day Marty called to tell me a script had arrived for me from *The Simpsons*.

"What?! Send it over right now."

I read through it and it was absolutely incredible. I called the producers to say I was in and they arranged to fly me down to tape my part. They treated me like I was Elvis — a limo at the airport, suite at a fine hotel, and everybody acting like I was Tom Cruise or someone. A very classy organization. They treated Fred Turner the same. He and I were the only ones in the band with speaking parts.

I was coached by the director on how to deliver my lines. They record your vocal first and as you do so, they secretly videotape you so the animators can get your body movements. This is done alone; you don't record your part with the ensemble cast because it would be too distracting. I would have been totally ga ga as out of the ordinary-looking person standing beside me comes the voice of Homer Simpson or from the lady next to me emerges Lisa. I later attended a table read with the entire cast and was dumbstruck. I couldn't have done it with them present.

The script required me to say "Hello Springfield" as if I was walking out onstage. So I said, "Hello Springfield." The director then came over and said to me, "Are you playing for an audience of one person? You're on stage, it's a concert."

"Hello Springfield!" I tried adding a bit more force.

"Randy, there's twenty thousand people in the audience."

"HELLO SPRINGFIELD!!"

"Perfect. Give me three more like that."

As the story line went, I come out and say, "Hello Springfield" and Homer says to Bart, "Watch these guys, they're BTO!" and Bart says, "BTO?" Homer tells him, "Yeah, they're Canada's answer to ELO. We didn't have a lot of time in the seventies so we only used initials."

I did all my lines alone and when I was done they gave me a big box of Simpsons merchandise for myself and my kids and sent me on my way.

Denise, Callianne, and I were later invited to the season premiere of *The Simpsons* in LA that fall and it was the Mel Gibson episode. We had a great time. Then on December 23rd I received a package by courier, a Christmas present from Homer Simpson with a card and a little shiny black shopping bag with a dog tag on the handle that read: "Merry Christmas, Randy Bachman, *The Simpsons* 1999." It's beautiful. Inside was a Swiss Army stopwatch with *The Simpsons* on the face in a beautiful leather case with the words "Merry Christmas from the Simpsons."

"True immortality," smiles Prairie Oyster's Joan Besen, "is being characterized in a cartoon and showing up as a clue in the *New York Times* crossword puzzle. Randy has achieved both. And people know enough about him to recognize him or answer the question. That's astounding to me. And the charm of it is I don't think Randy sees how significant or how big he really is."

Randy remains a staunch Canadian booster and endorses a variety of causes including environmental concerns and the plight of the family farm. He has donated songs to charity albums and recently performed at a benefit concert in aid of the Canadian farm community where, in typical Randy Bachman fashion, he supported several artists including Prairie Oyster, Big Sugar, and Burton Cummings as well as performing his own set. "It's so funny how he can be playing with all these artists and be astounding without being distracting," marvels Joan Besen. "If the point of him being there is to make you sound better, he's there without taking the spotlight away from you. Totally supportive. He's like a musical chameleon. Then he can step forward and do his own set and step back and support someone else."

Randy is a ceaseless flag-waver for Canadian music, championing our homegrown talent at every turn and lobbying the government for a fair royalty rate for writers and performers. On the other hand, he feels the Canadian government has gone about its support of its own talent in a contrary manner.

The evolution of the Canadian music industry over the last forty years has been remarkable. The Canadian music scene today evolved from so many regional pockets across the country that had their own unique artists, influences, and sounds. That's why today we have such a diversity of styles and sounds from coast to coast. It took a long time for us to have a truly national music industry and a star system, but things like the *Music Hop/Let's Go* weekly showcases from each major region helped to break down those barriers and create national markets. Kids in

Winnipeg could see and hear artists from Toronto, Vancouver, Montreal, and Halifax. For the Guess Who, it meant national exposure and name recognition beyond the prairies. Every kid in every little town knew who we were or Anne Murray, Gordon Lightfoot, and others.

When the CRTC came into effect in 1971, they had to fill the airwaves with Canadian content, which gave a further boost to a national scene. Initially it was a lot of Lightfoot and Murray and didn't do much for the Guess Who or BTO, but gradually it encouraged record companies to sign Canadian talent and get it played on the radio. Much Music has done the same by setting a priority of airing and promoting Canadian talent so artists like I Mother Earth, Sloan, Natalie McMaster, Moist, and Our Lady Peace have national exposure. It's good music; people like it and these artists can now tour across Canada and make a living right here. Much Music has become a unifying thread for Canadian music by creating a Canadian star system.

I was such a Canadian patriot that when I had the opportunity when we were living in Lynden, I didn't go down and say I wanted to become an American citizen. I just couldn't renounce my Canadian citizenship. When I moved back to Canada in the early eighties, I gave up my green card and now it's a pain every time I come down to the States to write songs. Even though I am not really working per se, I'm writing, I get the odd customs officer at the border who retorts, "Yeah, you are working and you need a permit." I do have permits when I am touring with my band, but if I have a week booked delivering demo CDs of my songs and somebody gets it in his head that I'm working, I need a permit. If I had my green card, which has evolved into a pink card now, there would be no problem. A lot of my kids live in the States. Tal is lucky. He has dual citizenship. He was born in Canada, but his mother was American so when we lived in the States he went in and got his naturalized citizenship papers. He has two passports and two residences. So do my other kids.

Years ago, I went through all sorts of tax shelter options with my accountants and tax lawyers looking here and there around the world. I seriously considered taking up official residence in places like the Isle of Man or Liechtenstein. But at the end of the day I realized: what climate do I like? The West Coast of Canada. Once you have paid for all your tax dodges, the extra residences and the extra accountants and lawyers, you are just breaking even anyway. So just pick where you want to live and pay the fare. And that's what I'm doing in Canada. But I'm lucky, I make a good living.

The Canadian government goes out of its way on the front end of your career offering FACTOR grants to produce videos, CIDO grants to record, and legislation to play your music on the radio. My pet peeve, however, is that when you achieve your success and make your millions of dollars, they tax you so heavily you are tempted to move to the US and not pay taxes in Canada. It's a self-defeating situation. If they would only lower the taxes in Canada, think of the money that would go back into Canada if Celine Dion, Alanis Morissette, Bryan Adams, Brad Roberts, and Shania Twain moved back to Canada? It would encourage others who are successful to stay here.

"Randy Bachman ranks right up there at the top of Canadian rock 'n' roll," maintains music journalist Larry LeBlanc. "He is a Canadian music icon. He's the only guy that has successfully launched two international acts from a Canadian base. They were international in the context of what Canadian music was at that time. Does it compare today with say Celine Dion, Shania Twain, or Bryan Adams? No. But in the context of the time it was quite a feat. He actually did it three times: first with the Chad Allan version of the Guess Who and *Shakin' All Over*, then with the *These Eyes* Guess Who with Burton, and a third time with Bachman-Turner Overdrive. Nobody's done that up here, ever. I used to say nobody has nine lives except Randy Bachman. Quite frankly it wouldn't surprise me tomorrow for him to have another hit record. He has an unparalleled string of successes. Randy has a boyish enthusiasm toward rock music that few others have. He had it back when I first met him in 1965 with *Shakin' All Over* and he still has it.

"Randy is an unlikely father figure in Canadian rock, but he is a link back to the early days. Randy is viewed as an authentic rock 'n' roller. He has an integrity about him. Burton Cummings has one of the finest rock 'n' roll voices that I have ever heard and he should have become a worldwide star on a level of say an Elton John. But for a lot of reasons he didn't. Randy achieved his goals. He secured his position in rock music."

Although Randy continues to be a practising Mormon faithful to all its tenets and determined to lead a good life under the Mormon doctrine, his commitment to the Church has waned slightly in recent years not due to any conflict of conscience but rather to expediency. "We were active Mormons the whole time we had the kids," admits Denise, "but I grew away from the Church after the kids left and now am no longer a member. Randy is still a member though not as involved as he once was. His kids are still very committed to the Church though. That's the way they were all brought up. The older ones all served their mission, even the girls, which is rare. The youngest, Emilie, is currently completing hers. Their mother is a very strong believer. The Church is the centre of her life."

I am not as active in the Church as I used to be because Denise isn't going and doesn't want Callianne to attend each week and be indoctrinated. She wants Callianne to find her own way, which I kind of agree with because that's what I had done. It has been heartbreaking for me though, because we made the commitment for time and eternity. Denise is okay with it and maybe someday she will come back. She simply responds, "Don't worry about it. We'll always be together. We don't need this to love one another."

That's true. People don't need a marriage certificate to be married. For some, that piece of paper means everything. But there are no guarantees in life. I thought I had it all with Lorayne forever — marriage, kids, the Church, sealed in heaven, but it all exploded in my face.

My life is a little different now with Denise, but we are both very happy and whether or not she is a member of the Church, she at least has the grounding and understanding of it. I still hope things will change, but if they don't that's okay too because she restored my life at a time when I thought I was doomed to live a miserable existence forever. I felt I did not deserve any more happiness, but she revived that in me. She healed that part of me.

Whether he attends church regularly or not will hardly alter the basic fabric of who Randy Bachman is. Long before he received his instruction in the Mormon faith, Randy had a solid grounding in the morality of Christian beliefs with a clear sense of right and wrong. On his journey through life in pursuit of his dreams Randy has left a few casualties strewn along the roadway; however, he has always been guided by his own innate sense of morality and justice. Though some may quibble with his methods, few would challenge the integrity of his motives. He is a moral man in an amoral business. "Randy is an honourable guy," attests former manager and confidante Bruce Allen. Big Sugar's Gordie Johnson has a deep respect for Randy. "There has never been any scandal swirling around Randy. He's never been arrested. He's not making a comeback after going through rehab. He's a guy who never succumbed to any of that. He has a nice family and when you visit him it's like going home. It's like going to visit your uncle. I haven't met that many musicians in my life that I have admiration for on a personal level. It's easy to admire someone on a musical level, but many of them you wouldn't trust with your car keys or bring them home to meet your family. To meet someone like Randy is so refreshing. It's enviable. With Randy, you get the feeling 'Yeah, the good guys do win sometimes. I want to be like that.'"

As the elder statesman of Canadian rock 'n' roll, a title he accepts with some reluctance, Randy just keeps rockin' along. His life-long commitment to music remains as firm as ever. "It's just instinct with him," notes son Tal. "I don't think he knows why he continues to do it, he just does it. He is all about music. He can't stop. He has a million ideas and wants to get things done. He's had successes and failures but he just keeps on."

Smiles Kezia, "When I was in college and people would find out who my Dad was, they would say 'Your Dad's a rock 'n' roll legend!' And I would think, 'Yeah, whatever. He's just my Dad.' It's only been in the last few years and I'll be in a grocery store and one of his numerous hits will come on and it'll catch me off guard and I'll think 'Whoa. That's my Dad.' It totally dawns on me that he really is a legend. They're still playing his music and I'm almost thirty!' It always surprises me. I don't even know who Prairie Oyster are, but I was watching videos recently and they came on and there was my Dad. I just thought 'Holy cow, there he is!'"

I keep peaking, then something new comes along. Every couple of years out of the blue, something will pop up. I thought it was all over after the last incarnation of BTO in the late eighties then *ANY ROAD* came along and the opportunity to pull Neil Young into it. After that came the call from Ringo Starr and that was unbelievable. When it ended, a couple of years later came the Pan Am Games offer completely out of left field.

If you ask me what I am doing next month or next year, my calendar is full. I have songwriting, publishing, recording, touring, other side business plans — they are all there. But whatever requires my immediate attention or is the most exciting thing that stimulates me or keeps me alive creatively, then that's what I'll do. If the phone rings today and it's something I'd like to do, I do it.

Do you want to do a Guess Who reunion? Or a BTO thing? Or tour with Ringo? Or come to Nashville and write? I can just stop everything and do it. I have this restless wandering spirit that is creative, and when one thing doesn't go I've got these other things going on. If something doesn't work out it's not the end of my life. There is always something new and that is what is so exciting.

Years ago I became fed up with hearing the saying "Where is he now?" I made up my mind that no one would ever say, "Where is Randy Bachman now?" "Where is he now? He's guesting on the new Prairie Oyster album, he's playing with Big Sugar, he's writing in London with Cher's writer who did *Believe*, he's producing, he's in Nashville. He's all over the place doing everything." That's what I want to hear.

My children keep asking me why I am still making music. It's like Neil Young once said to me, "The minute we stop doing this, we're not alive." Making music is the essence of our being. I'm still younger than Mick Jagger or Paul McCartney and they are still out there rockin'. We won't let rock 'n' roll go. We never had the slightest inkling as teenagers full of dreams that we would still be doing it into our twenties, never mind our fifties.

I was recently at a hospital using a Medicare card that had my wife's name on it but not mine. It didn't say Bachman. The fellow behind the counter looked at the card then up at me and with a puzzled expression inquired, "Is there something wrong with this card?"

"No."

"But you're Randy Bachman. You're one of the four or five most recognizable names and faces in Canada."

Curious, I asked him who the other recognizable characters were.

"Neil Young, Burton Cummings, Anne Murray, and Gordon Lightfoot."

RANDY BACHMAN

Not Jean Chrétien, John Diefenbaker, or Pierre Elliott Trudeau. Me, Neil, Burton, Anne, Gordon, we're like the Rolling Stones of Canada still rockin' on into the next millennium.

CHAPTER 12

You Ain't Seen Nothin' Yet

"It would be easier to negotiate peace in the Middle East than to broker a Guess Who reunion" carped a music scribe in one of Winnipeg's daily newspapers at the rumour that such talks were taking place during the spring of 1999. He was far closer to the truth than he ever imagined. Getting the four veteran Winnipeg rockers in the same room together, let alone reunited on one stage for an actual performance was a daunting task approached with great trepidation.

By early in the new year, Winnipeggers had already whipped themselves into a frenzy of enthusiasm over the much anticipation return of the Pan American Games to their fair city after a thirty-two-year absence. During Canada's Centennial year, 1967, the isolated prairie burgh of half a million or so had shown the Americas it knew how to throw a party in what was championed at the time as the best organized Pan Am Games ever — something not that hard to achieve given the rather lacklustre and low-key affairs mounted by other cities since the inception of the Games in 1951. Though hardly comparable to the Olympics in magnitude or significance, the 1999 Pan Am Games were nonetheless Winnipeg's chance to shine once again for a few weeks.

More than a year and a half earlier, the Pan Am Games' steering committee — consisting of various local luminaries, captains of industry, and movers and shakers — recognized that the success of Winnipeg's Games in the eyes of the country as well as two continents, rested in large measure on the extravagant opening and closing ceremonies. Whether anyone outside of Winnipeg bothered to tune into the two dozen or so athletic competitions over the two-week duration, it was these two televised galas that could make or break the public's perception of Winnipeg's efforts. Premier Gary Filmon and the governing Conservatives were hoping for a Pan Am triumph, and his wife Janice's presence on the Games' steering committee ensured the weight of the provincial government was placed squarely behind the event.

With so much hanging in the balance, the committee engaged the services of Los Angeles–based special events producer Chuck Gayton whose track record included the recent Olympic Games in Atlanta, as well as several awards specials. Known to be fond of employing big name celebrities in his gala presentations, Gayton promised a star-studded affair despite a meagre budget. "People have offered to go outside the parameters of the budget if that would help obtain name talent," assured committee member David Wolinsky, a noted Winnipeg attorney specializing in entertainment law whose clients included Fred Turner of Bachman-Turner Overdrive. "We're exploring every possibility." Names like Celine Dion, Shania Twain, Alanis Morissette, and Sarah McLachlan were bandied about in the media as potential draws capable of delivering the kind of ratings essential to validating Winnipeg's efforts. The only problem: the fees each of these mega-stars demanded. Dion's rumoured remuneration tipped the scales at a cool million, Twain just half that, with Morissette and McLachlan weighing in at a quarter to a half million. No one seemed to question the wisdom of parachuting any of these world-class artists into a Winnipeg event when none had the slightest connection to the city other than the fact that they may have graced a stage here once or twice.

Organizers even threw former Winnipegger Neil Young's name into the mix in an effort to inject local colour into the festivities, but they were rebuffed when Young's busy schedule precluded a Winnipeg visit.

While some committee members had stars in their eyes, Bob McMahon, the Games' chief operating officer, remained more pragmatic. "The budget excludes any big name talent," he announced in the midst of the fray. With a total budget of $2.3 million for both the opening and closing ceremonies combined, the likelihood of a Dion or a Twain seemed remote. In the end, McMahon won out and with just four months before the Games were slated to open, Gayton was summarily dismissed. With the clock ticking, panicked ceremonies' organizers returned to square one.

The focus now shifted to a "Made in Manitoba" solution. If Young, whose connections to Winnipeg were rather tenuous anyway, couldn't be persuaded to grace the Games with his presence, surely there were other local artists worthy of the event. Up and comer Chantal Kreviazuk's name was thrown into the ring along with bands the Crash Test Dummies and Watchmen. The pride of Morden, Manitoba, Celtic-flavoured artist Loreena McKennitt was put forward as a suitable candidate. With summer touring schedules well in place, time was a critical factor in booking any of these acts and the committee soon discovered only Kreviazuk was available. In the end, she was honoured with the singing of the national anthem only to back out two days before the opening when the pre-recorded accompaniment was not in a suitable key for her.

In the months preceding Gayton's dismissal, the Guess Who had been mooted as a potential headliner for the closing event. Although they had long since disbanded, in its heyday the quartet had been Winnipeg's most successful music export and Canada's first rock 'n' roll superstars. The original hit-making lineup had fragmented in the spring of 1970 and with a legacy of bitterness and legal entanglements hanging over the four members, a Guess Who reunion seemed a long shot at best. As everyone knew, these were men who no longer seemed to enjoy each other's company. Given all the water under their bridge, the media termed a Guess Who reunion "a complete wildcard" noting that it had taken the force of nature, 1997's Flood of the Century, to bring Randy and Burton together for a three-song mini set. No such natural disasters had been prophesied for the summer of 1999.

Nevertheless, a groundswell of interest remained, and factions within the organizing committee were warming to the idea of at least testing the waters with the four recalcitrant musicians. With little to lose and time rapidly running out, a trial balloon was floated and representatives contacted. Back in 1967, two years before *These Eyes* would catapult the local group to international acclaim, the Guess Who, the city's pride and joy, had performed for athletes at Winnipeg's first Pan Am Games. A return engagement seemed fitting, even though Burton maintained he couldn't remember playing the 1967 Games at all.

With the group having notched its last hit in 1974, no one, least of all the four Guess Who members themselves, could have envisioned that 1999 would see their return to the pop charts with a vengeance. Although most pop hits are conceived with a limited shelf life, the Guess Who's catalogue endured to be revived every few years in one form or another. Several heavy metal bands cut *American Woman* and that song, as well as *Undun* and *No Time*, appeared in the soundtracks to a number of hit movies, including *Jackie Brown, American Beauty*, and *Cable Guy*. Canadian rapper Maestro Fresh Wes scored a hit sampling *These Eyes* for *Stick to Your Vision*. Mike Myers' blockbuster summer movie hit *Austin Powers: The Spy Who Shagged Me* brought the group's greatest hit *American Woman* out of mothballs by featuring the original version in the movie. The subsequent soundtrack album included a cover of *American Woman* by hip heavy rocker Lenny Kravitz that raced up the charts in the wake of the movie's success. Kravitz also included the cut on his own album released that summer. This was followed by the Academy Award–winning film *American Beauty* featuring *American Woman* in its soundtrack. Guess Who was back.

American Woman and sixties-inspired rocker Lenny Kravitz

seemed like a perfect match. Kravitz liked his guitars heavy and distorted, and had a sneer to his vocals well suited to Burton's original
delivery. The choice of artist pleased Randy. Lenny Kravitz ultimately
took *American Woman* back to the top of the *Billboard* charts twen-
ty-nine years after it first rested there.

When I first heard that Lenny Kravitz was covering *American
Woman* for the movie soundtrack, I thought "Great!" I hadn't
heard his version yet but I was excited because I like Lenny
Kravitz. When he rocks, he has this incredible classic rock sound,
very Hendrix and Zeppelin. He is really into the old equipment
and getting the authentic sound, as I am, using tube amps and an
old board. He has become a diverse artist and in a Neil Young kind
of way has charted his own course without trying to curry favour
with the latest pop trends. He has integrity.

When I received a copy of Lenny's version though, I listened
and kept waiting to hear my signature guitar riff but it didn't
come. "Did someone forget to mix it in? Was an amp turned off
and no one noticed?" Then in came a lead guitar track playing a
solo, a different kind of solo, so I knew they hadn't mixed the
guitar out. I must confess the first time through, I didn't like his
version. I just didn't get it. After a few more listenings, it started to
grow on me and I realized the brilliance of Lenny's version. Other
renditions of *American Woman* and covers of some of my other
songs by artists have always been identical clones of the original.
As a writer you're flattered, but there is not another personality
in it so you don't really need to listen to it more than once. You
might as well hear the original as a clone copy. But here was
Lenny Kravitz leaving out my guitar line, adding a key change and
putting his own stamp on the song. It's his interpretation of
American Woman, not simply his cover of it and I appreciate
that approach.

Lenny made *American Woman* very modern. To have my

teenage daughter tell me she and her friends really think it rocks meant a lot to me. He had made me contemporary to a new generation of record buyers. The phones started ringing again.

I am continually amazed that my songs have longevity to them and keep reappearing. It proves that the music I created has transcended the generations and decades. Every eight or ten years, some new artist comes along and says, "I really like that song. My father played it when I was a kid and I want to record my version of it." And out comes one of my songs. For a songwriter, it's terrific; it's an ongoing tribute to what you created. You are lucky in life to be thanked once for doing something, but when you write a song that endures you get thanked every few years by someone redoing it and people buying it again. I am appreciative of the fact that there are these Canadian comedians like Mike Myers and Jim Carrey who want to use Canadian music in their movies.

In the wake of the film and soundtrack rejuvenation came the offer of the Pan American Games closing ceremony in Winnipeg. But could the group overcome decades of animosity and agree to reunite? "Portage and Main will have to be ninety degrees in January," Randy had earlier declared on the likelihood of a Guess Who reunion taking place. Despite public denials from Burton, on June 6 the *Winnipeg Sun* broke the story that the Guess Who were indeed short-listed for the coveted closing slot. With initial entreaties by the Pan Am committee having met with cautious response, Premier Gary Filmon stepped up to the plate in a last ditch bid to secure the group's participation. In a letter dated May 6 and delivered to Randy and Burton individually, Filmon played on the sentimentality of a Guess Who appearance. Publicly acknowledging *These Eyes* as his favourite song, the Premier wrote:

...*The Guess Who were the most significant musical group to emerge from Manitoba and Canada during the 1960s and 1970s...*

The Pan Am Games Ceremonies Committee wishes to request The Guess Who to rekindle the special magic of the group for a feature appearance at the Games closing ceremony. There can be no more fitting finale to the most important sporting event in Manitoba's history than a performance by Canada's original rockers. As a proud Manitoban and long-time fan of the band I would ask that you give their invitation your fullest consideration.

Yours sincerely,

Gary Filmon

Meanwhile, behind the scenes, the drama unfolding between the four and their respective representatives was typical of everything involving the Guess Who franchise. Though there was no doubting the flattery bestowed by the premier, major obstacles remained to be surmounted that jeopardized any confirmation of the group's appearance. Burton's manager, Los Angeles–based Lorne Saifer, a former Winnipegger and one-time business partner with Randy Bachman, fielded the request on behalf of his client but reserved a response until all his ducks were in place. Clearly he was not about to allow his client to participate unless certain conditions were guaranteed. Lorne initially favoured a Burton Cummings solo performance at the ceremonies. Randy's manager, another ex-Winnipegger and former Cummings confidante, Marty Kramer, discussed the options with his boss. Randy had American tour commitments pending around the date of the event and worried over the logistics of rehearsals and production, as well as the health of certain band members. Garry Peterson was fronting an ersatz Guess Who band in the US and would be on tour in the midst of the Games, while Jim Kale, who owned the Guess Who name and kept Garry out on the road under that banner despite his own retirement from the grind of one-night stands, was holed up in Winnipeg dealing with his own personal demons.

When I first heard about the offer I thought "They're dreaming. It'll never happen." With the rumours I had heard about certain members' personal and professional lives — some were booked on tour, I had dates booked around that time — I just never thought it would happen. But deep down I really wanted it to come about, so when the letter from the Premier arrived I said to Marty "Make this happen."

In a dreadful slight, neither Garry nor Jim were sent the Filmon letter. Nor did they have personal managers to champion their interests in the Games negotiations. Realizing the bargaining chip of three against one, Marty Kramer approached the two with an offer to represent them. Lorne Saifer soon found himself dealing with an empowered adversary. "The Pan Am Games reunion was all due to Marty Kramer," acknowledges Garry Peterson. "He worked his ass off. No one has any idea what he went through to get it to happen. He had the patience of Job." But despite holding more cards, Randy and Marty knew there could be no Guess Who reunion without Burton's voice and presence. While the other three agreed soon after to Filmon's offer, Burton and Lorne dragged their feet.

Band equipment, rehearsal space, sound, lighting and video equipment, support personnel, accommodation, transportation, seating for family members, and performance fee all had to be arranged in short order and to the satisfaction of the individual group members. Throughout it all, the four never spoke to one another directly. There was never a conference call between them to discuss the offer or even to say "Let's let bygones be bygones and do it for old time's sake." Instead, managers hashed out the details. Each of the four refused to confirm or deny the story as it hit the wire services across the country. Indeed, up until the last few weeks, their appearance could not be guaranteed. A lot of hair splitting was going on behind the scenes.

It was precarious. Even though to all appearances it is a four-man situation with 25 percent each, it doesn't matter what the three of us decide if Burton Cummings or his representative decide not to do it. There is no Guess Who without Burton Cummings singing those songs. It's a three-to-one vote but that one has the power because without his voice it isn't the Guess Who. It might be similar if I had that kind of power, but the fact is I don't.

But when I received the letter it was so late in the game. I had August booked, Burton had gigs, Garry was booked with his Guess Who in the States. They actually had to get another drummer to fill in for their gigs when Garry came up for the Games. If someone had approached us earlier and asked us to do it for nothing as an honour to close the Games and gave us something commemorative like a key to the city or the Order of the Buffalo or something like that, I'm sure we would have agreed to do it more quickly.

The Pan Am Games organization hired some high-paid entertainment hotshot from LA to get artists. All they needed from the start was someone like Marty Kramer who is a die-hard Winnipegger and knows all the Winnipeg and Manitoba entertainers to put it together. They should have had Loreena McKennitt and Tom Jackson, the Watchmen, Chantal Kreviazuk, Tom Cochrane, the Crash Test Dummies, BTO, the Guess Who, Burton and me. All those Manitobans to do a couple of their best-known songs so people could say "Wow, this is all from Winnipeg?!" Then maybe Neil Young might have come. Think of how incredible that show would have been? But none of us was ever booked early on. Instead, the money was squandered on this big entertainment consultant from LA who knew nothing about the history of Winnipeg music. He was going after Celine Dion and Sarah McLachlan, who have nothing to do with Winnipeg. Then he was dismissed and suddenly it got so late and there still hadn't been any big announcements about Canadian entertainment.

Burton's response remained elusive; phone messages and faxes went unanswered as the others waited impatiently for their singer to make up his mind.

Although a figure of $60,000 had been mooted for a possible Guess Who appearance back when Chuck Gayton was still at the helm, by the time Filmon dispatched his missive, the offer on the table was $100,000. It was met with a laugh from Marty who, when asked what it would take to put the four together on one stage, responded "double it." This eleventh-hour gambit paid off with the Pan Am committee agreeing to a staggering $200,000 fee for a twenty-minute, four-song set from a band that had not officially played together in sixteen years. The media tempered the news with speculation that the amount, in part, would go toward the cost of staging the group's performance, a position not denied by the band members or their representatives, leaving the four individuals considerably less at the end of the day. However, the truth was that the $200,000 pot was to be split four ways with each representative taking his percentage. Production costs added on top ballooned the total cost of a one-time Guess Who performance to upwards of $300,000.

> As it got down to the wire, they had to offer more and more money to induce us to cancel gigs and tour arrangements. They were so late. I had to tear up nonrefundable plane tickets. The Pan Am committee painted themselves into a corner and panicked. Had it been earlier we might have done it for nothing, but by that time it became "Don't ask us to do it for nothing now!"

The fee immediately became a public relations hot potato until it was pointed out that Canadian superstar sprinter Donovan Bailey had received the same figure to personally appear at the Games and to have his image grace the publicity. In the end, at least the Guess Who showed up. Bailey couldn't be bothered making an appearance at either the opening or closing ceremonies and refused to take part in his premiere event — the 100-metre run — after a placing glitch left him as an alternate. He did, however, keep his fee.

Technical demands and remuneration notwithstanding, a much more pressing concern further jeopardized confirmation of the group's appearance. Although there were certainly conflicts that divided the four, they had in the past managed to temporarily shelve those issues for the collective good. "We're not the best of friends," acknowledged Burton, "but we're not the worst of enemies either." Indeed, Randy and Burton had been in and out of court over ownership of the still lucrative Guess Who song catalogue. Burton legally owns the publishing rights to the songs he and Randy co-wrote, including *These Eyes, Laughing, No Time*, and Randy's own *Undun*.

It was made adamantly clear by Burton and Lorne that any attempt by Randy to press the issue could scuttle a Guess Who reunion. Randy chose not to do so.

A far more immediate and threatening problem, however, was the health of bass player Jim Kale. He had not picked up his bass in months when the Pan Am offer came up. Could Jim get through two days of rehearsals, a sound check, and the actual performance? Though no one alluded publicly to the situation, rendering it the best kept secret of the entire Games, Jim's ability to perform remained the greatest "if" to the Guess Who's acceptance of the offer. Promises of a strict regime of sobriety were demanded and assured before Jim was in.

Once the official announcement was made that the city's favourite sons would indeed reunite for a one-off performance on the evening of Sunday, August 8, the media across the country embarked on a feeding frenzy. Before the first note had been played concert promoters weighed in with hefty tour offers. Guess Who mania was rampant. What had seemed so implausible just weeks earlier was now looking possible.

With twenty tickets to the closing ceremonies allotted to each band member, Randy arranged for several of his children and grandchildren to attend the event. Many had never seen him with the Guess Who, and the opportunity might not come round again. "The Pan Am Games performance must be important to him," noted Randy's wife Denise two days before the event, "because he flew his kids in for it. 'I want my kids to see me in the Guess Who. This is once in a lifetime.' I just thought it was another of his projects but it is very important to him. The Guess Who was the band of his teenage years. It's like his first love and you always keep a warm spot in your heart for that. There was a special magic there and when he and Burton get together they just sparkle. It's like they are two halves of one perfect musician: Burton has the voice, the presence, and delivery and Randy has the musicianship and the creativity. But they have such divurgent personalities and lifestyles, it's like fire and ice. There are so many other things that get in the way, the egos, the control, the business issues, the alcohol and drugs. Randy cannot stand to be around that."

Arriving in Winnipeg five days before the closing ceremonies, Randy checked into a suite arranged for him and Denise at the Holiday Inn Crowne Plaza. Rehearsals would start the following afternoon at the venerable Winnipeg landmark, the Walker Theatre, the former downtown Odeon cinema. Initial plans to rehearse at a local sound equipment company's warehouse facility soundstage were nixed when that company was bumped from providing the sound system for the band's set despite having the exclusive contract for the closing ceremonies. Burton's entourage had insisted on using a Toronto-based company.

Burton's people flew in and informed the Games' organizers that the PA system they were providing wasn't good enough. They insisted on their own system. As a result, some really good people were offended and ultimately blamed the Guess Who, the four of us. I personally didn't know about it and I don't think Burton did either; he was in Winnipeg doing a daily radio show with Gary Maclean and getting ready for our performance. But there were a lot of shenanigans going on behind the scenes.

In the end, the Walker proved a suitable location. The former movie theatre that each of the members had attended as youngsters fostered an atmosphere of nostalgia appropriate for the task at hand.

Thursday's rehearsal was a closed-door affair. The media arrived to film the four arriving and entering, but were prevented from going any further than the parking lot. Randy and Garry showed up together, followed by Burton and lastly Jim who was shielded from any intrusive media glare by Marty Kramer, who took the bass player by the shoulders and led him into the theater. No one wanted the public to see the band stumble, as well it might have. By all accounts, the first day went surprisingly well, in spite of Jim's recent inactivity. Each of them had been playing the four chosen numbers in their own repertoires for years. All that was required was a fine tuning. For his part, Burton was in the trimmest, healthiest form he had been in for a decade, with his voice sounding strong and clear.

I had heard Burton was in shape, physically, mentally, and vocally. I knew I was ready and that Garry was ready, but that Jim was having his problems. You're only as good as your weakest link. But when it really counted, Jim came through and it was really good.

No one can play those songs perfectly except the four of us. At rehearsals, someone came up to me and asked if I could hear Jim and Garry in my monitors. And I replied, "I don't need to." I intuitively knew exactly what they were playing. I lived and dreamed those songs. They lived those songs, too, and created their parts and, sure enough, I walked over and they were playing them exactly the way they always did. It was such a comfortable feeling. And they're very weird parts. When you listen to the songs you can hear how simply Burton and I tried to write those songs and how basically complicated the bass and drum parts were. But somehow there's this magic when it all comes together.

One of the fun things that happened at the rehearsals was Burton and I trying to outdo each other with "Play That Tune." We would start a song and out of this mutual musical library stored in our heads there for thirty years or more, we would see if we could play every chord in the song and every note in the solo. We had a lot of fun playing old Moby Grape and Dion and Georgie Fame songs; some of this stuff we never even played onstage but we all had heard as kids. Burton even played *Back and Forth*, which was the flip side of *Tribute to Buddy Holly*, Chad Allan and the Reflections' first record, and I jumped right in and played the guitar solo note for note. He didn't think I would remember it! It was a really cool, kind of mental gymnastics trying to pull this stuff out of our collective memory banks like musical *Jeopardy*, each of us playing snippets of songs and seeing if the other could finish it. What a blast!

I also brought pictures along that they had never seen. When you take pictures yourself or if your family takes them, only you see them; they are for you. But the other guys may not have seen them. I had a picture of Burton in Tee Kay jeans writhing around on the stage at the Winnipeg Arena in 1966. I had shots of Jim with Bob Ashley from the early days of the Reflections that really meant a lot to Jim. And they in turn had photographs I had never seen.

The next day, selected guests, friends, and the media were invited to witness the historic moment as the group rehearsed their set. Imbued with a sense of camaraderie rarely witnessed between the four in decades, the band ran through *No Time, These Eyes, Undun*, and *American Woman*. When they hit those harmonies on *No Time*, the rocker that broke their soft rock run in 1970, it made the hairs on your neck stand on end. The elegantly cavernous Walker Theatre never shook so hard. It was 1970 all over again, as the four shared an unspoken language between them following lock step through the songs that had made their careers. Seated on a stool, his greying hair tied back in a ponytail, Jim seemed distant from the *joie de vivre* the other three enjoyed. Heavier than in his younger years, Garry beamed his ever-youthful grin from behind his kit, while Randy and Burton kibitzed out front. Having shed several pounds and sporting closely cropped locks, Burton's youthful presence belied his fifty-one years. Randy stood taller and heavier, dwarfing his baby blue Fender Stratocaster, in long grey hair and beard, prompting one journalist to dub him "Methuselah."

The playful banter continued nonstop as techies scurried about with cables and mikes. In their heyday, the Guess Who was Canada's most exclusive boys' club and only the four know the adventures they shared. Randy slipped in a few jazz standards like *Mr. Sandman* and *My Favourite Things*, invoking the memory of his early mentor Lenny Breau. Burton responded on piano with a rollicking *Bumble Boogie*. "It's like the Twilight Zone," he muttered, from time to time shaking his head in disbelief. Following a flawless rendition of *These Eyes*, Burton looked at his three mates and declared, "I've played *These Eyes* a thousand times since I left the band but it never sounds as good as when you guys do it." As the band launched into *American Woman*, Randy tore into an inspired guitar solo that would have made guitar guru Eric Clapton turn his head. Wiping the sweat from his brow, Burton raved, "Nobody can play *American Woman* like Randy." And he meant it. It was that good.

A hastily arranged local CBC television interview, the only one the group agreed to collectively, interrupted proceedings as the four gathered in one of the theatre loges to field questions. Investigative reporter Ross Rutherford evidently had his own agenda in mind and probed the group for cracks in their apparent unity, peppering the four with questions intended to elicit either a negative response at the very least or, hopefully, outright acrimony. "Would you do this for free? Everybody knows you don't get along so why are you doing this? Is it the money or the sentimentality?" He failed to incite any rancour or rattle the four. The bonhomie borne of two days of rehearsals was strong enough to resist even the most pointed query.

To Rutherford's assertion that the four weren't exactly holding hands and singing *We Are the World*, Garry bluntly responded. "On the road, Three Dog Night play together but travel in separate vehicles and stay in separate rooms. We have never done that, period." Added Burton, "There are always going to be power struggles and animosities in any successful entity." Barely containing his exasperation with Rutherford's line of inquiry, he spat out, "You can sit here and dig all day for dirt but you're not going to find it. The friendship outweighs whatever baggage there is."

Befitting the reflective spirit of the event, Saturday morning Randy rented a large, multiseat van and herded in family members — assorted children, spouses, and grandchildren — for his own magical history tour of West Kildonan, the north Winnipeg community he grew up in. Stops along the way included the houses he had lived in as a boy, former schools, the monkey trails he would ride his bike on in Kildonan Park, and the large two-storey home on tree-lined Scotia Street he and his first wife Lorayne bought with the first flush of Guess Who success. Lunch was at the North Winnipeg landmark, Kelekis's Restaurant, for hot dogs and chips. Clearly revelling in the sentimental mood, the former Winnipegger was bent on making the most of it.

I have wondered during this week what might have happened had I stayed with the band in 1970. If I hadn't left or been thrown out, what might have happened? If part of the band wasn't seriously into drugs and I could have taken a few months off to clear up my health problems and been able to come back healthy, I wonder what we might have done? But that didn't happen. They wanted to keep the party going and I needed to take care of myself.

That evening, the family gathered at brother Gary's luxurious

Tuxedo home for dinner. Randy's mother Anne Bachman and his Aunt Nerky also attended. The following night the Guess Who took the rain-soaked stage and with four songs proceeded to lay to rest any doubts as to their title as Canadian's premier rock superstars. In a dazzling performance, the four members delighted not only the hometown faithful and an entire nation but also themselves, exiting the stage arm in arm. The experience left Randy exhilarated, exhausted, and reflective.

In talking with my daughters after the Pan Am Games they told me they cried through the whole performance seeing me up there onstage. They didn't feel bad because everyone around them was crying too, but for a different reason. Over all the years, they had never seen me playing with the Guess Who. Although they had heard these songs thousands of times and been told by hundreds of people how much those songs meant to their lives, to my own kids they were simply "Dad's songs." To hear those songs played and to see the response from the crowd, twenty-five thousand people, they told me later how much that moment meant to them. It was a healing experience for them and in many ways brought everything full circle.

That whole week was so incredible. The build up to it really drained me — the four of us together again and my family being there and it being my old hometown. When I left Winnipeg the next day, I was a wreck. The pressure of worrying over Jim Kale and the shape he was in and just over how it would all fly that week gave me several sleepless nights. We went to Louisiana to resume my tour, and the next day I could not get out of bed. I was so emotionally drained that for the first time in my life I said, "I don't want to get out of bed. I want to stay here." I could feel every pore, every cell, in my body was fatigued. I had a catnap after the sound check and fell into a deep sleep and when I got up I felt re-energized.

My band — Colin Arthur Wiebe, Donnie McDougall, and Rogé

Belanger — and I went out and I probably did one of the worst shows in my life that night. I don't mean this as a put-down on my band — they are all talented guys and we play the songs well and always get rave reviews — but it was a big comedown after playing with the Guess Who. It was like making love with someone who looks like your wife but isn't your wife. It's an imitation. Your wife can get all the recipes but it won't taste like your mother's cooking because it isn't her. It's more than just the ingredients. The magic wasn't there.

I think it was pretty obvious to everyone, including Burton and me, that when we played the Pan American Games, Jim and Garry contributed a verve, energy, and strength to the songs and sound. Burton and I could play those songs, and we both have individually for years, but the sound of the Guess Who is the sound of those four individuals. While Burton and I gave that Guess Who entity a vehicle with our songs, we were like the quarterback and running back that cannot score the touchdowns without that solid frontline of blockers, Jim and Garry. What good is a quarterback without the rest of the team? We were like a team of four guys who played the music, walked the walk, talked the talk, drove the miles, starved, faced the crooks, paid the bills, did all that stuff together.

Buoyed by the overwhelmingly positive response to their Pan American Games triumph and with offers pouring in from across the country, the four members of the Guess Who weighed the possibility of mounting a full-scale tour in the summer of 2000 with the possibility of taking it into the US, something they had failed to do back in 1983. Such thoughts would have been sheer folly a mere six months earlier, but here they were fielding lucrative tenders. They were no longer young men, and there was plenty at stake. For Garry Peterson, the payday from a lucrative tour could not have come at a more propitious moment with his father seriously ill in the United States and

medical bills mounting. By year's end, the pot had swelled to a potential two-million-dollar windfall. Could the bonhomie of that August
week in Winnipeg sustain the group through a lengthy cross-country
jaunt?

Immediately following the Pan Am reunion, the Canadian media
made a big deal out of it across the country. Every radio, television, and newspaper ran a story about it. People are in love with
our music. The Pan Am reunion spread across the continent and
all the way to Japan and Australia. It was a flash in the night that
caused an explosion of interest in other pockets. Since the 1983
reunion, it has been extremely gratifying to discover that our
music means even more to people sixteen years later. All that time
has passed and the songs remain important and have even taken
on more meaning with the passage of time.

Despite the goodwill, reunion plans were tethered by a thin
thread. Burton spouted off incessantly on his buddy Gary Maclean's
local radio show that a tour was already in the works with offers from
as far away as Japan and Australia, but Jim's precarious health and personal problems continued to render him the wild card. With the
announcement that the group was to be honoured as the first-ever
recipients of the inaugural Prairie Music Hall of Fame Award in
Winnipeg in October, the four agreed to hold a summit meeting the
day before to lay all the reunion cards on the table.

On the afternoon of Saturday, October 16, the four met in a downtown Winnipeg hotel room sans managers for the first two hours to
speak frankly about the possibility of surmounting their many obstacles to proceed with a reunion tour. It was an emotional meeting. "We
were told beforehand that if the publishing issue was raised, Burton
and Jim were walking out of the meeting," acknowledges Garry
Peterson. "But was it a setup? The only one to bring it up was Lorne
Saifer at the start of the meeting before he and Marty Kramer left the

room. He took us totally by surprise by saying that nothing could go any further until the publishing issue was laid to rest. He told us it had been settled by the courts. Then he asked Randy, 'Are you okay with that because we have to put this aside before we can go on?' That took us totally by surprise because they were supposed to walk out if the issue was raised we had been told, but they were the ones who brought it up. Was that the most important reason for Burton and Lorne to be there? Is that all Burton was looking for? I said I had maybe lost a hundred thousand dollars on *American Woman* but I could make a million dollars if we got together again. That was a no brainer for me.

"We went around the room and told the others why we were there. When I had my chance I knew that there were certain members of the band, Jim and Burton in particular, that carried grudges against me for thirty years. That was a fact. Unfortunately, I was the last one to speak because we went in alphabetical order. I started out by saying that, first of all, I wanted to apologize to each of them for anything I had done in the past to cause them pain. You can't carry a grudge for so long without addressing the problem. I told them the only way a reunion could ever happen is with trust, faith, and love. I said a lot of things that I felt from my heart."

At the conclusion of the meeting, the four agreed to temporarily shelve the publishing issue for the sake of a possible reunion. The next evening as the four stood together to receive their Prairie Music Award, emotions ran high with Jim teary-eyed as he invoked the memory of his late mother. "I wish she could be here to see this," he intoned. Backstage questions about a tour in the new year were deflected diplomatically.

"Randy is keen to tour with the Guess Who, which is saying a lot because he really doesn't like to tour any more," remarks Denise Bachman. "That's a young man's game and it's hard for him to be away from home that long living out of a suitcase. He misses his home routine."

"Seeing the original Guess Who, those four guys, in their heyday

back in 1969-70, it simply didn't get any better than that," recalls journalist Larry LeBlanc, contemplating the possibility of a full-blown
reunion tour. "And I think Randy would give anything to have that
again. But on the other hand, they just can't seem to live together."

Following the October meeting several public appearances by
Randy and Burton onstage together pointed to a thawing in their tem-
pestuous relationship lending credence to a possible reunion. What
they hoped to draw from a successful reunion was both a validation
that they had truly accomplished something that, in Burton's own vernacular, cheated time, as well as a sense of closure going out on the
high of highs as the conquering heroes, the undisputed kings of
Canadian rock.

While talk of a tour remained speculative by year's end, the four
committed to a further round of talks in late January in Winnipeg to
discuss reunion possibilities once again.

During two lengthy sessions on January 26 and 27, a tentative itinerary was placed before the group for consideration. As before, personal baggage remained the first order of the day. This time the four left
with a feeling of cautious optimism with concrete plans in place for
possibly mounting a summer assault on Canada. Once again, Randy
accepted a truce regarding the publishing issue for the sake of a
reunion tour.

With this whole reunion project, not only is it one step at a
time, it's one step forward, two steps back. I come out of these
meetings feeling both exhilarated and beaten up at the same time.
Feeling good and bad simultaneously. Some of us are exorcising a
lot of demons at these meetings. After one such shouting match
one of the lawyers present said to us, "You guys have beaten the
crap out of each other for three decades. When is it going to end
and when are you just going to play a gig?" We all laughed, but he
was correct. We have been mentally, physically, and emotionally
beating each other up for years.

I sat down at the January meeting and said to the other guys, "Much to my amazement, we are all here again. From the last time we met until now, the things that have happened, the phone calls, the rantings and ravings, would not be believable even in a Hollywood movie. It's been beyond words. Yet here we are together again talking about it." Lorne Saifer then asked each of us once again why we were here. I replied, "In those twenty minutes on stage at the Pan Am Games I felt like I was twenty-five years old again. It was the most incredible, trance-like sensation. I didn't even realize it was raining or that I had a backache. It was a trance of emotion and love packing forty years of musical experience and every ounce of energy in my being into twenty minutes. If I can get that feeling once more, great! Twice more? Wonderful! A hundred times more? Incredible! This is like a youth drug for me that makes me feel young, playing with these guys. And if it makes them feel the same way then we will play together."

No matter how many problems we have, when we play together something special occurs. You can search the world over to find the right musicians to play with and when you do that's a very magical thing. I found it with those three guys.

With *American Woman* featured in the Austin Powers movie, *The Spy Who Shagged Me* and in *American Beauty* (which won the Academy Award for best picture in 1999) and now we've learned that Lenny Kravitz's version is up for a Grammy Award, the timing is right for us to come together and do something.

Burton made a rough set list and it had thirty-eight songs and that didn't even include my BTO songs. It was literally mind boggling all the great songs we can draw on.

For us to go out on tour, though, it needs an event, a catalyst. It isn't like we have an album coming out and are touring to support it.

"We need an event," I suggested.

"What kind of event?" the other guys asked.

"This may sound stupid but I would really like to play where it all started for us: a community club. Take it back to the beginning."

"Wow, what a great idea!"

So we began talking animatedly about playing places like St. Martin's-in-the-Field church hall in the north end of Winnipeg or River Heights or Crescentwood Community Clubs in the south end. We became so excited, throwing out ideas like charging $2.50 and just putting up those dumb-looking old Hungry I Agency posters around town. It was so silly, but on the other hand so obvious. A community club appearance would generate a tremendous public buzz, a groundswell that would continue to grow right up to the tour itself, followed by the actual tour opening in St. John's and going across Canada. We could also record every show for a live CD.

When I spoke to Denise after the first day of meetings, I told her we had a three-year plan. That was met with dead silence at first.

"Three years?!"

"Well, if we're going to do this we have to lay down some plans that offer more than just a one-off thing."

A lot of this is to get what we deserved, what we never received when we were together. What has survived throughout the whole mess is the music. The songs live on.

With latter-day Guess Who member and current Bachman sideman Donnie McDougall signed on as utility man on guitar and vocals and holds placed on several prominent venues, the Guess Who were to be ready to rock again. Nineteen-seventy was the year of the Guess Who. Miraculously, thirty years later, 2000 was shaping up to be their Second Coming.

I have found in the last five or six years that my life has come round in a circle. No matter where I've gone I seem to be bumping into people from my past and rekindling those relationships. My life circle seems to be getting smaller — to go to London and meet up with Tony Hiller again and develop a close personal relationship with him; to go to Nashville and connect with Ralph Murphy right off the bat or to run in to Bob Sabellico there; to bring former Winnipegger and ex–Guess Who member Donnie McDougall into my band; and to keep coming back to these three guys in the Guess Who with the Pan Am Games and now a reunion tour.

As for this whole Guess Who reunion thing, I have never been on a ride like this in my life! It's exhilarating and at the same time I don't know where it is going. It could end tomorrow or be three years of the most extraordinary time travel. As Burton says, we're cheating time, especially if we get to play a community club. That's where the dream began for us.

On April 1, a Guess Who reunion tour, dubbed "Running Back Thru Canada," was announced to great fanfare. It opened in St. John's, Newfoundland, on May 31 and continued for twenty-six dates. Tickets immediately sold out at virtually every venue. Several surprise dates were hinted at as well, including the much-anticipated community club appearance. With rehearsals convening in Winnipeg on May 1 at the cavernous Transcona Golf and Country Club, Randy's roller-coaster ride was about to take him for quite a spin.

All five participants and their retinue of crew members arrived suitably pumped for the event. The first week's rehearsal went so well that Burton boasted to the media that the group's upcoming performances would out do the original recordings. A massive two-and-a-half-hour show was being prepared that would not only feature the group's considerable catalogue of hits, but also lesser-known tracks like *Road Food* and *Guns Guns Guns*. An acoustic interlude would feature the rare *Talisman*, not performed since Randy's departure in 1970, plus a stripped-down arrangement of BTO's *Let It Ride*, surprisingly arranged by Burton. Indeed, it was Cummings who took on the leadership role at rehearsals, calling out the songs, assigning the harmony notes, and spurring the others on.

One week later, however, Burton walked out in a huff after accusing each member of not being adequately prepared or sufficiently healthy. He even fired long-time manager and confidante Lorne Saifer who had assumed duties as the group's de facto manager for the tour. Plagued by the rigours of a gruelling daily rehearsal schedule, of singing a lengthy set, and complaining of media pressure, Burton lashed out before retreating. Phone calls went unanswered as the remaining members continued rehearsing without their lead singer. Talk of cancelling the tour was accompanied by the threat of legal action for breach of contract. The group had been advanced $200,000 to defray the cost of rehearsals. Over 100,000 tickets had already been sold. Everyone waited for the next move. It was up to Burton.

We sat around for three days waiting to see what was going to happen next. It was costing us money to keep a crew and equipment on standby. I ran the band through the numbers just to tighten the arrangements. We sounded fine. Both Donnie and I had been feeling under the weather the previous week, but that had not hampered progress. Burton just got it into his head that we had somehow sabotaged the rehearsals by not being in tip-top form. He, too, was suffering from a raw throat and sniffles. It was like the end of the Beatles when everybody fired everyone and sued each other. Burton claimed the daily schedule, which began at noon was unsuited to his routine of staying up all night then sleeping until mid-afternoon. So we changed the times to evenings. But he still didn't show.

On Friday evening, May 12, we arrived at 6 p.m. only to sit around once again. No one had heard from Burton. I decided that we might as well run through *Takin' Care of Business* so I counted it in. As I started singing, the door swung open and in mid-song Burton waltzed up onstage, took his place behind his piano, and joined us, taking the song to its end.

"Is that the key you always do it in? C?" he asked, sheepishly, when we had finished.

"Yes."

"I thought you did it in A?"

"Sometimes, if I do it acoustically."

"Oh. Let's run through the whole show."

And we did, top to bottom. Nothing was ever said about Burton's fit of pique. We simply carried on. Lorne was back calling the shots and the next day rehearsals resumed again. The only concession was that we cancelled a couple of low-profile Toronto warm-up gigs and a television appearance in order to stay in Winnipeg another week to tighten up the set. The surprise gig, now slated for Crescentwood Community Club in Winnipeg's south end, would remain. There we would do a selection of cover tunes, some of our old favourites. The gig was being billed as Herbie and the Moonglows. Maybe it would be the spark we needed to get over the nerves of the upcoming trek across Canada.

In the back of my mind though, I couldn't help but wonder if this was 1983 déjà vu all over again.

Randy's fears were well founded. Looking, as the journalist from the *Globe and Mail* suggested, like Keith Richards of the Rolling Stones, Jim Kale was having trouble keeping up. Family issues and his continuing to rehearse after-hours with his local jam band Dinkboy compounded his problems. The others began to doubt Jim's ability to handle a two-month tour, and even Jim expressed his own trepidation. A secret call was placed to Jim's original Guess Who replacement back in 1972, Bill Wallace, to test the waters. If Bill could come onboard on short notice, the tour might still be salvaged. There were several obstacles: Jim owned the Guess Who name and would have to be compensated; time was a significant factor with the community club gig already advertised for four days hence and the full tour commencing a week later; Bill Wallace was a school teacher and not officially available until the end of June; and, more importantly, was it still the Guess Who — three originals and two substitutes? How would the media and public react to a quick personnel shuffle after touting the original four? A meeting was convened with the principals on Wednesday afternoon. Clearly the stakes were high with few options.

We didn't discuss it at first, but the four of us — Burton, Garry, Donnie, and myself — felt an unease about Jim's participation. Playing four songs in your hometown for the Pan Am Games was one thing, but playing thirty-plus songs sometimes four times in a week with travel in-between was a whole other matter. With all Jim's problems, I couldn't see him being able to handle it.

After two weeks of rehearsals, we did not feel we were ready to go out before an audience and present our best. We all knew in our hearts what had to be done.

At the meeting Burton looked squarely at Jim.

"We don't think you can handle what lies ahead of us. I'm frightened for you and for us that something might happen and you'll miss a show. We can't afford to do that. There's too much at stake." I admired Burton's resolve in confronting Jim.

Jim was on medication and with the wrong combination he could possibly jeopardize a performance. If we cancelled a show, we would be crucified in the media.

Garry couldn't bear to tell Jim, and I was waffling. It was a tough thing to face. We had to call Jim back for another meeting a few hours later and resolve it once and for all. This time I spoke. I supported Burton's assertion that we couldn't go on with Jim.

"Before, I thought you couldn't do it. Now I know you can't."

"If you guys feel that way, you gotta do what you gotta do."

We were all sobbing and there were hugs all round. There was no bitterness or name-calling. Jim handled it in a professional manner. After he left he told one of his friends that he felt a sense of relief that he could now deal with all these other issues distracting him.

That same night, Bill Wallace came down to rehearsals, plugged in, and it just felt right. Burton admitted that if he could have picked his dream lineup of the Guess Who this would be it. Now we could let the music do the talking.

With a heavy heart, Jim admitted he was in no shape, either physically or emotionally, to carry on. Family problems mixed with his ill health were just too much for him. It was a heart-rending meeting. "That was one of the toughest things I've ever had to do," lamented Burton the following day. "But as much as we love Jim it was just too risky to go out for two months and have him cave in halfway through."

Rehearsals picked up where they had left off with Bill jumping in headfirst (after negotiating a leave of absence from his teaching post). His solid playing, precise harmony singing, and onstage joie de vivre so invigorated the others that they found themselves bouncing about the small stage, infusing each number with a renewed intensity and enthusiasm that had been missing in the weeks before. In many respects, the group was now a unique Guess Who hybrid spanning the early years with Randy, Garry, and Burton, as well as the post-Bachman period with Donnie and Bill, lending songs from both eras a sense of integrity. Although Donnie and Bill might not have recorded *No Time* or *These Eyes*, they had played them in the latter lineups. And though Randy was not on hand for *Clap for the Wolfman* or *Star Baby*, Bill and Donnie were. All bases were covered.

The exclusive Crescentwood Community Club engagement, a much-anticipated media event intended to kick off the upcoming tour with a bang, would still belong to Jim though. As the band took the tiny stage to a packed house of three hundred or so who had been selected at random from over four thousand entrants, the loudest cheers were saved for Jim. Taken aback by the reception, he nonetheless pulled out all the stops, mugging to the crowd and cavorting across the stage. The band charged into a mini-version of the full-tour show spiced up with several chestnuts from their early days on the community club circuit. Opening with *Louie Louie*, the five made it clear this night was for fun. They followed that with the Deverons' 1965 ballad *Blue Is the Night* before a thundering *Runnin' Back to Saskatoon* and all the Guess Who favourites. *Saskatoon*'s line "This band is homegrown, don't come from Hong Kong" elicited a roar of approval from the crowd. Randy dug deep into his own past for the nimble Ventures instrumental *Walk, Don't Run*. A rare treat was Jim taking the mike to sing the Larry Williams' rocker *Short Fat Fanny*. But the highlight had to be Randy and Burton alone performing *Talisman*, a song neither of them or the band had performed since May 16, 1970, at the Fillmore East.

Following the show, Jim thanked his band mates, bid them good luck on the impending tour, and quietly slipped into the night. Though he acquitted himself admirably throughout the two-hour set, there was little doubt that Jim could withstand a lengthy outing. Though he retained his percentage of the tour take, it was now up to Bill Wallace to carry the load.

Burton was so nervous about the Crescentwood gig that he couldn't sleep the night before. He always gets worried before the hometown crowd. He called us that morning to say he couldn't make the sound check, went home, and slept from noon to six. The rest of us did the sound check and ran threw a few numbers. Jim seemed up for the gig. Before we left for the club that evening, Burton came to my room and was still visibly anxious. I kept reassuring him that it was no big deal even though we all knew it was a big deal. I don't get nervous before shows because I feel a confidence in what I'm supposed to do, but I do get nervous about the other guys and whether they know what they're doing. All I wanted to do was get on that stage.

I surveyed the crowd and it was so neat to see people in their forties or fifties with their teenage kids beside them. They had brought their children to experience what the community clubs were like. And the night was like the old days. Throughout the entire set, there was a guy in his mid-fifties over by the speaker column watching the show fairly unemotionally until we began *Share the Land*. I looked at him then and he had tears streaming down his cheeks. It was very moving.

It was a special night for several reasons. It was a shared experience for us and the audience, and for Jim. It was his night. It took a lot of courage for him to come out after that unfair article and photograph in the *Winnipeg Sun* newspaper the day before. We had the old vibes again onstage, smiling, joking, and laughing. He held his end up well.

The Crescentwood gig did everything the band and manager Lorne Saifer had anticipated it would and more. It generated national coverage in the television and print media, got the band over the initial apprehension of facing an audience again, and gave a huge boost to the impending tour. Indeed, Lorne had fielded over 2,000 requests from the media across Canada for access to the exclusive Crescentwood venue to cover the show. Afterwards, the unanimous consensus was that the group sounded better than their original recordings. Burton's boast had been well founded. Now with Bill Wallace onboard, the band had the confidence they needed to conquer Canada all over again.

The hand of fate seems to be guiding this whole reunion thing. It was thirty years ago to the month, May of 1970, that I left the Guess Who, and twenty-eight years ago to the month that Bill Wallace replaced Jim in the band. Bill told us that he had a premonition a few days before we called him that he would be involved with this tour.

I feel really secure now about the tour because Burton feels good about it. When you're as close as we are in a band, you can sense when one of the members isn't feeling one hundred percent. It's an intuitive thing, but it affects everyone. However, with this lineup, Burton feels confident now and therefore we all do. Because if he doesn't feel ready, it can't happen. He's the guy up front doing the singing. He is the voice of the Guess Who. And he has, without doubt, the greatest voice in rock 'n' roll. He hasn't lost a note in his range over the years. What he has been doing at our rehearsals has been simply amazing. I have been knocked out by him. And him taking the reins at the rehearsals makes sense. He has a lot riding on his shoulders. Without Burton there is no show. He's done a terrific job running us through our paces.

We all realize that if this tour isn't successful, it'll be the end of all our careers. It would be deemed a national disgrace. We would all have to go into hiding. We could never work again. There is so much riding on us, not just our own pride, but the country's pride.

As I look to the weeks ahead, I'm really looking forward to this tour. To go right across Canada, which we haven't done since the late sixties, is so exciting. We didn't do that in 1983. With this tour, we are taking our show to the people, not just in Toronto, Winnipeg, and Vancouver, but places like Kitchener, North Bay, Saskatoon, Lethbridge, Thunder Bay, Grande Prairie, and Red Deer. It really touches our hearts that the people in all these towns and cities want us. We were never that big in Montreal but they begged us to play there on this tour. That's very gratifying.

We always saw the Guess Who not only as a Canadian band, but also as a band for the ordinary people, for ordinary Canadians everywhere across this land, and this tour is taking our music to those people. They're the ones we owe our success and our longevity to. In the early years, we played literally everywhere in

Canada. Every stop on this tour will be like a coming home for us because there are fans in every part of Canada who came to see us in the early days and supported us through thick and thin. We were embraced first in the smaller cities and towns before the bigger cities picked up on us.

How often does anybody get a second chance? We, the Guess Who, have a second chance with this tour, and it's better than ever. Whatever happens afterwards really doesn't matter to me. Once the last curtain falls I can go home feeling that I have accomplished something worthwhile. It will have fulfilled a dream and given me a sense of closure to an important part of my career, a part that is now resolved.

CHAPTER 13

EPILOGUE:
Running Back to Saskatoon

Rarely are music critics unanimous in their praise of a concert act. Yet that has been the case right across the country for the Guess Who's "Running Back Thru Canada" tour 2000. With accolades bestowed on the group at every stop and sellout arenas filled with ecstatic fans young and old, the tour has taken on mythical proportions. A flag-waving jingoism unseen in this fair land has left little doubt that the Guess Who are truly Canada's band.

Opening on May 31 at St. John's Memorial Stadium in Newfoundland, the media went wild over the group's hit-packed two-and-a-half-hour set, marvelling at the five-man group's onstage energy and power. "I feel a lot of closure," Randy postulated to *Toronto Sun* reporter Jane Stevenson following the group's St. John's performance. "I think the band feels closure. I think tempers were high, and emotions were high when I left the band. I feel very fortunate, and possibly they agree, that we're able to go back and rebuild this bridge that we burned between us. I feel like I'm with my buddies again." Burton reinforced the mutual admiration society sentiment. "I've never heard Randy play guitar this well. The solo he did on *Glamour Boy* was amazing. He just blows me away."

Reviewers never failed to acknowledge the eclectic crowd mix. Noted the *Halifax Daily News*' Sandy Macdonald, "The full house at the Metro Centre — from grey-haired bikers and businessmen to young kids in bellbottoms and bandannas — grasped the spirit of the Guess Who reunion." That spirit was nothing short of a Canadian love-in. "Canadian nationalism is getting another boost, and for once it isn't in the form of a fervent beer commercial rant from some hoser named Joe," wrote *For the Record*'s Nick Krewen. "No, the fearless flag-wavers currently swelling homegrown hearts with domestic pride are five 50-ish Winnipeggers who are storming 22 cities [sic] from St. John's, Nfld., to Kamloops, B.C., with 2 1/2 hour musical marathons down memory lane." Added *Halifax Chronicle-Herald* entertainment critic Stephen Cooke, "The songs of the Guess Who are as tightly woven into the fabric of Canadian culture as Glenn Gould's piano or Pierre Berton's bow tie. Rooted in fertile prairie soil, the music of the Winnipeg quartet grew to bridge the passage from the Summer of Love to the years of the FLQ crisis, Watergate, and Vietnam. But it was nostalgia of the rosy-hued kind that hung in the air at the Halifax Metro Centre on Friday night, as a reunited Guess Who came to call." Enthused the *Vancouver Sun*'s John Mackie, "The two-hour show was like a Canadian celebration, a musical version of the 'I am a Canadian' TV commercial. Opening with the hoser anthem *Running Back to Saskatoon* and closing with the hippie anthem *Share the Land*, the Guess Who reeled off a veritable soundtrack to Canadian life. When Burton Cummings proudly announced the band members were all born and raised in Winnipeg, Manitoba, the roar from the crowd was unbelievable. When he followed it up by stating that Canada was the greatest country on earth, the roar from the crowd nearly blew the roof off." The *Edmonton Sun*'s Mike Ross termed the tour "the biggest comeback in Canadian rock history. After all, they are Canadian rock history."

While the taut musicianship and invigorated playing empowered their set, it was the Guess Who's string of familiar favourites that carried each performance. "It's the staying power of the songs," stated Burton early into the tour. "The songs have never gone away. They're still on the radio. I think that's the main reason for this tour, why tickets have been selling like mad across the country. No matter what city I'm in in Canada, I can't go more than a couple of hours without hearing something by the Guess Who on the radio. I know a lot of people in their mid- to late-twenties who tell me the Guess Who is their favourite band. I think that speaks volumes for the power of the songs. They don't sound dated. They don't sound as old as they are. I heard *No Time* the other day and it sounded pretty damn good."

Burton's voice is in the best shape in decades; Garry Peterson's rock-solid beat keeps the familiar arrangements tight; and Donnie McDougall and Bill Wallace offer steady support and strong harmony voices. Nonetheless, it is Randy who draws much of the attention. "It was Bachman's presence that added the most credibility to last night's show," stated the *Ottawa Sun*'s Ian Nathanson in reviewing the group's stellar show at the Corel Centre. "In fact, things didn't kick into high gear until three songs in with the first Bachman–Cummings composition *These Eyes*, the song that got the whole ball rolling for the band back in 1969. Same goes for the remaining Bachman-era tunes: An unplugged-style *No Sugar Tonight/New Mother Nature, No Time, Undun, Laughing* and a raucous, eleven-minute rendering of *American Woman*." Indeed, Randy's extended soloing in that number brought audiences to their feet every single night as he wrenched out searing guitar licks from his Fender. "Song after song, Randy Bachman demonstrated why he was, and still is, Canada's guitar god," boasted Sandra Sperounes, in *The Edmonton Journal*. "During a show-stopping, floor-stomping rendition of *American Woman*, Bachman decided to play his axe with a drum stick, running it up and down the frets to create a frenzied, distorted effect. Even when Bachman played acoustically, as on an awesome unplugged version of *No Sugar Tonight*, he still found a way to make it electric." Suggested *The Vancouver Sun*'s John Mackie, "Having Randy Bachman back in the group is key. There really is no one in the world who can play *American Woman* like him, and adding BTO nuggets like *Lookin' Out for Number #1* and *Takin' Care of Business* to the Guess Who's set makes it even stronger. *Takin' Care of Business*, in fact, was the biggest crowd-pleaser: all 7,000 people in the audience were standing and clapping and singing along. It's Canada's real national anthem." "The high point," confirmed Sandy Macdonald of the *Halifax Daily News*, "came as Bachman took the vocal mike for his anthemic *Takin' Care of Business*. The Metro Centre was absolutely thunderstruck by stompin' feet for that timeless headbanger." Each evening, Burton paid respect to Randy by praising his songwriting and playing, genuflecting before him during *American Woman*.

In the midst of all the hoopla surrounding the tour, a survey was conducted by Universal Music Canada and the *Sun* chain of newspapers in Toronto, Calgary, Edmonton, Winnipeg, and Ottawa asking Canadians to nominate their selections for the top Canadian songs of all time. To no one's surprise *American Woman* easily topped the informal poll with BTO's *Takin' Care of Business* pulling in the second spot. Score two for Randy Bachman. Further evidence of the power of Randy's songwriting pen came with *These Eyes* at #9 and *You Ain't Seen Nothin' Yet* logging #19 out of the one hundred entries.

The Guess Who's June 15 appearance at Toronto's Molson Amphitheatre became the heftiest payday in the group's history, but their return to Winnipeg, inaugurating the recently completed CanWest Global Park's first rock concert, was to be the pinnacle. The hype surrounding the impending performance and pressure felt by the group as a whole, and Burton in particular, intensified as the June 30 date neared. Arriving the day before to a media frenzy, Burton had been unable to sleep the two nights prior to the show. Missing the afternoon sound check, he had worked himself into such a state of anxiety by show time that he likened the group's appearance before the hometown faithful to John Lennon coming back to life or the return of Jesus Christ. Remaining calm, Randy attempted to reassure his partner that despite the presence of nine cameras filming a CBC television special and recording facilities set up for a live album, it was just another gig. When the band hit the stage at 9:30, Burton was noticeably tense as the crowd of 13,000 greeted the group with a standing ovation before the first note had even been played. Determined to enjoy the moment, the other four members revelled in the adulation. By the third number Burton had loosened up. Heavy rains forced the group to the wings and halted the concert for an hour. But the crowd remained in their seats and gave their heroes a rousing welcome on their return to the stage, whence they proceeded to lay waste to the rain-soaked mass. "Only in Winnipeg would the crowd stay," shouted Burton as the band resumed its set. In the end, the Guess Who left in triumph and once again the critics rewarded their performance with five stars. Following the post-concert soiree, Burton collapsed. Then, finally, he got a good night's sleep before the tour resumed.

With a live album in the works, as well as a CBC television special, potential American dates, and talk of new material emanating from a renewed Bachman–Cummings team, the Guess Who's prospects look surprisingly bright. Although Randy remains cautious about the future, he does hold out hope that this will be more than a one-off spectacle. "We all knew this would stir up some interest," admits Burton, "but good Lord, it's way beyond what any of us comprehend. I haven't heard Bachman this fired up in a long time, I tell you."

With over 120,000 paying to see the reunited Guess Who, the Running Back Thru Canada tour's gross revenues including merchandising were estimated at close to $6 million, making it the most lucrative Canadian tour of the year. "Who could have predicted this would be happening?" marvelled Randy.